Conflict, Identity and Economic Development

Ireland and Scotland, 1600–1939

Conflict, Identity and Economic Development

Ireland and Scotland, 1600–1939

edited by
S. J. Connolly,
R. A. Houston
and R. J. Morris

Carnegie Publishing, 1995

Conflict, Identity and Economic Development:
Ireland and Scotland, 1600–1939

edited by S. J. Connolly, R. A. Houston and R. J. Morris

First edition

Published by Carnegie Publishing Ltd,
18 Maynard St., Preston PR2 2AL.

Copyright © Carnegie Publishing, 1995
Text copyright © individual authors, 1995

Typeset by Carnegie Publishing
Printed and bound by Cambridge University Press

British Library Cataloguing in Publication Data
A catalogue record for this book is available from the British Library

All rights reserved
Unauthorised duplication of material in this book contravenes current legislation

Contents

	Preface	vii
	List of Abbreviations	viii
	Members of the Conference	ix
1	Identity, conflict and economic change: themes and issues S. J. Connolly, R. A. Houston and R. J. Morris	1
2	Scottish and Irish urbanisation in the seventeenth and eighteenth centuries: a comparative perspective I. D. Whyte	14
3	The Scottish Exchange on London 1673–1778 L. M. Cullen	29
4	The economy of Edinburgh 1694–1763: the evidence of the Common Good R. A. Houston	45
5	Contrasting regimes: population growth in Ireland and Scotland during the eighteenth century R. E. Tyson	64
6	Why the Highlands did not starve: Ireland and Highland Scotland during the Potato Famine T. M. Devine	77
7	The fertility transition in Ireland and Scotland c. 1880–1930 Cormac Ó Gráda and Niall Duffy	89
8	Popular culture: patterns of change and adaptation S. J. Connolly	103
9	Corporate values in Hanoverian Edinburgh and Dublin Jacqueline Hill	114
10	Scotland, Ireland, and the antithesis of Enlightenment Gerard O'Brien	125

11	Ownership of the past: antiquarian debate and ethnic identity in Scotland and Ireland *Clare O'Halloran*	135
12	Land, the landed and relationships with England: literature and perception 1760–1830 *Stana Nenadic*	148
13	Permissive poor laws: the Irish and Scottish systems considered together *Rosalind Mitchison*	161
14	Rural protest in the Highlands of Scotland and in Ireland, 1850–1930 *Charles W. J. Withers*	172
15	Inequality, social structure and the market in Belfast and Glasgow, 1830–1914 *R. J. Morris*	189
16	Irish Catholics in Belfast and Glasgow in the early twentieth century: connections and comparisons *A. C. Hepburn*	204
17	Working-class housing in Scottish and Irish cities on the eve of World War I *M. E. Daly*	217
18	Financial institutions and the Scottish financial centre in the inter-war years *C. W. Munn*	228
19	Wages and employment in Northern Ireland and Scotland between the wars: the case of shipbuilding *F. Geary and W. Johnson*	239
20	Employers and policymaking: Scotland and Northern Ireland, *c.* 1880–1939 *Eleanor Gordon and Richard Trainor*	254
	Index	269

Preface

THIS VOLUME contains the papers given at the fourth conference of Scottish and Irish Economic Historians, held at St Andrews on 25–28 September 1990. The first of these conferences, intended to bring together specialists in the histories of two societies whose histories present both striking similarities and marked contrasts, was held in Trinity College, Dublin, in 1976. Two further conferences were held at Strathclyde in 1981 and at the Derry campus of the University of Ulster in 1985. The proceedings of all three have been published: L. M. Cullen and T. C. Smout, eds., *Comparative Aspects of Scottish and Irish Economic and Social History 1600-1900* (Edinburgh, 1977); T. M. Devine and David Dickson, eds., *Ireland and Scotland 1600–1850: Parallels and Contrasts in Economic and Social Development* (Edinburgh, 1983); and Rosalind Mitchison and Peter Roebuck, eds., *Economy and Society in Scotland and Ireland 1500-1939* (Edinburgh, 1988).

The fourth conference, like its predecessors, was made possible by the generous financial support of the Economic and Social Research Council, which we gratefully acknowledge. We should also like to thank the University of St Andrews, and especially the Dean of the Faculty of Arts, Andrew Dawson, for their hospitality and support for the venture. Particular thanks must go to Mrs Norma Porter, whose help was crucial to the smooth running of the conference.

We would like to thank Dorothy Kidd (Scottish Ethnographic Archives), Mungo Campbell (National Galleries of Scotland), Ian McIvor (National Library of Scotland) and Dr Vivienne Pollock (Ulster Museum) for help in finding illustrations. For permission to reproduce illustrations we are grateful to the National Galleries of Scotland, The National Library of Ireland, the National Library of Scotland, the National Museums of Scotland, the Royal Society of Antiquaries of Ireland, and the Ulster Museum.

S. J. Connolly
R. A. Houston
R. J. Morris

Abbreviations

Cullen & Smout	L. M. Cullen and T. C. Smout, eds, *Comparative Aspects of Scottish and Irish Economic and Social History 1600-1900* (Edinburgh, 1977)
Devine & Dickson	T. M. Devine and David Dickson, eds., *Ireland and Scotland 1600–1850: Parallels and Contrasts in Economic and Social Development* (Edinburgh, 1983)
Ec. Hist. Rev.	*Economic History Review*
Ir. Ec. & Soc. Hist.	*Irish Economic and Social History*
Mitchison & Roebuck	Rosalind Mitchison and Peter Roebuck, eds., *Economy and Society in Scotland and Ireland 1500-1939* (Edinburgh, 1988)
P.P.	Parliamentary Papers
Scot. Econ. & Soc. Hist.	*Scottish Economic and Social History*
S.R.O.	Scottish Record Office

Members of the Conference

Dr Richard Anthony	Department of Economic and Social History, University of Edinburgh
Dr Thomas Bartlett	Department of History, University College, Galway
Dr S. J. Connolly	Department of History, University of Ulster
Dr W. H. Crawford	Institute of Irish Studies
Prof. L. M. Cullen	Department of Modern History, Trinity College, Dublin
Dr M. E. Daly	Department of Modern History, University College, Dublin
Prof. T. M. Devine	Department of History, University of Strathclyde
Dr David Fitzpatrick	Department of Modern History, Trinity College, Dublin
Mr Frank Geary	Department of Applied Economics, University of Ulster
Dr Raymond Gillespie	Department of History, St Patrick's College, Maynooth
Dr Eleanor Gordon	Centre for Business History in Scotland, University of Glasgow
Dr Elspeth Graham	Department of Geography, University of St Andrews
Prof. A. C. Hepburn	School of Social and International Studies, University of Sunderland
Dr J. R. Hill	Department of History, St Patrick's College, Maynooth
Dr Rab Houston	Department of Modern History, University of St Andrews
Ms Jennifer Ingram	Department of Geography, University of St Andrews
Dr W. Johnson	Department of Banking and Commerce, University of Ulster

Dr Liam Kennedy	Department of Economic and Social History, Queen's University, Belfast
Dr W. W. Knox	Department of Scottish History, University of St Andrews
Dr Ros McClean	Department of Economic and Social History, University of Edinburgh
Prof. R. J. Morris	Department of Economic and Social History, University of Edinburgh
Dr Graeme Morton	Department of Economic and Social History, University of Edinburgh
Dr C. W. Munn	Chartered Institute of Bankers in Scotland
Dr Stana Nenadic	Department of Economic and Social History, University of Edinburgh
Dr Gerard O'Brien	Department of History, University of Ulster
Prof. Cormac Ó Gráda	Department of Economics, University College, Dublin
Dr Clare O'Halloran	Clare Hall, Cambridge
Dr Vivienne Pollock	Ulster Museum, Belfast
Prof. Eric Richards	Department of History, Flinders University of South Australia.
Mr Iain Robertson	Cheltenham and Gloucester College of Higher Education
Prof. T. C. Smout	Department of Scottish History, University of St Andrews
Dr Richard Trainor	Centre of Business History in Scotland, University of Glasgow
Mr R. E. Tyson	Department of Economic History, University of Aberdeen
Dr Ronald Weir	Department of Economics, University of York
Dr I. D. Whyte	Department of Geography, University of Lancaster
Dr C. W. J. Withers	Department of Geography, University of Edinburgh
Mr Donald Woodward	Department of Economic and Social History, University of Hull

I

Identity, conflict and economic change: themes and issues

S. J. Connolly, R. A. Houston and R. J. Morris

'THIS BEING ST ANDREW'S DAY the Scotsmen about the town here are as drunk as beggars.'[1] The comment of a Dublin Castle official conveys, across an interval of more than three centuries, what has remained a characteristic blend of national distinctiveness and close association. Three earlier collective explorations of the parallels and contrasts in the development of Scotland and Ireland concentrated on economic questions. This fourth venture extended that agenda. To the consideration of population growth, agriculture, manufacturing industry and financial services was added an exploration of other points of comparison in areas of social relationships, intellectual history and cultural change. In both countries, the process of economic development was closely bound up with social and cultural change. All three were influenced by interaction with religion, class and growing national identity. Concern was expressed, both before and after the conference, at the analytical dilution that might result from this wider focus. There were dire warnings of the widening methodological gap between the economic history practised in Ireland and Scotland, and that practised in the United States.[2] Against this must be set the equally serious problem of fragmentation of historical method and subject area that, in Ireland and Scotland as elsewhere, threatens to call into question the whole coherence of our project of seeking to understand the past. In the end the organizers rest their case, not just on the quality of the papers offered on topics brought into the remit of this conference for the first time, but also on the connections that emerged between these papers and those dealing with more familiar economic themes. One purpose of this introduction is to highlight the more important of these connections.

* * *

---

[1] *Calendar of State Papers Ireland 1669–70*, p. 29 (30 November 1669).
[2] Cormac Ó Gráda in the plenary session.

Several major themes ran through the conference and are worth isolating. In part, these hint at tentative conclusions but they also provide starting points for future debate.

It was clear that the nature of authority in both countries was very different. This was most explicit in the discussion of the failure of the Irish landlord class to act as effective regulators of economic behaviour, a topic which is further discussed below. The difference was also apparent in political institutions. Despite the absence of representative institutions, the Scottish local state emerged during the eighteenth century as a coherent and integrated set of structures, which were often able to shrug off or isolate themselves from London influence. Edinburgh acted as a filter for patronage and a base for the law courts and for local managers who provided the links to London. In Ireland the state apparently had a stronger central focus in Dublin. But this state—despite the pretensions of its parliamentary rhetoric and the grandiose scale of its official architecture—had in practice only a limited ability to direct and control civil society. The contrast was clear in the operation of the poor laws. At national level, Scottish judges used their powers of creative interpretation to nullify unwanted Westminster legislation and create conditions in which local provision was superior to anything found in Ireland. At local level, the kirk session was the basis of an effective administrative framework for poor relief. The failure of the parish in Ireland, outside Protestant Ulster and the larger towns, to take on comparable functions reflects the legacy of religious division and uneven political evolution that made authority in Ireland so problematic.[3]

After 1707 Scotland remained in the same formal relationship with England, but the Irish state underwent repeated transformations: the emergence of the Irish parliament as an effective institution from the 1690s, integration with the United Kingdom in 1801, and in the early 1920s self government and devolution. These drastic redefinitions were symptom and cause of underlying weakness. After 1801 government in Ireland increasingly sought to maintain a posture of religious neutrality, and was by contemporary standards very active in the direct promotion of economic development. But this was a London centred state, whose response to the problem of sectarian divisions was to resort to centralised, bureaucratic institutions directly answerable to itself.[4] The result was structures of government that were superficially powerful, but lacked roots. This background helps to explain how levels of economic intervention far in excess of anything that would have been considered on the other side of either the Irish Sea or the North Channel achieved so little. A similar contrast in the degree of integration between state and society was evident in the twentieth century. By the 1920s, the Scottish state and the local business leadership were closely integrated. This helped preserve social and political stability in a period of intense economic strain. The same sort of integration was achieved in Northern Ireland, but with only one part of a divided society, so that long term political and social stability

---

[3] See David Dickson, 'In Search of the Old Irish Poor Law' in Mitchison and Roebuck, pp. 149–59.
[4] Oliver MacDonagh, *Ireland* (Eaglewood Cliffs, NJ, 1968), chap. 1.

was weakened and threatened.[5] Independent Ireland developed more stable institutions, but only within a political culture dominated by localism and clientism of a kind which arguably militated against successful economic management at national level.[6] At all periods, the problem of authority in Ireland was not that it was strong and 'oppressive', but rather that it was weak and ineffective.

Behind this discussion of the nature of the state, as with many other topics, there was a 'ghost at the feast'. England acted as a direct influence on both Scotland and Ireland and as a point of comparison for historians and contemporaries.[7] Scotland and Ireland were both subordinate partners in a dynamic centre–periphery relationship. Superficially, Scotland's subordination seemed to be the more complete. Representative national institutions were extinguished in 1707 and effective political nationalism emerged only in the 1960s.[8] Yet in cultural terms it was Scotland which emerged as capable of holding its own. Although contributions to the conference showed that Ireland had an active and creative cultural life, it was a culture produced by and for specific sections of Irish society. Ireland was never able, as Scotland was, to generate cultural products which were exported beyond its own society. There was no Irish equivalent of *Wealth of Nations* or *Self Help*. But Ireland and Scotland were not simply at the periphery of a cultural and political universe, they were subordinate parts of an economic system increasingly dominated by England and London-led finance and trade. Discussions of national political and cultural identity too often remain trapped in the notion that these ought to be related to independent statehood. Independence was as circumscribed by the proximity of Ireland and Scotland to the growing power of the English-centred commercial and industrial economic system as by the lack of 'state' institutions. Scotland's more effective political subordination and geographical proximity may have had material dividends. Echoing recent literature and re-opening an old debate, many participants doubted that a famine on the scale experienced by Ireland in the late 1840s would have been 'allowed' to take place in Scotland.[9]

---

[5] Paul Bew, Peter Gibbon and Henry Patterson, *The State in Northern Ireland, 1921–72* (Manchester, 1979); Tony Dickson, ed., *Scottish Capitalism: Class, State and Nation, from before the Union to the Present* (London, 1980).

[6] Mart Bax, 'The Small Community in the Irish Political Process', in P. J. Drudy, ed., *Ireland: Land, Politics and People* (Cambridge, 1982). On planning and sectional politics, see Paul Bew and Henry Patterson, *Sean Lemass and the Making of Modern Ireland, 1945–66* (Dublin, 1982).

[7] 'England hovers around the conference like Banquo's ghost: but perhaps she should be brought into focus.' Tom Bartlett in discussion.

[8] Indeed Scotland's growing sense of nationhood in the nineteenth century was firmly bound to asserting identity within the Union of 1707. See H. J. Hanham, *Scottish Nationalism* (London, 1969).

[9] Joel Mokyr, *Why Ireland Starved: A Quantitative and Analytical History of the Irish Economy, 1800–1850* (London, 1985), pp. 291–2; Cormac Ó Gráda, *The Great Irish Famine* (London, 1989), pp. 50–8. T. C. Smout's account of Paisley suggests the quiet way in which the Westminster government overrode market forces in times of Scottish crisis. T. C. Smout, 'The strange Intervention of Edward Twistleton: Paisley in Depression, 1841–3', in T. C. Smout, ed., *The Search for Wealth and Stability* (London, 1979).

This shared position as small nations in the shadow of a more powerful neighbour has always been part of the justification for the exercise in sustained comparison represented by the Irish–Scottish conferences. Discussion indicated that many participants felt that the national framework needed to be supplemented by a regional perspective. This was important in Devine's paper, where a well defined region in Scotland was being compared with a large part, although not the whole, of Ireland. Fitzpatrick argued that a study of the south east of Ireland would reveal an elite responding to the crisis in much the same way as Devine's Highland landlords.[10] Tyson's survey of eighteenth-century population identified the Western Isles and adjacent areas as a region where, in contrast to other parts of Scotland, the demographic regime approximated to that of Ireland as a whole. Gordon and Trainor were able to explore similarities in government–industry relationships by comparing the Belfast region with the west of Scotland. The feeling that comparison should operate at below the national level was summed up by Withers's phrase: discussion should be ecologically rather than politically bound. The different sizes of various regional elements in the two economies were important. Scotland had its vulnerable famine-struck region and Ireland had a prosperous, industrializing region, but the size of these zones and hence their overall impact on their national histories was very different.[11] Both Woodward and Daly suggested that Ireland as a whole was an 'outlier', with a demographic regime that produced growth on a scale and of an extent not seen elsewhere in the British Isles. There are periods within which different regions, like the Highlands or west of Ireland, have driven the historiography of both countries, but it is not clear if this means that they have driven historical development.[12]

Time and again the great fracture of Irish society, religious division, emerged as a feature of discussion and explanation. In eighteenth-century Scotland, laws against a small Catholic minority served to enhance the authority of the dominant groups.[13] By contrast, the Irish ruling class were not able to build a hegemonistic culture based upon religion. Religious rules and structures operated in different ways to exclude. Property, politics and the professions all had different degrees of closure. Official celebrations that elsewhere provided the opportunity for ritualised expressions of reciprocity, such as November the Fifth, were, in Ireland, triumphalist celebrations of the victory of one faction over another.[14] The double-edged rhetoric of the 'freeborn Englishman' which bound all elements of a paternalistic society in England was not available. The safety

---

[10] Cullen in this discussion questioned whether regional divisions in landlord response were in fact so clear cut.

[11] 'What was in Scotland the minority problem [the Highlands] was, in Ireland, quite simply, the majority problem.' L. M. Cullen, T. C. Smout and A. Gibson, 'Wages and Comparative Development in Ireland and Scotland, 1565–1780', in Mitchison and Roebuck, p. 114.

[12] Comparison with other European countries may help to pinpoint issues which require regional, national or international comparisons.

[13] Callum Brown, *The Social History of Religion in Scotland since 1730* (London, 1987).

[14] J. R. Hill, 'National Festivals, the State and "Protestant Ascendancy" in Ireland, 1790–1829', *Irish Historical Studies*, XXIV, 93 (1984), pp. 30–51.

valve of an 'open society' based upon short-distance social mobility was again fractured by religious exclusions.[15] There were other less obvious consequences. O'Brien's analysis of the failure of the Irish Enlightenment indicated large-scale misapplication of human capital consequent upon religious exclusion. Scottish intellectuals of the eighteenth century were able to use the political and cultural conflicts of the recent past to construct a general model of economic development and the progress of civility.[16] Their Irish counterparts remained shackled and fenced in by the continued need to uphold conflicting partisan interpretations of past and present.[17] Scotland also had religious divisions, parallel to and partly imported from Ireland. But in a context where neither side could hope to modify state structures to its own advantage, these conflicts were less threatening to the social fabric and generally took second place to the divisions of class and status. The comparison of Scotland and Ireland suggests that class divisions, despite the apocalyptic potential attributed to them by theorists and historians, have generally proved to be negotiable in a way that religious divisions have not.[18] As a result, when both countries experienced political crisis in the early twentieth century there were very different outcomes.

Finally, many discussions identified an element of convergence in the twentieth-century experience of both societies. Both were part of the widespread demographic transition which took place in the late nineteenth and early twentieth centuries. Ó Gráda's paper highlights some of the common features concealed behind the apparent singularities of the Irish case. Both societies also experienced substantial out-migration. This resulted in the establishment of communities in many parts of the world which not only retained but developed their Irish or Scottish culture and remained a substantial influence on the 'home' country. In both countries the twentieth-century crisis involved a decline in export industries which were major employers. In both cases the immediate reaction was for employers and owners of capital to seek a corporate relationship with the state. These and other features may be grouped together as they are often shared by societies influenced by the spread of a capitalist world economy. The power of that economy and the technology and culture

---

[15] Douglas Hay, Peter Linebaugh, John Rule, E. P. Thompson and Cal Winslow, *Albion's Fatal Tree: Crime and Society in Eighteenth-Century England* (London, 1975); H. J. Perkin, *The Origins of Modern English Society, 1780–1880* (London, 1969).

[16] Nicholas Phillipson, 'Politics, Politeness and the Anglicisation of early Eighteenth-Century Scottish Culture', in R. A. Mason, ed., *Scotland and England, 1286–1815* (Edinburgh, 1987).

[17] J. R. Hill, 'Popery and Protestantism, Civil and Religious Liberty: The Disputed Lessons of Irish History, 1690–1812', *Past and Present*, 118 (1988), pp. 96–129; Clare O'Halloran, '"The Island of Saints and Scholars": Views of the Early Church and Sectarian Politics in Late Eighteenth-Century Ireland', *Eighteenth-Century Ireland*, V (1990), pp. 7–20; Joseph Liechty, 'Testing the Depth of Catholic–Protestant Conflict: The Case of Thomas Leland's "History of Ireland" 1773', *Archivium Hibernicum*, XLII (1987), pp. 13–28.

[18] James D. Young, *The Rousing of the Scottish Working Class* (London, 1979); W. Knox, 'The Political and Workplace Culture of the Scottish Working Class, 1832–1914', in W. H. Fraser and R. J. Morris, eds., *People and Society in Scotland*, vol. II: *1830–1914* (Edinburgh, 1990).

which accompany it may provide for elements of convergence which become more powerful as the twentieth century comes to an end.

* * *

Considerable attention was paid to the long-term character and chronology of economic growth in the two societies. Gillespie rightly drew attention to the dangers of neglecting the seventeenth century. If the Scottish and Irish economies diverged at some point in the eighteenth century, was there an earlier period during which they developed along parallel lines or even converged? In 1978, Cullen and Smout proposed convergence, as Ireland, less developed than Scotland in 1600, grew more rapidly during the following century.[19] At first sight Whyte's figures on urbanisation provided little support for this picture of more rapid growth in Ireland, but Gillespie argued that the minimum size of an effective marketing centre was well below the 2,500 limit used by Whyte. Gillespie restated the case for rapid commercialisation and export-orientated growth. There remained the question of why growth did not translate itself into higher living standards and more extensive urbanisation. William Nicolson, travelling through south Ulster to his new diocese of Derry in 1718, reported that he had 'never beheld, even in Picardy, Westphalia or Scotland, such dismal marks of hunger and want'. Yet Irish exports around 1700 amounted to about 6s. per head of population, compared with 4s. in Scotland.[20]

Contemporaries were clear that these two points were linked in some way. 'No two million of people besides of any country in Europe,' the speaker of the Irish Commons noted around 1747, 'consume so little of the commodities which they raise themselves'.[21] A satisfactory modern analysis would have to uncover the mechanisms which diverted such a high proportion of Irish output to export-orientated markets. The traditional answer, exploitation by a uniquely rapacious landed class, carries little conviction, given the evidence of the relative weakness of landlord authority. One approach would focus on the closer integration of Ireland with the powerful English economy which forced Ireland into patterns of unequal exchange, in which bulk exports of primary goods were traded for manufactures. Another answer might lie in the uneven and ambiguous character of commercialisation in seventeenth- and eighteenth-century Ireland.[22] In either case, the question remains as to why Scotland, with a similar starting point in the seventeenth century, did not come to exhibit the same characteristics. More work is also needed on the distribution of wealth in the two societies, an issue opened

---

[19] Cullen and Smout, pp. 3–4.
[20] Dublin Municipal Library, Gilbert Mss, vol. 27, p. 179, Nicolson to Wake, 24 June 1718; Cullen and Smout, p. 5.
[21] PRONI D2707\A1\12\3, 'observations' in the handwriting of Henry Boyle, c. 1747.
[22] Devine and Dickson, pp. 265–7.

up by Whyte in an earlier conference and touched upon in Houston's paper below.[23]

Cullen's account of the Scottish exchange on London provided a basis for rejecting earlier claims of a crisis-ridden early eighteenth century. But the traditional picture of a less dynamic Scottish economy in the first half of the eighteenth century is confirmed by Houston's study of Edinburgh, where conditions remained significantly less buoyant than in Dublin until about 1750, at which point a marked 'take off' occurred.[24] Cullen also drew attention to the marked strengthening of Scotland's position from around 1760. Devine noted that a series of other indicators—linen production, tobacco imports and the restructuring of land tenure, to which Munn added banking—all pointed to the 1750s and early 1760s as a moment when Scottish economic development accelerated. The impact of the Seven Years' War was relevant here. In Ireland the 1750s are also generally taken as a turning point, separating the difficult first half of the eighteenth century from the more prosperous second half. Arthur Young, in 1780, believed that Ireland 'has since the year 1748 made as great advances as could possibly be expected, perhaps greater than any country in Europe.'[25] But existing accounts give an uneven chronology for growth. A spectacular leap forward in 1747–52 was followed by bank failures and poor harvests later in the '50s, renewed growth in the 1760s, followed by signs of a loss of momentum thereafter.[26] Detailed comparison of the chronology of growth in the two societies is necessary. The origins of future divergence may lie in the period when both economies were making unprecedented advances.

The interaction of economic, social and political factors became obvious when the conference considered population and resources. Tom Devine's comparison of the very different impact of the potato famine on the Western Highlands of Scotland and on large parts of Ireland emphasised the vigorous and effective response from Highland landlords. As discussion noted, this reflected a revolution during the eighteenth century in the attitudes of the Scottish governing class. Faced with earlier social crises, most notably in the 1690s, Scottish landlords had shown the same inability or unwillingness to act as their counterparts in Ireland in the 1840s. Even more striking were points raised in the discussion of Tyson's comparison of the eighteenth-century demographic history of the two societies. Attention centred on the manner in which a more rigid Scottish tenurial system helped to produce a pattern of late marriage, high levels of permanent celibacy, and the progressive removal of 'surplus' population from the land. This was very different from the rapid population growth, and consequent unchecked expansion of the landless and land-poor, which lay behind Ireland's slide into Malthusian disaster. At the heart of the problem was the inability of the landlords

---

[23] I. D. and K. A. Whyte, 'Debt and Credit, Poverty and Prosperity in a Seventeenth-Century Scottish Rural Community', in Mitchison and Roebuck, pp. 70–80.

[24] Dickson in Devine and Dickson.

[25] Arthur Young, *A Tour in Ireland, 1776–1779* (London, 1972), II, p. 258.

[26] L. M. Cullen, *An Economic History of Ireland since 1660* (London, 1972), p. 74; David Dickson, *New Foundations: Ireland 1660–1800* (Dublin, 1987), pp. 102–3.

to exercise real control over patterns of land occupation and land use on their estates.[27] By contrast, it was suggested, Scottish landlords in the late eighteenth century saw their estates as a 'chessboard' on which families and holdings could be rearranged at will.[28]

This line of argument echoes a central conclusion advanced in Devine and Dickson's review of the second conference in the series. On this occasion, however, some participants warned against turning some unspecified deficiency in Irish landlordism into an all-purpose explanation of economic failure or difficulty. There were references to the long leases that had to be granted in the late seventeenth and early eighteenth centuries in order to attract tenants and raise ready cash, as well as to the social, cultural and political gulf that divided the landed class from the majority of tenants and dependants. But assertions that landlords failed to manage their estates in such a way as to maintain a profitable balance between population and resources seemed to run ahead of explanations as to why this should have been so. If the reason was fear of agrarian violence, we still have to explain why the Irish rural population should have been more ready than their Scottish counterparts to resort to violence as a means of preventing unwelcome economic change, and why they were more successful in doing so. Nor should the power and authority of the Scottish landlords be taken as a universal truth for all regions during the whole eighteenth century. Scottish proprietors had only limited influence over tenant behaviour in the late seventeenth and early eighteenth centuries when good farmers were in short supply. Indeed tenants, as Whyte has shown, were in general richer, better informed and more able to bargain than is often allowed.[29] The fact that leases, at least up to the later eighteenth century, were made to head tenants, who then decided what cottars should be allowed on the land, means that the differences in the proliferation of landless and land-poor cannot have been a function of landlord attitudes alone. It remains vital to look at the economic fortunes and social attitudes of classes below the well-documented landlords. It is also important to acknowledge that population trends in the second half of the eighteenth century were only partly related to changes in the economic environment. The lower age of marriage and higher levels of permanent celibacy that prevailed in Scotland must be seen as reflecting not just landlord policy, but cultural differences and preferences. The fall in mortality that seems to have accounted for much of the growth in population after c. 1750 was partly due to human action, notably vaccination, but autonomous changes in patterns of disease may also have played a part.[30]

The conference then moved to the wider issue of how eighteenth-century Ireland might be seen in relation to Scotland. In commenting on groups of papers on the theme of social relationships and cultural production and interchange,

---

[27] This endorsed a central conclusion of the earlier conference; Devine and Dickson, pp. 46–57, 257–8.

[28] Tom Devine in discussion.

[29] Ian D. Whyte, *Agriculture and Society in Seventeenth-Century Scotland* (Edinburgh, 1979).

[30] R. A. Houston, 'The Demographic Regime', in T. M. Devine and Rosalind Mitchison, eds., *People and Society in Scotland*, vol. I: *1760–1830* (Edinburgh, 1988).

Bartlett and Smout both drew attention to central differences in perspective. On the one side were those who tended to stress the violence, the insecurity and the chronic social, religious and political tensions of Irish society. Mitchison, for example, characterised early nineteenth-century Ireland as 'colonial'. O'Halloran and O'Brien portrayed a society in which intellectual development was inhibited or even stifled by the divide between Protestant and Catholic. By contrast, Hill stressed the affinities between the political discourse of Hanoverian Dublin and that of contemporary Edinburgh. For her, Ireland was a typical ancien régime society. Connolly sought to demonstrate the applicability to Ireland of Peter Burke's model of elite and popular culture in pre-industrial Europe. In a substantial paper, which we are not able to publish here, Fitzpatrick presented an analysis of the mentality revealed in Irish emigrant letters from Australia, in which he emphasised the deferential attitude often expressed towards landlords and the absence of the sense of oppressed nationality commonly assumed.[31]

This provoked a lively discussion on the question of law and order. After a rapid review of events in England and other European countries, Morris suggested that Scotland rather than Ireland might be an exception and that it was the low levels of political violence in Scotland after 1745 which were in need of explanation. Urban and labour protest existed in Scotland but tended to be within the bounds of the existing political system.[32] Fitzpatrick wondered to what extent successive British governments exaggerated the lawlessness of Irish society. Indeed the styles of policing adopted may actually have created crime. The paper by Withers included an example of a temporary increase in agrarian outrage produced by an equally temporary redefinition of terms for statistical purposes. In a careful analysis of published tours, Nenadic demonstrated that the image of Ireland as a landscape full of a teeming and unruly people presented in this fashionable medium was as much a cultural construct as the perception of Scotland as a land of thriving manufactures, fine views and improved estates. Official statistics on crime and violence might provide some check on these perceptions, although such figures often conceal as much as they reveal. Figures for Irish trial committals suggest that violence against the person was more common than in England, although this is hard to reconcile with an apparently lower homicide rate.[33] There was a general feeling that there was a real qualitative difference between the two societies. A major reason, Hill suggested, was that in Ireland social protest was often organised and encouraged by a sizeable portion of the middle classes, namely the Catholic bourgeoisie, in a way that did not happen in either England or Scotland. There was real disagreement over the extent to which the religious and political conflicts

---

[31] David Fitzpatrick, '"That Beloved Country, that no Place Else Resembles": Connotations of Irishness in Irish-Australian Letters, 1841–1915', *Irish Historical Studies*, XXVII (1991), pp.324–51

[32] Ken J. Logue, *Popular Disturbances in Scotland, 1780–1815* (Edinburgh, 1979); W. H. Fraser, *Conflict and Class: Scottish Workers, 1700–1838* (Edinburgh, 1988).

[33] S. H. Palmer, *Police and Protest in England and Ireland, 1780–1850* (Cambridge, 1988) reviewed by S. J. Connolly, *Irish Historical Studies*, XXVI, 103 (1989), pp. 308–9.

of the nineteenth century could be read back into earlier periods. Nor was there agreement on the value of calling Ireland a 'colony'. Connolly believed that this was in a sense the core of the Irish problem both for historians and for contemporaries. Ireland had many of the built-in structural weaknesses of a colony, such as a history of dispossession and a legal system that favoured 'settlers' at the expense of 'natives', but it became increasingly difficult for Ireland's rulers to regard the Catholic lower classes as 'natives' outside the bounds of civil society. Ireland hovered ambiguously between the status of a particularly troublesome province and a foreign territory held by force.

Intellectual history was considered here for the first time in these meetings and yielded a variety of fruitful comparisons. With the exception of the Irish Presbyterians, the cultural interchange between Scotland and Ireland was surprisingly limited. Both kingdoms, it was argued, interacted with England rather than with each other. But the exchange between Scotland and England was, as Smout emphasised, a two-way traffic. That between England and Ireland was predominantly one-way.

O'Brien's view that there was no Irish Enlightenment provoked lively debate. Several participants proposed the distinction between a producer's Enlightenment which involved Scotland, and a consumer's Enlightenment which involved both societies. Lenman took the economic analogy furthest. The Scottish universities, notably Glasgow and Edinburgh, less rigid in their structures, were able to market the Enlightenment to an eager public in all three kingdoms in a way that neither Oxford, Cambridge nor Trinity College, Dublin, were able to do. Smout drew attention to the political implications of intellectual traditions. Irish radicals were able to look to myths of native antiquity for slogans and legitimation. Scottish radicals had no way of using Ossianic and related cultural production in the same way. Instead they took their pseudo-history from England, adopting mythologies like that of the Norman yoke. A closer reading of the use made of the histories of Wallace and Bruce by various Scottish political groupings would be needed before this argument could be followed through. Nenadic's study of published tour diaries raised important questions of method and interpretation in relation to material which historians of both societies have tended to use in an uncritical manner. In Ireland, Cullen noted, travel writers tended to become mouthpieces for political factions. Thus, Young's celebrated *Tour* articulated the political ideas of Edmund Burke and his associates and, as a result, fell foul of the Irish conservative establishment.

* * *

Both societies approached and experienced a period of crisis between 1900 and 1930. The challenges to the Irish state grew in substance and assertiveness, Scotland's rapid export-led industrial growth slowed and both were involved in the traumatic fighting in the Great War of 1914–18. The 1920s brought the break-up of the Irish state and the decline of the export industries. Alongside this the pressures of 'modernisation' affected two cultures which lay between the twin shadows of England and the United States. Traditions were invented, re-invented and transformed. Minority languages were defended and retreated.

Papers on housing and the labour market sought to combine local cultural and economic variations with features common to urban industrial economies as a whole. Daly contrasted Glasgow, Edinburgh and Dublin, dominated by crowded tenements, with Belfast, where cheap land and cheap bricks enabled a much better level of provision for individual family dwellings. Low working-class incomes, already seen as a major cause of housing problems in Scotland, emerged as a key explanation for Dublin's poor tenement housing.[34] In Scotland there was not only a tradition of a strong local state but also there was none of the political and sectarian paralysis evident in Dublin. The supply of public housing was negligible in both cities but tighter official regulation had been important in Scotland since the 1860s.[35] The singularity of the Belfast labour market reflected a complex interplay of market and sectarian forces. Late nineteenth-century skill differentials were greater than anything found in the comparable west of Scotland economy. This was attributed to the pool of cheap labour always available in the Irish countryside, as well as to the 'attractions' of Belfast's relatively cheaper housing for the unskilled working class. The existing inequalities and bias in the religious composition of the workforce were increased by the riots of the 1880s.[36] There was some suggestion that this interplay of high differentials and sectarian structuring could be represented as a dual labour market, which had grim implications for the ability of market forces to overcome sectarian inequalities.[37] But inequalities were not always a simple matter of sectarian exclusion. Informal recruiting practices based upon kin and neighbourhood networks, evident in many areas of Britain, limited access to certain jobs to closed groups within the Protestant population.[38] Numerically there were more poor Protestants in Belfast than there were poor Catholics. Several skilled and petit bourgeois occupations did gain a Catholic identity. Most important of all were the publicans who by 1911 were 80 percent Catholic. Hepburn's paper explored the links between the Catholic Irish culture of Belfast and Glasgow. His examination of the career of Joe Devlin showed the value of case studies for revealing the social mechanisms behind the statistics presented in earlier papers.

Two papers on the inter-war period used Scottish and Irish material to contribute to wider debates. Johnson and Geary used data from Belfast's two major shipyards to sustain their claim that wage rates had little influence on levels of unemployment in shipbuilding, although they were reminded in discussion that

---

[34] Richard Rodger, 'The Invisible Hand: Market Forces, Housing and the Urban Form in Victorian Cities', in Derek Fraser and Anthony Sutcliffe, eds., *The Pursuit of Urban History* (London, 1983).

[35] M. E. Daly, *Dublin, The Deposed Capital: A Social and Economic History, 1860–1914* (Cork, 1984), chap. 7; R. J. Morris, 'Urbanisation and Scotland', in Fraser and Morris, eds., *People and Society*, pp. 73–102; R. G. Rodger, 'The Law and Urban Change', *Urban History Yearbook*, 1979, pp. 71–91.

[36] Morris in this volume.

[37] Weir in discussion.

[38] Geary in discussion.

their argument depended on the context of a capital intensive industry.³⁹ Gordon and Trainor documented the close links between Scottish industrialists and government, and the even closer involvement of Ulster industry with the Stormont government of the 1920s and 1930s. This does seem to counter the claims of many British historians that government policy served the financial sector against the interests of industry. The context of their evidence was again relevant. Both the west of Scotland and Belfast industrial organisations they examined were concerned with export industries and thus might be expected to follow the free trade and stable exchange rate policies of the London government. Munn's reminder of the importance of the growth of financial services brought comments akin to the political economy of the 1970s which suggested that in some way such services were not 'real'.⁴⁰

The common pressures of a modernizing world economy were felt in cultural as well as in economic life. The response was most marked in Ireland. Earlier 'discoveries of the people' had been elitist and—apart from the Young Ireland movement of the 1840s—apolitical. From the 1880s cultural nationalism acquired a broader social base and increasingly close links with separatist politics. For some, particularly the Catholic clergy and their lay allies, movements of cultural defence such as the Gaelic League were a negative response to the commercialisation of leisure and the growing penetration of Irish society by 'alien' influences. But there were others whose concern was with finding ways in which the modernisation of Ireland's economy and society could be combined with the preservation of a distinct Irish identity.⁴¹ It is also important to recognize that commercialisation and technological change provided not just the threat against which cultural nationalism reacted, but also the means for its development and growth. The Scottish experience was more diffuse than the Irish. Tradition was invented at venues like the Highland Games, but the same period saw the enthusiastic import of 'English' games like association football.⁴² But even such cultural imports, as Connolly suggests in the example of popular music, involved a degree of choice between rival possibilities. Diverse elements could be combined, as in the Irish showband, into a distinctive national style.

Historians still need to locate the importance of these debates in the context of the development of the two countries involved. The difficulties of the historians perhaps reflect the struggle within both countries to develop and sustain an independent and viable economic system controlled from within the country concerned. In recent literature, Foster and Woolfson have identified the efforts of a key group of Clyde employers to use links with an increasingly corporatist state,

---

³⁹ Liam Kennedy in discussion.

⁴⁰ Robert Bacon and Walter Eltis, *Britain's Economic Problem: Too Few Producers* (London, 1976).

⁴¹ Joseph Lee, *The Modernisation of Irish Society, 1848–1918* (Dublin, 1973), p. 137ff; John Hutchison, *The Dynamics of Cultural Nationalism: The Gaelic Revival and the Creation of the Irish Nation State* (London, 1987), pp. 168–78; Tom Garvin, *Nationalist Revolutionaries in Ireland 1858–1928* (Oxford, 1987), pp. 67–75.

⁴² Connolly in this volume; Fraser in Fraser and Morris, *People and Society*.

especially links forged through the Scottish Unionist Party, to sustain both the Scottish economy and the Scottish Unionist national identity. The Northern Ireland state developed a similar but much more divisive client corporatism.[43] Historians remain divided on the degree to which strategies of economic nationalism were a possible way forward for the Irish state. An earlier orthodoxy in which post-1932 protectionist policies were seen as a self-inflicted disaster, has begun to be called into question.[44] A recent study by Lee attributes the dismal economic performance across the whole period since 1922 less to specific policies than to culture and institutions. His suggestion that 'Small states must rely heavily on the quality of their strategic thinking to counter their vulnerability to international influences', must leave historians wondering if Irish independence or Scottish dependent corporatism was the most effective base for such thinking.[45] In his commentary on the *New Forum Report*, produced in Dublin in 1984 in response to the Northern Ireland crisis, Lee notes, 'the report rightly detected the gap between the potential and the performance of the Dublin state . . . It produced no compelling evidence to suggest that partition was a factor in the slovenliness of the national performance.'[46] In contrast to this, recent debate in Scotland which was centred on the Constitutional Convention and the run-down of the Scottish steel industry has argued over the nature, extent and impact of Scottish dependency. The common assumption that Scotland relied upon subsidies had been challenged by the suggestion that government spending which involves a net transfer to Scotland is expressed in regional terms, whilst other forms of spending, like defence, which involve net transfers to England, are rarely calculated this way. Hence public and political perceptions of dependency are fundamentally distorted.[47] *The Economist*, however, claimed that 'the union . . . involves bribing the Scots to eschew nationalism and stay loyal to Westminster'.[48] Much work needs to be done before it is clear how far twentieth-century Scotland has been subsidised or exploited by unionism, and the degree to which this contrasts with the experience of economic sluggishness under the direction of the 'intense centralisation of the Dublin state'.[49] It is clear after this conference that progress will only be made by a continued willingness to pursue forms of analysis in which the economic, the cultural and the political are integrated rather than partitioned.

---

[43] John Foster and Charles Woolfson, *The Politics of the UCS Work-in* (London, 1986); Bew, Gibbon and Patterson, *The State in Northern Ireland*.

[44] M. Daly, 'The Employment Gains from Industrial Protection in the Irish Free State during the 1930s: A Note', *Ir. Econ. and Soc. Hist.*, XV (1988), pp. 71–5; J. P. Neary and Cormac Ó Gráda, 'Protection, Economic War and Structural Change: The 1930s in Ireland', *Irish Historical Studies*, XXVII, 107 (1991).

[45] J. J. Lee, *Ireland, 1912–1985* (Cambridge, 1989), p. 627–31; Craig Beveridge and Ronald Turnbull, *The Eclipse of Scottish Culture* (Edinburgh, 1989).

[46] Lee, *Ireland*, p. 678.

[47] *Scotland on Sunday*, 25 November 1990.

[48] *The Economist*, 26 May 1990.

[49] Lee, *Ireland*, p. 678.

2

Scottish and Irish urbanisation in the seventeenth and eighteenth centuries: a comparative perspective

I. D. Whyte

URBANISATION has been identified as a key element in the modernisation of Europe's economy and society between the sixteenth and seventeenth centuries. Its outlines have been sketched by de Vries[1] and there have been some more detailed studies of changing patterns of urbanisation in different countries.[2] Despite recent comparative research into the social and economic development of Ireland and Scotland during the seventeenth and eighteenth centuries little attention has been paid to the processes of urbanisation in the two countries. Reasons for this are not hard to seek. Irish urban history, particularly its social and economic dimensions, has been slow to develop compared with England.[3] In Scotland, until recently, urban studies for the pre-industrial period focused on the institutional development of burghs rather than on their economic and social development. Although recent research has begun to explore the socio-economic structures of Scottish towns in greater depth much of it has concentrated on individual towns rather than adopting a comparative perspective.[4]

In looking at the urban systems of Scotland and Ireland before the nineteenth century one immediately faces problems caused by the paucity of available data. Information on urban populations in Scotland before the 1801 census is variable in nature and quality making comparison difficult. Estimates of the populations of the larger towns can be made back to the late sixteenth century but information on

---

[1] J. de Vries, *European Urbanisation 1500–1800* (London, 1984).
[2] E.g. B. Lepetit, 'Event and Structure: The Revolution and the French Urban System 1700–1840', *Journal of Historical Geography* 16 (1900), pp. 17–37.
[3] L. A. Clarkson, 'The Writing of Irish Economic and Social History since 1968', *Economic History Review*, XXX (1980), p. 104.
[4] However, for a true comparative viewpoint see M. Lynch,'Continuity and Change in Urban Society 1500–1700', in R. A. Houston and I. D. Whyte, eds., *Scottish Society 1500–1800* (Cambridge, 1989), pp. 85–117.

the sizes of smaller centres is much scarcer and less reliable. The problem is even worse for Ireland. Before the census of 1821 only the hearth tax returns of the late seventeenth and eighteenth centuries provide suitable data. They have been analyzed at a county level[5] but so far they have not been examined systematically for the purpose of reconstructing the sizes of Irish towns.

Nevertheless urbanisation is a key topic in relation to the development of both countries during these two centuries. Cullen and Smout have argued that the economies of Ireland and Scotland did not begin to diverge significantly before the 1780s.[6] On this basis one might expect considerable comparability between the urban systems of the two countries in earlier times with indications of growing contrasts during the eighteenth century. The purpose of this paper is first to attempt a reconstruction of the Scottish and Irish urban hierarchies during the seventeenth and eighteenth centuries. Similarities and differences between the urban systems of the two countries are then considered in relation to their economic and social development.

THE BROAD PATTERN OF URBANISATION

It is useful to start with de Vries's figures while acknowledging, as he does, the imperfections of the data that he used.[7] His data base included towns with estimated populations of 10,000 or over, largely because of the problems of trying to reconstruct the lower levels of the urban hierarchy, even for part of Europe. It provides a good measure of the approximate proportions of the population living in large towns and cities. From de Vries's data (Table 1) it is clear that in 1500 Ireland and Scotland were very lightly urbanised. Ireland had no urban centres with over 10,000 inhabitants and Scotland had only Edinburgh. The proportion of the Scottish population in towns with over 10,000 began to rise during the later sixteenth century and increased steadily thereafter. A comparison of the rate of growth of the urban population shows that in the second half of the sixteenth and seventeenth centuries the rate of growth of urban population in Scotland matched that south of the border and during the eighteenth century significantly exceeded it. In Ireland the rise in the proportion of the population in towns with populations over 10,000 began later. There was a dramatic growth of urban population during the seventeenth century but a slackening of the rate of increase in the eighteenth. During the first half of the eighteenth century the Irish urban population grew at a slower rate than in Scotland (though faster than in England and Wales) but rose to match the Scottish rate of growth during the second half of the century.

---

[5] D. Dickson, C. Ó Gráda and S. Daultry, 'Hearth Tax, Household Size and Irish Population Change 1672–1821', *Proceedings of the Royal Irish Academy*, C, LXXXII (1982), pp. 125–81.
[6] L. M. Cullen and T. C. Smout, 'Economic Growth in Scotland and Ireland', in Cullen and Smout, pp. 3–18.
[7] De Vries, *European Urbanisation*, pp. 21–2.

Table 1: Urbanisation in Scotland, Ireland and England & Wales (after de Vries)

Percentage of total population in towns with over 10,000 inhabitants

	1500	1550	1600	1650	1700	1750	1800
Scotland	1.6	1.4	3.0	3.5	5.3	9.2	17.3
Ireland	0	0	0	0.9 *(1.1)	3.4 (5.3)	5.0 (7.0)	7.0 (7.38)
England & Wales	3.1	3.5	5.8	8.8	13.3	16.7	20.3

Total population in towns with over 10,000 inhabitants (thousands)

	1500	1550	1600	1650	1700	1750	1800
Scotland	13	13	30	35	53	119	276
Ireland	0	0	0	17	96	161	369
England & Wales	80	112	255	495	718	1021	1870

* Based on revised population estimates: see text.

However, the growth in the urban proportions of the total population tells a different story. By 1800 Scotland was, by this definition, almost as urbanised as England, having started from a baseline almost as low as Ireland in 1500. The level of Irish urbanisation was much lower. It was below that of France and Portugal though not as low as Germany, Scandinavia or Eastern Europe.[8] On this basis Scotland was, with England, far along the path towards becoming an urbanised society while Ireland was still clearly a rural one. The reason for the difference lay in the much faster growth of the Irish rural population during the seventeenth and especially the eighteenth century. The total Scottish population only doubled between 1500 and 1800 against a five-fold increase for Ireland.

Given the broadly similar character of the Irish and Scottish economies in the seventeenth and early eighteenth centuries, how does one explain the seemingly marked difference in levels of urbanisation between the two countries? First, it should be noted that de Vries's calculations are based on estimates of Ireland's total population which are now widely considered to be too high.[9] The revisions of Connell's and Cullen's figures now favour slower population growth in the seventeenth century and the first half of the eighteenth.[10] If the more recent lower revised estimates are used the proportion of the Irish population that was urbanised is substantially increased for 1650, 1700 and 1750 (Table 1). On these new calculations

---

[8] *Ibid.* p. 39.

[9] L. A. Clarkson, 'Irish Population Revisited, 1687–1821', in J. M. Goldstrom and L. A. Clarkson, eds., *Irish Population, Economy and Society* (Oxford, 1981), pp. 13–36; Dickson *et al*, 'Irish Population Change', p. 156.

[10] K. H. Connell, *The Population of Ireland 1750–1845* (Oxford, 1950). Revised figures are suggested in: L. M. Cullen, 'Population Trends in Seventeenth-Century Ireland', *Econ. & Soc. Rev.*, 6 (1975), pp. 149–65.

the proportion of Ireland's population in towns of over 10,000 had risen rapidly during the second half of the seventeenth century to match that of Scotland. Scotland had moved ahead slightly by 1750 and the gap widened rapidly in the later eighteenth century. This interpretation of Irish urbanisation fits more closely the pattern of economic growth outlined by Cullen and Smout,[11] with Irish exports per capita being well ahead of Scotland at the end of the seventeenth century, only slightly ahead by the 1750s but well behind by 1800.

SCOTTISH AND IRISH URBAN HIERARCHIES

So far, we have been considering only the upper levels of the urban hierarchies of Scotland and Ireland. As in other European countries, notably Germany, smaller towns were far more numerous in both countries and contained a significant proportion of the total urban population. Smaller local and regional market centres must have represented the normal urban experience for most Scottish and Irish rural dwellers. A more realistic appraisal of the progress and character of urbanisation in the two countries is needed.

In Table 2 an attempt is made to calculate the proportions of the population of Scotland and, more tentatively, of Ireland, living in smaller as well as larger towns at various dates during the seventeenth and eighteenth centuries. An arbitrary lower limit of 2,500 inhabitants has been used. It is appreciated that many centres with small populations in both countries had urban characteristics. However, the difficulty of differentiating between the urban and rural components of the populations in sources based on parishes makes it impossible to determine the size of smaller centres with any accuracy for most periods. The percentage of the population in towns with more than 2,500 inhabitants is a better overall measure of urbanisation than de Vries's figures. In Scotland the growing demographic importance of smaller centres is particularly notable.

As a further aid to comparative analysis, changes through time in the rank/size distribution of the larger towns in each country can be considered. Although empirically based, this method has been used widely in the comparison of urban systems.[12] Rank/size distributions for Scottish towns in the seventeenth and eighteenth centuries can be calculated from a number of sources. First there is the 1639 tax on burgh rents which has been used by Lynch.[13] Then there are the hearth and poll tax data for the mid-1690s.[14] For the mid-eighteenth century Webster's census of

---

[11] Cullen and Smout, pp. 3–8, 54.
[12] The nature of rank/size distributions is discussed in P. Hagget, *Geography: A Modern Synthesis* (New York, 1975), pp. 356–62.
[13] Lynch, 'Continuity and Change', pp. 101–5.
[14] Population data calculated from these data and the 1639 tax are presented, and problems of calculation and interpretation reviewed, in I. D. Whyte, 'Urbanisation in Early-Modern Scotland: A Preliminary Consideration', *Scottish Economic and Social History* 9 (1989), pp. 23–6.

Table 2: Percentage of total population in Scottish and Irish towns

Scotland	1560[a]	1639[b]	1690s[c]	1755[d]	1790s[e]	1801[f]	1821[g]
Capital	1.1	2.7	4.5	4.5	5.6	5.1	6.6
Other towns over 10,000	0.0	3.5	2.7	4.4	10.8	12.8	19.2
5,000–9,999	0.6	3.3	1.6	3.2	3.2	8.9	6.3
2,500–4,999	0.8	2.2	3.1	4.2	6.4	9.3	6.4
Total	2.5	11.7	11.9	17.3	26.0	36.1	38.5

Ireland	1600[h]	1660[i]	1680s[j]	1700[j]			1821[k]
Capital	0.5	1.5	3.5	3.9			2.7
Other towns over 10,000	0.0	0.8	3.8				4.7
5,000–9,999	0.0	0.5	2.3				2.7
2,500–4,999	1.1	1.8	2.7				2.4
Total	1.6	4.6	12.3				12.5

Sources:

a. S. G. E. Lythe and J. Butt, *An Economic History of Scotland 1100–1939* (Glasgow, 1975), pp. 5–6.
b. M. Lynch, 'Continuity and Change in Urban Society 1500–1700' in R. A. Houston and I. D. Whyte, eds., *Scottish Society 1500–1800* (Cambridge, 1989), pp. 102–3.
c. 1690s Hearth and poll taxes: see I. D. Whyte, 'Urbanization in Early-Modern Scotland: A Preliminary Analysis', *Scot. Econ. & Soc. Hist.*, 9 (1989), pp. 21–37.
d. Webster's census.
e. Statistical Account.
f. 1801 census.
g. 1821 census.
h. and j. R. A. Butlin, 'Irish Towns in the Sixteenth and Seventeenth Centuries', in R. A. Butlin, ed., *The Making of the Irish Town* (London, 1977), p. 93.
i. S. Pender, *A Census of Ireland c. 1659* (Dublin, 1939).
k. W. E. Vaughan and A. J. Fitzpatrick, *Irish Historical Statistics* (Dublin, 1978), pp. 28–41.

1755 provides a useful reference point while towards the end of the century the Statistical Account contains detailed population figures for most towns.[15] Finally, there is the census of 1801.[16] Attempts to assess the rank/size distribution of Scottish burghs as early as the fourteenth century have been made by Fox[17] using the proportions of burgh taxation paid by various towns. However, in view of the evidence that the relationship between volume of trade, size of tax assessment and population was not always a close one,[18] this work should be treated with caution.

[15] J. G. Kyd, *Scottish Population Statistics* (Scottish History Society, Edinburgh, 1952); Sir John Sinclair, ed., *Statistical Account of Scotland*, 21 vols (Edinburgh, 1791–7).
[16] 1801 census.
[17] R. Fox, 'The Burghs of Scotland 1327, 1600, 1670', *Area*, 13 (1981), pp. 161–7.
[18] M. Lynch, 'The Social and Economic Structure of the Larger Towns 1450–1600', in M. Lynch, M. Spearman and G. Stell, eds., *The Scottish Medieval Town* (Edinburgh, 1988), pp. 269–70.

THE RANK/SIZE DISTRIBUTION OF SCOTTISH TOWNS, 1639–1801

Figure 1 shows the changing rank/size distribution between 1639 and 1801. Comparison of the graphs for 1639 and the mid 1690s suggests that some growth of population in Glasgow and Edinburgh, and a good deal of growth among smaller towns, was offset by decline in some of the main regional centres. This supports Lynch's theory of later seventeenth-century urban stagnation and decline,[19] though clearly it was far from universal. Overall the total population living in burghs with more than 2,000 inhabitants grew between these two periods. The graphs for the 1690s, 1755 and the 1790s suggest a modest expansion of population in the larger centres during the first half of the eighteenth century followed by more substantial growth in the second half of the century. It should be noted that the 1755 data, unlike those from the Statistical Account, are for parishes containing towns and not for towns themselves. Thus the 1755 populations for smaller towns are inflated. The degree of expansion in the lower part of the urban hierarchy during the first half of the eighteenth century has probably been exaggerated, and during the second half underestimated. Between the 1790s and 1801 the distance between the lower levels of the urban hierarchies has probably been widened artificially by the inclusion of a proportion of non-urban inhabitants in the parish totals from the 1801 census. As far as the populations of smaller towns are concerned, the data from the Statistical Account are more accurate than those from the 1801 census.

Over the two centuries the trend is for the rank/size distribution of Scottish towns to move from a shallow convex curve towards a slightly concave one. This has been caused by a greater expansion of population in the larger towns compared with the smaller ones. In 1639 Scotland's larger burghs were slightly smaller in relation to the remainder of the urban hierarchy than would have been expected with a linear rank/size relationship. Given that several larger burghs, especially Edinburgh, grew substantially in the later sixteenth and early seventeenth centuries,[20] it is likely that the rank/size distribution in the mid-sixteenth century was even more convex. Such a distribution was characteristic of much of Europe and was a symptom of an immature pre-modern urban system with a low level of economic integration between different regions.[21]

During the seventeenth century the slope of the graph steepens reflecting a tendency for larger centres, and possibly smaller ones too, to grow at the expense of middle-rank centres. During the eighteenth century, while the entire urban system experienced growth, the tendency was for much of it to be concentrated in the larger towns and some of the middle-rank centres. De Vries has characterised

---

[19] Lynch, 'Continuity and Change', pp. 104–5.
[20] M. Lynch, *Edinburgh and the Reformation* (Edinburgh, 1981), pp. 9–11.
[21] De Vries, *European Urbanisation*, p. 95.

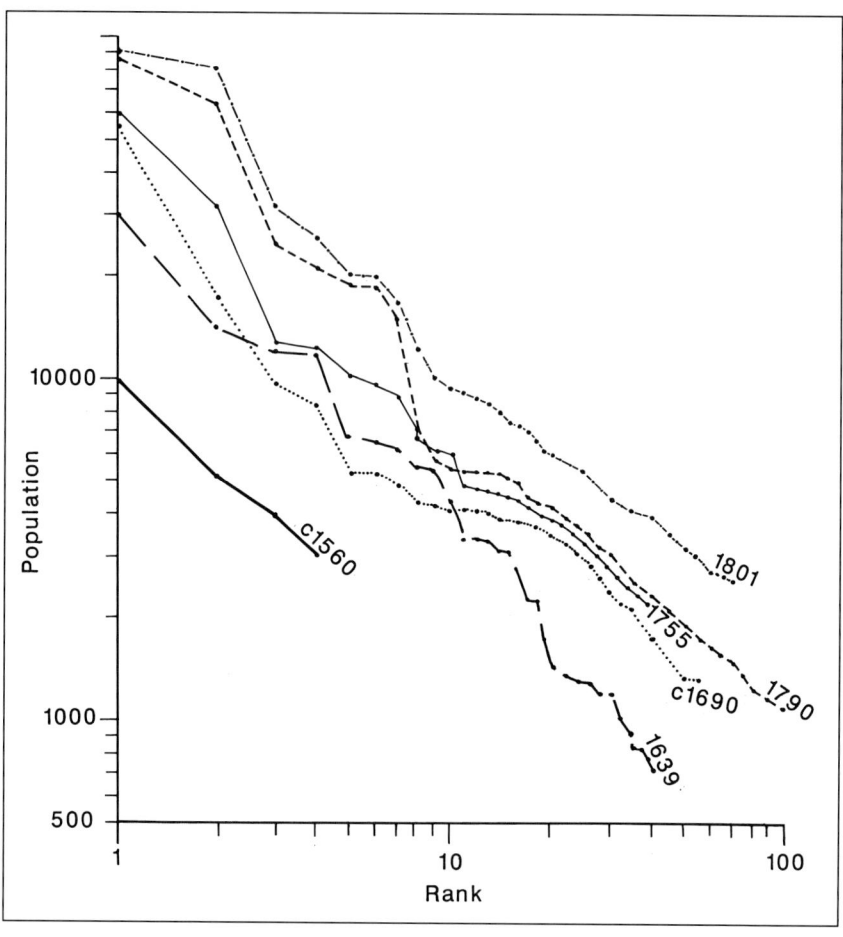

Figure 1: Rank/Size distributions of Scottish towns c. 1560–1801

the century after 1750 as one in which there was disproportionate growth among individual smaller centres.[22] Although there were some impressive growth rates among smaller Scottish towns, there is little sign of this disproportionate growth by the 1790s. Throughout this period the rank/size graph for England remains much more markedly concave due to the extreme dominance of London in terms of size and importance over the rest of the urban hierarchy.[23]

---

[22] *Ibid.*, pp. 98–101.
[23] *Ibid.*, p. 118.

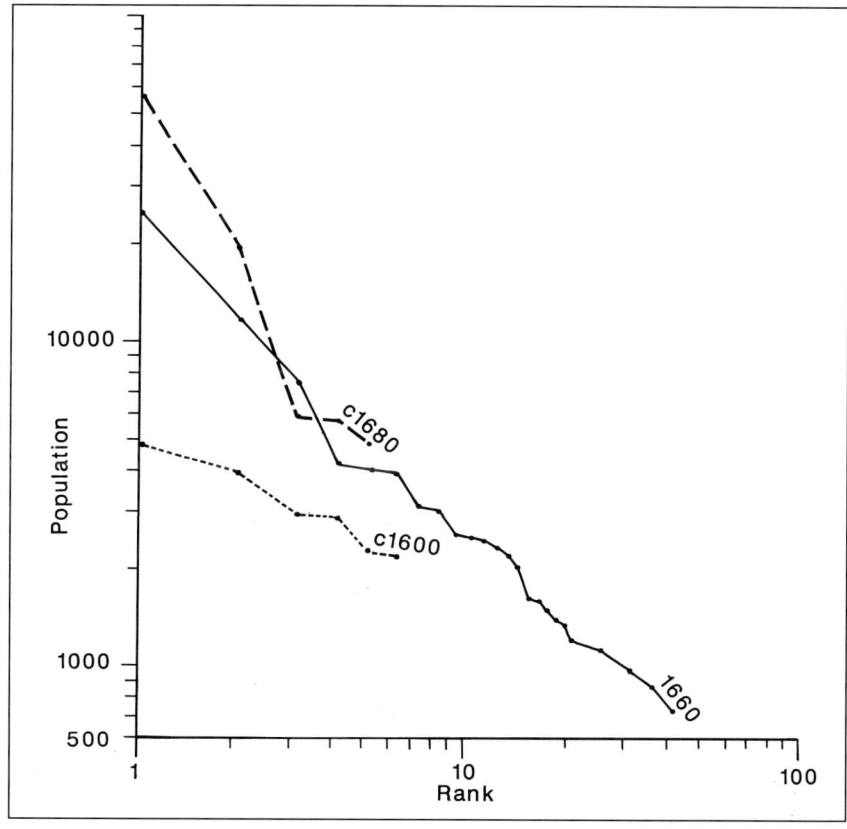

Figure 2: Rank/size distributions of Irish towns in the seventeenth century.

THE IRISH URBAN HIERARCHY IN 1660 AND 1821

For Ireland the construction of rank/size graphs for the seventeenth and eighteenth centuries is hampered by the lack of readily accessible data on urban populations compared with Scotland. The manuscript returns for the hearth taxes would, if analysed in detail, provide a good picture of urban development but such a large-scale research programme lies beyond the scope of the present study. However, the so-called '1659 census', actually an abstract of the 1660 poll tax returns, has been published.[24] Despite problems of interpretation,[25] the returns

---

[24] S. Pender, *A Census of Ireland c. 1659* (Dublin, 1939).

[25] W. J. Smyth, 'Society and Settlement in Seventeenth-Century Ireland: The Evidence of the "1659 Census"', in W. J. Smyth and K. Whelan, eds., *Common Ground: Essays on the Historical Geography of Ireland* (Cork, 1988), p. 56.

provide a more complete picture of Irish urbanisation at this time than is available for Scotland. Data are missing for counties Carlow, Galway, Mayo, Tyrone and Wicklow as well as for parts of Cork and Meath. This means that a few sizeable towns, including Galway, Strabane and Wicklow, are omitted. Nevertheless, using estimated population values for these a virtually complete rank/size distribution can be constructed (Figure 2). A multiplier of 2.5 has been used to convert hearth tax populations to total populations.[26] The figure for Dublin calculated on this basis is only slightly below the estimated one of more than 25,000 suggested by Butlin for this date[27] and discrepancies are likely to have been less pronounced for smaller towns.

Estimates of the populations of the larger Irish towns c. 1600 suggest that at this time the rank/size distribution was probably more gently sloping in its upper levels than the Scottish one with no clear primate city which was disproportionately large, as London was within the English urban hierarchy (Figure 2). This fits Butlin's interpretation of the Irish urban system at this time being poorly integrated and characterised by a series of isolated ports, each with a high degree of autonomy and its own distinct hinterland.[28] It also matches Haggett's interpretation of an undeveloped urban system,[29] and is mirrored in the overall pattern of Irish population distribution in the mid-seventeenth century with a number of distinct concentrations of higher population density focusing on the main coastal towns.[30] The Scottish urban hierarchy had exhibited similar features in the fourteenth century but had achieved greater cohesion by the early seventeenth century.[31] This probably reflected the earlier rise of Edinburgh, in terms first of trade and later of population, compared with Dublin,[32] and contrasting political conditions, as will be discussed below.

THE SCOTTISH AND IRISH URBAN HIERARCHIES COMPARED

It is instructive to compare the rank/size distributions for Scotland in 1639 and Ireland in 1660 (Figure 3). Caution is necessary for the distributions are derived from different sources. Moreover the Scottish urban hierarchy is seen at the end of a relatively prosperous period before the onset of civil war and plague while the Irish one relates to a date when towns were only just beginning to recover from these disasters. However, there are indications that the recovery of trade, and hence of urban prosperity, was well under way in Ireland by the end of the Cromwellian regime,[33] so that comparison with Scotland in 1639 is not unrealistic.

[26] *Ibid.*
[27] Butlin, 'Irish Towns', p. 93.
[28] *Ibid.*
[29] Haggett, *Geography*, pp. 356–62.
[30] Smyth, 'Society and Settlement', pp. 57–8.
[31] Fox, 'The Burghs of Scotland'.
[32] Lynch, 'Social and Economic Structure'.
[33] P. Corish, 'The Cromwellian Regime 1650–60', in T. W. Moody, F. X. Martin and F. J. Byrne, eds., *A New History of Ireland,* Vol III: *Early Modern Ireland 1534–1691* (Oxford, 1976), p. 373.

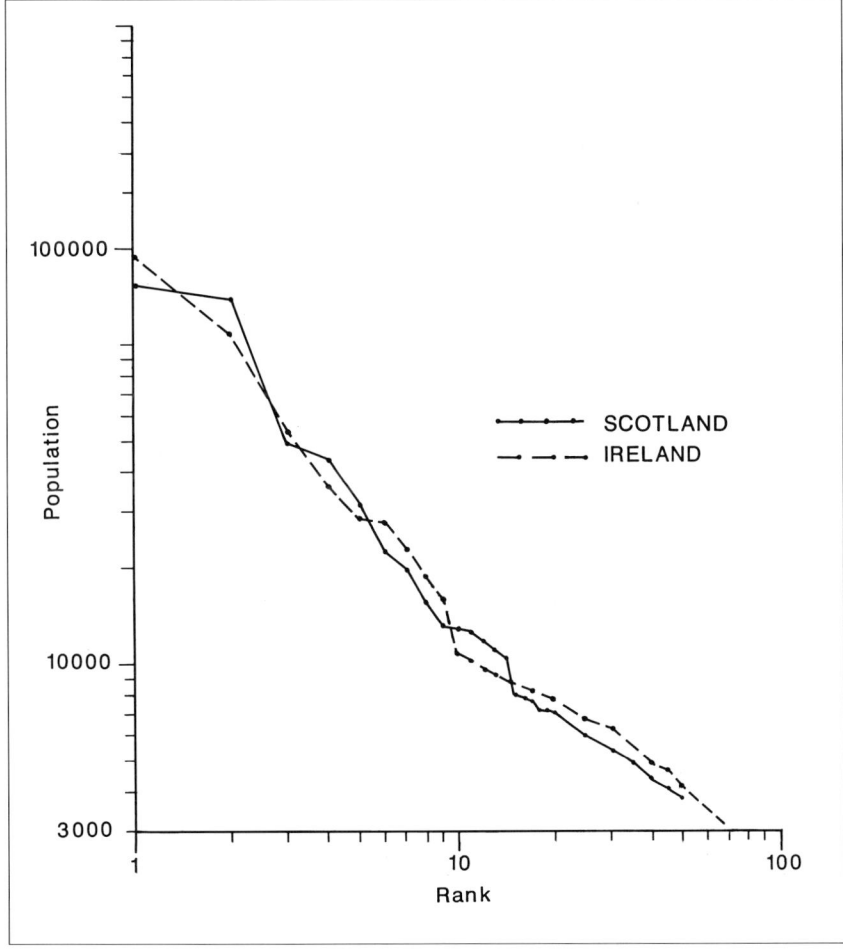

Figure 3: Rank/size distributions of Scottish towns, 1639 and Irish towns, 1660.

The graph shows that the urban hierarchies of the two countries match quite closely though with an overall higher level of urban development in Scotland. The merging of the lower ends of the graphs suggests a similar distribution of small market and agricultural service centres in countries with many similarities in agricultural and rural settlement patterns. At the top the graphs parallel each other, suggesting that Dublin and Cork had comparable levels of importance compared with Edinburgh and Glasgow. It is in the middle that the graphs diverge most, the relative strength of Scottish regional centres, notably Aberdeen, Dundee and Perth, contrasting with the smaller relative populations of their Irish rank equivalents. This may emphasise the degree to which Dublin had already begun to dominate the Irish urban system. However, given that Dublin suffered less during the disturbed 1640s and early

Table 3: Comparative sizes of twelve Scottish and Irish towns at various dates

Scotland

	1639		c. 1690		1755	
1.	Edinburgh	30,000	Edinburgh	54,000	Edinburgh	57,215
2.	Glasgow	14,000	Glasgow	17,100	Glasgow	31,840
3.	Aberdeen	12,000	Aberdeen	9,900	Dundee	12,427
4.	Dundee	12,000	Dundee	8,250	Aberdeen	10,785
5.	St Andrews	6,750	Musselburgh	4,800	Inverness	9,730
6.	Dumfries	6,250	Kilmarnock	4,400	Perth	9,019
7.	Perth	6,000	Ayr	4,200	Dunfermline	8,552
8.	Inverness	5,200	Perth	3,800	Elgin	6,300
9.	Montrose	5,200	Inverness	3,800	Alloa	5,816
10.	Ayr	4,250	Stirling	3,700	Jedburgh	5,816
11.	Stirling	3,250	Montrose	3,600	Musselburgh	4,645
12.	Haddington	3,250	Kirkcaldy	3,500	St Andrews	4,590
	c. 1790–95		1801		1821	
1.	Edinburgh	84,880	Glasgow	84,102	Glasgow	150,818
2.	Glasgow	64,743	Edinburgh	82,266	Edinburgh	138,241
3.	Dundee	24,000	Paisley	31,179	Paisley	47,003
4.	Aberdeen	20,067	Dundee	26,804	Aberdeen	44,796
5.	Paisley	19,903	Aberdeen	17,597	Dundee	30,575
6.	Perth	19,500	Greenock	17,458	Greenock	22,088
7.	Greenock	15,000	Perth	14,898	Perth	19,068
8.	Dumfries	6,902	Stirling	12,118	Stirling	15,387
9.	Kilmarnock	5,670	Dunfermline	9,980	Dunfermline	13,861
10.	Ayr	5,560	Peterhead	9,019	Kilmarnock	12,769
11.	Montrose	5,194	Falkirk	8,838	Inverness	12,264
12.	Dunfermline	5,192	Inverness	8,732	Falkirk	11,536

Ireland

	c. 1660		1821	
1.	Dublin	21,950	Dublin	185,881
2.	Cork	12,065	Cork	100,658
3.	Limerick	7,763	Limerick	50,045
4.	Kilkenny	4,305	Belfast	37,270
5.	Waterford	4,118	Waterford	28,679
6.	Drogheda	4,013	Galway	27,775
7.	Kinsale	3,350	Kilkenny	23,230
8.	Carrickfergus	3,278	Drogheda	18,118
9.	Athlone	2,688	Clonmel	15,590
10.	Londonderry	2,630	Bandon	10,179
11.	Galway	2,625	Newry	10,013
12.	Youghal	2,390	Londonderry	9,313

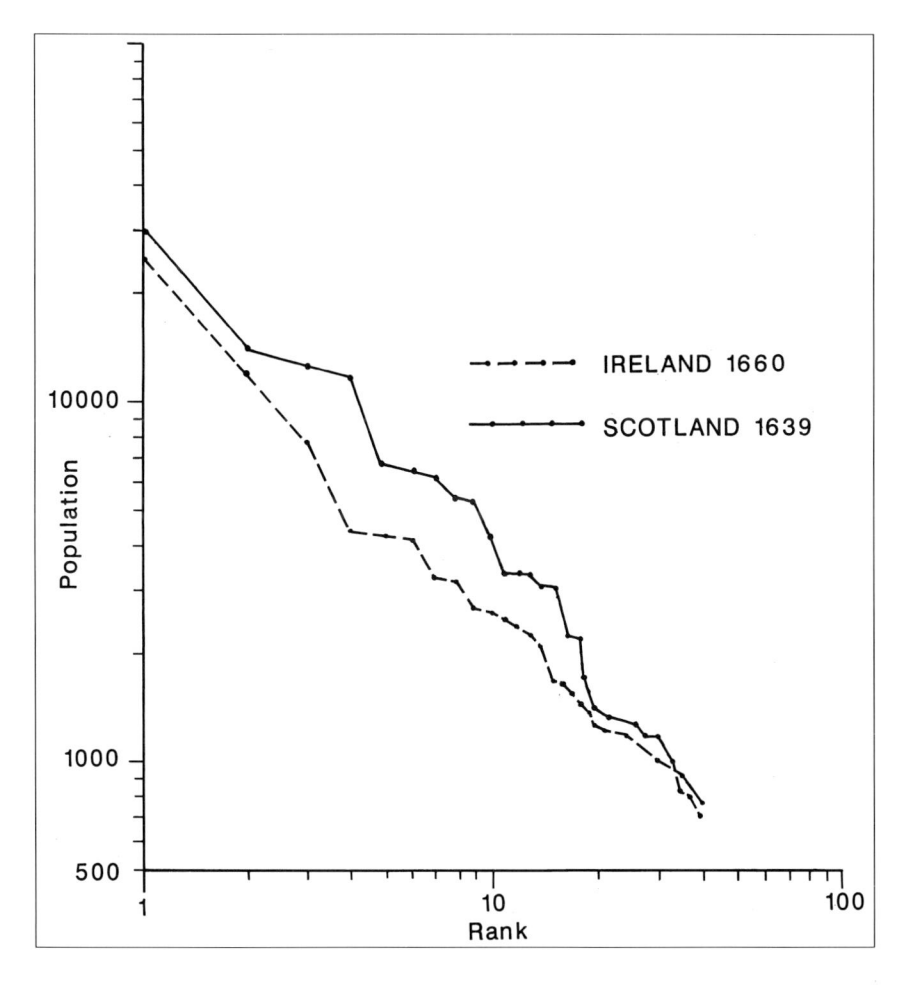

Figure 4: Rank/size distributions of Scottish and Irish towns, 1821.

1650s than other major Irish towns, it may also reflect a short-term situation in which there was a time-lag in the recovery of some Irish regional centres.

A comparison of the Irish rank/size distribution for 1660 with the estimated populations of major towns around 1680 shows a marked steepening of the upper part of the graph, with Dublin—and to a lesser extent Cork—continuing to pull away from other towns, moving towards a more markedly primate pattern. In Scotland a similar trend occurred between 1639 and the 1690s, but here the growth of Edinburgh and Glasgow was modest and the steepening of the graph was achieved by the stagnation or decline of a number of middle-rank centres.[34]

---

[34] Lynch, 'Continuity and Change', pp. 91, 104.

The next available Scottish and Irish rank/size distributions which are closely comparable are derived from the 1821 census (Figure 4). The graphs are still broadly similar although the primacy of Dublin over other Irish towns is replaced in Scotland by the combined dominance of Edinburgh and Glasgow. Lower down the graph there are clusters of towns in both countries which are larger or smaller in relation to their rank than their counterparts but the overall trend of the graphs is very similar. However, Scottish towns in the 10,000–99,999 class were more important in terms of total urban population and percentage of the total population than their Irish counterparts. This reflects the rise of new industrial centres like Paisley, Kilmarnock and Falkirk as well as the continuing strength of old-established regional centres like Aberdeen and Dundee.

THE CHRONOLOGY OF URBAN DEVELOPMENT

The contrasting influence of political conditions upon urban development, both directly and indirectly, provides some explanation of differences in the pace of urbanisation between Scotland and Ireland. The unstable political situation during the second half of the sixteenth century undoubtedly helps to explain the relatively low level of urbanisation in Ireland. At the opening of the sixteenth century many towns had been ravaged by war and were partly ruined. Armagh and Galway were among the major centres which had been devastated.[35] By contrast the later sixteenth century and the early years of the seventeenth were for Scotland a period of demographic and economic growth during which many larger burghs, especially Edinburgh, expanded rapidly.[36]

The relative stability of Scotland during the reign of James VI gave urban development a major boost following the late-medieval urban decline.[37] In both countries towns suffered severely from the crisis of the mid-seventeenth century. Towns like Aberdeen and Dundee suffered directly from military action leading to loss of life, plundering and damage to property.[38] More generally high levels of taxation and disruption of trading patterns hit most larger centres,[39] as did high mortality due to outbreaks of plague during the 1640s.[40]

Irish towns suffered similarly. The campaigns of the early 1640s and to an even greater extent those of Cromwell involved many sieges. Some towns, notably Drogheda and Wexford, were stormed with heavy loss of life.[41] To war was added

---

[35] Butlin, *Making of the Irish Town*, p. 158.
[36] S. G. E. Lythe, *The Economy of Scotland in its European Setting, 1550–1625* (Edinburgh, 1960).
[37] M. Lynch, 'Introduction', in Lynch *et al.*, eds., *Scottish Medieval Town*, pp. 6–7.
[38] D. Stevenson, 'The Burghs and the Scottish Revolution', in M. Lynch, ed., *The Early Modern Town in Scotland* (London, 1987), pp. 179–87.
[39] *Ibid.*, pp. 180–1, 186–7.
[40] M. Flynn, ed., *Scottish Population History* (Cambridge, 1976).
[41] P. J. Corish, 'The Rising of 1641 and the Catholic Confederacy 1641–5', in Moody *et al.*, *New History of Ireland*, III, pp. 339–43.

the scourge of plague in the early 1650s.[42] During Cromwell's campaigns large areas of the countryside were devastated and agriculture was brought to a standstill, dislocating urban food supplies and trade.[43] Some towns fared less badly, notably Dublin which was never besieged or stormed, but in other major centres urban life and administration virtually broke down.[44]

For both countries the Restoration era represented a period of urban growth and revival. However, the overall buoyancy of the Irish economy contrasts with the slower pace of Scottish economic development, something which was mirrored in demographic trends and the pace of urban development. The greater overall dependability of Irish trade, heavily oriented as it was to England,[45] contrasts with the greater variability of conditions in Scotland, much of whose trade was tied to continental markets and liable to sharp and sudden dislocations due to changing political conditions.[46] Involvement in wars with France and Holland during the 1660s and 1670s did have significant short-term effects on Irish trade but recovery was fairly rapid.[47]

The Jacobite campaigns in Ireland in 1689-91 brought some temporary dislocation but the scale of disruption was far less than during the 1640s and 1650s. The effects of the Revolution of 1688 were more serious for Scotland. The Revolution did not have a major effect on Irish trade, the greater part of which was linked with England. In Scotland, however, there was a major trade and industrial slump as the country was dragged into war with France, one of her major trading partners. To this was added serious losses of capital in the ill-fated Darien Scheme.[48] Following the Union of 1707 the Scottish economy and the pace of urban growth remained sluggish for a considerable time, but by the middle decades of the eighteenth century the Scottish economy was starting to perform better against the Irish one and urban growth was starting to accelerate in a trend which was to transform the pattern of Scottish urbanisation by the early nineteenth century.

CONCLUSION

In the space available it has been possible only to outline some general frameworks for the comparative study of Scottish and Irish urban development in the seventeenth and eighteenth centuries. The Scottish urban system seems to have reached

---

[42] L. M. Cullen, *An Economic History of Ireland since 1660* (London, 1972), p. 9.
[43] P. J. Corish, 'The Cromwellian Regime, 1650–1660', in Moody *et al.*, *New History of Ireland*, III, p. 357.
[44] *Ibid.*, p. 373.
[45] L. M. Cullen, *Anglo-Irish Trade, 1660–1800* (Manchester, 1968), p. 1–39.
[46] T. C. Smout, *Scottish Trade on the Eve of Union* (Edinburgh, 1963), p. 240.
[47] Cullen, *Economic History*, pp. 10–11.
[48] Smout, *Scottish Trade*, pp. 244–56.

a more advanced stage with a closer degree of integration by the early seventeenth century compared with Ireland. By the later seventeenth century, however, the Irish system had developed rapidly and had caught up with Scotland in terms of the proportion of the population living in towns and the rank/size distribution of urban centres. During the eighteenth century more rapid population growth in Ireland reduced the relative demographic importance of Irish towns compared with Scotland where population growth was slower and urban expansion more rapid. By 1821 the two countries possessed urban systems with closely comparable rank/size distributions. Scotland had, however, moved towards a much more urbanised society with over three times the proportion of the population living in centres with over 2,500 inhabitants compared with Ireland. Patterns of urbanisation cannot be considered in isolation from the changing demographic, economic and political fortunes of both countries during this eventful period. It is hoped that this exploratory essay has highlighted the potential for further more detailed comparative research into urban development in Scotland and Ireland. Topics which might be pursued with profit include the contrasting processes of foundation of new towns in both countries during the seventeenth century, variations in urban occupational structures, the development of functional specialisation in the urban hierarchies of the two countries during the eighteenth century, as well as differences in the social structure of the respective capitals, larger regional centres, and the smaller towns in each country. A comparison of the roles of Scottish and Irish towns as centres from which new ideas, fashions and trends in consumption were diffused throughout their respective societies would also be of interest, as would a more detailed analysis of the effects of the growth of the major urban centres in each country on the rural economies of their hinterlands.

3

The Scottish Exchange on London, 1673–1778

L. M. Cullen

IF THE CONDUCT OF THE EXCHANGES is obscure before the late seventeenth century, even more obscure are the actual rates. The inland exchange, as opposed to the foreign exchange, remains obscure even into the eighteenth century: for instance, in Herbert Luthy's study of banking in France, it merits a single reference.[1] The Scottish exchange on London is of course singular. With a separate customs administration (though, post-1707, with a free internal market and common external tariff), its own commercial law and a separate economy in some respects, the Scottish exchange has some of the elements of a foreign exchange as well as of an inland exchange. It was also seen as a national issue. This distinctive character accounts for some commentary on the exchanges and for some public quotations, all too rare for the inland exchanges in western Europe at large.

The apparently high exchanges of some years have been the source of rather serious misapprehensions about economic conditions. A premium of 10 to 15 per cent on London in 1681 has been quoted for instance.[2] Though they fell thereafter, high rates occurred again between 1696 and 1707. In both periods the high rates, if not interpreted aright, give an impression of an economy in chronic difficulty, and the sharp rise in the premium in 1696–1707 would seem at first sight to justify a pessimistic conclusion about the state of the Scottish economy. The fact that the onset of a run of high exchanges coincided with the four hungry years of the late 1690s would seem equally to reinforce this gloomy interpretation.

The exchanges rose quite sharply again in 1761–3 in circumstances which are complex and rather interesting. This was the first occasion in which the exchanges got extensive attention—there was much pamphlet writing on the subject in 1762–4. In consequence it might be easy to assume that the economy either had

---

[1] H. Luthy, *La banque protestante en France de la révocation de l'Edit de Nantes jusqu'a la Révolution* (Paris, 1959–61), II, 32–3. For a broader discussion, see L. M. Cullen, 'Luthy's La banque protestante: A Reassessment', *Bulletin du Centre d'histoire des espaces Atlantique*, nouvelle série, no. 5 (Bordeaux, 1990), pp. 229–63.

[2] S. G. Checkland, *Scottish Banking: A History, 1695–1973* (Glasgow, 1975), p. 11.

remained in dire straits or at least regularly lapsed into prolonged phases of difficulty. Indeed this is a point sometimes made in modern books, and no less a person than the late Sydney Checkland entitled a section of his book on banking 'The continuing exchange crisis 1764–71'.[3]

There is no study of the Scottish exchange on London, if one excepts an excellent account entitled 'The Royal Bank and the London-Edinburgh Exchange Rate in the Eighteenth Century' which appeared in 1958.[4] This attempts to give maximum and minimum rates for the years 1760 to 1778. While it is a judiciously written account, it is in some error in its conclusion that for the years 1756–63 'the net result was a significant worsening of the Scottish balance of payments'.[5] Added to the Checkland concept of a continuing exchange crisis in 1764–71, we would have for Scotland a curiously persistent balance of payments crisis.

Edinburgh prices on London begin to occur regularly from the mid-1670s.[6] A London merchant seeking a correspondent in Edinburgh observed in 1673 that 'there is no constant current of exchange yet I should think it should bear some proportion with that here which has been for time at 5 per cent advance'.[7] The implication is that quotations on Edinburgh were already familiar in London. A well-defined exchange would in fact correspond to the growth of trade at this time, and coincides also with a rapid spread in the Scottish trade network in London and overseas. While purely domestic settlements with London, predictable to some degree, could be geared to the provision of both bills and specie by drovers, foreign trade could be conducted only on the basis of a regular course of exchange. The increase in the Scottish business community in London was prompted not only by internal settlements with England but, as Scottish trade grew, by external settlements. Indeed, far from the background to the Darien Company being one of Scottish desperation, it may have reflected ambition whetted by increasing contact with the outside world.

Not only was Scotland a tobacco consuming region, but Scots had already passed into the tobacco trade, both in Maryland and in England. The Edinburgh house of Coutts in 1698 already had a member of the family trading in Maryland.[8] The business between Patrick Coutts in Edinburgh and Thomas in London can be linked to the commodity interests of Scotland, as there is no evidence of a particular gentry clientele of the house at this stage. Other houses can be identified

---

[3] *Ibid.*, p. 121.

[4] Anon., in *The Three Banks Review* (June 1958). I am indebted to Ms Christine Hunter Robinson, former archivist of the Royal Bank of Scotland, for bringing this article to my attention.

[5] *Ibid.*, p. 32.

[6] I am especially indebted to Dr Gordon Jackson who at the outset of this research brought the CS96 series in the Scottish Record Office to my attention.

[7] S.R.O. West Register House, Edinburgh, CS96/3264, London, 29th of the 5th month (i.e. July) 1673, to John Mothmorland.

[8] S.R.O. CS96/3309, John Watson to Thomas Coutts, 9 September 1698.

in the same years.⁹ In particular the bill business of another London house, Frazer, with Edinburgh was already a very extensive one.¹⁰ While gentry and peers can be identified in Frazer's business, the house's origins lay in mercantile business, emphasising that the maturity of the exchanges had been attained less in the gentry demand for remittances than in trade. Frazer had an interest in commodity trade with Scotland, including tobacco. So had one of his correspondents, John Watson of Edinburgh, who dealt in a range of goods as well as in a bill trade with Frazer. Frazer's other correspondent was the house of Blackwood.

Of course the Union in 1707 played a role in developing the exchanges with London. Its effects were two-fold. It required the regular presence of some gentry and peers in London, and hence enlarged a non-mercantile demand for bills. It also created a demand for bills to remit the proceeds of taxes to London. These new developments may have been responsible for the Drummonds opening a London house in 1717 with a gentry focus in contrast to the more versatile and cosmopolitan operations of the Coutts and Frazers. In fact the Edinburgh bankers did not issue notes in the first half of the century.¹¹ What they were, was simply specialised bill houses, both selling and buying bills of exchange. They handled only part of the actual bill business; the Royal Bank itself likewise had a small bill business on London. The great bulk of the Scottish exchange was conducted without any recourse to the bankers, a fact reflected in the growing importance of Glasgow's bill business with London.

The exchange business in any market revolved around the transfer of bills of exchange from sellers to buyers. The bill of exchange was in essence a claim to cash balances in another centre. While most bills originated in commodity trade, the balances they transferred made it possible in turn for the new owners of the balances to finance the drawing of fresh bills at a later date. Officials or gentry in Edinburgh needing balances in London found it more convenient to buy bills from an intermediary than from merchants: these also began to give them bills at sight or short date in contrast to the longer-dated paper that merchants traded with one another and with the bill intermediaries. The Edinburgh exchange contrasted with the Glasgow exchange on London. As Edinburgh ran a deficit on its balance of payments at least in post-1707 times, it acquired from Glasgow houses many of the bills necessary to keep up its London balances. This dependence on Glasgow arbitraged the exchange rates in the Glasgow and Edinburgh markets, as a rise or

---

⁹ S.R.O. RH 15/14 is especially informative in illustrating both the exchange business of Alexander Campbell of Edinburgh with James Foulis and others in London in the 1680s and his exchange ties with several London houses in the 1690s. Other sources also illustrate the exchange business with London, e.g. S.R.O. CS 96/1726, and some such as CS 96/3264, S.R.O. RH 15/106, are useful on the widespread pattern of Scottish trade with the continent, which enhanced the London balances of Scottish houses. For particularly informative later sources see especially Mitchell Library, Glasgow Room, Bogle letter book, and Strathclyde Regional Archives, TD170, 1755–65.

¹⁰ S.R.O. CS 96/524. This account book contains innumerable exchange quotations or bill transactions between 1700 and 1711. CS 96/3309 contains copies of Watson's letters from 1697 onwards.

¹¹ Checkland, *Scottish Banking*, p. 84.

fall in the Edinburgh exchange on London, determined by the state of demand for balances in London, triggered off a corresponding rise or fall in the flow of bills from Glasgow to Edinburgh. The powerful Glasgow house of Bogle for instance disposed of London bills both to Glasgow houses, and also to the Alexanders in Edinburgh.[12] The Alexanders both used these bills in their own business and were the principal suppliers of the Royal Bank's limited requirements. In the merchant exchange in Glasgow all the customers were familiar on a daily basis with the exchange on London; in Edinburgh many were not. In the Glasgow exchange, almost invariably one between merchants or with Edinburgh bill intermediaries, the exchange was well known and the local exchange was never quoted in the press: in contrast as non-specialists bought bills in Edinburgh, the exchange there was an object of some public comment and quotation.[13] There was also an exchange on transfers between provincial centres and Glasgow or Edinburgh. This was of course a smaller and less perfect market: it can not be documented regularly and rates were more erratic. All transactions at the Scottish end were denominated in sterling, though within accounts in the seventeenth century the actual proceeds of smaller transactions are occasionally denominated in Scottish money of account.

An exchange existed on France, Holland and, late in the eighteenth century, in Glasgow on Dublin and Belfast. The volume of transactions was small. Most of the merchants who engaged in it held balances in London as well as in the overseas centres. This arbitraged the rates, and the direct transactions were numerous only with Holland where there was a large two-way direct flow of payments, usually for smaller transfers.

From surviving quotations on London it is possible, with gaps especially between 1712 and 1755, to build up a picture of the exchanges. The rates were moderate in the 1670s, until they rose sharply in late 1679. It is only between 1680 and the mid-1680s that high rates existed: by 1688 rates were back at a low premium of 1 and 2 per cent. Even within the plateau of high exchanges between London and Edinburgh, rates of 10, 11 and 12 per cent were recorded only in two months, February and March 1681. However, in June 1682, while the exchange in London was 7½ per cent, James Foulis seemed to anticipate a rise as he noted the exchange in London 'condescending rather to about 10 or 15 per cent.'[14]

The effective par seems to have altered with the raising of the price of bullion in March 1680.[15] Coin should have flowed into Scotland, and expectation of this

---

[12] Glasgow Room, Mitchell Library, George Bogle letter book, 1729–42, and letters. I am indebted to Professor T. M. Devine for bringing this collection to my attention.

[13] In fact from the time of the 1762 exchange crisis public awareness of the exchange was greatly enhanced, and it is this rather than the crisis in subsequent years which accounts for more information and comment in the newspapers. There were in particular extensive runs of exchange quotations in the *Edinburgh Advertiser*, and *Glasgow Journal* in 1766–8 and frequent though irregular quotation in subsequent years up to 1773.

[14] S.R.O. RH 15/14/37¹, Foulis to Campbell, 3 June 1682.

[15] R. W. Cochran-Patrick, *Records of the Coinage of Scotland* (Edinburgh, 1876), I, p. cxci.

is implied in the statement that 'the exchange I hope will be lower within a week or so for [that] is the time our drovers comes [sic] down from England'.[16] Moreover, the bill business itself on London remained active in 1681–2, which is hardly consistent with an acute exchange crisis. Significantly, the specie outflow in 1682 was entirely one of Dutch dollars (rex, legs and cross), whose attraction was the demand for them in London. This may suggest that one result of the currency operation in 1680 was an undervaluation of foreign silver: undervalued Dutch silver must have been replaced by other (also silver) coins, Scots (either unintentionally or wilfully overvalued in the hope of the profits in seignorage) and to a lesser extent English. The unilateral revaluation in Scotland would inevitably be reflected in a raising in the par of exchange on London money by several percentage points, and only the major reissue in Scotland in 1686 must have put the precious metals at the old par again.[17] Thus for the interval of 1680–6 there is the task of disentangling an effective alteration of the par of exchange from, in some years, a real worsening of the exchanges. In the second half of 1681 however the premium on the exchanges was as low as 2½, which was probably close to the new par level. While marks of 5¼ per cent or more occurred in five months in 1682, in November a Scottish house in London, that of James Foulis, 'guessed' that the Edinburgh exchange was 3½ per cent.[18] The high rates were all in May and June 1682, months which preceded an expected seasonal fall in the premium.[19] The effective par in Edinburgh would seem to have been of the order of 3½ per cent as Foulis instructed Campbell in 1682 that 'if you find exchange at 3½ or thereby, it will be more acceptable than the silver or the others . . .'[20] As the rates rarely exceeded 9 per cent, a prolonged crisis existed only from late 1679 into the outset of 1681, and even within the crisis period, if the rates are assessed with reference to a par of 3½ per cent, the effective rise in the exchange was significantly more modest than a crude comparison with the earlier or later course of exchange might suggest. In late 1681 and in 1682 the rates were close to the new par, possibly even at a discount at times in the second half of 1681, and rarely above it by more than 1 or 2 percentage points. A secondary peak in rates seems to have occurred briefly towards mid-1682.

The next period in which exchanges seem to have taken on a life of their own was in 1695–1707. We have no quotations for 1695 and 1696 earlier than January 1696. However it is likely that overvaluation of the coinage in England between June 1695 and April 1696 would have resulted in the appearance of a favourable exchange between Scotland and London,[21] even allowing for an increase in the

---

16 S.R.O. RH 15 14/32, copy letters 1681–2, Campbell to Joseph Short, –November 1681.
17 Cochran-Patrick, *Records*, II, pp. 209–10.
18 S.R.O. RH 15 14/37 iii, 8 November 1682. In CS96/2015 in September 1682 and January 1683 the exchange was 6 and 8 respectively.
19 S.R.O. RH 15 14/37^i, Foulis to Campbell, 24 June 1682.
20 S.R.O. RH 15 14/37^{iii}, 26 October 1682.
21 L. M. Cullen, *Anglo-Irish Trade 1600–1800* (Manchester, 1968), p. 156.

rated valuation of silver in 1695 to keep it in Scotland.[22] However, uncertainty about silver in London by January had serious consequences for a de facto silver standard country like Scotland. A fall in the exchange, described as 'sudden', in fact occurred in January,[23] and with the exchange in London at 3½, a London merchant had an expectation of 'the exchange . . . at parr with you or better as I am told with you'.[24] English guineas appear to have circulated in 1695-6 and to have been regulated in value. In turn their presence resulted in a Scots issue of gold coin in 1701, 'the first for a long tyme'.

While the reduction of coins in England by April 1696 would have re-established a premium in London's favour, the fact that the Scots did not re-tariff gold in step with London ensured that much higher nominal valuations in Scotland inevitably were reflected in a greatly enlarged premium as coins and bullion now stood at higher prices in money of account in Scotland. This meant a new par of exchange. Despite the superficially high exchanges the remitting of specie between Scotland and England was, on the evidence of the correspondence of the period, slight, which is a clear proof of technical overvaluation, and in so far as it took place, it should have tended, outside periods of short-lived economic crisis, to be in the direction of Scotland. In fact in Frazer's very large business with Scotland, coin was moved very rarely to England, e.g. from Edinburgh through Newcastle in October 1702 when the exchange premium rose rather abruptly. Periods of pressure against Scotland occurred in 1701-2, 1704, 1706 and 1709-10. When order was restored to the English currency in 1696 the overvaluation would have been crudely of the order of ten per cent, i.e. approximately the percentage increase in the valuation of gold in 1695-6 which in Scotland had not been removed in 1696. In other words the par was in Edinburgh a premium of 10 per cent (or in London approximately 11 per cent). That an altered par was at the root of the problem is seen in the fact that with the Union the exchanges fell immediately. In February 1707 the exchange in Frazer's accounts was 9 and 11 per cent. It was down to 2 per cent in April; Frazer himself moved guineas to Scotland in May and the exchange was actually at par in London on several occasions in 1708 (which would suggest a discount in Edinburgh). Of course some of the immediately following years were years of difficulty. Rates of 3 to 4 per cent occurred in the three months in 1710 for which quotations exist and the exchange premium rose again in May 1711. These are very high rates reflecting real pressures on the exchanges in what had been some of the most difficult seasons of the century. We have to go forward to the exchanges of 1761-3 to witness comparable rates (or back to the exchanges in the early 1700s or 1680-1).

What periods of large swings can we detect after 1711? There is a comparative dearth of exchange quotations for the years 1712-55. Within this period, while the

---

[22] Cochran-Patrick, *Records*, I, p cxcv. The value of English silver and of Scottish silver was cried down in 1696. This still left foreign coins and all gold unchanged.

[23] S.R.O. RH 15/14/54, Crawford and Hunter, 18 January 1696.

[24] S.R.O. RH 15/14/54, Hunter and Crawford to Alexander Campbell, 28 January 1696.

possibility of adverse upturns can not be excluded, they can for the most part be ruled out, as the Royal Bank, a marginal performer in the exchange market, which set its rate for the sale of sight bills from time to time from 1731, never exceeded one per cent within the period. There was certainly a recurrence of adverse exchanges in 1732 in Glasgow, though as rates are not quoted we can not put a precise figure on them.[25] In May 1741 the rates in Glasgow on London were 2¼ and 2½: however, the rate was lower in Edinburgh.[26] In early 1756 the exchange temporarily rose and rates of 1½ per cent were recorded.

This movement in 1756 was followed, however, by the longest run, and largest rates, of discount in the history of the exchange. Rates were still remarkably favourable in the course of 1759, even if the discount on London of preceding years was converted in the spring of 1759 into a premium, though by historic standards the modest levels of ¼ to ⅝ per cent. However, when the agent for the French tobacco trade, George Fitzgerald, failed in London in December 1759 and Alexander held £20,000 of his paper, apprehensions sent the premium upwards.[27] On 26 December bills on London at thirty days shot up to 1¼ per cent[28] (the equivalent of 1¾ for a sight bill). But the rate quickly declined, and in early February 1760 a merchant noted that 'I can always get bills here at thirty days for a half per cent excepting the time Mr Fitzgerald stopt when provost Alexander had to replace his drafts which is now over'.[29] In March the exchange was only ⅝ to ¾ per cent at thirty days date.[30]

This was less than the astonishingly favourable exchanges of the war years so far, but still favourable. The argument at this point underlines the need of appreciating that the Scottish exchanges over time had not deteriorated, and more specifically that they had not seriously worsened for the first five years of war. In fact only in the course of 1761 did Scotland's fortunes on the exchanges really alter. In July 1761 the ominous note occurred in a merchant's letter that 'the exchange to London still continues enormously high with us',[31] and the usance of many bills had lengthened to an exceptional seventy or eighty days. In September the exchange on a bill on London at twenty one days sight was almost 1 per cent, the equivalent of 1½ on a sight bill, and the complaint in November was of long bills.[32]

---

25 Glasgow Room, Mitchell Library, George Bogle letter book, 1729–42, Bogle to John Govan, London, letter between 10 and 16 February 1732.

26 *Ibid.*, to David Edie, 1 May 1741, 10 June 1741.

27 The Bank held £20,200 of Alexander's bills drawn on Fitzgerald in favour of the Bank. See Minutes, Royal Bank of Scotland, 15 December 1759.

28 S.R.O. CS96/1197, Glasgow, 26 December 1759, to James Russell, London. Rates of 1 per cent at thirty and forty days are quoted in another source. S.R.O. 96/507, Glasgow, letters to Robert Patrick Company, 26 December 1759, and to Fairhold and Malcolm, same date.

29 S.R.O. CS96/1197, 6 February 1760, to James Russell, London.

30 S.R.O. CS96/507, Glasgow, 10 March 1760, to Robert Patrick and Company, Dublin.

31 S.R.O. CS96/507, 23 July 1761, to Anthony Perrier, Dublin.

32 S.R.O. CS96/507, 3 September 1761, to Robert Nevin; 25 November 1761 to James Buchanan and Company, London.

An upswing of this sort, though uncommon, would not be significant of itself. What was significant on this occasion is that the upswing proved persistent and was prelude to two years of remarkably high exchanges. By January and February 1762 the rate had even reached 5 per cent, the peak rate for a sight bill during the crisis.[33]

A concern with private bank paper as a cause of the exchange rise reflected the novelty of bank notes. It had however been in circulation for some years without damaging the exchanges. The Glasgow merchant Gavin, who did not like paper, as early as June 1756 had written that 'money is at present very scarce here but paper very plentiful. I cannot say for my own part I am very fond of it.'[34] In August he attributed the discount in the exchanges to many bills being sold to pay off bank credits which were being drawn in.[35] However the exchanges remained favourable for several years, and it was only from mid-1760 that a radical change began to take place. The sudden nature of the crisis in 1761 would seem to reflect real circumstances in the external business environment rather than a rise in the volume of paper.

Severe crisis had already set in in London in 1759. Scotland, with its boom in recruitment (perhaps 90,000 Scottish recruits in all received a bounty), and with its advantage in American trade, was slower to experience the crisis than London. It could not be deferred indefinitely of course, and it eventually took effect with devastating impact in Glasgow, terminating the war boom. The situation had still been strong enough for the Scottish economy to adjust quickly to the Alexander crisis in December 1759: the exchange in February 1760 on bills at thirty days date was ½ per cent (the equivalent of 1 per cent on sight bills), only fractionally above the rates of the preceding years, but it had edged up to ⅝ and ¾ by March.[36] However, something which was not immediately apparent at the time, this marked the end of the run of remarkable exchanges. In the case of the Glasgow merchant Semple the confidence or resilience, still evident in the spring, gradually vanished.[37] The really acute exchange crisis, with sight bills reaching 4 to 5 per cent, seems to have been confined to January and February 1762. However, although the premium fell quite sharply by April 1762, it trended upwards again in the autumn with a peak in September 1762 of 3 per cent on sight bills.

---

[33] Strathclyde Regional Archives, Glasgow, TD170, Glasgow, 8 February 1762, to Chas. Cowan, Leith. Rates of four-and-a-half and five per cent are first noted in the *Scots Magazine* in January 1762. (p. 64)

[34] Strathclyde Regional Archives, Glasgow, TD170, Gavin to Hercules Skinner, Campheer, 26 June 1756.

[35] Strathclyde Regional Archives, Glasgow, TD170, Gavin to A. Livington, Aberdeen, 3 August 1756.

[36] S.R.O. CS96/1197, Semple, Glasgow, to James Russell, 6 February 1760; CS96/507, Glasgow, to Robert Patrick and Company, 10 March 1760.

[37] S.R.O. CS96/1197, Semple to Davidson, 29 August 1760; to Russell, 9 April 1761; to Semple, 23 April 1761. See for another source of comment, S.R.O. CS96/507, especially letter to Anthony Perrier, Dublin, 23 July 1761.

The 'Checkland' exchange crisis of 1764–71 is a myth. It cannot be traced in the exchanges. All that can be said is that the remarkably strong exchanges of 1756–9 did not recur, but these were something quite unique, reflecting an unprecedented inflow of funds to Scotland as it benefited both from the commercial and non-commercial transactions of the war. However, if the premium had been high at the outset of 1764 it moved downwards very sharply in the remainder of the year. By October it was down to 1 per cent, and indeed in the remainder of the 1760s was frequently below 1 per cent. Indeed, far from this being a period of crisis in the exchanges, it was a period of favourable exchanges with some interruption only in 1766 and early 1767. This favourable profile of the exchanges should not cause surprise, as it squares with the evidence of a boom in commercial paper, and with the physical expansion of trade and the remarkable extension of tobacco production in America, now more than ever geared to Glasgow custom. Indeed the exchanges on London remained favourable even through the stormy years of the early 1770s, showing an upward turn only in 1773. It is illuminating to compare the Edinburgh exchange with the Irish exchange on London: the Irish one in fact moved more adversely and more frequently than the Scottish one in these years and for longer periods. A corollary of these events is that the favourable turn in the exchanges, post-1773, which has been recognised, is not a novel phenomenon, but one which had been anticipated not only in the 1760s but in the late 1750s. The exchanges certainly in the mid-1770s were remarkably favourable: bills on London traded at times at a discount. This itself was not a novelty: as we have seen it was a feature, and more markedly, of the years 1756–8.

It is not at all obvious that there had been an overissue of paper or that this had caused the rise in the exchanges at the outset of the 1760s. It is true that the exchanges did rise in 1762 and by more than the cost of remitting specie. But this had been brought about by the combination of an adverse balance of payments (which did require an outflow of specie) and the costs of converting bills into specie for Scotland on the tight London market. In addition, with a downturn in activity, the real cost of the exchanges was not simply the cost of remitting specie but the cost of borrowing as the usance of paper had extended beyond the usual outside limit of ninety days by as much as twenty days. If we regard the established par of exchange as around 1 per cent, the cost of remitting would have added a further percentage point, and borrowing for two months (as the standard drawing and redrawing expedients were too slow and uncertain in a tight market), a further percentage point. This would represent a more meaningful specie point of 103 in a situation where both the Edinburgh and London markets had become illiquid in crisis. There were specie inflows, in part financed by the banks. The total in 1762 would have been of the order of £165,000[38] in the case of the Royal Bank. This was large in relation to the bank's turnover in bills and the specie need had in fact inflated the turnover (which would explain the ferocity of the chartered banks in

---

38 Royal Bank of Scotland, Minutes, various dates from 29 January to 10 December 1762.

attacking the private circulation) but not so large in relation to the total value of exports (which would have represented a turnover in bills of perhaps £1 million). The Royal Bank's quotations for its own bills on London had risen to a rate of $2\frac{1}{4}$ for sight bills in November 1762, and they came down to 1 per cent only by a decision on 8 March 1763. However the Bank did not always offer bills at sight, and its rate was not the effective market rate in any event as even on these terms it dealt only with the shrinking number of holders of its own notes. Put into circulation through the Bank's own operations, the specie inflow ensured the operation of a specie point around the 3 per cent mark. This is borne out in the operation of the exchanges. Sight rates of 4 and 5 per cent were short-lived, and over the period March 1762 to January 1764 the exchanges oscillated towards a more regular peak of 3 per cent.

Given the unusual situation, it is easy to understand why the novel fact of private paper money might be singled out as a cause of the high exchanges, though the popularisation of the issue owed more to the self-interest of the chartered banks than to any other factor. With the phenomenal expansion of the Ayr Bank in and after 1769, the comfortable but conservative policy of the two chartered banks was in danger of having the unwanted result of forcing customers in Scotland into the hands of other houses. This banking challenge is of course sometimes lost sight of in the emphasis on the Douglas Heron link to Fordyce in London, and the celebrated speculation which brought down both the Ayr Bank and Fordyce in 1772. This speculation was however much broader than the individual interests of Heron and Fordyce. It is a very interesting episode and far more complex than meets the eye (Adam Smith for instance recognised this). In some respects it reflects the upsurge in the Scottish economy in the 1760s which resulted both in cash surpluses and in the confidence which tempted some into speculative investment. It also coincided with peaks of economic activity and speculation throughout Europe. The network of Scots houses in London which collapsed in 1772 was a secondary or new group rather than the longer-established group involved in Edinburgh finances or in the prime circuits in the Glasgow tobacco trade.

The combination of the unwinding of the Fordyce affair and the separate but related Colebrooke debacle in London did create problems. Indeed, the Colebrooke affair, less axed on Scotland and more closely tied to Amsterdam and to the Dublin-London axis, was more damaging, and the unwinding of the Colebrooke collapse also explains why the exchange crisis occurred in 1773 rather than 1772. There was an acute shortage of money in March 1773; exchange tightened and as late as July 1773 sight bills were at $1\frac{3}{4}$ and 2 per cent.[39] This however was the only period of real crisis in the exchanges. It was also short-lived. The Fordyce and Colebrooke failures in 1772–3 had not been preceded by high exchanges on

---

[39] S.R.O. CS96/2250, Inglis to Edie and Laird, London, 30 March 1773; to James Johnston, Glasgow, 31 March 1773; to Robert Hunter, 2 July 1773; to Hamilton and Company, Newcastle, 10 July 1773.

London, which shows that Scotland was somewhat less involved in the heart of the speculative ventures. As a consequence the exchanges quickly reverted to favourable rates, indeed remarkably favourable rates, in 1774 and 1775. This underlines the need to avoid giving too much attention to the economic dimensions as opposed to the political character of the Ayr bank episode. In fact, in many ways its results were constructive. The Ayr Bank episode was not as damaging as was suggested, partly because the resources of its backers, especially the titled backers, reduced the losses to the creditors and more importantly, given the fact that the unwinding of the bank was to prove long-drawn-out, because the expectation of a favourable outcome kept up confidence in the crucial short-term period when a crisis of confidence could have fed on itself.

The Scottish exchange on London was usually at a premium. This does not in itself reflect a weak exchange. The premium on sterling reflected the intensive demand within Scotland for working balances: hence balances in London outran demand and a slight premium was the norm. The same pattern seems to have existed within provincial England.[40] In France and Ireland by contrast, despite higher interest rates than in Britain, balances on the centre were normally at a discount. The belief that the Scottish exchange was against Sctland and that it reflected an adverse balance of trade was however generalised in the aftermath of 1762. Some of the accounts in 1765 are colourful and interesting, but they are not well-grounded in fact, and should be disregarded.[41] Moreover, the rents to absentee Scots south of the border were small, and assumptions about them in modern literature exaggerate them. Even Scots with London residences spent a good deal of time in Scotland, and by comparison with some of the major Irish absentees spent much of their funds in Scotland, as the accounts in the Buccleuch and Breadalbane papers show.[42] Absenteeism was not the structural feature which Irish absenteeism was. In fact, remarkably few complaints were made about absenteeism, and they seem to occur to an extent in the aftermath of 1762. The absentee drain was put at rather small amounts, £100,000 in one source; another commentator declared that 'these I will call by the Irish term of absentee, and rate their folly so low as £150,000'.[43] Rents in Scotland were said to be £1,150,000.[44] In that case absentee remittances amounted to one eighth to one twelfth of the total rental. This contrasted with the Irish situation where they were one eighth in the 1770s. However the fewness of Scots estimates of rents and remittance, compared with the obsessive interest on the Irish side, itself is a telling measure of the comparative

---

[40] A. H. John, 'Aspects of English Economic Growth in the First Half of the Eighteenth Century', in E. M. Carus-Wilson, ed., *Essays in Economic History*, Vol. 2 (London, 1962), p. 372.

[41] See letter by Christopher Crabtree junior in *Glasgow Journal*, 12/19 September 1765, and by 'A lover of Great Britain, of truth and of the public peace', in *Glasgow Journal*, 17/24 October 1765; *Glasgow Journal* 4/11 December 1765.

[42] S.R.O. GD112, Breadalbane papers; Calendar of Buccleuch papers.

[43] *Glasgow Journal*, 12/19 September 1765; 17/24 October 1765.

[44] *Glasgow Journal*, 12/19 September 1765.

lack of concern on the Scottish side. Moreover, the estimates for rents, by comparison with the estimates for Ireland, seem uncommonly low, and the actual rental was in all probability higher. Expressed as a proportion of foreign trade, the Scottish remittances paled in importance beside the Irish: the Scottish remittances would have taken up one fifteenth of the Scottish bills generated on London by trade, the remittances from Ireland one quarter of the Irish bills on London.[45]

The exchange was quoted somewhat differently in London from Edinburgh. Again, this was a technical feature common to all exchange circuits, and not a peculiarity of the London–Edinburgh exchange. A bill at one months' date should trade for roughly £1 per cent more in London than in Edinburgh. If the rate was the same in the two centres, an accommodation bill on London typically would realise £101 in Edinburgh; at the end of the month the correspondent of the Edinburgh house would draw in London to obtain the cash to honour the bill on the account of his Edinburgh partner. A month later this bill in turn would become due in Edinburgh, and the Edinburghman would pay out £101. In this hypothetical illustration, the original Edinburgh drawer had the use of money for two months without incurring any interest charge. Once the London rate stood at £102 compared with £101 in Edinburgh, the situation was entirely different. The Edinburgh drawer realised £101 in Scotland for the bill on London, but when the London correspondent drew a month later, it was for £102 in Scotland. At the end of the two month period, the Edinburghman's outlay of £102 for the original £101 two months previously contained in effect an interest element of £1 for the two month period. In this situation an equilibrium existed; an accommodation bill had its price, and if the exchanges moved towards equality in either centre, bankers or merchants, quick to spot the change, sold bills and had their correspondents draw on them, and the exchange reverted to equilibrium.

This is the theory illustrated for a one-month bill. In practice it was much more complicated as the paper on the market was so varied. There are not enough price quotations to work out the variations between the two exchanges on sight bills. The gap between Edinburgh and London quotations appears in fact to have been a large fraction of 1 per cent, as for much of the period sight bills were a small part of the circulation, and a redrawing operation in sight bills, a very limited market in itself moreover, could not be conducted on a scale which eliminated a substantial and sometimes unpredictable time interval. In fact it would seem likely that a differential of ¾ to 1 per cent between the quotations in the two centres represented an equilibrium position.[46] The differential was already evident in the quotations in the Frazer account book in the first decade of the eighteenth century. Indeed it existed in 1682, although its operation was not at that stage perfectly smooth. A house in

---

[45] These calculations are based on the Irish figures for foreign trade in 1770, and for Scottish trade at the same date, enlarged by an estimate of £500,000 for Scottish exports to England. The absentee remittances for Scotland are taken at the level of £150,000, for Ireland at the figure of £732,000 given in Arthur Young.

[46] S.R.O. CS96/1835, to Mansfield and Hunter, Edinburgh, 20 January 1759.

Edinburgh refused to allow the higher premium on a bill drawn from London when it was presented: 'the exchange current from Edinburgh to London was all he would give, for he would have had it at 5 or 5½ here if he had been to remit it'.[47] The Edinburgh rate at the time happened to be 3½ per cent. In the still imperfect market of the day the gap could widen further. In November 1698, when the London exchange on Edinburgh was 10 to 12 per cent, John Watson drew on London at 8 or 9 per cent.[48] In such a situation, bills on London could easily be resold in Edinburgh, though it was at this time unusual because when a bill was drawn on Frazer to Thomas Coutts at 9½ per cent and Coutts lost no time in reselling the bill to a further customer for 10½, Watson observed in December 1703 that 'this way of dealing I do not understand if true'.[49] In a very tight exchange market—as in late 1703—the differential tended to widen, because a shortage of bills slowed down the process of arbitraging the exchanges. In the early stages of war in 1756, when the gap widened temporarily, drawings on London were at 1½ short sight, while the London exchange on Edinburgh was at 2½ to 3 per cent for forty to forty-five day bills.[50] Deducting ¾ per cent from the London premium for a sight bill (were it available), this would amount to a differential of at least 1¾ per cent.

There was a very large number of difference usances in employment in the remitting of funds between Edinburgh and London. Bills at sight occur at least from 1696. They gradually became more common, but they were not invariably available even in the more developed exchanges of the 1760s and 1770s. At times when they were not available in the 1760s, quotations were given for 'short-dated' bills or on occasion short-dated bills and sight bills as a composite category. Strictly speaking, as the shortest bill was simply the shortest that a drawer was prepared to draw, if it was the only paper available, it would command as high a premium as sight paper simply on that basis. However, because sight bills commanded a higher premium, remitters unless in a hurry did not seek them out, and they were not important in dealings from merchant to merchant.

In contrast to the emergence of a trade in sight bills in Edinburgh, merchant usance in Glasgow grew longer in the course of the century, and by the second half the bulk of the paper was for the equivalent of two usances (usance conventionally denoting a period of one month), less frequently for three. Strictly speaking the term usance was rarely employed in the Edinburgh–London exchange, and quotations did not always fit into neat intervals of months. As the exchange moved increasingly to long-dated paper, the exchange came to be expressed frequently, not in the exchange rate, but in a variation in the usance of the paper sold at par; paper was in effect offered at par at a variable date, lengthening to seventy or eighty

---

[47] S.R.O. RH 15/14/32, copy letters 1681/82, Campbell to Foulis, 8 June 1682.
[48] S.R.O. CS96/3309, Edinburgh, 22 and 24 November 1698, John Watson to William Frazer, London.
[49] S.R.O. CS96/3309, Watson, Edinburgh, 27 December 1703, to Frazer, London.
[50] Strathclyde Regional Archives, TD170, Glasgow, 22 April 1756, Gavin to Robert Hogg, Campheer.

days (in other words movement beyond the more regular quotation of two usances) or even longer.

A longer usance on bills between Scotland and London went hand in hand with a greater volume of discounting in the true sense (i.e. not simply lodging the paper with a correspondent to be credited to the account when honoured on the due date, but as security for an advance of its face value less the discount or interest). This was very common in London, where perhaps half of the paper passing through the drawing ledgers at the Bank of England was discounted.[51] It was quite common in Scotland as well, especially in Glasgow. On occasion a merchant finding only a long-dated bill to remit to Glasgow would offer to allow his correspondent a benefit in the exchange to match the cost of discount. There is not much cost difference in the end between short-dated paper bought at a premium and longer paper discounted when it comes to hand.

In bill sales between merchants a distinction between buying and selling rates did not exist, but, where an intermediary handling bills as part of an exchange business existed, a clear distinction between buying and selling rates quickly emerged. Intermediaries took bills at a lower premium than they were prepared to draw at. Thus, Watson in Edinburgh in 1698, keen at the time to dispose of bills, had to report to London that 'there's great odds betwixt selling and buying for if I would offer to buy Newcastle bills, [I] could not get any under 6 and yet I am afraid will be necessary to sell at 5'. Even that was hopeful as 4½ per cent was the highest offer he had. The differential at this time was as large as 1½ or even 2½ per cent.[52] In remitting bills to London there was also a difference in rates between houses. In January 1759 a London house were somewhat surprised 'at no uniform price from your place': Mansfield and Hunter drew at ¼ per cent, Alexander and Company at ⅜ per cent, and the Royal Bank at ½ per cent.[53] The Royal Bank dealt in the market only to a limited extent: it drew to the demands of its regular customers, but was not really competing in the market as a seller of bills in a significant way. On the other hand, as they depended on bill purchases for their London funds, banks offered a higher premium than other exchange dealers in buying bills. One of the Edinburgh banks was buying at ¼ per cent above the exchange in the crisis month of February 1762.[54]

It is quite misleading to suggest, as has been done, that the Royal Bank arbitraged the Edinburgh rate on London.[55] It was not even interested in doing so. It sold bills at a rate which was fixed by court decision from time to time (on some

---

[51] Bank of England Record Office, Threadneedle Street, London, ledgers.

[52] S.R.O. CS96/3309, Edinburgh, 30 December 1698, to Thomas Frazer, London. See also John Watson, Edinburgh, 24 November 1698, to William Frazer, London.

[53] S.R.O. CS96/1835, London, 2 and 20 January 1759 to Mansfield and Hunter, Edinburgh.

[54] Strathclyde Regional Archives, TD170, Glasgow, 27 February 1762, Gavin to Cowan.

[55] Anon., 'The Royal Bank and the London–Edinburgh Exchange Rate in the Eighteenth Century', *The Three Banks Review*, (June 1958), pp. 30–1.

eleven occasions in all between 1737 and 1761);[56] and in consequence its price was frequently above the market rate. In fact, so little was the Royal an arbiter of the exchanges that when in 1761 it contracted to take bills on London from a particular house, it did so 'at the current rate of exchange to ascertain which it shall be adjusted as valued by Messrs Coutts Brothers and Company's house here'.[57] The Bank of Scotland was even less in touch with the London market, as Checkland has observed.[58] The interest of the Royal Bank of Scotland was not in operating extensively in the market but in servicing its own customers. The Bank's only significant exchange business in the early decades was in the remitting of the proceeds of excise duties to London,[59] and it acquired important private customers only with the accession of Buccleuch and Dalkeith by 1749. To meet these commitments, it needed funds in London, which it held at the Bank of England. As the demands on this account could be anticipated, the exchange business was confined to taking bills to create the required balances. Its bill buying business in mid-century was confined largely to taking prime bills at long dates, largely bills of William Alexander (on George Fitzgerald), of the Coutts, and of Breadalbane on Drummond. It operated buying and selling rates, contrary to what is implied in the Royal Bank article. Its selling rate was usually 1 per cent. In buying bills, it took short paper at par, and usually deducted ½ per cent on bills above a month. However, the longdated paper of houses such as Alexander was taken at preferential rates: it is marked at par: in other words it was paying the bill drawers a hefty price above what merchants would have offered.

Such bills would accrue only at particular times (in the case of the Alexanders in tobacco selling) and hence it was necessary to build up funds in London beforehand, and on occasion to discount in London. This, not the management of the currency, was the purpose of opening an account with the Bank of England. Of course the Bank also had in mind the use of its London account in a crisis to draw on it to remit specie to Edinburgh.[60] In the case of the Royal, despite the absence of its customer ledgers, the 'dealers in exchange and others who have large credits in cash account with the bank' can be identified in 1761: a mere nine dealers in exchange and seven other houses.[61] What is immediately obvious is that, apart from the Alexanders, the huge business in bills generated by Glasgow commodity business scarcely touched the Royal Bank at all.

The turnover in the Royal Bank account with the Bank of England was not large, a mere shadow for instance of the huge Irish accounts, and even in mid-century did

---

56 *Ibid.*, p. 31.
57 Royal Bank of Scotland, Minutes, 11 September 1761.
58 Checkland, *Scottish Banking*, pp. 37, 63–4.
59 The Royal Bank records are specific that the funds remitted in its early decades are on excise account. According to Checkland, the Royal in the 1760s was remitting customs receipts (Checkland *Scottish Banking*, pp. 104, 166), and the Coutts from the 1740s remitted the excise (p. 69).
60 Royal Bank of Scotland, Court Minutes, 11 March 1737.
61 *Ibid.*, 11 May 1761. The nine dealers become twelve, if associated houses are not aggregated.

not rise in proportion to the growth of Scottish foreign trade. It arranged an overdraft with the Bank of England, at the outset £30,000 raised later to £50,000.[62] It was down to £20,000 in the 1750s but was fixed at £37,000 in 1760 so that 'they might enlarge their transactions in the article of the exchanges'.[63] The actual turnover amounted to £80,185 in the year to September 1748, £95,118 in the year to September 1749 and £103,772 in the year to September 1750.[64] It was actually less active in the late 1760s than in the 1740s, indeed singularly so. It had virtually abdicated its role in the London business. Indeed it was the competition of the Ayr Bank which forced the Bank into expansion. Its turnover in its London account grew sharply in 1771 and 1772. Interestingly it reversed its policy of not dealing in the paper of its rivals. It was taking bills on Fordyce in quantity in 1771 and on Colebrooke in 1772. For the first half of 1772 the total turnover in the account reached £250,000.[65] In other words, the lesson of the past had been learned. It took rival paper in large quantity. A result of this was that for the first time it became a large force in the bill market: its London turnover in 1768 would have been only 2 per cent of the value of Scottish exports (including estimated exports to England); in 1772 it would have been of the order of 20 per cent. Undoubtedly the growth in the Bank's capacity to draw on London would have added to the forces tending to stabilise the market. Whether that was the intention is not clear. Moreover, the effect of stabilising the market was achieved not simply by the growth in its funds but by the fact that, failing to hold a monopoly position in the Scottish market, the Bank's acquiescence in the role of other houses and a termination to the destructive war on private bankers' notes greatly increased the aggregate strength of the Scottish banks. However, the reduction in exchange fluctuations may not have been primarily a result of activity by banking institutions, private or chartered, but simply an offshoot of the strengthening and deepening—often underestimated in the literature because of an unhealthy preoccupation with crises—of the Scottish economy during the 1760s and 1770s.

---

[62] J. H. Clapham, *The Bank of England: A History* (Cambridge, 1944), I, p. 121.
[63] Clapham, *Bank of England*, I, p. 122.
[64] Royal Bank of Scotland, ledger 1747–50.
[65] Bank of England Record Office, Roehampton, drawing ledgers.

4

The economy of Edinburgh 1694–1763: the evidence of the Common Good[1]

R. A. Houston

THE ECONOMIC HISTORY OF SCOTLAND in the first half of the eighteenth century is dominated by discussions of the effects of Union.[2] A partial picture of Scotland's short- and long-term response to changing political rules has emerged. In economic history in general, more is known about production than consumption.[3] For its part, Edinburgh in this period has always been seen as a centre of consumption. A capital city with little industry, it was perceived mainly as a service centre offering legal, administrative, medical and educational facilities. While the extent of metropolitan reliance on selling rather than making has been exaggerated, few attempts have been made to measure patterns of consumption and the overall economic health of the city in the early eighteenth century.[4]

What follows is not a comprehensive overview of Edinburgh's economic life but it is a direct contribution to that subject and to the political economy of the city. Indirectly, it bears on the economic history of Scotland during the first half of the eighteenth century.

---

[1] I should like to thank Michael Lynch, Christopher Smout and Chris Whatley for earlier comments on this paper, and also those who commented on the paper during the conference, especially Raymond Gillespie and (by written communication) David Dickson.

[2] C. Whatley, 'Economic Causes and Consequences of the Union of 1707: A Survey', *Scottish Historical Review*, LXVIII, 2 (1989), pp. 150–81.

[3] For example, C. Gulvin, *The Tweedmakers* (London, 1973); the forthcoming volume from Gibson and Smout on Scottish diet, wages and prices will help to fill the gap.

[4] H. Arnot, *The History of Edinburgh from the Earliest Accounts to the Year 1780* (Edinburgh, 1816); P. Thestrup, *The Standard of Living in Copenhagen, 1730–1800* (Copenhagen, 1971) is a good example of this work on the continent.

The main source used here is the offers made to rent elements of the Common Good of Edinburgh.⁵ The Common Good comprised about twenty taxes, rights, rents and teinds (tithes), originally purchases and grants from sovereigns, from the income of which the city was supposed to pay for public works and, hopefully, pay off its substantial debts. The components were auctioned or 'rouped' yearly at the end of October, usually for a term of one year until the 1730s when longer leases of three to six years began to be negotiated. One of the town drummer's duties was to announce the roups at the cross and throughout the city.⁶ Bids were open to all burgesses and there were no restrictions on an existing holder of the farm renewing a lease. Most elements were leased to individuals but the most lucrative tended to be bid for by partnerships, probably because of the costs of collection. One Patrick Campbell was awarded £1,191 Scots in a law suit as a half of one fifth of the profits of the tack of the imposition on wines taken out by his kinsman Alexander Campbell, merchant in Edinburgh, and his four partners on 1 November 1706.⁷ 'Earnest money', a non-refundable deposit, had to be paid by the highest bidder to secure his lease and he had also to find a cautioner that the amount he had offered would be paid at the specified date(s). After 1729 all bids are recorded but prior to that only the name of the successful candidate and his or her payment or 'tack duty' is set down.

Comparison of the sums offered over time gives an indication of the way in which bidders, active crafts and trades burgesses (merchants, skinners, tailors, vintners, fleshers, shoemakers, masons), perceived the health of different elements of the city economy. The amounts offered represent direct or secondhand knowledge of how well the last farmer or tacksman had done from his enterprise coupled with a projection of what the applicant thought of his abilities to collect, and an assessment of the state of the urban economy over the coming year. For its part, the council recognised that proceeds from the Common Good were linked to economic and political circumstances. Landed estates were purchased in 1717 and 1718 to generate a steady income for the city since 'the expense was regular and certain, but several branches of the revenue were in their nature entirely precarious'.⁸ Unexpected shortfalls in revenue to the tacksman occasioned by war or weather might be compensated by the town council but the

---

⁵ Edinburgh City Archives [hereafter E.C.A.], Conditions of the Roup of the Common Good, 1694–1740; E.C.A. Treasurer's Accounts; E.C.A. Town Council Minute Books (hereafter *Minute Books*). The majority of the city's income came from the Common Good, the annuity tax and seat rents (the largest single source of revenue in the early eighteenth century), and by the proceeds of Edinburgh's position as landlord and feudal superior; S.R.O. GD5816/1.

⁶ The petty customs on the House of Muir were amalgamated with those of the sheep pens or 'flecks' at the West Port in 1695; the merk on the pack with the imposition on wines in 1740 'so small a branch of the revenue that if it is set separately . . . it cannot well bear the charge of collection' (*Minute Books*, vol. 61, p. 144). Items amalgamated at any stage 1694–1763 have been grouped together from the outset; J. Mackay, *History of the Burgh of the Canongate* (Edinburgh, 1879), p. 56.

⁷ S.R.O. RH15/14/128/iv.

⁸ National Library of Scotland [hereafter N.L.S.]. 3.2848[4]:12.

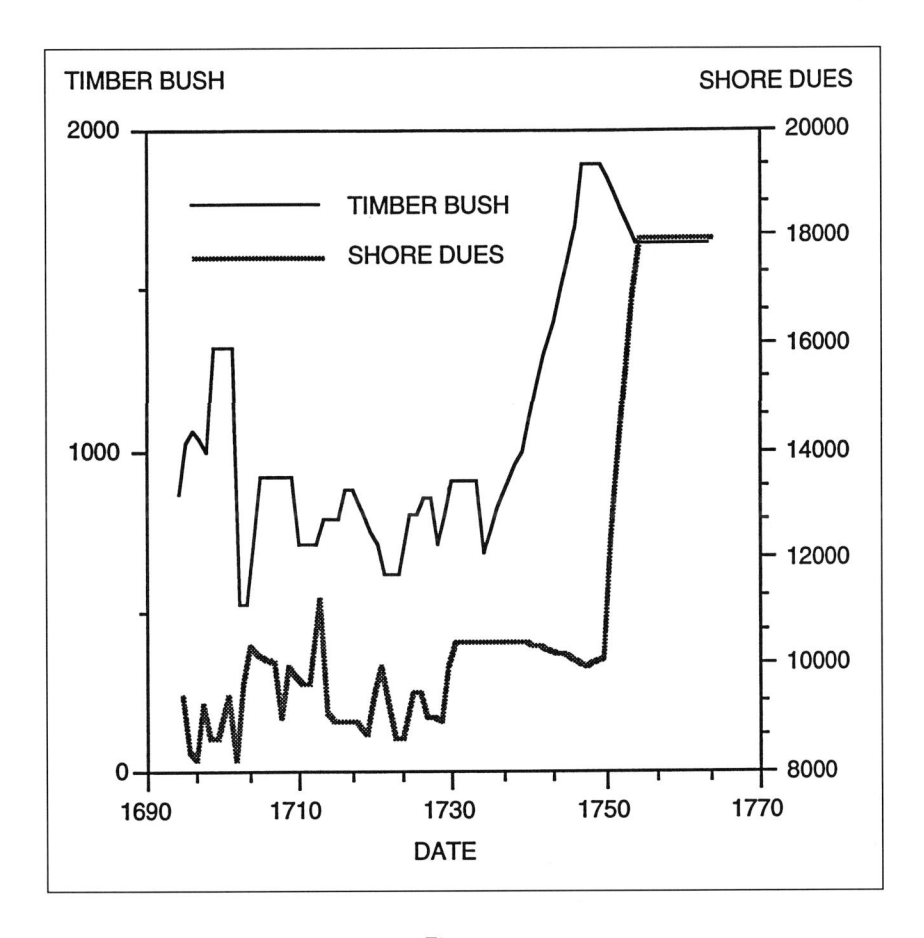

Figure 1.

burden of collection and of risk was effectively transferred to the tacksman. The city lacked the administrative machinery to collect all indirect taxes on a regular basis though there were years when this was tried. 'Collected' is sometimes filled in as an entry for the old imposition on wines in the 1690s and 1700s, perhaps indicating that the council had not farmed it out for that year. If a bid was seen to be too low or the terms unfavourable the council would collect the dues itself or repeat the auction. In 1758 the shore dues were offered at 18,000 merks but there were no takers.[9]

The components graphed represent the basic needs of the city for foodstuffs; its consumption of certain luxury items; its coastal and overseas trade links through Leith; and its need for building supplies. Only the fuller and more important series

---

[9] *Minute Books*, vol. 75, pp. 101–3.

are graphed. The graphs are of nominal sums offered and make no allowance for inflation, probably close to nil at this period. All are in merks Scots unless otherwise stated. Sums offered do not show the absolute level of total consumption, let alone that per capita. Estimates of Edinburgh's population are fraught with difficulties which cannot be discussed fully here. However, the population of 'greater Edinburgh' was probably not increasing much (if at all) in this period. Whyte and Tyson's estimate of just over 50,000 in the early 1690s can be compared with Webster's reasonably reliable figure of 57,195 for the metropolis in 1755. The number of communicants in the central Tolbooth parish remained almost constant between the 1730s and 1770s.[10] Suburban growth, notably in St Cuthbert's or West Kirk, was stronger. It is likely that most of the trends graphed here were related less to absolute numbers living in Edinburgh and its suburbs than to its changing wealth and social composition.

Interpretation is not, however, entirely straightforward as political and institutional factors could influence trends as well as changes in demand or supply of the goods traded. One problem lies in exemptions from duties. The lease of shod carts and hackney coaches did not include coal carts or others with metal-rimmed wheels which were carrying food, drink or furniture for nobles, lords of session, gentry and burgesses for their own family use. Carts carrying stones for building were to pay 6d. Scots but paving stones and any masonry for the city's projects were exempt, as were muck carts. Brewers who were burgesses could claim exemption for personal loads but since they were also the main payers of these duties for their ale shipments serious disputes could arise with the tacksmen and their employees. Dues were payable only on ale and beer for sale, not for domestic consumption.[11] Exemptions create problems but as long as the same thing is being measured over time the comparisons are valid.

As with any indirect tax based on consumption, smuggling and evasion were practised. As early as 1667 the town council recorded widespread evasion of the wine duty by carters and sledders bringing wines into the city and in February 1685 the tacksman of the wine impost asked for a reduction of 5,000 merks in his year's payment because the Nor Loch had been frozen for four months and he had suffered from widespread smuggling across the ice at night.[12] If smuggling suddenly increased or decreased—with the imposition or removal of a duty, for example—there would be a short term 'blip' but probably little effect on the long term trend.

Petitions for exemption show the significance of short term political, administrative or meteorological factors on the profitability of the leases. Short term crises could seriously influence revenues and therefore future bids. In 1714 the tacksman of the shore dues received a rebate on his payments because the expected growth

---

[10] S.R.O. CH2/140/2.
[11] H. Armet, ed., *Extracts from the Records of the Burgh of Edinburgh, 1701 to 1718* (Edinburgh, 1967), p. 157.
[12] M. Wood, ed., *Extracts from the Records of the Burgh of Edinburgh, 1665 to 1680* (Edinburgh, 1950), p. 34; M. Wood and H. Armet, eds., *Extracts from the Records of the Burgh of Edinburgh, 1681 to 1689* (Edinburgh, 1954), p. 137.

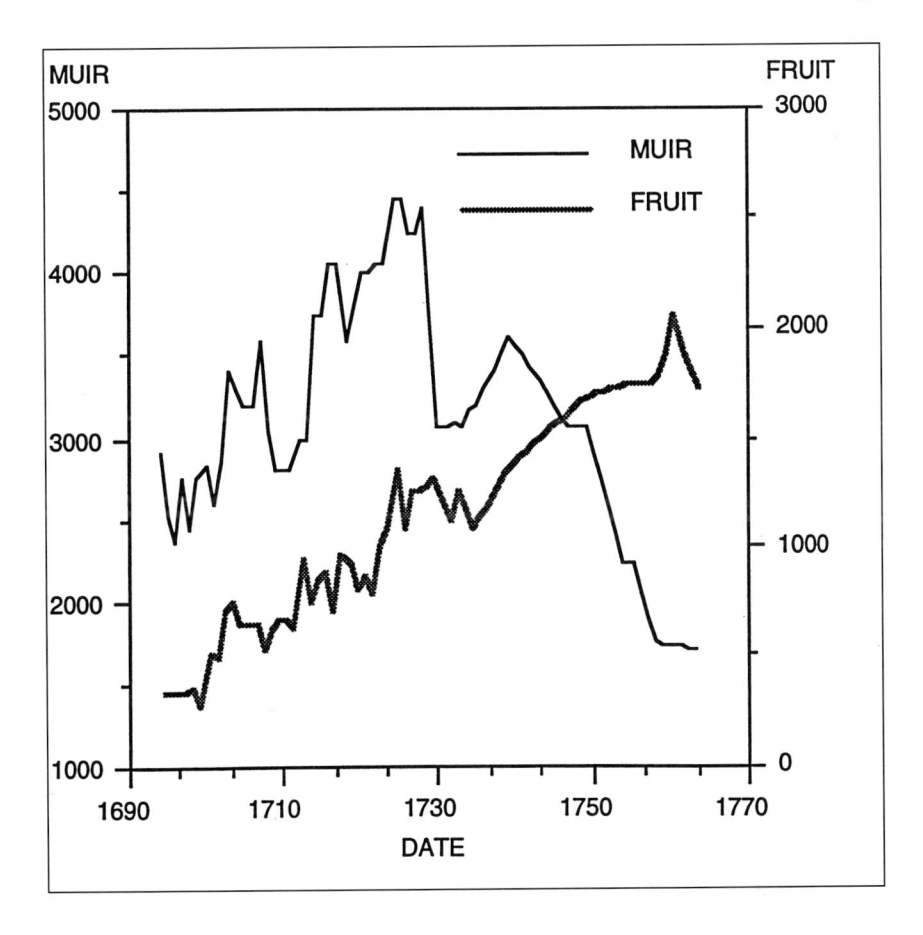

Figure 2.

in trade following peace with France had not materialised and trade had actually declined.[13] Marion Mitchell, tackswoman of the Netherbow customs, received a rebate on her contracted payments to the council because of problems in collecting dues during the 'tumults' of 1685 and because of the depredations of soldiery in subsequent years.[14] These and other petitions for rebates primarily cite changes in consumption and thus reinforce the credibility of the indicator.[15] The council occasionally granted exemptions from particular branches of the customs to stimulate trade. In September 1662 they waived the merk on the tun payable on Norwegian timber 'being so necessary a commodity for this

[13] Armet, *Extracts . . . 1701 to 1718*, p. 267.
[14] Wood and Armet, *Extracts . . . 1681 to 1689*, p. 266.
[15] Armet, *Extracts . . . 1701 to 1718*, p. 254; N.L.S. MS 17, 602, ff.74–9.

country of great bulk and small value' because the duty 'is such a burden on the same as all strangers forebear to bring in their ships and timber to the port of Leith but carry the same to Fisherraw and other ports to the great prejudice of that trade in this city and town of Leith and of the citizens and inhabitants who have occasion to build houses'.[16] Better that some customs were collected than no customs at all. Short term fluctuations, related to unexpected events, are interesting in themselves, but long term trends are probably well represented.

Collection of the dues was farmed out to men and women whose profit on the enterprise depended on the successful and economical collection of indirect taxes from those importing or selling goods in the city and its jurisdictions. When names are recorded, there were usually less than a dozen bidders. Given the relatively small number of burgesses—about 2,000 after the Restoration and perhaps 1,200 in the 1750s[17]—it might have been possible for potential bidders to 'ring' the auction and keep offers low but again it would be difficult to conceal collusion from the authorities. The accounting of the Common Good was often subject to inquiry by the auditors.[18] The council had an idea of what a tack was worth since its members were themselves active traders. It is the very closeness of the burgh's business community and the council's determination to promote open competition which makes the Common Good such a sensitive indicator.

Desire for longer leases suggests a perception that the contract was likely to become more lucrative. If too many eager bidders drove up the price, an unlikely scenario given the hard-headed businessmen involved, this would not be sustained unless the winner had developed some novel method of extracting more from the concession or, more probable, unless objective conditions had improved. The price would fall back quickly once potential tacksmen saw their profit margins being eroded. Short shrift was given in 1661 to the 'frivolous pretences' of John Arthor, tacksman of Edinburgh and Leith weigh-houses, that a cabal of ten or twelve wool merchants had 'bid so much for it in the rouping ... of intention to disappoint the town and tacksman of the benefit of the table' of customers on wool and other goods.[19] While it is dangerous to argue from silence about a topic like corruption, it is surprising how few comments there are in the sources about cartels. There was a lively debate about placemen, corruption and misuse of funds from c. 1720 but almost no evidence of this kind of malpractice surrounding the Common Good. The city's debt burden and its reliance on all sources of income made strict control of financial practices essential on both practical and moral grounds.

[16] *Minute Books*, vol. 21, f.171v.

[17] J. MacMillan, 'A Study of the Edinburgh Burgess Community and its Economic Activities' (unpublished Ph.D. thesis, University of Edinburgh, 1984), p. 37; J. Gilhooley, *A Directory of Edinburgh in 1752* (Edinburgh, 1989), p. viii.

[18] Wood, *Extracts . . . 1665 to 1680*, pp. xxxiv–v.

[19] *Minute Books*, vol. 21, ff.55–v.

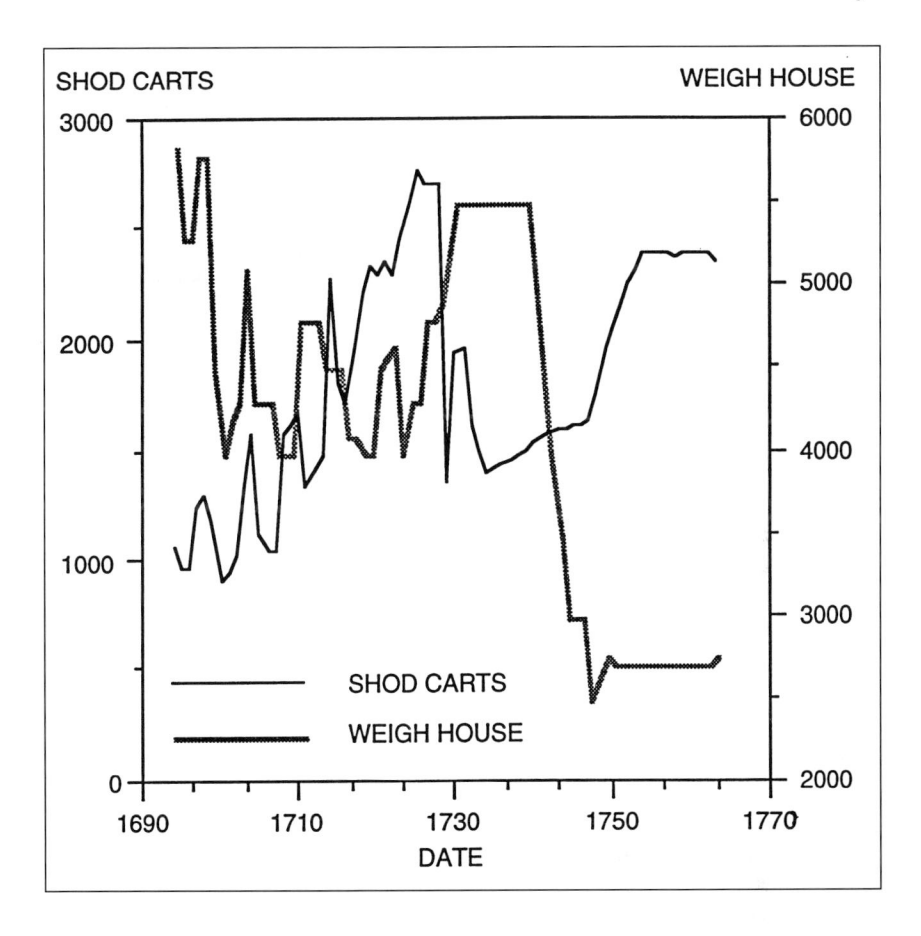

Figure 3.

The effect of cartels on the value of the common good as an indicator should also be weighed up closely. If auctions were 'ringed' throughout the period, trends would be unaffected but the absolute level of sums offered would be consistently lower than if bids were completely open. If cartels formed and then broke down, this could account for some short term fluctuations; the dissolution of a 'ring' would probably raise bids. However, cartels did not operate in a vacuum. They might form to exploit improving conditions in one branch of the common good and melt away when times got bad and few wanted to risk collection. In other words, cartels might dampen the effect of swings in objective circumstances observed in sums offered. But the trends shown in the graphs are almost certainly robust indicators of the underlying state of elements of Edinburgh's economy. And they are plausible economic reasons for many of the short term movements in the series.

It is as plausible to argue that offers were determined by market forces while bidders looked to exploit both public and traders rather than the city to bump up their profits. Their methods were sometimes direct and forceful. An early eighteenth-century petition by the city's brewers, a powerful lobby group not known for being diligent payers of the excise, spoke of arbitrary action by the tacksman: 'under cloud of night they called for their keys, and by fifteen or sixteen vagabond fellows . . . they have kept possession of their houses, drunk ale at pleasure, gaming all the night at cards.'[20] Corruption among employees charged with levying the taxes was seemingly extensive. Complaints against the supervisor of the collection of the impost on wines, John Straiton, spoke of his irregular practices and of 'the general clamour against his carriage to the people'.[21] The sub committee of the council delegated to investigate also mentions a not infrequent event: 'since the servants were last purged'. Granting unwarranted exemptions to friends, bribery and extortion were all mentioned: a problem for tacksmen as well as the city's people.

In short, while considerations other than economics may have influenced short term fluctuations, the overall trends indicate consumption and economic conditions in the city, providing pointers to the wellbeing of its inhabitants and the condition of certain important parts of its economy. The trends can be compared with other economic indicators such as interest rates and fiars for Midlothian—the prices of grains set (in relation to the previous harvest) every February by a court of landowners.[22] Oatmeal fiars, the mainstay of everyday diet, have been graphed here in shillings sterling per boll (Fig. 6), as have the sums collected for the poor at church doors 1663–1743 in pounds Scots (Fig. 7).[23]

Changes in economic conditions determined the sharp surge in dues payable on the Leith timber yard in the 1740s (Fig. 1). Dues for this and those payable for the use of the harbour there show the state of imports into the Edinburgh area and the demand for building timber. Shore dues and petty customs of Leith included weighing and measuring, 'gold penny', dock silver, beaconage, payments for the ballast boats and ballasting duty (Fig. 1). The graph of shore dues reveals a 'blip' between 1698 and 1701, possibly because of rebuilding after the disastrous fires at the head of the Canongate in 1698 and in the heart of the city in 1700. Of 150 cases before the Dean of Guild court 1697–8, 32 per cent concerned rebuilding or extensive repairs and alterations compared with

---

[20] N.L.S. 6.692 [25].

[21] *Minute Books*, vol. 21, ff.112–14.

[22] M. W. Flinn, *Scottish Population History* (Cambridge, 1977), pp. 492–5; Arnot, *History of Edinburgh*, pp. 482–5.

[23] E.C.A. Kirk Treasurer's Accounts, 1663–1743; the yield on 3 per cent funds 1731–70 and valuation of the city 1749–81 (E.C.A.) have not been graphed. Unbroken series are not available for any of the Common Good elements in the figures. All figures are extrapolations for the years 1735–8, 1740–6, 1750–3, 1756–7, 1759–60, 1761–2.

```
MERK ON PACK
```

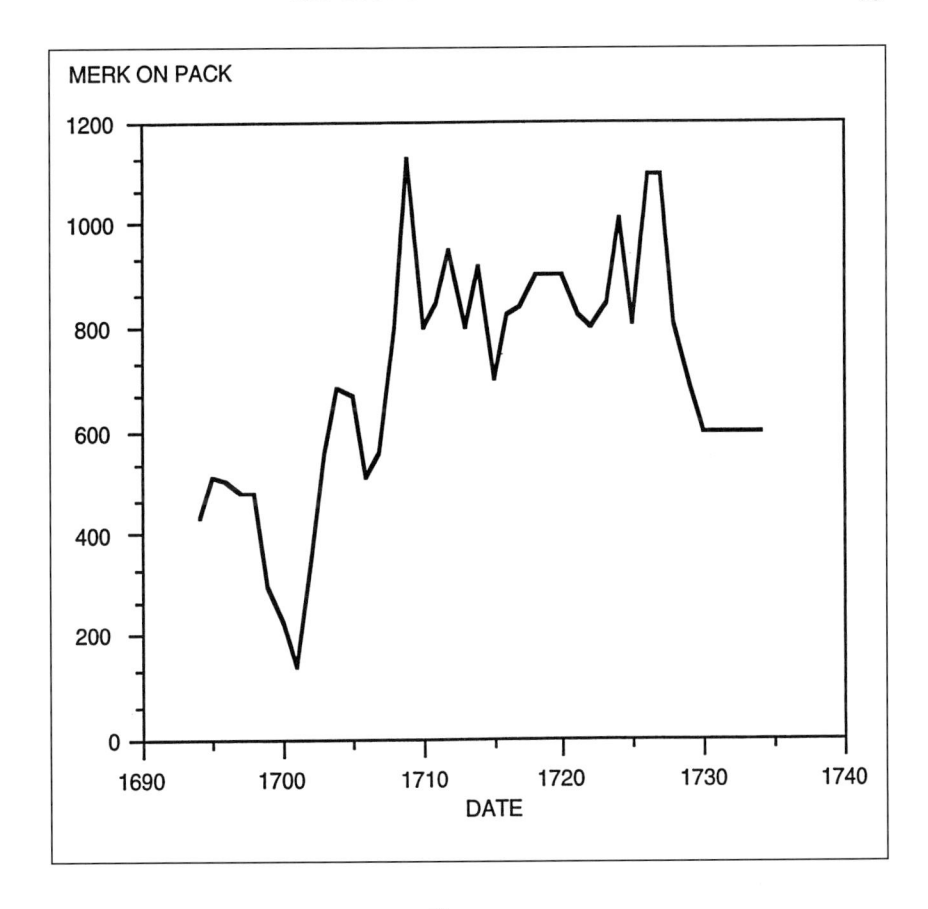

Figure 4.

17 per cent for the 1687–8 sample (from a total of 134 cases) and 8 per cent in the next available year of 1737 (107 cases).[24] The trough after 1701 may be because the rebuilding pre-empted what would have taken place anyway. At the same time, the Darien aftermath hit confidence within the city: sums offered fell from 1,320 merks in 1701 to just 525 merks in 1702. In March 1702 the council minuted increasing debt problems 'occasioned through the many annual rents (interest payments) that were resting by the good town upon the consigned money and other old debts and the great poverty of the place by reason of the several fires, famine and the burdens occasioned by the desolations made by the late dreadful fires'.[25] Social dislocations and a loss of confidence may have been as significant as absolute poverty between 1695 and 1702. The opening years of the eighteenth century were not auspicious. Indeed,

[24] E.C.A. Dean of Guild Court.
[25] Armet, *Extracts . . . 1701 to 1718*, p. 8.

Whatley notes a decline in timber imports into Dundee beginning before 1707 and culminating in none at all brought in during 1710 thanks to English restrictions.[26]

The relative stagnation in the value of trade through Leith from the beginning of the eighteenth century to the end of the 1740s and its rapid development in the early 1750s is much more striking. A 1725 Court of Session case about construction provoked the defendants to complain of a lack of building in the Canongate because of 'the growing poverty of the place'.[27] All this seems to have changed during the 1740s. The volume of timber imports must have been increasing prior to this since sums offered for the Bush rose from the end of the 1730s and had broken out of the 1700–35 trading range by 1740. The county's heritors minuted in 1753 that within the last eight years the sums offered for the tack of shore dues had risen from 8,000 merks to 16,500 merks.[28] In fact, the amount offered rose by three-quarters between 1749 and 1753 from 10,200 to 18,050, and the lowest it had ever been was 8,300 merks in 1696 and 1701. The increasing volume of trade at this time is shown in a broken series of Leith shore dues, which offer a rare insight into Edinburgh's mid-eighteenth century commerce.[29] The number of vessels varied within a narrow range from 1,239 a year to 1,352 between 1727–8 and 1735–6, dipping to 1,185 in 1736–7 but recovering to 1,436 in 1737–8. After a gap, the 1752–3 volume shows 1,826 vessels paying dues. Numbers fell to 1,558 and 1,500 in 1753–4 and 1754–5 but picked up to 1,702 in 1755–6. The average of 1727–38 was 1,306 vessels a year compared with 1,647 in the 1750s, an increase of a quarter.

It was this expansion of trade which produced the announcement in December 1753 that the town council would pay up to £2,000 sterling towards buying land for the harbour project, 'being sensible of the advantages that will arise to that city and to the public'.[30] This was not before time since a new pier funded by the impost on ale had been proposed as early as 1720 and a pamphlet of 1721 spoke of a pressing need to improve the harbour.[31] In January 1744 the masters of Trinity House, Leith, petitioned that the lack of a west pier blocked ships in harbour when unfavourable winds were blowing.[32] In 1745 complaints surfaced about the need to improve the heavily used roads from Leith to Edinburgh.[33] Serious discussions about enlarging the harbour had been under way since the summer of 1750 and in July 1753 it was acknowledged that the constraints of the small harbour were made increasingly apparent by the recent extension of the Greenland trade; a whale oil processing plant existed next to the Bush

---

[26] Whatley, 'Economic Causes', pp. 170–1.
[27] S.R.O. CS271/66, 639.
[28] S.R.O. SC39/69/3, f.90.
[29] E.C.A. Shore Dues.
[30] S.R.O. SC39/69/3, f.77.
[31] S.R.O. SC39/69/2, f.6v; N.L.S. 1.7[38], p. 2.
[32] *Minute Books*, vol. 64, p. 171.
[33] *Ibid.*, vol. 65, p. 200.

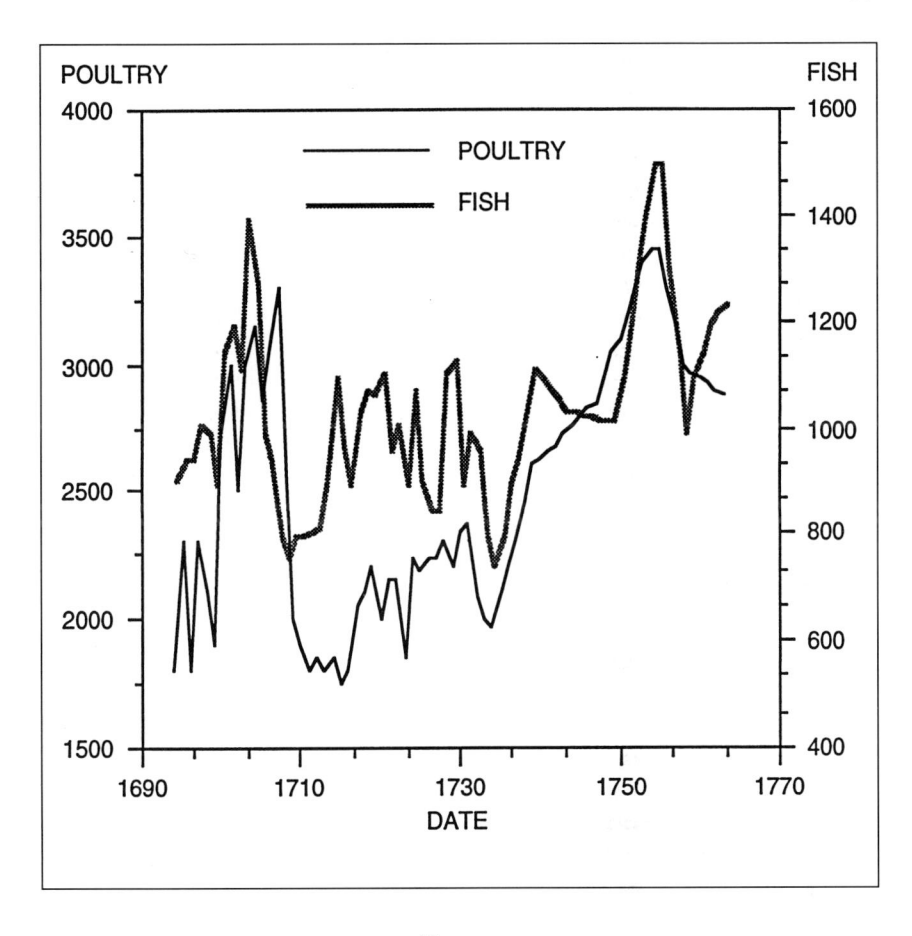

Figure 5.

in 1750.³⁴ Other evidence confirms the expansion of trade. The number of metsters at Leith was raised from ten to eighteen (plus four widows) in February 1747 'in regard that business at the port of Leith for the metsters is pretty much increased'.³⁵ Grants of land at Leith for shipbuilding become increasingly common at this time.³⁶

In April 1752 the city looked at recovering certain land grants in the timber bush because of a need for more space 'to promote and encourage the trade of the said port and to provide suitable and convenient repositories'.³⁷ In July of the same year Mr Adam Drummond, surgeon, offered to take an abandoned feu there

---

[34] *Ibid.*, vol. 71, p. 180; vol. 69, pp. 64–7.
[35] *Ibid.*, vol. 66, p. 81.
[36] For example, *ibid.*, vol. 69, pp. 258–9.
[37] *Ibid.*, vol. 70, pp. 123–4.

for a lime store, and in December the reorganisation of the whole site was announced 'whereby it is thought that the Bush will contain twice as much as it now does'.[38] A new table of duties based on the number and size of planks was drawn up. By then, the boom in timber bush rentals was over. With eleven or twelve private entries to the site people recognised that it was almost useless as a safe place to keep goods and 'no tacksman for many years past has received any dues for goods lodged there, the people always losing or pretending to have lost a greater value of their timber than all the dues amounted to'.[39] Lead for roofing and piping was also kept in the Bush, much to the detriment of the roads leading to and from it.

Other elements show very different trends. Sums offered for the house of muir and sheep pens (all quadruped livestock) rose strongly between 1695 and 1725 (Figure 2). Cattle prices may have been rising after the Union but if bids are indicative of the rising value of the trade the trend seems already to have been in place.[40] The next major development was a fall of 30 per cent between 1728 and 1730. After a brief respite, proceeds declined to less than half their peak of 1724–5 by the 1760s. The city was erecting new sheep pens on the north side of the Grassmarket in 1733 and seems to have been responding to increased trade and a desire to prevent livestock running loose in the Grassmarket.[41] The reason for the fall seems to have been changes in marketing practices and in particular the development of wholesale buying and selling of livestock outside the town markets. At the 1739 roup 'all fleshers or drovers are hereby prohibited to buy or sell the cattle brought into the city or liberties anywhere else except in the said market or on the pasture where they have been fed at least six weeks and particularly from buying or selling them in Dalkeith, Musselburgh or Leith under pain of being punished as forestallers'. The poor performance of this element may be due to the flouting of the regulations. Certainly, the city's demand for meat was prodigious by the 1770s. For 1776–7 Hugo Arnot estimated Edinburgh's inhabitants consumed 10,000 oxen, 8,300 calves, 49,000 sheep and 78,000 lambs.[42]

Graphs of the weigh house and shod carts or 'calsey dues' give insights into the volume of business in the city since they involved duties on movements of items for sale (Fig. 3). The weigh houses at Edinburgh and Leith charged duties on wool and cloth, and foodstuffs such as butter brought into the city for sale. Whatley speaks of a sharp decline in wool and woollen cloth exports from Dundee and elsewhere after 1707 but the weigh house figures again suggest that a downturn

---

[38] *Ibid.*, vol. 70, pp. 218–21; vol. 71, p. 3.
[39] *Minute Books*, vol. 71, p. 103.
[40] Whatley, 'Economic Causes', p. 169.
[41] S.R.O. CS237/E/1/18; *Minute Books*, vol. 54, p. 387.
[42] Arnot, *History of Edinburgh*, p. 264; A. Lottin and H. Soly, 'Aspects de l'histoire des villes des Pays–Bas meridionaux et de la principute de Liege', in A. Lottin *et al.*, eds., *Etudes sur les villes en Europe occidentale*, tome 2 (Paris, 1983), p. 232.

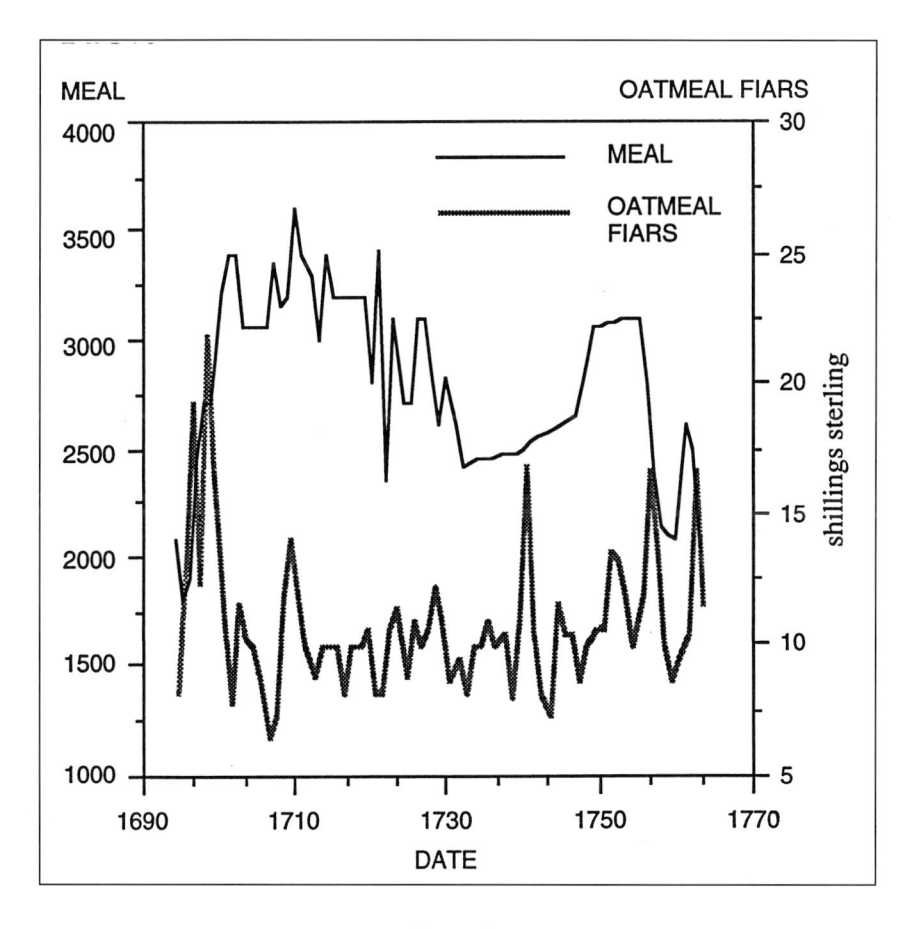

Figure 6.

was already in place.[43] Duties on exported and printed linens in 1711 and 1715 may explain the stagnation of dues from the 1700s to the 1720s. The weigh house graph gives no sign of the depression in the woollen cloth industry 1752–7.[44]

Calsey dues included hackney coaches which were an increasingly important means of transport. The sharp rise in amounts offered in 1713 may have been influenced by the inclusion of the new duty on ale, noted in a Court of Session declarator of 13 January of that year, with it, but the jump was part of a strong uptrend in this element between 1694 and 1725. The collapse between 1728 and 1729 was the result of three factors. First, there was an attempt to extend the customs on shod carts and the 2d. impost on ale to brewers outside the

---

[43] Whatley, 'Economic Causes', p. 173.
[44] Flinn, *Scottish Population*, p. 225.

city.⁴⁵ One voice among many raised against the move, that of Robert Mitchell feuer and brewer at Fountainbridge, complained that 'the inhabitants of the city have twenty ways of making gain by their residence therein', compared with suburban producers who had to shoulder transport costs as well.⁴⁶ Second, there were ambiguities stemming from an act of parliament in 1727 about what goods should pay 'petty port customs'. This also hit the merk on the pack and cannot have helped the port customs though these are not recorded after 1722. Third, there may well have been a decline in consumption of 2d. ale. Ale duty was realising £7,188 a year in 1725 compared with £6,802 in 1731 and £6,209 in 1735.⁴⁷ Spirit consumption rose from the early eighteenth century. 'Glasgow rum' was being passed off as brandy in 1711, and in 1731 the council passed an act discouraging the sale and consumption of foreign spirits.⁴⁸ In 1745 efforts were being made to tax native distillers because of their greatly increased numbers and 'a much greater consumption.'⁴⁹ Disputes over who should pay calsey dues had flared up intermittently in the first quarter of the eighteenth century and in 1726 the burgh had to borrow money to take the coachmasters to the Court of Session for failing to pay.⁵⁰ The 1729 conditions of roup notes a wider range of exemptions than formerly, including the Edinburgh-Leith stage coach, British wool and linen cloth, and, apparently, all building materials, combustibles and household furniture.

The merk on the pack included foreign goods coming overland from England or elsewhere into the city except packs of wool (Fig. 4). In the 1700 'conditions' it was specified that 'all liquors imported over land from the country are to pay as the merk upon the tun and that a pack of other goods is understood at least sixteen stone weight which is to pay a merk and so proportionately for lesser weight'. Goods belonging to the Africa and India trading companies were exempt and Leith was free of this duty. From 510 merks in 1695 and 500 in 1696 the offers fell to 140 merks in 1701 before staging a strong rally to reach an all time high of 1,130 merks in 1709. Thereafter it fluctuated between roughly 800 and 1,100 before breaking downward out of this range; the last recorded offer is 600 merks. As an indicator of luxury goods which could bear the heavy costs of overland transport, this suggests that the first decade of the eighteenth century was perhaps not as bad as has been painted—at least for those able to buy such goods.

Tolls on the markets for fruit, fish, meal and livestock can be seen as indicators of food consumption in the city and liberties. The fruit market tolls were on 'such fruits as are of the growth of the kingdom', specified as potatoes, artichokes, strawberries, gooseberries, cherries, apricots, peaches, plums, kail, herbs and radishes (Fig. 2). Of

---

45 Arnot, *History of Edinburgh*, p. 256.
46 S.R.O. SC39/69/2, ff.15, 21–21Av.
47 E.C.A. Ale Duty Journal, 1718–32; S.R.O. SC39/69/2 ff.28, 33v.
48 Armet, *Extracts . . . 1701 to 1718*, p. 216; Edinburgh City Libraries qYHU 5080.
49 *Minute Books*, vol. 65, p. 116.
50 E.C.A. Acts of the Canongate Bailies, vol. 4, p. 235.

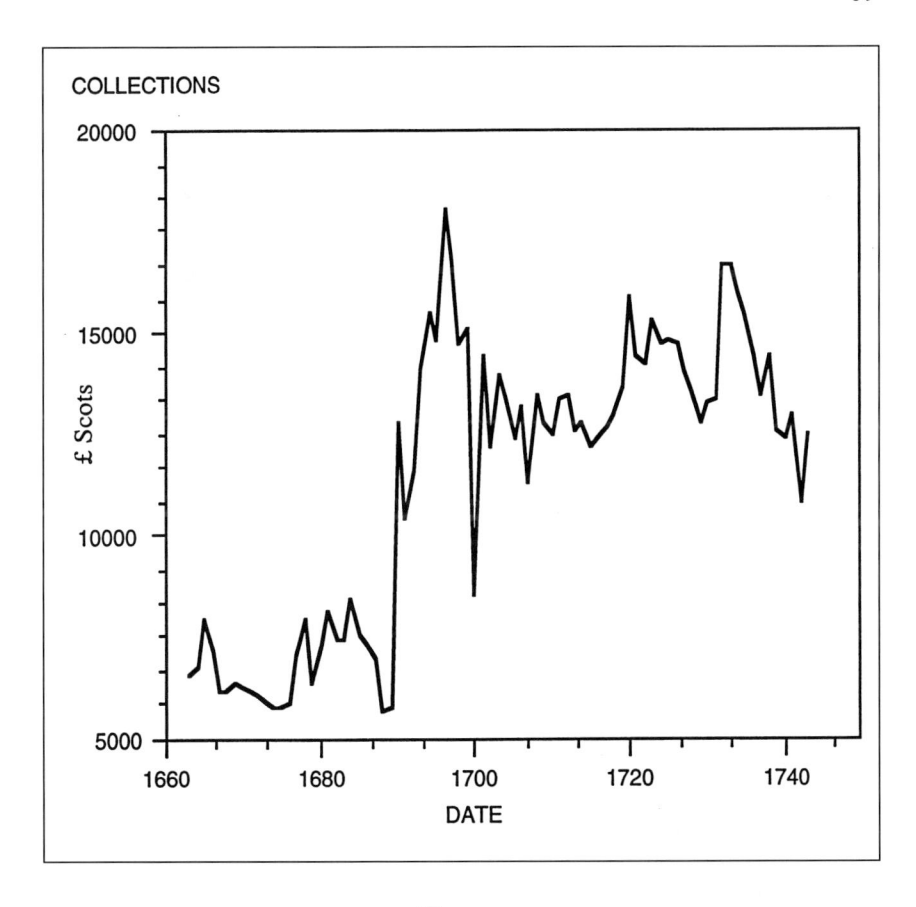

Figure 7.

those elements of the Common Good for which a relatively unbroken run of auction prices are recorded, the fruit 'metts and measures' rose strongly from 1694 to 1763. When, as in 1729, the bids are itemised, the fruit market and calsey dues were the most closely contested. In that year, Thomas Chalmers first bid 1,120 merks for the fruit market customs but had to raise his offer twice to 1,340 merks to secure the tack. Arnot reported of the 1770s that vegetable prices were low and supplies good.[51] Potatoes were being brought into the city in January 1743.[52] *The Thistle* newspaper number 46 for Christmas day 1734 advertised that only one cargo of fruit had arrived that year—lemons and 'China oranges' from Malaga—and that these were to be sold by the importer, William Carmichael, at his shop in

---

[51] Arnot, *History of Edinburgh*, pp. 266, 514.
[52] S.R.O. JP35/4/3.

Edinburgh or from his warehouse in Leith. Many Midlothian parishes were involved in fruit production according to the Statistical Account.

Suggestive though the graph of fruit market offers may be, it is difficult to place the produce in the mouths of ordinary people. In eighteenth-century Madrid fresh vegetables and fruit were mainly found in the diet of the better-off middling and upper classes, though in England there seems to have been a general increase in consumption after the Restoration.[53] The relative stability of Edinburgh building wages before the mid-eighteenth century implies growing consumption among a restricted clientele, unless the price of fruit and vegetables had fallen steadily in real terms.[54] The slight effect of the 1695–1700 dearths on the fruit market implies a clientele with a low income elasticity of demand at this period. Arnot saw demand from the General Assembly and the Court of Session exerting a pronounced influence on prices with a heavy premium on early season fruit and vegetables.[55]

Fish market offers rose sharply from 950 merks in 1695 and 1696 to peak at 1,400 merks in 1703 (Fig. 5). Arnot observed salmon being brought from Perth and Stirling while herring was so plentiful that it was used as a fertiliser around the city.[56] The early 1750s peak may have been the result of a project by James and Thomas Walker in 1751 to outfit boats for deep sea fishing thus increasing the supply of good fish for the gentry and other inhabitants; they also asked for the right to sell it through the city.[57] For sale in the poultry market in 1732 were veal, rabbit, hare, wild and domesticated geese, turkey, wildfowl, hens, ducks, pigeons and larks (Fig. 5). The growth in sums offered was neither as steady nor as large as for fruit. Furthermore, the poultry market shows two distinct chart patterns: a rise from 1,800 merks to 3,300 merks in 1707 followed by a 40 per cent fall in the next two years. The chart bottomed out at 1,750 merks in 1715 then began a slow rise which accelerated in the early 1730s to reach a peak of 3,450 merks in 1754–5. The pattern relative to the fish market in the 1690s and 1700s is puzzling. In bad times, consumption of fish would rise and that of poultry decline.[58] Why both rose in the period of dearths and why the effect lasted into the 1700s before tailing off is hard to explain unless there were two distinct sets of buyers for the different commodities.

Another pattern is evident in the graph of sums offered for the meal market where grains were sold (Fig. 6). The rise of 77 per cent 1695–1700 was

---

[53] D. Ringrose, *Madrid and the Spanish Economy, 1560–1850* (Berkeley, 1983), p. 82; J. Thirsk and J. P. Cooper, eds., *Seventeenth-Century Economic Documents* (Oxford, 1972), p. 80.

[54] L. Cullen, A. Gibson and T. C. Smout, 'Wages and comparative development in Ireland and Scotland, 1565–1780', in Mitchison and Roebuck, pp. 106, 111.

[55] Arnot, *History of Edinburgh*, pp. 264–6.

[56] *Ibid.*, p. 265.

[57] *Minute Books*, vol. 69, pp. 230–3.

[58] S. Rappaport, *Worlds within Worlds: Structures of Life in Sixteenth-Century London* (Cambridge, 1989), p. 51.

presumably related to the serious dearths in those years. The council was anxious that sales take place in the open market rather than outside the city or elsewhere within it. As late as 1739 retailers were forbidden to deal with grain suppliers within four miles of the city and the tacksmen had the incentive of double duties from convicted forestallers. A customs exemption for seven years declared in May 1716 to encourage people to use the new corn market in the Grassmarket had little short-term effect but from 1719–21 sums offered fell by approximately a quarter, not recovering to their 1719 level until 1726 and languishing thereafter.[59]

Comparisons can be made with other economic indicators such as the level of long term interest rates shown by the proxy measure of the yield on 3 per cent consols from 1731 (not graphed).[60] Before that, official interest rates (set in connection with the usury laws) fell from a ceiling of 10 per cent in the early seventeenth century to 5½ per cent by 1700, remaining within 0.5 per cent of that level until the end of the eighteenth century.[61] Eighteenth-century comparisons between official ceilings and actual rates show the problems of using the former and the same is true of the seventeenth century. The 1660s 'showtrials' (mostly of Edinburgh people) for usury before the Justiciary court reveal actual interest charges of 10 to 15 per cent *per annum* during the troubled 1640s and 1650s when the official maximum ranged between 6 per cent and 8 per cent.[62]

It might be thought that elements like the timber bush would be susceptible to interest rate fluctuations which would influence building work.[63] This does not appear to be so. Nor is there any obvious connection between any of the other parts of the Common Good and long term interest rate changes, judged by linear regression correlations. The only exception is the strong inverse relationship ($r = 0.9$) between the weigh house and interest rates. The food market offers turned down during the period when the yield on consols rose from 2.9 per cent in 1754 to 4.3 per cent in 1762 but it is hard to see what mechanism could have connected inelastic basic food consumption and interest rates. Perhaps potential bidders felt they could get a better return in some other form of business, though it is hard to imagine the council tolerating artificially low offers. In any case, it is difficult to see any other obviously better opportunities. Residential property yielded 6 to 7 per cent a year in the 1740s and 1750s but the capital value of the

---

[59] Armet, *Extracts* ... *1701 to 1718*, pp. 313–14.
[60] T. S. Ashton, *Economic Fluctuations in England, 1700–1800* (Oxford, 1959), p. 187. This is only one, long-term interest rate and it is possible that shorter term ones would be more appropriate for comparison, were they available. K. J. Weiller and P. Mirowski, 'Rates of Interest in Eighteenth-Century England', *Explorations in Economic History*, XXVII, 1 (1990), 1–28. While there was an exchange on London, the rates presented may not be appropriate to the Edinburgh capital markets.
[61] G. C. Mathemat, *An Almanac and New Prognostication for the Year of our Lord, 1701* (Edinburgh, 1701); Ashton, *Economic Fluctuations*, p. 86.
[62] Mathemat, *Almanac*; S.R.O. JC6/6, 7.
[63] Ashton, *Economic Fluctuations*, pp. 85–9.

buildings was relatively low: ten years purchase compared with fourteen to sixteen years in the late seventeenth and early eighteenth centuries. The real return on heritable property rented out was perhaps 3 to 4 per cent *per annum* during 1660–1760.[64] Foreign trade was risky as was speculative building: both could be lucrative but both were more likely to end in bankruptcy than many other investments.

Sums collected at church doors can be seen as an indicator of perceived poverty and may give an oblique sign of who was consuming what (Fig. 7). The sharp rise in 1690 is easily explained by changes in poor relief after the Revolution, and the rise after 1695 by the dearth, but the level did not drop off again the way fiars prices did (Fig. 6). The drastic fall in 1700 was the result of 'donor fatigue' and the crisis of confidence associated with Darien. A stable cost of living in the first half of the eighteenth century alongside collection levels nearly double the 1663–89 average suggests that the poor were seen as a permanently larger problem. The 1711 workhouse scheme and reorganisation of out-relief in 1743 reinforce this impression. Seen alongside the steady rise in the fruit market, the recovery in the merk on the pack 1700–9 and the valuation of the city, which shows an almost uninterrupted rise in assessments from £309,440 in 1749 to £520,440 in 1781, this suggests that wealth polarisation in the city was becoming more pronounced.

What conclusions can we draw from analysis of the Common Good? First the value of trade through Leith was static for the first three decades of the eighteenth century but experienced rapid growth in the fourth. This confirms received wisdom about slow economic growth in early eighteenth-century Scotland.[65] The rise in Edinburgh labourers' real wages identified by Cullen, Gibson and Smout in the 1760s followed these developments.[66] Second, the steady growth in fruit market offers suggests increasing disposable income for those buying fruit and vegetables. This and other indicators point to a marked, and possibly growing, wealth polarisation within the city, though probably not as pronounced as in contemporary Dublin. Third, the short term impact of harvest crises in the 1690s on meal, fish and poultry markets was pronounced. By the next serious dearth in 1740 the effect is negligible and masked in the graphs by other trends, though it is still visible in the fiars prices of 1740–1.

Finally, what can the Common Good not tell us? It shows overall patterns better than precise details, interesting as these are and closely as they fit the wider economic context available from other sources. It is not a 'pure' economic indicator for its interpretation depends in part on the nature of social and political relationships within the city. It says little directly about Edinburgh's role in Scotland's economic

---

[64] J. Dambruyne, 'De Gentse immobiliënmarkt en de economische trend, 1590–1640', *Bijdragen en Mededelingen*, CIV, 2 (1989), pp. 157–83 is a rare northern European study of the real estate market in a wider economic context.

[65] Whatley, 'Economic Causes', pp. 168–9.

[66] Cullen, Gibson and Smout, 'Wages', pp. 106, 111.

development. Edinburgh was Scotland's biggest city until the middle of the eighteenth century yet its importance for national society and economy awaits full study.[67] The capital's catchment area for apprentices declined from being truly national in the seventeenth century to being much more regionalised as Glasgow grew in size and importance.[68] Edinburgh, like Dublin, was for a time, in the early and mid-eighteenth century, economically as well as socially and politically significant in a national context. Like Dublin, it was increasingly overtaken by economic growth elsewhere.[69]

---

[67] Except at a general level, and with conspicuous exceptions, such analyses are rare in European urban history: E. A. Wrigley, 'A Simple Model of London's Importance in Changing English Economy and Society, 1650–1750', *Past and Present* 37 (1967), pp. 44–70; Ringrose, *Madrid*; Thestrup, *Standard of Living*.

[68] A. A. Lovett, I. D. Whyte and K. A. Whyte, 'Poisson Regression Analysis and Migration Fields: The Example of the Apprenticeship Records of Edinburgh in the Seventeenth and Eighteenth Centuries', *Transactions of the Institute of British Geographers*, new series 10 (1985), pp. 317–32.

[69] D. Dickson, 'The Place of Dublin in the Eighteenth-Century Irish Economy', in Devine and Dickson, p. 189.

5

Contrasting regimes: population growth in Ireland and Scotland during the eighteenth century

R. E. Tyson

ALTHOUGH there is a distinct shortage of relevant data, Irish demographic historians in recent years have proved remarkably ingenious at providing estimates of the population of pre-censal Ireland from 1687 onwards. The result is a somewhat different picture of national and provincial population from that produced by Connell in his great pioneering study.[1] The purpose of this essay is to compare trends there with those in Scotland during the eighteenth century and to offer some explanation of why, despite their proximity, the two countries differed so markedly, for while Irish population growth after 1750 was the most rapid in Europe, that of Scotland was one of the slowest.

The study of Scottish population has been seriously handicapped by the absence of any estimate of total numbers before Webster's private census of 1755. However, it is possible to provide a figure for 1691 by making use of records which give the number of paid hearths for most of the Lowlands and a large part of the Highlands. Adamson suggests that normally 65 per cent of households paid the tax, rising to 67 per cent in Edinburgh, the remainder of Midlothian, and West Lothian, and that there were on average two hearths per household in Edinburgh, 1.5 in the counties around the Firth of Forth 1.4 in the remaining Lowland areas, and 1.2 in the Highlands.[2] Recent research on Aberdeenshire in the 1690s indicates that in that county there was an average of 1.3 hearths per household, ranging from 1.7 in Aberdeen to 1.1 in Highland parishes, and that 63 per cent of households paid

---

[1] K. H. Connell, *The Population of Ireland, 1750–1845* (Oxford, 1950); L. A. Clarkson, 'Irish Population Revisited, 1687–1821', in J. M. Goldstrom and L. A. Clarkson, eds., *Irish Population, Economy and Society* (Oxford, 1981), pp. 13–35; S. Daultrey, D. Dickson and C. Ó Gráda, 'Eighteenth-Century Irish Population: New Perspectives from Old Sources', *Journal of Economic History*, XLI (1981), pp. 601–28; D. Dickson, C. Ó Gráda and S. Daultrey, 'Hearth Tax, Household Size and Irish Population Change 1672–1821', *Proceedings of the Royal Irish Academy*, C, LXXXII (1982), pp. 125–81.

[2] M. Flinn, ed., *Scottish Population History* (Cambridge, 1977), pp. 189–200.

Table 1: The population of Scottish counties, 1691–1755

County	Paid hearths	Hearths per household	% of households paying hearth tax	Mean household size	Population 1691	Population 1755
Aberdeen	24,089	1.3	63	4.2	124,122	116,100
Angus	14,100	1.5	65	4.5	65,511	68,883
Argyll*	4,990	1.2	60	4.8	33,336	35,376
Ayr	12,744	1.5	65	4.6	59,864	59,009
Berwick	5,470	1.5	65	4.7	26,312	23,987
Bute	1,065	1.2	60	4.8	7,115	7,125
Caithness	3,348	1.2	60	5.6	24,413	22,215
Clackmannan	1,252	1.3	65	3.8	5,630	9,003
Dumfries	7,368	1.4	65	4.9	39,386	39,788
Dumbarton	2,589	1.4	65	4.7	13,343	13,857
East Lothian	7,904	1.5	65	4.2	34,291	29,709
Fife and Kinross	19,395	1.5	65	4.2	82,752	86,459
Kirkcudbright	3,220	1.4	65	4.7	16,525	21,205
Lanark	15,351	1.5	65	4.2	65,498	81,726
Midlothian—Edinburgh and Leith	14,727	2.0	67	4.4	48,687	57,220
Midlothian—other than Edinburgh and Leith	9,553	1.5	67	4.2	40,208	33,192
Peebles and Selkirk	2,951	1.5	65	4.7	14,104	12,929
Perth	22,713	1.3	65	4.3	115,043	120,116
Renfrew	5,019	1.5	65	4.4	22,701	26,645
Ross and Cromarty†	4,049	1.2	60	4.6	26,024	27,590
Roxburgh	6,419	1.3	62	4.5	35,519	34,704
Shetland	1,200	1.1	60	5.9	10,673	15,210
Stirling	7,492	1.5	65	4.5	34,425	37,014
Sutherland	2,175	1.1	60	5.6	18,455	20,774
West Lothian	5,226	1.5	67	4.2	21,996	16,829
Wigtown	3,340	1.4	65	4.8	17,764	16,466

* 22 parishes only
† 19 parishes only

Sources:
D. Adamson, ed., *West Lothian Hearth Tax, 1691* (Scottish Record Society, 1981); M. Flinn, ed., *Scottish Population History* (Cambridge, 1977), pp. 187–200; Sir John Sinclair, *The Statistical Account of Scotland, 1791–99* (new edn, Wakefield, 1975–83), vols. II–XX; J. G. Kyd, *Scottish Population Statistics* (Scottish History Society, 1952).

Table 2: Population of Scottish regions, 1691–1801

Region	Population 1691	Population 1755	Population 1801	% increase (+) or decrease (-) 1691–1755	1755–1801
Borders	150,140	149,079	184,949	- 0.7	+24.1
Eastern Lowlands	448,542	458,425	557,041	+ 2.2	+21.5
Western Lowlands	161,406	181,237	331,110	+12.3	+82.7
North East	222,788	214,001	220,712	- 6.5	+ 3.1
Highlands and Islands	245,699	262,638	314,608	+ 6.9	+19.8
Scotland	1,234,575	1,265,380	1,608,420	+ 2.5	+27.1

For definition of regions see Flinn, *Scottish Population History*, p. xxii.

the tax (60 per cent in the Highlands).[3] It is likely, therefore, that Adamson's estimates of hearths per household and the percentage paying the tax are too high for the North East and the Highlands.

As regards mean household size, the final variable needed to produce a population total, Adamson can only say that it was somewhere between 4 and 4.5. It is possible to be more precise than this since the *Old Statistical Account* gives the household size of 219 parishes in every county except Nairn. In all there were 104,079 households containing 468,596 people (30.1 per cent of the population) which gives a mean of 4.5 people per household. This figure, however, conceals wide differences since mean household size was less than 4.0 in Clackmannan and Kinross but 5.6 in Sutherland and 5.9 in Shetland.[4] Assuming that, as in England, mean household size remained relatively unchanged during the eighteenth century, it is possible to estimate the population of the Lowlands (apart from a number of counties in the Jacobite North East where there appears to have been widespread tax evasion) and a considerable part of the Highlands (see Table 1). On the further assumption that the omitted areas had the same population growth between 1691 and 1755 as neighbouring ones where it is possible to provide totals, we have a population for Scotland in 1691 of 1,234,575, only 31,000 fewer than in 1755. Growth between these two dates was a miserable 2.5 per cent and though the increase in the Western Lowlands was a more respectable 12.3 per cent, in the North East there was a decline of 6.5 per cent (see Table 2).

These figures, particularly for the Highlands, are highly speculative but they support Flinn's guarded statement that 'it is not impossible . . that Lowland Scotland in 1691 had much the same population as it had in 1755'.[5] The main explanation for this was the famine of 1696–9 which, Flinn suggested, led to a fall in Scotland's population of between 5 and 15 per cent. This is probably correct for

---

[3] R. E. Tyson, 'The Population of Aberdeenshire, 1695–1755: A New Approach', *Northern Scotland*, VI (1985), pp. 113–31.

[4] Sir John Sinclair, *The Statistical Account of Scotland, 1791–95* [hereafter *O.S.A.*] (new ed., Wakefield, 1975–83), II–XXI.

[5] Flinn, *Scottish Population History*, p. 200.

most Lowland parishes but a recent study of Aberdeenshire, where the famine was particularly severe, argues that in that county there was a decline of 20 per cent, with the Highland and Upland areas losing more than a quarter of their population and even the relatively fertile coastal parishes 10 per cent.[6] Between 1700 and 1755 the population of Aberdeenshire grew by 18 per cent (almost exactly the same as England during the same period). If representative of Scotland as a whole, this woud give a population for the country at the beginning of the eighteenth century of 1,072,000, or a decline of 13 per cent since 1691.[7] This figure is remarkably similar to Sir John Sinclair's estimate of 1,048,000 and the 1,093,000 of George Chalmers, in his *Caledonia* for about the same date.[8] When the estimates for 1691 and 1700 are added to those from Webster and to the 1801 census, they provide a set of figures which can be compared with those compiled by Irish demographic historians for roughly the same years (see Table 3).

Table 3: *Rates of population growth, Ireland 1687–1791 and Scotland 1691–1801*

Year	Ireland		Year	Scotland	
	Population (millions)	Annual rate of growth (%)		Population (millions)	Annual rate of growth (%)
1687	1.97		1691	1.23	
1706	1.75–2.06	−0.5 to +0.2	1700	1.07	−1.2
1753	2.22–2.57	+0.5	1755	1.27	+0.3
1791	4.42	+1.4 to +1.9	1801	1.67	+0.6

Sources:
S. Daultrey, D. Dickson and C. Ó Gráda, 'Eighteenth-Century Irish Population: New Perspectives from Old Sources', *Journal of Economic History*, XLI (1981), pp. 624–54; Kyd, *Scottish Population Statistics, passim* (for 1755 and 1801).

The data in Table 3 reveal a number of differences between the two countries. Although the Williamite wars and the severe depression of 1701 led to little or no growth in Ireland's population between 1687 and 1706, despite heavy immigration from Scotland, there was nothing comparable to the famine of 1695–9 which caused such a massive decline in the Scottish population. There were no nation-wide crop failures after 1700 in Scotland but growth was slow and uneven until after 1742, when it began to accelerate. Ireland experienced quite impressive growth between

---

[6] R. E. Tyson, 'Famine in Aberdeenshire, 1695–9: Anatomy of a Crisis', in D. Stevenson, ed., *From Lairds to Louns* (Aberdeen, 1986), pp. 32–52.
[7] R. E. Tyson, 'Famine in Aberdeenshire', pp. 49–50; J. G. Kyd, *Scottish Population Statistics* (Scottish History Society, 1952); E. A. Wrigley and R. S. Schofield, *The Population History of England 1541–1871* (London, 1981), pp. 528–9.
[8] Flinn, *Scottish Population History*, p. 241.

1706 and 1725 (which in the early part of the period reached over 2 per cent a year) but this was followed by two decades of stagnation or even decline as a result of the severe harvest crises of 1727–9 and the disastrous famines of 1740–1 and 1744–6. However, although that of 1740–1 was particularly severe and may have reduced the population by 10 per cent or more, its long term consequences were less serious than the Scottish famine of the 1690s since the 1746 level of population was regained by 1753. This supports the view of Daultrey *et al*, that until the middle of the eighteenth century the potential for growth was frustrated by a combination of wars, harvest crisis and migration to the port cities. Even so, Ireland still managed an annual growth rate of 0.2–0.4 per cent between 1687 and 1755, while that for Scotland during the same period was almost non-existent.[9]

It was in the second half of the eighteenth century that the difference between the two countries became marked. The Irish potential for growth was now fully realised, so much so that population rose perhaps three times as fast as in Scotland (see Table 3). In Ireland between 1753 and 1791 only the province of Leinster had a growth rate of less than 1.5 per cent a year, and it still managed an impressive 1.0–1.4 per cent. In Scotland the Western Lowlands equalled this with an annual growth rate of 1.3 per cent but the remainder of Scotland grew by 0.3 per cent a year and in the North East growth was only 0.1 per cent.[10]

Scotland differed in other ways from Ireland. For example it urbanised more rapidly. In 1801 seven towns there had over 10,000 inhabitants and these accounted for 45 per cent of all population growth between 1755 and 1801. Although Dublin in 1800 was larger than Edinburgh and Glasgow combined and Cork as big as either, urban growth in Ireland during the second half of the eighteenth century did not match that of Scotland (which was probably unequalled in Europe). The proportion of Scots living in these large towns rose from 9.2 per cent to 17.2 during that period, whereas for Ireland the comparable figures were 5.0 and 7.0 per cent.[11]

Scottish mean household size was also considerably smaller and subject to greater regional variation than in Ireland, where in 1791 it was 5.9 in Leinster and Ulster, 5.8 in Munster and 5.3 in Connaught. In Scotland only the Highlands and Islands, with a mean household size of 5.4, were comparable and elsewhere it ranged from 4.7 in the Borders to 4.3 in the Eastern Lowlands. It is also probable, though the evidence is admittedly slight, that mean household size did not change much during the eighteenth century, whereas in Ireland there was a significant increase from 1750 onwards which, except in Ulster, continued until after 1820.[12]

---

[9] Dickson *et al*, 'Hearth Tax, Household Size and Irish Population Change', pp. 156–75.
[10] Dickson, *et al*, 'Hearth Tax, Household Size and Irish Population Change', p. 155; J. G. Kyd, *Scottish Population Statistics*, p. 82.
[11] L. M. Cullen, *An Economic History of Ireland since 1660* (London, 1972), pp. 84–5; T. M. Devine, 'Urbanisation', in T. M. Devine and R. Mitchison, eds., *People and Society in Scotland*, Vol I: *1760–1830* (Edinburgh, 1988), pp. 27–31.
[12] Dickson, *et al*, 'Hearth Tax, Household Size and Irish Population Change', p. 153; *O.S.A.* II–XXI.

Thus the two countries appear to have had quite different demographic regimes. Even when conditions in both became more favourable to population growth, that of Scotland was slower and probably subject to greater regional variations. How this growth was achieved is still a matter for debate. Mitchison, using Webster's population structure and the Princeton life tables, estimates that in 1755 the Scottish crude birth rate was 35 per 1000, the crude death rate 31 and expectation of life at birth 31 years (which was also the figure calculated from the same source by the Reverend David Wilkie in 1792). England by contrast had a somewhat lower birth rate, a considerably lower death rate, and a life expectancy of thirty-seven years (see Table 4).[13]

The difference in life expectancy was not simply the result of higher infant and child mortality since life expectancy at thirty in England between 1700 and 1749 was 4.6 years higher. The life expectancy of the still predominantly rural Scottish adults, in fact, was remarkably similar to that of unskilled and semi-skilled workers in seventeenth-century Geneva though at birth it was far higher (see Table 5).

In the 1790s the birth rate for Scotland was more or less unchanged from that in 1755 but there had been a considerable fall in mortality and improvement in life-expectancy. The figures for the 1790s, derived from the age structure of parishes in the O.S.A., have been criticised but they link up quite well with the first accurate ones following civil registration in 1855, which show a still unchanged birth rate but a somewhat lower death rate. By this time (1861) there was very little difference between England and Scotland but the demographic revolution had been achieved by different means. It is still probable that the decline in mortality, particularly infant mortality, was largely responsible for the increase in Scotland's population, despite rapid urbanisation.[14]

Unlike England, there appears to have been no significant fall in the average age of first marriage. Houston suggests that it was twenty-six to twenty-seven years for women during the first half of the eighteenth century and twenty-six years during the 1820s, with no apparent change in the intervening years. This is supported by a partial reconstitution study of the Central Highland parish of Laggan which indicates that in the period 1775–1811 women usually married between twenty-six and twenty-eight. Celibacy also appears to be higher than in England, where fewer than 10 per cent of women were still single by the age of fifty between 1750 and 1861. In Scotland, however, 20–25 per cent of women appearing in a sample of Lowland burial registers between 1740 and 1790 had never been married and in the 1790s it was 15–20 per cent for the country as a whole. This combination of a late age of marriage and relatively high celibacy must have acted as a powerful check on fertility. Thus, while those aged 14 or less in England

---

[13] R. Mitchison, 'Webster Revisited: A Re-Examination of the 1755 "Census" of Scotland', in T. M. Devine, ed., *Improvement and Enlightenment* (Edinburgh, 1989), p. 71; *O.S.A.* I, p. 151.

[14] Flinn, *Scottish Population History*, pp. 270, 340, 382.

Table 4: Population indices in England and Scotland, 1755–1861

	Scotland 1755	England 1756	Scotland 1790s	England 1791	Scotland 1861	England 1861
Crude birth-rate	34.7	33.6	35.1	38.4	34.8	36.2
Crude death-rate	30.7	25.7	24.1	25.4	21.5	21.9
Expectation of life	31.0	37.3	39.4	37.3	41.0†	41.3
Infant mortality	222	195*	164	166†	127	148

* 1700–49   † 1750–99   ‡ 1871

Sources:
R. Mitchison, 'Webster Revisited: A Re-Examination of the 1755 "Census" of Scotland', in T. Devine, ed., *Improvement and Enlightenment* (Edinburgh, 1989), p. 71; E. A. Wrigley and R. S. Schofield, 'English Population History from Family Reconstitution: Summary Results 1600–1799', *Population Studies*, 37 (1983), p. 177; E. A. Wrigley and R. S. Schofield, *The Population History of England 1541–1871* (London, 1981), pp. 250, 529, 530; Flinn, *Scottish Population History*, pp. 270, 338, 382, 385.

Table 5: Expectation of life in Scotland, Geneva and England

	Scotland 1755	Geneva * 1625–84	England 1700–49
e 0	31.0	18.9	–
e 20	31.7	30.4	–
e 30	25.8	26.2	30.4

* Unskilled and semi-skilled workers.

Sources:
The Statistical Account of Scotland, I, p. 151; A. Perrenoud, 'L'Inegalité sociale devant la mort a Geneve au XVII siècle', *Population*, 30 (1975), p. 236; Wrigley and Schofield, *The Population History of England*, p. 250.

rose from 33 per cent of the population in 1756 to 48 per cent in 1821, in Scotland the increase was only from 33 per cent to 38.[15]

The Western Isles and adjacent areas of the mainland were a significant exception to this general picture. Despite some emigration their population grew by 1.0 per cent a year in the second half of the eighteenth century.[16] Mean household size there was 5.3 in the 1790s, and in mid-Argyll and Tiree in 1779 those aged fourteen or under were 42 and 44 per cent respectively of the population,

---

[15] R. A. Houston, 'The Demographic Regime', in Devine and Mitchison, *People and Society in Scotland*, pp. 18–20; R. A. Houston, 'Age of Marriage and Scottish Women, circa 1660–1770', *Local Population Studies* (1989), 43, pp. 63–6.

[16] Kyd, *Scottish Population Statistics*, passim.

compared with 35 per cent in England at that time and 33 per cent in Scotland in 1755. On the Argyll estates in Mull in 1779, where mean household size was 5.2, 80.8 per cent of households had children and there were 2.53 children (excluding resident kin) per family; for the 100 English communities the comparable figures were 74.6 and 2.03. These figures support the traditional view that the age of marriage and celibacy in this area of Scotland were low and families large.[17]

At the other extreme was the North East where fertility and eventually mortality appear to have been lower than elsewhere, though the figures for the 1790s in *Scottish Population History* may exaggerate the difference. Just before the famine of 1696–9 the crude birth rate in a sample of twenty-one Aberdeenshire parishes was twenty-nine and the crude death rate in Aberdeen and the neighbouring parish of Old Machar (which contained the burgh of Old Aberdeen and the suburbs of Aberdeen) was thirty.[18] Between 1753 and 1777 the minister of the Kincardineshire parish of Benholm kept a record of all births, deaths and marriages, and took a count of the population for every year between those dates. Although it would be unwise to build too much upon the figures for a single parish which never had more than 1,715 inhabitants, they may well be typical of the North East as a whole. Compared with England in the same period, they reveal lower birth and marriage rates, though with more births per marriage. The crude death rate in Benholm was far lower than in England and life expectancy a good three years higher; the difference in mortality between Benholm and Scotland in 1755 was even greater

Table 6: Population indices of Scotland, Benholm (Kincardineshire), England and the North East of Scotland

	Scotland 1755	Benholm 1753–77	England 1753–77	N E Scotland 1790s
Crude birth-rate	34.7	31.1	34.6	28.2
Crude death-rate	30.7	24.0	27.1	18.2
Crude marriage rate	–	7.2	8.9	–
Births per marriage	–	4.3	3.9	–
Infant mortality	222	173	166*	122
Life expectancy	31	39	36	48

* 1750–99

Sources: Mitchison, 'Webster Revisited', p. 71; *The Statistical Account of Scotland*, XIV, pp. 38–9; Wrigley and Schofield, *The Population History of England*, pp. 528–9, 533–4; Flinn, *Scottish Population History*, p. 270.

---

[17] E. E. R. Cregeen, ed., *Inhabitants of the Argyll Estate, 1779* (Scottish Record Society, 1963), pp. 26–65, 70–115; Wrigley and Schofield, *Population History of England*, p. 529; Kyd, *Scottish Population Statistics*, pp. 80–1; P. Laslett, ed., *Household and Family in Past Time* (Cambridge, 1972), pp. 80, 83.
[18] Tyson, 'The Population of Aberdeenshire', p. 126; Tyson, 'Famine in Aberdeenshire', pp. 43, 49.

(see Table 6). The comparable figures for the North East in the 1790s show an even lower death rate (it was actually the same as in 1861) but a birth rate in line with Aberdeenshire in 1691–5 and Benholm in 1753–77.[19]

The first comparable figure that we have for Ireland as a whole is an estimated crude birth rate of 41 to 42 per thousand in the early years of the nineteenth century, which was probably about the same as in the Highlands and Hebrides in the 1790s. By contrast the first estimate of the crude death rate, 24 per thousand just before the Great Famine, was slightly higher than for England and Scotland.[20]

Before the nineteenth century the most complete statistics available are for Irish Quakers, at first sight hardly a representative group. However, they had a quite different demographic regime from that of English Quakers, although the two groups resembled each other closely in their socio-economic composition and life-style. Compared with those in England, Irish Quakers married earlier, had a longer child-bearing period, and shorter birth intervals. It seems likely that this pattern of nuptiality and fertility was broadly similar to that of the Irish population as a whole, though the Quaker age of first marriage for women, 24.9 years in 1750–99, was higher than the 21.8 years of women in the Ulster parish of Killyman between 1771 and 1810 who belonged to the Church of Ireland.

Table 7: *Expectation of life of English and Irish Quakers and of the population of Scotland*

Age group	English Quakers 1700–49	Irish Quakers 1700–49	Scotland 1755
20–24	34.2	30.6*	30.1
30–34	29.5	29.6	24.5
40–44	24.4	24.8	19.8
50–54	18.9	19.0	15.6

* Males only

Sources:
D. E. C. Eversley, 'The Demography of Irish Quakers, 1650–1850', in J. M. Goldstrom and L. A. Clarkson, eds., *Irish Population, Economy and Society* (Oxford, 1981), p. 83; *The Statistical Account of Scotland*, I, p. 151.

The fertility of Irish Quakers rose from 1725 onwards to reach its peak between 1775 and 1825, when the Irish population was growing most rapidly and mean household size was also increasing. The improvement in mortality was less dramatic,

---

[19] *O.S.A.* XIV, pp. 38–9. Life expectancy has been estimated by using A. Coale and P. Demeny, *Regional Model Life Tables* (Princeton, NJ, 1966).

[20] J. Mokyr and C. Ó Gráda, 'New Developments in Irish Population History, 1700–1850', *Econ. Hist. Rev.* XXXVII (1984), pp. 473–88.

particularly in the case of adults, whose life-expectancy was about the same as that of English Quakers and for England in 1700–49. For those in their early twenties it was only a little higher than for Scotland as a whole in 1755 but thereafter the gap widened considerably (see Table 7). The decline in infant and child mortality among Irish Quakers was more rapid than that of adults, although the main decrease came in the first half of the nineteenth century; infant mortality, for example, was 117 in 1700–49, 108 in 1750–99, but only 48 in 1800-49.[21]

These figures may well be much lower than for the remainder of the population, though Mokyr's estimate of an infant mortality rate of 220–5 in 1841 seems improbably high (it is, in fact, about the same as for Scotland in the middle of the eighteenth century).[22] As in Scotland, where life expectancy rose seven years between 1755 and 1791, it appears likely, if what happened in Killyman is typical, that there was a substantial fall in mortality, particularly among infants after 1750. However, what really distinguishes the two countries, and largely explains their differing rates of population growth, was the exceptionally high Irish birth rate (which may well have risen if the experience of the Quakers was typical) and the low Scottish one, which stubbornly refused to grow.

In the case of Ireland, increasing sub-division (made possible by the growing dependence upon the potato and earnings from rural textile industries) and the reclamation of waste made it relatively easy to acquire land and therefore to marry at an early age. Moreover, unlike in Scotland, the great majority of rural labourers were married and had their own households, complete with some land for growing potatoes. It can be argued that the absence of serious famines, the increasing commercialisation of agriculture (which in Ireland encouraged sub-division) and the rapid expansion of rural industries combined to maintain or even reduce an already low age of marriage after 1750.[23] The same forces operated in the Hebrides and along the western seaboard north of Argyll where the burning of kelp, an extremely labour intensive industry which encouraged landlords to sub-divide their land more and more, was the main by-employment.[24]

Elsewhere in Scotland economic conditions were less favourable to population increase, particularly in the North East, whose population grew by only 3.1 per cent between 1755 and 1801. During these years there were two distinct sub-periods. The first, from 1755 to 1782, saw the population of Aberdeenshire (which accounted for over half that of the region) grow by 0.5 per cent a year or about the same as Scotland between 1755 and 1775 (if a contemporary estimate for the latter

---

[21] D. E. C. Eversley, 'The Demography of Irish Quakers, 1650–1850', in Goldstrom and Clarkson, *Irish Population, Economy and Society*, pp. 57–88; W. Macafee, 'Pre-Famine Population in Ulster: Evidence from the Parish Register of Killyman', in P. O'Flanagan, P. Ferguson, and K. Whelan, eds. *Rural Ireland 1600–1900: Modernisation and Change* (Cork, 1987), pp. 142–61.

[22] J. Mokyr, *Why Ireland Starved* (London, 1983), pp. 237–8.

[23] This section is based on L. M. Cullen, *The Emergence of Modern Ireland 1600–1900* (London 1981), particularly pp. 83–108, and D. Dickson, *New Foundations: Ireland 1660–1800* (Dublin, 1987), pp. 96–127.

[24] M. Gray, *The Highland Economy* (Edinburgh, 1956), chapters 2, 3.

year of 1.4 million can be believed). Since there was hardly any emigration abroad from Aberdeenshire and the remainder of the region between 1763 and 1775, when 1 per cent of Scotland's population left for North America, and little economic development to attract immigrants, this figure of 0.5 per cent is probably about the rate of natural increase. The second sub-period was between 1782 and 1801, during which the population fell by 0.5 per cent a year.[25]

Before Improvement, most of those living in the countryside, perhaps as many as two-thirds in Aberdeenshire, were sub-tenants who received some land or grazing rights in return for providing tenants with their labour. Although figures are difficult to find, the amount of land held was small. Thus an unusually large farm of two hundred acres in the Aberdeenshire parish of Monymusk had six sub-tenants in 1753 of whom two held about seven acres each, one sub-tenant three, another one and a half acres, and two more only an acre each.[26] These amounts were not enough to provide a full-time living and some by-employment was needed. The North East had been a major producer of cheap woollen cloth for sale abroad, but following its collapse sometime before 1750 this trade was replaced by the knitting of worsted stockings in most of Aberdeenshire and the northern part of Kincardineshire, and by linen spinning elsewhere. At its peak c. 1790, knitting alone employed an estimated 30,000 part-time workers out of a combined population for the two counties of just under 147,000.[27] The region also had considerable tracts of waste which were capable of being brought under the plough. These were conditions ostensibly similar to those prevailing in much of Ireland and which should have encouraged early marriage and large families.

However, the North East and indeed Lowland Scotland generally differed from Ireland in a number of ways which combined to delay or even prevent marriage. Before the middle of the eighteenth century slow population growth and low agricultural prices meant that there was probably not much incentive for landlords to sub-divide or to reclaim waste. Young men thus found it more difficult to obtain land, whether as tenants, sub-tenants or cottars, than did their counterparts in Ireland, and potatoes were rarely grown. Tenant farmers relied for much of their labour on farm servants who lived-in and remained unmarried until they could acquire some land and establish their own households. Finally by-employments do not seem to have provided much of a stimulus to population growth. In the sixty-six Aberdeenshire and Kincardineshire parishes that had knitters in 1761, the

---

[25] For the population of Aberdeenshire in 1782 see W. Kennedy, *Annals of Aberdeen* (London, 1818), p. 313, and of Scotland in 1775 T. C. Smout, 'Where had the Scottish Economy Got To by 1776?', in I. Hont and M. Ignatieff, eds., *Wealth and Virtue* (Cambridge, 1983); B. Bailyn, *Voyagers to the West* (London, 1986), pp. 110–12. Out of 3,872 emigrants leaving Scotland for North America between December 1773 and March 1776, only eighty were from the North East (including twenty from Aberdeenshire).

[26] H. Hamilton, *Selections from the Monymusk Papers (1713–1755)* (Scottish History Society, 1945), p. xxv.

[27] R. E. Tyson, 'The Rise and Fall of Manufacturing in Rural Aberdeenshire', in J. S. Smith and D. Stevenson, eds., *Farmfolk and Fisherfolk* (Aberdeen, 1989), pp. 63–82.

population actually fell by 8 per cent between 1755 and 1801, while in the thirty-three which relied mainly on the spinning of linen yarn there was an increase of only 4 per cent. These were overwhelmingly female occupations and earnings were low; knitters earned 2s.–2s. 6d. a week at the most, probably averaging 1s. 6d. a week for the whole year, and linen spinners a little more.[28] Although an important part of the family income, this was probably not enough to encourage early marriage, let alone support a household with little or no land, unlike the earnings of male linen weavers in Angus who lived for the most part in villages and small towns. The population of the latter increased by 32 per cent between 1755 and 1801, but even this is modest compared with Ulster, where the weavers lived mainly in the countryside and rented land.[29] Similar conditions to Ulster may have been found in rural Aberdeenshire between 1600 and 1640 when the woollen industry was at its peak and there is some evidence of rapid population growth.

Between 1760 and 1782 there appears to have been a movement in the North East towards some sub-division as landlords created crofts of usually between ten and sixteen acres to take advantage of rising rents, which may have been the consequence of some pressure on land following the acceleration in population growth after 1742 and the start of rising prices.[30] However, after the harvest failure of 1782 (and perhaps earlier in Kincardineshire, the southern half of which is really an extension of Angus), agricultural prices seem to have become high enough to stimulate agricultural improvement. Unlike Ireland, where similar forces had occurred earlier in the century, many landlords stopped creating crofts and instead increased the size of their farms, which relied even more on unmarried servants for labour since new leases insisted on the removal of sub-tenants. Moreover, in the North East the early stages of improvement involved putting down land to grass at the expense of arable. Not only did it become more difficult to acquire land but there was also less demand for labour. The result was a mass exodus of people from the countryside which in Aberdeenshire may have started with th bad harvest of 1783 and after 1793 was hastened by the collapse of the knitting industry. Although Aberdeen and a few small towns, notably Peterhead, grew rapidly and landlords built numerous planned villages, they did not provide sufficient employment to fully absorb the flow of people from the land. In 1801 there were 10,000 fewer people in Aberdeenshire than in 1782, when a contemporary and probably

---

[28] For agriculture in the North-East of Scotland before Improvement see I. D. Whyte, 'Agriculture in Aberdeenshire in the Seventeenth and Early Eighteenth Centuries: Continuity and Change', in Stevenson, *From Lairds to Louns*, pp. 10–31, and M. Gray, 'Scottish Emigration: The Social Impact of Agrarian Change in the Rural Lowlands, 1775–1875', *Perspectives in American History*, VII (1973), pp. 107–11; Aberdeen District Archives, Guildry Minute Book, 25 March 1761; Tyson, 'Manufacturing in Rural Aberdeenshire', p. 69.

[29] T. M. Devine and D. Dickson, 'In Pursuit of Comparative Aspects of Irish and Scottish Development: A Review of the Symposium', in Devine and Dickson, pp. 264–5; M. Gray, 'Migration in the Rural Lowlands of Scotland, 1750–1850', in Devine and Dickson, p. 114; W. H. Crawford, *Domestic Industry in Ireland* (Dublin, 1972), pp. 24–6.

[30] G. S. Keith, *A General View of Agriculture in Aberdeenshire* (Aberdeen, 1811), pp. 148–9.

accurate estimate put the population at 131,000.[31] Most of those who left were probably young adults, which would automatically lead to a decline in the birth rate and increase in the death rate. In Benholm, where the population began to decrease from 1773 onwards, the crude birth rate fell from 31.3 in 1763–7 to 27.9 in 1773–77 while the crude death rate rose from 19.4 to 23.3.[32] In a few parishes there was a contrary movement as large farms continued to be sub-divided (in New Deer, for example, where the population rose by 30 per cent between 1755 and 1801), but these were still areas of predominantly infield-outfield agriculture.[33]

Although the exodus of people was greater from the North East than elsewhere, there was a similar movement from most of eastern Scotland (Angus was a notable exception) whose main beneficiary was the industrializing areas of the west of Scotland, particularly the towns. The latter may have had a higher natural increase than elsewhere but it was probably well below that in Ireland.

These differing demographic regimes, particularly marked in the case of fertility, had very different consequences. In Scotland the rate of population growth, except in the Western Isles and nearby areas of the mainland, was slow enough not to outstrip the modest economic growth of the period under discussion. Indeed, all the evidence points to a rise in *per capita* growth and in the standard of living of most Lowland counties, while agricultural improvement and modern industrial development brought about an even greater increase in both, though not until after 1800.[34] The much more rapid growth of population in Ireland meant that although the economy probably grew more rapidly than that of Scotland, its *per capita* output eventually fell, leading to a decline in the standard of living and an increase in poverty.

---

[31] Gray, 'Scottish Emigration', pp. 166–7; Gray, 'Migration in the Rural Lowlands of Scotland', pp. 113–14; *O.S.A.* XIV and XV, *passim*; Tyson, 'The Rise and Fall of Manufacturing in Rural Aberdeenshire', pp 78–80.
[32] *O.S.A.* XIV, pp. 38–9.
[33] *O.S.A.* XV, p. 118.
[34] J. Treble, 'The Standard of Living of the Working Class', in Devine and Mitchison, *People and Society in Scotland*, pp. 188–226.

6

Why the Highlands did not starve; Ireland and Highland Scotland during the Potato Famine

T. M. Devine

IN MANY WAYS THE FAILURE OF THE POTATOES in Ireland and Highland Scotland in the 1840s had remarkably similar effects. The dependency on this single crop was such that blight plunged entire districts into profound crisis. In both the Western Highlands and the west of Ireland, where famine was most acute and its social consequences most serious, the emigration of the poor accelerated beyond all previous levels, landowners promoted mass clearance and set up schemes of assisted passage across the Atlantic. External agencies, whether government or private charities, were forced to establish extensive programmes of relief for distressed districts.[1]

The failure of the potato crop over successive years in the 1840s and early 1850s was, of course, not unique to the Highlands and Ireland. The fungal disease which devastated their subsistence agriculture also wrought havoc throughout western Europe and beyond. But in two senses, the catastrophe in both northern Scotland and Ireland was exceptional. Firstly, the crop deficiency in several years in the two areas was abnormal by standards elsewhere in Europe. Recent estimates suggest that the shortfall in potato yields throughout

---

[1] Key works on the Irish potato famine include E. M. Crawford, ed., *Famine: The Irish Experience 900–1900: Subsistence Crises and Famine in Ireland* (Edinburgh, 1989); M. Daly, *The Great Famine in Ireland* (Dublin, 1986); J. S. Donnelly, 'The Great Famine', in W. E. Vaughan, ed., *The New History of Ireland*, Vol. V: *Ireland Under the Union 1801–70* (Oxford, 1989); R. D. Edwards and T. D. Williams, eds., *The Great Famine: Studies in Irish History* (Dublin, 1956); J. Mokyr, *Why Ireland Starved: A Quantitative and Analytical History of the Irish Economy, 1800–45* (revised edition London, 1985); C. Ó Gráda, *Ireland Before and After the Famine* (Manchester, 1988); C. Ó Gráda, *The Great Irish Famine* (London, 1989). The Highland famine is analysed in T. M. Devine, *The Great Highland Famine: Hunger, Emigration and the Scottish Highlands in the Nineteenth Century* (Edinburgh, 1988); M. W. Flinn, ed., *Scottish Population History from the Seventeenth Century to the 1930s* (Cambridge, 1977); James Hunter, *The Making of the Crofting Community* (Edinburgh, 1976); T. C. Smout, 'Famines and Famine Relief in Scotland', in Cullen and Smout, pp. 21–31.

Europe, even during the period of blight, was usually no more than one third.² The 'largest observed deficiency' in potato yields in France throughout the nineteenth century was 36 per cent, in Germany 31 per cent and in the Netherlands 50 per cent. However, three quarters of the crop was lost in Ireland in 1846 while in the same year, in a sample of distressed Highland districts, 67 per cent experienced complete failure and in another 20 per cent blight destroyed the potatoes 'almost entirely.'³

In the second place, the crisis was protracted over several seasons. In both Ireland and the Highlands 1846 was a terrible year but it was not unique. Blight also struck in Ireland, especially in the west, in 1845, 1848, 1849 and 1850. Crops continued to be badly affected in the Hebrides and the western coastlands of the Highlands until 1855; only in the following season did clear evidence emerge of sustained recovery from the ravages of the famine years. The moist and moderately warm summers of both regions were ideal for the propagation and perpetuation of *Phytopthora Infestans*.

In one fundamental sense, however, the experience of the two societies diverged dramatically in the 1840s. Between 1,000,000 and 1,200,000 died during the Irish famine through starvation or famine-related disease. In the Scottish Highlands mortality rates did start to climb above 'normal' levels in the latter months of 1846 and early 1847 but the crisis was eventually and successfully contained.⁴ The potato blight had profound demographic effects in north west Scotland. A huge emigration was precipitated from the distressed districts. Between 1841 and 1861 Uig in Lewis lost about half of its population, Jura almost a third, the Small Isles nearly a half and Barra about a third.⁵ In addition there was a pronounced fall in both the rate of marriage and the number of births in many affected parishes.⁶ These demographic measures illustrate the scale of the social crisis triggered by crop failure. But unlike their counterparts across the Irish Sea the people of the region survived. Misery and suffering increased but contemporary comment, government reports, estate correspondence and surviving burial records all indicate that there was no crisis of mortality.⁷

The purpose of this paper is to outline some of the influences which might help to explain the contrasting fate of the Irish and the Highlanders who were exposed to crop failure on an equally massive scale but with somewhat different results.

---

² Peter M. Solar, 'The Great Famine was No Ordinary Subsistence Crisis', in Crawford, ed., *Famine*, pp. 112–33.
³ *Report to the General Assembly of the Free Church of Scotland regarding Highland Destitution* [hereafter *Free Church Reports*] (Edinburgh, 1847), pp. 6–13.
⁴ Devine, *Great Highland Famine*, pp. 57–67.
⁵ Calculated from the published census, 1841, 1851, 1861.
⁶ Based on calculations from General Record Office, Edinburgh, Parish Registers for Kilfinichen, Tiree, Ardchattan, Glenorchy, Iona, Ardnamurchan, Dornoch, Creich, Clyne, Stornoway, Portree, North Uist, Moidart, Arisaig, Bracadale, Strontian.
⁷ The evidence is sifted in detail in Devine, *Great Highland Famine*, ch. 3.

SCALE AND POTATO DEPENDENCY

Why Ireland starved and the Highlands survived is in part a question of numbers. In much of Ireland and particularly in the poorer districts of the far west the population dependent on potatoes in whole or in part was enormous. Recent estimates suggest that on the eve of the Great Famine, potatoes accounted for about one-third of all tilled ground, three million or so people consumed them as the major element in diet and the crop formed a cornerstone of the agrarian system by which plots of potato-land were let 'on conacre' by farmers to labourers on an annual basis.[8] Such was the scale of dependency that some argue effective control of the crisis was beyond the powers of the contemporary state, especially one so thoroughly imbued with such doctrinaire *laissez-faire* principles as that of early Victorian Britain.[9] Others contend that even given the ideological and administrative constraints of the time much more could have been done to save life.[10]

Self-evidently, however, the management of relief was much easier in the Highlands because there the potential victims of crop failure could be numbered in thousands rather than millions. In late 1846, the estimates of those seriously at risk from starvation ranged from 600,000 to 200,000.[11] By 1847 and thereafter it became apparent, however, that the disaster was less extensive. The southern, eastern and central Highlands attracted external relief in 1846 and 1847 but operations were wound down in subsequent years. The blight rapidly diminished in ferocity in these inland districts. In addition, the balance between population and employment opportunities was much better than further west and potatoes were not so much a principal subsistence crop as an important element within a more diverse system of food supply which included grains, fish and vegetables.[12]

Furthermore, as the famine persisted, destitution became concentrated not only in the western maritime districts of croft agriculture but even more emphatically on the islands of the inner and outer Hebrides.[13] The potato blight in the Highlands endured for a long period but gradually became confined to a particular corner of

---

[8] P. M. A. Bourke, 'The Use of the Potato Crop in Pre-Famine Ireland', *Journal of the Statistical and Social Inquiry Society of Ireland*, 12 (1968), pp. 72–96; Ó Gráda, *Great Irish Famine*, pp. 24–5.

[9] Daly, *Famine in Ireland*, p. 84.

[10] Mokyr, *Why Ireland Starved*, p. 292; Donnelly, 'Great Famine'; Ó Gráda, *Ireland Before and After the Famine*, pp. 116–17.

[11] *Scotsman*, 19 December 1846; P.P. 1847 LIII, *Correspondence relating to the Measures adopted for the Relief of Distress in Ireland and Scotland*, Sir J. Riddell to Sir G. Gray, 24 August 1846; Sir J. McNeill to Sir G. Gray, 27 September 1846.

[12] *Reports of Edinburgh Section of the Central Board* (Edinburgh, 1847–50), Second Report for 1850 of the Committee of Management, p. 11.

[13] *Report on the Outer Hebrides by a Deputation of the Glasgow Section of the Highland Relief Board* (Glasgow, 1849), p. 9.

the northern region. As a result, the crisis was much more easily managed than in the west of Ireland. In 1851, the population of the four main Highland counties was almost a quarter of a million. About half of this number lived in areas in receipt of consistent supplies of external aid in the later 1840s while the numbers of inhabitants of parishes 'seriously at risk' (defined as having up to one third of their population on the relief lists between 1847 and 1850) was 66,000 or about 28 per cent of the Highland population.[14] By 1848/9, in only Tiree, South Uist, Barra, Skye, Harris and Mull, were conditions similar to the distressed west of Ireland. The administrative problems associated with famine relief in that region were not replicated in the Highlands after 1847. Partly because the crisis could be more easily controlled in Scotland, government in that year was able to delegate responsibility for the entire relief operation to the private and church charities co-ordinated by the Central Board of Management for Highland Destitution.

It may also be that dependency on the potato was not as complete as in the poorest districts of Ireland. One Scottish historian, A. J. Youngson, has described the Highlands as 'almost a potato economy' and R. N. Salaman thought the crop was 'the cornerstone of the social structure' of the region in the nineteenth century.[15] These assertions are probably exaggerated. In 1846 the Free Church investigated the importance of potatoes in the West Highland diet and concluded that they accounted for up to four fifths of popular food consumption in only one third of the districts surveyed.[16] Both its research and the reports of other contemporary observers describe a Highland diet in which potatoes were very important but which also still included meal, from both oats and barley, milk and, above all, fish.[17] Even in some of the poorest communities along the west coast, the *New Statistical Account* described how potatoes and herring were consumed twice a day while oatmeal gruel was a common dish for supper.[18] There also seem to have been interesting dietary variations within the social structure of the peasant community. Most crofting (or full tenant) families ate meal and fish regularly whereas semi-landless cottars were more likely to depend on potatoes as their main source of subsistence.[19] The complexity of Highland diet ensured that the potato blight created shortages for some and the threat of starvation for the very poor but did not necessarily threaten the mass catastrophe which engulfed entire areas of Ireland after 1845.

---

[14] Devine, *Great Highland Famine*, pp. 43–8.
[15] A. J. Youngson, *After the '45* (Edinburgh, 1973), p. 164; R. N. Salaman, *The History and Social Influence of the Potato* (Cambridge, 1949), p. 362.
[16] *Free Church Reports*, Second Statement of Destitution Committee, pp. 6–12.
[17] P.P. 1851 XXVI, *Report to the Board of Supervision by Sir John McNeill on the Western Highlands and Islands*, Appendix A, *passim*; Dr J. Macculoch, *The Highlands and Western Islands of Scotland* (London, 1824), p. 338; A. Fullarton and C. R. Baird, *Remarks on the Evils at Present Affecting the Highlands and Islands of Scotland* (Glasgow, 1838), p. 15.
[18] *New Statistical Account of Scotland*, 15 vols. (Edinburgh, 1845), Ross and Cromarty, pp. 110–11.
[19] P.R.O. T1/4201s R. Grahame to Fox Maule, 3 April 1837; S.R.O. Lord Advocate's Papers, AD58/84, W. H. Sitwell to Countess of Dunmore, 1 October 1846.

ECONOMY AND SOCIETY BEFORE THE FAMINE

Superficially there were pronounced similarities between the development of the Irish and Highland economies before the 1840s. Both areas suffered from 'deindustrialisation' as textile and other manufactures collapsed after 1815: contemporary economists suggested that each also demonstrated the horrors of 'over-population' and confirmed the validity of Malthus's arguments. The west of Ireland like the western Highlands was a region of 'redundant' population and chronic poverty which persistently succumbed to a cycle of subsistence crises which had long disappeared from the rest of Britain. Not surprisingly, therefore, both Scottish and Irish historians, in endeavouring to explain why a biological disaster became a social catastrophe in the later 1840s, tend to argue that the potato blight was but the pretext for a crisis ultimately conditioned by an imbalance between resources and population which became steadily worse after the Napoleonic Wars. Malcolm Gray's *Highland Economy 1750–1850*, in particular, presents the postwar Highlands in dark colours as a society becoming more vulnerable to crop failure and economic disaster.

Perhaps, however, the pessimistic analysis has been taken too far. The crumbling of the structure of bi-employments which had grown up in the later eighteenth century is undeniable. But not enough attention may have been given to the re-adjustment of west Highland society and economy in the generation after Waterloo which probably gave it more resilience than the poorest districts of western Ireland by the time of the potato famines.

First, in both Ireland and Highland Scotland, the decades before the 1840s saw a deceleration in population growth due primarily to an increase in out-migration. In Ireland growth fell from 1.6 per cent in 1780–1821 to 0.9 per cent by the 1820s and had dropped to 0.6 per cent in 1830–45.[20] But there was considerable regional variation within the national trend and in those areas badly hit by the Great Famine growth, though slowing down, was still occurring in the 1820s and 1830s. Emigration was very significant before the 1840s but mainly confined to Ulster, Sligo, Leitrim and some parts of eastern Ireland. Outward movement from the poorest counties of the west, the districts later most ravaged by the potato blight, was still relatively slight.[21] It was a different story in the western Highlands. In the period 1810 to 1840 Scottish average population increase per annum was 1.48 per cent in 1811–20, 1.23 per cent between 1821 and 1830 and 1.03 per cent between 1831 and 1840. The West Highlands experienced an even more dramatic fall from 1.46

---

[20] S. G. Daultrey, D. Dickson and C. Ó Gráda, 'Eighteenth-Century Irish Population: New Perspectives from Old Sources', *Journal of Economic History*, XLII (1981); J. Lee, 'On the Accuracy of the Pre-Famine Irish Censuses', in J. M. Goldstrom and L. A. Clarkson, eds., *Irish Population, Economy and Society* (Oxford, 1981), pp. 37–56.

[21] D. Fitzpatrick, *Irish Emigration 1801–1921* (Dublin, 1984).

per cent in 1811–20 to 0.51 in 1821–30. Between 1831 and 1840, however, population was actually falling with a decadal rate of -0.03 per cent.[22] The safety-valve of emigration operated more effectively in the Highlands than in the poorer parts of Ireland. From the middle decades of the eighteenth century chain migrations linked communities in the Hebrides with specific areas in the U. S. A. and Canada. The dislocation imposed by the creation of the crofting system and later the clearances associated with sheep farming produced a considerable increase in movement.[23] The sheer scale of recruitment to the British Army between 1756 and 1815, perhaps unparalleled in Europe, cannot but have accustomed men to mobility.[24] The inflation of cattle prices in the later eighteenth century provided the resources for sea migration, while landlords after the Napoleonic Wars were increasingly anxious to promote depopulation through assisted emigration.[25] In more general terms, however, the much greater rate of Highland emigration in the pre-famine decades may also suggest a less impoverished society than the west of Ireland, one where many crofters still had enough stock and goods to sell to raise the necessary capital to start a new life across the Atlantic.

Secondly, the Highland adjustment involved a huge increase in temporary migration in the first half of the nineteenth century. This may be seen as a substitute source of income and employment after the collapse of the kelp manufacture, the decline in army recruitment and the crushing by the state of illicit whisky-making in the 1820s and 1830s.[26] On the eve of the potato famine temporary migration occurred from all parts of the western Highlands with the exception of some areas in the Outer Hebrides. Of course, temporary migrants also came in large numbers from the poorer districts of Ireland and increasingly from the 1820s Irish harvesters became an important source of labour in Scottish agriculture.[27] But the impression is that Highland temporary migration was more extensive, more diverse and more significant to local economies in the north west. Both young men and women were involved and they worked in Lowland agriculture, fisheries, domestic service, urban construction and railway building. Equally importantly, before 1840 most temporary migrants seem to have been drawn from the cottar class, the group most dependent on potatoes for subsistence. As will be seen later,

---

[22] Eric Richards, *A History of the Highland Clearances* (London, 1982), p. 99.

[23] J. M. Bumstead, *The People's Clearance: Highland Emigration to British North America, 1770–1815* (Edinburgh, 1982).

[24] This point was suggested to me by Professor Louis Cullen.

[25] James M. Cameron. 'A Study of the Factors that Assisted and Directed Scottish Emigration to Upper Canada, 1815–55' (unpublished Ph.D. thesis, University of Glasgow, 1970).

[26] This paragraph is a summary of Devine, *Great Highland Famine*, pp. 146–70 and T. M. Devine, 'Temporary Migration and the Scottish Highlands in the Nineteenth Century', *Econ. Hist. Rev.* 2nd series, XXXII (1979).

[27] James H. Johnson, 'The Two "Irelands" at the Beginning of the Nineteenth Century', in N. Stephens and R. W. Glasscock, eds., *Irish Geographical Studies in Honour of E. Estyn Evans* (Belfast, 1970), pp. 224–43; Cormac Ó Gráda, 'Seasonal Migration and Post-Famine Adjustment in the West of Ireland', *Studia Hibernica*, 13 (1973), pp. 48–76.

the growing connection between this class and seasonal work opportunities in the Lowlands was very relevant to their survival when the potatoes failed in the 1840s.

Thirdly, commercial fishing (especially for cod and ling) and subsistence fishing probably persisted longer in some parts of the Highlands than some commentators have suggested.[28] The *New Statistical Account* is certainly full of references to stagnation in fishing and the disappearance of the herring from the sea lochs by the 1820s and 1830s. But the evidence of estate papers and the experience of some districts during the potato famine itself are partly in conflict with the pessimistic view. Many communities still depended on the sea rather than the land and proprietors made determined efforts to consolidate their position while dispossessing crofting townships which had mainly relied on kelp manufacture.[29] Relief officials during the famine pointed out that such areas as Wester Ross, eastern Lewis and parts of Mull were not seriously distressed because of their fishing traditions.[30] Similar patterns can be detected in the west of Ireland, where both Patrick Hickey and Cormac Ó Gráda suggest that the offshore islands were less affected than mainlanders partly because of the opportunities for fishing.[31] On the other hand, the riches of the sea were more easily harvested by the majority of Highlanders. The region most vulnerable to blight was the Hebrides and the western seaboard. Sheep clearances in earlier times had pushed even the people of the inland glens towards the coast. As Sir John McNeill concluded after his survey of the distressed areas in 1851: 'Of fresh fish they can almost always command a supply, for in those districts there are few crofts that are far from the coast.'[32]

Fourthly, the Highlands developed a more effective system of internal communications in the years after the end of the Napoleonic Wars. Irish historians argue that famine relief in the 1840s was constrained by the primitive nature of transport and communications, the isolation of many communities and the under-developed nature of trade in the far west.[33] Thus the depth of the famine crisis was conditioned not only by a shortage of food in absolute terms but in some localities at least by poor structures of distribution and marketing. Few of these arguments are applicable to the western Highlands. Connections between the region and the Lowlands had expanded on a huge scale since the later eighteenth century as the

---

[28] See for example, Malcolm Gray, *The Highland Economy, 1750–1850* (Edinburgh, 1957), pp. 158–69.

[29] MS Diary of J. M. Mackenzie, 1851 (in private hands); Conon House, Conon, Rosshire, Mackenzie of Gairloch MSS Bundle 53, Correspondence re estate affairs, 1847–53; Macculoch, *Highlands and Western Islands*, IV, p. 341; Fullarton and Baird, *Remarks*, p. 16; P.P. 1847 XXVIII, *First Annual Report of the Board of Supervision for the Relief of the Poor*, p. 39.

[30] *Reports of Edinburgh Section of the Central Board* (Edinburgh, 1847–50), Captain H. B. Rose to Captain Eliot, 1 May 1848.

[31] Ó Gráda, *Ireland Before and After the Famine* p. 121; P. Hickey, 'A Study of Four Peninsular Parishes in Cork, 1796–1855' (unpublished M.A. thesis, National University of Ireland, 1980), p. 603.

[32] *McNeill Report*, p. ix.

[33] Daly, *Famine in Ireland*, p. 51; Ó Gráda, *Great Irish Famine*, pp. 54–5.

north west developed as a major source of meat, wool, mutton, fish, kelp, timber, slate and whisky for the southern economy. A tourist trade flourished from the early nineteenth century.[34] These trends were both cause and effect of the revolution in communications. From the 1820s steam propulsion began a new erain Highland navigation: 'a bridge of boats now unites the southern mainland with the northern coast and very specially with the Western Isles.'[35] A traveller took five weeks to make the journey from Edinburgh to Tiree in the 1770s; by the 1840s, the round trip from Glasgow to Mull by steamship took less than three days.[36] Partly because of the transport revolution, but more basically because the region had long had an historic dependency on grain imports, the trade in meal from the south was extensive before the 1840s. A structure of retail markets did exist through which the much enhanced supplies of the famine years could flow.[37] Proprietors and many large tenants kept grain stores. Fish merchants provided meal on credit and local traders supplied grain to temporary migrants.[38]

THE LANDLORD RESPONSE

To the British government and some later historians Irish landlords were the great villains of the Famine years. More recent judgements suggest that some landowners were very active, a few went bankrupt in the struggle to keep the distressed people of their estates alive and the vast majority did little, either through choice or circumstances.[39] Considerable emphasis is placed in the literature on the poverty of many proprietors which prevented them playing an energetic role in the Famine: 'By 1843 an estimated one thousand estates, accounting for a rental of over £700,000, one twentieth of the country, were in the hands of the receivers. This figure increased to £1,300,000 by 1847 and £2 million by 1849.'[40] Systematic research on the Irish landed class during the Famine has yet to begin but enough is already known to point to significant differences between their response and that of the Highland elite.

The activities of 77 per cent of landowners in the affected areas of the western Highlands in 1846–7 are known.[41] Almost 30 per cent were singled out for special

---

[34] T. C. Smout, 'Tours in the Scottish Highlands from the Eighteenth to the Twentieth Centuries', *Northern Scotland*, 5 (1983).

[35] Thomas Mulock, *The Western Highlands and Islands Socially Considered* (Edinburgh, 1850), p. 160.

[36] Compare E. R. Cregeen, ed., *Argyll Estate Instructions, 1771–1805* (Edinburgh, 1964), p. xx and J. Bruce, *Letters on the Present Condition of the Highlands and Islands of Scotland* (Edinburgh, 1847), p. 5.

[37] *Relief Correspondence*, Sir J. McNeill to Sir G. Gray, 27 September 1846; S.R.O. Treasury Correspondence, Coffin to Trevelyan, 28 September 1847.

[38] *Edinburgh Section Reports*, First Report (1849), pp. 20, 46.

[39] Donnelly, 'Great Famine'.

[40] Daly, *Famine in Ireland*, p. 109.

[41] This paragraph summarises T. M. Devine, 'Highland Landowners and the Highland Potato Famine', in Leah Leneman, ed., *Perspectives in Scottish Social History: Essays in Honour of Rosalind Mitchison* (Aberdeen, 1988), pp. 141–62.

praise by government officials for their private relief efforts while only 14 per cent were censured for their negligence. Charles Trevelyan was warm in his praise:

> ... the Treasury have been quite delighted with the whole conduct of the Highland proprietors ... it was a source of positive pleasure to turn from the Irish to the Scotch case. In the former, everything with regard to the proprietors is sickening and disgusting.

A key factor in the difference was almost certainly the contrasting financial position of the two groups. Highland landowners also experienced a steep increase in crofter rent arrears in 1846–9 and many contributed much to famine relief schemes on their estates. On the island of Tiree, the Duke of Argyll's outlay on relief turned a pre-famine surplus of £2,226 into a deficit in 1847 of £3,170. Yet there was no spectacular increase in bankruptcies. Only an estimated 6 per cent of the eighty odd estates in the distressed districts were sold or placed under trust during the famine years as a consequence of landlord insolvency.

The Highland elite may have been in a much stronger position to aid their people than many of their counterparts in the west of Ireland. This relief did not simply take the form of meal distribution and the provision of work. From the middle years of the famine several proprietors also established ambitious schemes of assisted emigration and these, together with private charities in which landlords participated, led to the resettlement of over 16,000 people, mostly from the Hebrides, in Canada and Australia.[42] Potential emigrants were selected with meticulous care: the poorest, the most destitute and the weakest were given the highest priority. The overwhelming majority belonged to the cottar class.[43] As one landlord put it in 1851: 'I wish to send out those whom we would be obliged to feed if they stayed at home—to get rid of that class is *the object*'.[44] By removing many of the most vulnerable in the society by coercive means some landlords achieved lasting infamy and opprobrium.[45] But they also reduced the chances of a crisis of mortality in the Highlands. Irish proprietors were also active in assisted emigration but the total supported by Highland landowners was a much higher proportion both of the regional population and of the famine emigrations from northern Scotland as a whole.[46]

Two factors probably explain the solvency of the Highland aristocracy. First, a great transfer of estates took place between 1810 and 1840 from the old, indebted hereditary class to new owners who were principally rich tycoons from the

---

[42] T. M. Devine, 'The Flight of the Poor: Assisted Emigration from the Scottish Highlands in the Nineteenth Century', in C. J. Byrne, M. Harry and P. O'Siadhail, eds., *Celtic Languages and Celtic Peoples* (Halifax, Nova Scotia, 1992).

[43] See Inveraray Castle, Argyll Estate Papers, Bundles 1335, 1531, 1558, 1804, Correspondence of John Campbell; MS Diary of J. M. Mackenzie, Chamberlain of the Lews, 1851.

[44] Inveraray Castle, Argyll Estate Papers, Bundle 1558, Duke of Argyll to ?, 5 May 1851.

[45] A. Mackenzie, *The History of the Highland Clearances* (Inverness, 1883).

[46] Fitzpatrick, *Irish Emigration*, pp. 19–20.

Lowlands and England. They were merchants, bankers, lawyers, southern landowners, financiers and industrialists who were attracted to the Highlands for sport and recreation and by its romantic allure. An estimated 74 per cent of estates in the famine zone changed hands in the four decades before 1840.[47] Second, there had been a radical restructuring of estate economies in many parts of the western Highlands and islands over the same period. As the labour-intensive economy founded on kelp, fish and cattle stagnated or collapsed, proprietors increasingly laid down more land to more profitable sheep-farming. By the 1840s commercial pastoralism was dominant on the majority of estates.[48] The income of most landlords came to depend on the rental of the big sheep ranchers rather than the petty payments of the crofters.[49] Mutton and wool prices rose during the famine years, sheep rentals were maintained and most proprietors were therefore insulated from the sharp increase in arrears within the crofting sector which occurred in 1846–9.[50] This resilience allowed many to play an active and energetic role in the provision of relief during the same period.

THE CRISIS OF 1846–7

The potato blight affected Ireland for the first time in 1845, a year earlier than the Highlands, but late 1846 and early 1847 was probably the period of most acute distress in both societies.[51] Close study of these two years provides further insights into the reasons for Scottish resilience. Two key differences between the experience of the two societies at this time emerge. First, the role of the state in Ireland was more significant in the relief effort than private charity. A principal agency was the creation of a Board of Works which in return for labour in relief schemes provided work for the needy. The public works carried out in the autumn and winter of 1846–7 cost the huge sum of £4,848,123. The scale of the Irish crisis was such, however, that even this was not enough to prevent a massive increase in mortality. In addition, scholars have criticised the schemes because money spent on the works did not necessarily have a decisive impact as local organisation was often lacking in the areas of most acute distress. Moreover, the system of payment in return for labour penalised the weakest and the unhealthiest who were most in need of support.[52] Government intervention was much more limited in the western Highlands in 1846–7 and was confined to the establishment of meal depots, maintaining

---

[47] T. M. Devine, 'The Emergence of the New Elite in the Western Highlands and Islands, 1800–60', in T. M. Devine, ed., *Improvement and Enlightenment* (Edinburgh, 1989), pp. 108–42.

[48] This generalisation is based on a survey of the relevant entries in the *New Statistical Account*.

[49] See, for example, Conon House, Conon, Mackenzie of Gairloch MSS, Report by Thomas Scott on accounts of Dr Mackenzie as factor, 1843–6; National Library of Scotland, Sutherland Estate Papers, Dept. 313/2159–60; *McNeil Report*, Appendix A, *passim*.

[50] Devine, 'Highland Landowners', pp. 150–2.

[51] Ó Gráda, *Great Irish Famine*, p. 46.

[52] *Ibid.*, pp. 54–5; Daly, *Famine in Ireland*, p. 84.

pressure on landowners to provide succour for the poor and sponsoring relief works through the promotion of the Drainage Act.

Ironically, however, the more muted response of the state was probably to the advantage of the stricken Highland population. The Whig government of Lord John Russell would have done everything possible to avoid free or lavish distribution of meal. But the first agency to provide relief in the north west, the Free Church of Scotland, seems to have had a more liberal policy.[53] The government's initiatives in Scotland, especially those in the far west, have been criticised for poor organisation. But the Free Church in the Highlands was in an excellent position both to guide funds to the worst hit areas and at the same time to attract subscriptions from its mainly middle class adherents in the Scottish cities. It was in essence an embryonic relief organisation which through its local parishes, synods and ministers could be activated to provide ready assistance. All contemporary observers agreed that its response was immediate, generous and vigorous and showed no sign of denominational prejudice. In fact, the Catholic islands of Barra and South Uist were among the first to receive succour. A further telling illustration of the church's imaginative effort was its scheme for transporting 3,000 Highlanders to the labour markets of the Lowlands for seasonal employment in 1847.

A second important distinction between the two societies in this phase of crisis was the general economic context in Scotland and Ireland. Dr Ó Gráda states that:

> Unfortunately for Ireland, the height of the Famine period—late 1846 and early 1847—was one of financial crisis in Britain. The 'railway mania' which began in 1845 had run its course, and bad harvests in both Ireland and Britain in 1846 led to a huge trade deficit and consequent drain of bullion. The ensuing sharp rise in the cost of credit embarrassed many companies. The value of cotton output fell by a quarter.[54]

The economic depression therefore massively intensified the problems caused by crop failure. The Highland population was again more fortunate. Only in the latter months of 1847 and early 1848 was Scotland plunged into industrial recession. At the end of 1846 the Board of Supervision of the Scottish Poor Law confirmed that 'there was an unusual demand for labour at rates of wages probably unprecedented'.[55] The greatest railway construction boom of the nineteenth century was under way and did not abate until the late autumn of 1847.[56] Wages in the east coast herring fishery in the season of 1846 were 'at least one third higher than was

---

[53] The Free Church's activities are chronicled in *Report of the General Assembly of the Free Church of Scotland Regarding Highland Destitution* (Edinburgh, 1847) and its newspaper *The Witness* for 1846 and early 1847.

[54] Ó Gráda, *Great Irish Famine*, p. 46.

[55] P.P. 1847–8 XXXII, *Second Annual Report of the Board of Supervision*, p. xv.

[56] *Scotsman*, 3 February 1847; *North British Daily Mail*, 1 May 1847.

customary' and in the same year the agricultural labour market in the Lowlands 'was never better able to bear the influx of Highlanders'.[57] Prices for Highland black cattle were also buoyant in 1846 and the first few months of 1847.[58]

Throughout the worst period of the potato failure, the vigour of the Lowland economy was therefore able to absorb increasing numbers of Highland temporary migrants who on their return released a great stream of income throughout the north west. It was the boom in 1846 and 1847 in temporary migration which provides one answer to the question which puzzled relief officials in the destitute districts, namely why so many of the poor were able to pay cash for meal.[59] Amartya Sen's familiar argument suggests that some famines are caused less by an absolute shortage of food than by the absence of 'entitlements' to food through the inability of the population to buy that which is available.[60] One probable reason therefore why the Highland population survived was that a higher proportion than in the west of Ireland in 1846–7 had the purchasing power to make good some of the deficiencies in subsistence brought about by the failure of the potatoes.

CONCLUSION

The stark contrast in the fate of the Irish and the Highlanders during the potato famines is partly explained by the enormous difference in scale and the numbers affected in the two societies. However, this paper has argued that west Highland society was also more resilient than the poorer districts of Ireland. Potato dependency was not as great and population pressure not as acute; the landlord class was more active in relief and the peasant economy more diverse. The proximity of an industrialised society to the south and east was also of singular importance. The advanced economy of the Lowlands provided a host of seasonal work opportunities for Highland temporary migrants. It produced the surplus wealth which allowed the very rich to acquire insolvent Highland estates before the 1840s and also enabled the philanthropic organisations to raise the necessary funds to alleviate the threat of starvation in the north west.

---

[57] S.R.O. HD16/101, Minutes of Committee appointed to watch the progress of events connected with the potato failure (1847); *Inverness Journal*, 20 August 1847.

[58] West Highland cattle prices are recorded in the *Inverness Courier*, *Scotsman* and *Witness*, 1846–8.

[59] *Edinburgh Section Reports*, Fourth Report (1848), R. Eliot to W. Skene, 3 February 1848; S.R.O. HD6/2, Treasury Correspondence, Sir E. Coffin to Mr Trevelyan, 28 September 1847 and Captain E. Rose to Sir E. Coffin, 28 March 1847.

[60] A. Sen, *Poverty and Famines* (Oxford, 1981).

7

The fertility transition in Ireland and Scotland c. 1880–1930[1]

Cormac Ó Gráda and Niall Duffy

I am just 28 years old married 9 years today and the mother of six children so I feel I have done my bit and only wish I could be in London to go to your clinic.

Limerick woman to Marie Stopes, 1923[2]

A woman like you would find it hard to believe I am sure but I was close to twenty years of age before I understood the process of human reproduction. That is God's truth. I was born in a remote country district of Ireland and I always thought that if you talked too much with girls or made chums with them too much God would send a child.

Irishman to Marie Stopes, 1920

IRELAND'S status as a half-hearted participant in the nineteenth-century European fertility decline is well-known. The standard perception is of a rural and devoutly Catholic society relying on emigration, low nuptiality, and late marriage instead of family limitation as a means of raising living standards.

The data on emigration (one third to one half of each generation) and celibacy (from about one tenth before the Famine to one quarter on the eve of the Great War) are striking enough, but the contours of the Irish fertility decline are in dispute. Independently-derived estimates of a standard measure of marital fertility—the Coale–Henry I_g—by Fitzpatrick and Ó Gráda[3] indicate stasis (or

---

[1] This is an amended and abbreviated version of the paper presented at St. Andrews, 'Fertility Control in Ireland and Scotland c. 1880–1930: Some New Findings' (U.C.D. Centre for Economic Research Working Paper 1989/14). We are grateful to Paul David, David Fitzpatrick, Joel Mokyr and conference participants for their comments on the earlier version.

[2] This and the following quotation are taken from letters in Marie Stopes Papers, Contemporary Medical Archives Centre, Wellcome Institute for the History of Medicine. See section 6 below.

[3] We are grateful to David Fitzpatrick for showing us his unpublished data. Ig is defined as $I_g = B/(H_i m_i)$, where B is the annual number of legitimate births, m_i is the number of married women in age-cohort i, and H_i is the fertility schedule (see A. J. Coale and S. C. Watkins, *The Fertility Decline in Europe* (Princeton, 1986), pp. 33–4. The derivation of Ó Gráda's I_g estimates is explained in his *Ireland Before and After the Famine* (Manchester, 1988), pp. 168–9.

even some rise) at the national level in the 1860s and 1870s, but a modest drop thereafter to 1911. However, in his contribution to the Princeton project on the European fertility transition, Michael Teitelbaum[4] tells a different story: he reports national (weighted) estimates for Ig of 0.708 in both 1871 and 1911, with hardly any variation in between. Teitelbaum's contribution has been influential, consolidating Ireland's reputation as demographic 'oddball': it has prompted Francine van de Walle to allude to Ireland as 'an extreme case . . . where marital fertility did not decline before the 1920s', and Coale and Treadway to report that 'the [fertility] declines that occurred after 1920 were in Ireland and the southern and eastern periphery of Europe'.[5]

The details of the gaps between Teitelbaum's and Ó Gráda's Irish county estimates for 1881 and 1911 have been reported elsewhere.[6] Only in four cases out of sixty-four are Teitelbaum's estimates higher, and the differences in the case of western counties in 1881 are particularly glaring. However, the unweighted average gap narrows from 0.111 in 1881 to 0.025 in 1911. The gap is accounted for as follows: Ó Gráda's estimates, like Fitzpatrick's, are derived entirely from censal data, whereas Teitelbaum relies on the census for the number of married women, and on civil registration data for the number of births—data well-known to be of dubious quality in this period.[7] In effect, Teitelbaum has mistaken improved statistical coverage over the period in question for fertility stasis.

Teitelbaum's estimates of Irish marital fertility in 1871 imply levels that were by no means high by contemporary European standards.[8] Ó Gráda's estimates go some distance towards restoring Ireland's reputation for rather high pre-transition marital fertility. The paper explores various aspects of the Irish fertility transition denied in Teitelbaum's figures. The second part analyses the variation in marital fertility within Ireland and Scotland before World War I; the third part applies a new approach to fertility measurement, cohort parity analysis, to aggregate Irish and Scottish data; the fourth part turns to a qualitative archival source for more insight into the fertility transition in Ireland and Scotland; and the fifth part applies the same technique of cohort parity analysis to three specially-constructed micro data-sets.

---

[4] *The British Fertility Decline* (Princeton, 1984), p. 129.
[5] In Coale and Watkins, *Fertility Decline*, pp. 40, 220.
[6] Cormac Ó Gráda, 'New Evidence on the Fertility Transition in Ireland 1880–1911', *Demography*, XXXVIII, 4 (1991), 535-48.
[7] See, for example, Brendan M. Walsh, 'Marriage Rates and Population Pressure: Ireland, 1871 and 1911', *Econ. Hist. Rev.* XXXIII (1970), pp. 148-62; John Coward, 'Birth Under-registration in the Republic of Ireland During the Twentieth Century', *Economic and Social Review*, XIV, 1 (1982), pp. 1-28. Because they rely on censal data only, Fitzpatrick's and Ó Gráda's estimates obviate the need for the corrections suggested by Pantelides and Coale in an appendix to Teitelbaum (*British Fertility Decline*, pp. 228-45).
[8] Compare Coale and Watkins, *Fertility Decline*, Map 2.2.

Table 1a: Accounting for the cross-county variation in Irish I_g, 1881–1911

Dependent > Variable	IG_{11}	IG_{11}	$DIG81$	$DIG81$
	(1)	(2)	(3)	(4)
Constant	858.0	680.1	-0.004	0.216
	(43.0)	(50.8)	(-0.10)	(0.49)
CATH	116.6	105.9	0.078	0.052
	(37.5)	(30.0)	(1.97)	(1.39)
BIGFARM	-348.9	-240.7	-0.364	-0.311
	(70.8)	(60.4)	(-5.35)	(-6.38)
NONAGR	-116.4	–	–	–
	(58.9			
EMIG	–	1211.2	–	–
		(264.2)		
URBAN	–	–	-0.100	–
			(-1.79)	
DUBLIN	–	–	–	0.116
				(2.75)
R^2	0.83	0.89	0.63	0.67

Note: variables defined in text, t-statistics in parentheses.

Table 1b: 'Explaining' the variation in I_g

Dependent Variable	$>IG1881$	$DIG51$	$DIG81$
CONST	529.91	-0.448	-0.286
	(15.81)	(-3.58)	(-6.09)
LOWVAL	–	0.00368	0.00374
		(3.09)	(4.32)
DCOH81	97.71	–	0.074
	(3.18)		(0.86)
DCOH51	–	0.678	–
		(3.44)	
CATH	384.09	–	–
	(6.86)		
R^2	0.735	0.448	0.500
$F(3, 28)$	40.19	11.75	14.49

Note: t-statistics in parentheses. LOWVAL refers to 1911, must be amended. DCOH81 and DCOH51 are cohort depletion measures of migration. The latter is the proportionate loss in the 17–24 year cohort of 1851 by 1881 (using the 45–54 year cohort in 1881). The former is measured analogously.

EXPLAINING INTER-COUNTY VARIATION IN I_g

(a) *Ireland*

The decline in Irish marital fertility—and from now on we rely on Ó Gráda's estimates—was neither uniform nor universal: between 1881 and 1911 there were increases in counties Galway, Mayo, Roscommon and Donegal, while the decline in several other counties was small. Despite their high overall average, the regional variation in I_g suggests that rural Ireland contained many couples practising some form of contraception. The variation in marital fertility across Irish counties, as measured by I_g, was substantial and seemingly by no means fully explained by some rural/urban split. For example, Laois (I_g = 0.752) or Meath (0.724) were about as rural in 1911 as Kerry (0.911) or Galway (0.909). A map of I_g levels in 1911 would show a high-fertility zone encompassing Connacht and north Munster, a swathe of counties down the middle of the country where I_g ranged from 0.7 to 0.8. and an area including east Ulster, Dublin, and Louth, where fertility was 'light'.

Most of the cross-county variation is easily accounted for, however. This should be evident from the results of the regression analysis in Tables 1a and 1b. Regression 1 shows that three variables—the Catholic share in the total population (CATH), the proportion of farmers residing on farms of a valuation greater than £15 (BIGFARM), and the proportion of the population not resident on farms (NONAGR)—explain over four fifths of the variation in I_g. The corresponding elasticities are 0.18, 0.20, and 0.07. The finding that the strength of Catholicism has considerable explanatory power is in interesting contrast to the finding that there was little difference between Catholic and non-Catholic fertility in rural Ulster in this period.[9] Perhaps CATH is simply a proxy for something else, but the inclusion of proxies for urbanisation and literacy failed to reduce the size of the CATH coefficient appreciably.

Adding EMIG, the emigration rate,[10] and omitting NONAGR produces Regression 2.[11] Note that emigration was positively associated with fertility. In Regression 3, a similar mix of variables also accounts for a substantial part of the variation in DIG81, defined as (I 1911–I 1881)/I 1881. Substituting a Dublin dummy for URBAN (Regression 4) improves the fit and reduces the coefficients on other variables.

The results for 1881 and 1851–81, reported in Table 1b, bear comparison. Religion still works in the same direction. Again, note that the coefficient on DCOH, our proxy for outmigration in 1851–81, is positive. Thus high emigration

---

[9] Cormac Ó Gráda, 'Did Irish Catholics Always Have Larger Families?', *Ir. Econ. and Soc. Hist.* XII (1985), pp. 79–88.
[10] As defined in B. M. Walsh, 'Marriage Rates and Population Pressure', p. 159.
[11] Compare Ó Gráda, *Ireland*, pp. 163–4.

was associated with high and rising fertility in this period. This interesting result may be compared with the findings of Sundstrom and David[12] that outmigration prompted a reduction in fertility in American farming areas in the early nineteenth century. Note that while both in 1851–81 and in 1881–1911 the outcome is analogous for the fertility rate, the coefficient on emigration in the fertility change regression was small and insignificant.[13]

(b) *Scotland*

Teitelbaum's Scottish estimates do not seem to suffer from the same defective registration data as the Irish. In 1911 at least there is no problem. An alternative estimate of I_g, using the number of children of less than a year reported in the census rather than the number of births registered as a basis for the denominator, produces a very similar answer.

Teitelbaum reports I_g, in Scotland as rising slightly in the 1860s, then falling from 0.752 in 1871 to 0.733 in 1881, 0.696 in 1891, 0.632 in 1901, 0.565 in 1911, and 0.480 in 1921.[14] This is consistent with the assessment of Flinn *et al.*, based on general fertility rates by regions (i.e. live births per thousand women).[15] The decline applied to all counties. Flinn *et al.* raised the problem of 'the enormous apparent contrast between the fertility of the far north and Highland counties, on the one hand, and that of the rest of Scotland, on the other'.[16] This is an allusion to the puzzlingly low fertility of the north implied by crude birth rate data. However, according to Teitelbaum's data, in 1911 the unweighted average of I_g was 0.588 in the eleven northernmost counties, 0.527 in the other twenty-two.[17]

Cross-section explanations of the variation in Scottish fertility are harder to come by. For example, CATH and RUR combined account for only about one-quarter of the variation. Variables failing to explain much of the cross-county variation included the proportion of Irish-born, the proportion Gaelic-speaking, and the proportion of the male labour force in mining. Variables with explanatory power included ILL (the percentage of men signing their marriage register with a mark in 1910), and PCCOAL (percentage of male employment in coal-mining).

I_g = 456.2 + 19.0ILL + 3.18CATH + 1.00RUR + 1.69PCCOAL
       (34.4)   (8.2)   (2.38)   (0.58)   (1.01)

R^2 = 0.423; $F(4, 28)$ = 5.13; s.e.s in parentheses.

The elasticities are small (e.g. 0.03 for CATH, 0.3 for ILL). The dubious strategy of omitting Bute and Caithness, two outliers, yielded a better result:

---

[12] William Sundstrom and Paul A. David, 'Old-age Security Motives, Labour Markets, and Farm Family Fertility in Antebellum America', *Explorations in Economic History*, XXV, 2 (1988), pp. 164–97.
[13] See also, Ó Gráda, *Ireland Before and After the Famine*, ch. 5.
[14] Teitelbaum, *British Fertility Decline*, p. 129.
[15] Michael Flinn, *et al.*, *Scottish Population History* (Oxford, 1977), pp. 341, 348.
[16] Flinn *et al.*, *Scottish Population History*, pp. 340–1.
[17] Teitelbaum, *British Fertility Decline*, Table 6.4b.

$$I_g = 455.9 + 18.7\text{ILL} + 3.95\text{CATH} + 0.95\text{RUR} + 1.51\text{PCCOAL}$$
$$(28.8) \quad (6.9) \quad (1.99) \quad (0.48) \quad (0.84)$$
$R^2 = 0.543$; $F(4, 26) = 7.72$; s.e.s in parentheses.

COHORT PARITY ANALYSIS

Cohort Parity Analysis (C.P.A.), an alternative approach to the measurement of fertility control devised by Paul David and his research associates, provides a means of inferring the extent and timing of birth control within marriage from distributions of married women by number of children born. An important aspect of C.P.A. is the extent to which married couples resort to contraception in order to 'space' births. Traditionally, according to David, historical demographers have focused on an unnecessarily restrictive definition, viz. the parity at which some form of birth-control is introduced. That definition presumed a period free of control followed by 'stopping'. But if methods of averting births are unreliable, the distinction between 'spacing' and 'stopping' becomes blurred, and 'precautionary parity-independent birth-spacing behaviour among couples who sought to limit their completed family size' is more plausible.[18] In addition, David argues that C.P.A.'s choice framework is more consistent with the optimizing behaviour of economic theory. Factors such as seasonality in the demand for female labour, career considerations, and the gender mix of children already born, are likely to affect 'spacing'. However, as a measure of fertility, C.P.A. does not preclude forms of control that do not result in a concentration of births early in marriage or at low parities: it allows for either 'spacing' or 'stopping' behaviour. The methodology of C.P.A. has been explained fully elsewhere.[19] A brief non-technical outline must suffice here. Like the alternative Coale-Henry measure, C.P.A. sets a 'target' population against some benchmark non-controlling model population (analogous to the Hutterites in the derivation of I_g). Both populations contain women marrying in some defined age-range, who have been married for a specified number of years. C.P.A. generates lower and upper bound estimates—C_L and C_U—of the proportions of women in the target controlling births. The Irish example has played an important part in the development of C.P.A. since David and his colleagues believe that 'the rural Irish of 1911 provide a suitable model, not only in urban Ireland in 1911 and the United States around the turn of the century, but also for Western Europe, Canada, Australia, and New Zealand, from the mid-nineteen

---

[18] Paul A. David, 'On Stopping vs. Spacing and Historical Fertility Transitions', Stanford Project on the History of Fertility Control, Working Paper No. 25 (1987), p. 10.

[19] This explanation closely follows Paul A. David and Warren C. Sanderson, 'Measuring Marital Fertility Control with C.P.A.', *Population Index*, LIV, 4 (1988), pp. 691–713. For an alternative formulation see Paul A. David, Thomas A. Mroz, Warren C. Sanderson, Kenneth W. Wachter and David R. Weir, 'Cohort Parity Analysis: Statistical Estimates of the Extent of Fertility Control', *Demography*, XV, 2 (1988), pp. 163–88.

FERTILITY TRANSITION 95

Table 2a: Lower- and upper-bound estimates of the percentage of 'urban' Irishwomen controlling c. 1900–1910, using 'rural' Ireland as a model population.

	Model: 'Rural Ireland'				Target: 'Urban' Ireland			
	Age at Marriage							
Duration of Marriage	<20		20–24		25–29		30–34	
	C_L	C_U	C_L	C_U	C_L	C_U	C_L	C_U
0– 4	11.4	27.4	15.7	31.9	21.4	38.7	22.0	29.1
4	20.9	25.5	28.7	34.9	33.0	41.1	30.1	38.7
5– 9	16.3	24.6	20.6	30.7	30.4	42.8	31.9	40.3
10–14	12.5	19.7	19.8	29.1	33.7	48.9	34.9	45.6
15–19	9.5	15.5	23.4	40.5	32.6	48.0	37.6	50.9
20–24	10.5	14.1	20.4	31.7	33.4	48.9	–	–
25–29	10.8	14.4	20.2	30.1	–	–	–	–

Table 2b: Lower- and upper-bound estimates of the percentage of Irishwomen controlling c. 1900–1910, using 'rural' Ireland as a model population.

	Model: 'Rural' Ireland				Target: Ireland			
	Age at Marriage							
Duration of Marriage	<20		20–24		25–29		30–34	
	C_L	C_U	C_L	C_U	C_L	C_U	C_L	C_U
0– 4	8.2	10.0	10.0	12.1	7.4	9.3	4.4	5.6
5– 9	6.5	9.8	6.6	9.9	6.1	8.6	4.6	5.9
10–14	5.0	7.9	6.0	8.8	6.6	9.6	4.7	6.2
15–19	3.6	5.9	6.7	11.7	6.1	9.0	4.6	6.2
20–24	3.9	5.3	5.5	8.5	5.6	8.2	–	–
25–29	3.8	5.0	4.9	7.3	–	–	–	–

Note: 'urban' and 'rural' are defined as in David et al., 'Cohort Parity Analysis'.

Table 3: Lower- and upper-bound estimates of the percentage of Scottish women controlling c. 1900–1910, using 'rural' Ireland as a model population.

	Model: 'Rural' Ireland				Target: Scotland			
	Age at Marriage							
Duration of Marriage	<20		20–24		25–29		30–34	
	C_L	C_U	C_L	C_U	C_L	C_U	C_L	C_U
<1	-100.0	-100.0	-100.0	-100.0	-100.0	-100.0	-100.0	-100.0
1– 4	-9.7	-15.3	3.8	9.1	22.1	35.9	24.3	39.9
5– 9	8.7	13.3	27.1	38.7	44.5	60.8	41.1	56.2
10–14	11.0	18.1	30.3	43.4	44.5	63.6	44.1	66.9
15–19	9.6	15.3	30.7	51.8	41.8	60.6	40.8	62.6
20–24	7.2	10.2	27.9	43.8	39.1	56.3	–	–
25–29	7.5	10.1	26.4	33.3	–	–	–	–

Table 4: Lower- and upper-bound estimates of the percentage of Scottish women controlling c. 1900–1910, using 'urban' Ireland as a model population.

	Model: 'Urban' Ireland				Target: Scotland			
	Age at Marriage							
Duration of Marriage	<20		20–24		25–29		30–34	
	C_L	C_U	C_L	C_U	C_L	C_U	C_L	C_U
0– 4	-27.0	-58.5	-19.1	-36.5	-6.1	-6.8	-6.2	12.7
1– 4	-30.2	-60.6	-19.9	-36.7	-3.4	-5.5	-2.1	14.6
5–9	-8.8	-14.9	8.0	11.5	19.1	31.4	10.7	26.6
10–14	-1.8	-2.1	12.4	20.1	14.8	28.7	9.4	39.3
15–19	0.1	-0.2	9.2	19.0	12.5	24.2	2.0	29.7
20–24	-3.6	-4.5	8.7	17.7	7.7	14.6	–	–
25–29	3.6	-5.1	7.2	13.2	–	–	–	–

through the early twentieth centuries'.[20] The interest in Ireland is motivated in no small part by the inclusion of requisite data in the Irish census of 1911. Using fertility data published in the census as the basis for a 'model', David and his collaborators were able to show that a substantial minority of married couples in the main cities of Ireland were practising birth control early in marriage in 1911.[21]

Table 2 applies the same definitions of 'urban' and 'rural', but broadens the canvas. The entries refer to lower- and upper-bound estimates of the percentage of 'controlling' couples for a range of bridal ages at marriage and marriage duration. Using 'rural' Ireland as a model population, a substantial proportion of controllers in 'urban' Ireland is indicated. The results in Row 3, describing the extent of control in marriages of 5–9 years' duration match those in Tables 2 and 4 of David et al.[22] Broadly speaking, those marrying later were more likely to restrict births. Table 3 uses the entire population as a target, and indicates that 5 to 10 per cent were controllers.[23]

Tables 3 and 4 apply C.P.A. to 1911 Scottish data. They show that taking 'rural Ireland' as the model non-controlling population, the percentage of controllers in Scotland was already high by 1911. Even using urban Ireland as a model, the estimated percentage of Scottish controllers is high except in the case of early marriages.

One anomaly concerns marriages of 0–4 years' duration, where the Irish seem the controllers. The reason for this seems to be the much higher incidence of bridal

---

[20] David and Sanderson, 'Measuring Marital Fertility', p. 695.
[21] The 'generation of 1911' (in Scotland at least) was the second to be exposed to a widespread knowledge of birth-control technology. Thus, as Bob Morris has reminded us, 'stopping' may well be a better description of the state of play in the 1880s. The point is worth further investigation.
[22] David et al., 'Cohort Parity Analysis', pp. 175, 178.
[23] Row 3 confirms the results reported in David et al., Table 3.

pregnancy (and perhaps pre-marital births) in Scotland.[24] Flinn and his collaborators found that as far back as the 1855–69 period one third of a large sample of rural births were the outcome of bridal pregnancies. The illegitimacy ratio in Scotland was 7 per cent in the 1890s and 1900s,[25] but only about 2 per cent in Ireland. In 1911, 28 per cent of 20–24 year-old brides married less than a year were reported as having at least one child; for 25–29 year-old brides the percentage was 16. In Ireland the percentages were 11 and 6. The outcome reported above may therefore be spurious, and raises a question-mark over the appropriateness of C.P.A. comparisons in cases such as this.[26]

THE MARIE STOPES CORRESPONDENCE, 1918–40

The thousands of surviving letters received by the English family planning pioneer Marie Carmichael Stopes[27] between 1918 and the early 1940s include several hundred from Scotland and Ireland. In this section we draw on the contents of one important set of letters to Stopes from Irish and Scottish correspondents—letters prompted by Stopes's *Married Love* and related works—for comparative insight into the fertility transition in both countries.[28] The set contains over one hundred letters from Ireland and twice as many from Scotland.

Individually, the letters reflect a wide variety of experience and problems. Most obviously, they indicate a strong desire for confidentiality in sexual matters, and a widespread ignorance about sexual problems. Some of the letters—a case in point being those from an Ulster schoolteacher who 'simply devoured' *Contraception* (one of Stopes's pamphlets) and read a chapter of *Married Love* every night in bed, finding it 'absorbing'—reflect eccentricity and male prurience. Such letters generally eschew the personal histories found in the bulk of the letters. Yet most of

---

[24] Compare N. F. R. Crafts, 'Duration of Marriage, Fertility, and Female Employment Opportunities in England and Wales in 1911', *Population Studies*, XLIII, 2 (1990) pp. 325–35, fn. 10.

[25] Flinn *et al.*, *Scottish Population History*, pp. 350–1, 359.

[26] David Fitzpatrick has reminded us that the effect might be due in part to the differing seasonality of marriages in Scotland and Ireland. The point is taken, but the effect was very small (c.f. Ó Gráda, 'New Evidence').

[27] Marie Carmichael Stopes (1880–1958), author of *Married Love*, *Enduring Passion*, and many other popular works, publicist for contraception and the eugenics movement. Through her journalism, clinics, and libel actions, more responsible than anyone else for breaking the taboo against public discussion of fertility control in Britain. See Ruth Hall, *Marie Stopes* (London, 1977). For more on Stopes and her correspondence see Leslie A. Hall, 'The Stopes Collection in the Contemporary Medical Archives Centre at the Wellcome Institute for the History of Medicine', *The Society for the Social History of Medicine*, Bulletin 32 (1983), pp. 51–2.

[28] The letters are to be found in the Contemporary Medical Archive Collection, Wellcome Institute, London, ML Series, Folios A1–A259. Names and precise references have been avoided to maintain anonymity. For an earlier study based on another set of correspondence, using a much larger sample of letters for insight into birth-control methods practised in interwar Britain, see Claire Davey, 'Birth Control in Britain During the Interwar Years', *Journal of Family History*, XIII, 3 (1988), pp. 329–45.

the letters seem genuine and to-the-point. A few examples must suffice here. The quest for secrecy is represented by the woman from the Dublin suburb of Blackrock who pleaded that literature about contraception not be sent in wrappers—'people might open them and misunderstand'—or the young Glasgow woman who wrote because 'I am very ignorant in these things and I don't like to ask any of my friends'. Several letters betray a limited knowledge of the 'facts of life'. Thus in 1938 an elderly Glasgow man wondered, his wife in mind, if 'there [is] any instance of a woman of 58 conceiving'. Some years earlier, a man from Oban wrote to ask (allegedly on behalf of a friend) whether merely stimulating a woman's vagina might induce pregnancy. A Glasgow woman desiring 'a little time to adjust [her]self to the new life', and not reassured by her husband's confidence that 'there may be no child for some time naturally', sought advice about a Vaseline-based concoction. Stopes wisely proposed a pessary instead. A recently-married Belfast woman wanted to know in 1919 whether if she and her husband 'reach[ed] the climax simultaneously would there be any chance of having a child?' Two different correspondents wanted to know if couples could choose the sex of their children. Another wondered whether red-haired men were more highly sexed than others. A twenty-one year-old Offaly woman betrayed such ignorance that Stopes met her request for information about *Married Love* with the advice that she 'should start by reading *The Human Body*'. A well-heeled Scots woman wondered whether horse-riding, appropriately timed, was a safeguard against pregnancy. A belief in quack methods of averting births and inducing abortions (hot baths, Dr Patterson's pills, etc.) is also evident.

To rely on the Marie Stopes correspondence as a window on the demand for birth control invites some obvious criticisms. Clearly, middle-class, literate demand is likely to have been over-represented.[29] Also problematic are the influence of the activities of rival family planning pioneers and the banning of Stopes's works in the Irish Free State after 1928 on the flow of letters to Stopes. Any general points made on the basis of such a small number of observations must therefore be doubly tentative. Still, Stopes was widely known and easily contacted through her publishers. The letters are surely a useful guide to the extent that the postal service provided a voice to some of those living far from the early family planning clinics, that it guaranteed confidentiality, and that it was inexpensive. We think the following points worth making:

(i) In Ireland men were more likely to write than women, but in Scotland the reverse was true. However, the women were more likely to seek information on birth control, whereas male queries were more concerned with recurrent sexual problems such as impotence and premature ejaculation. Most of the letters came from 'respectable' married people or from those about to be married. In Ireland, middle and upper class people constituted the bulk of the correspondents. Thirty-six of the Irish requests came from such people, as against three from identifiably

---

[29] Compare Davey, 'Birth Control', p. 336.

working class people. The latter consisted of a soldier in Kilworth camp, a Limerick woman with six children, and a Coleraine woman who wondered in 1943 whether cod liver oil was a safe substitute for olive oil, 'now that olive oil is unavailable'. By contrast, of the Scottish correspondents whose socioeconomic status could be ascertained, one third hailed from a poor background.

(ii) Over the period as a whole, the Scots were far more likely to write to Stopes than the Irish. Scotland, with a population only marginally greater than Ireland's in this period, accounted for over two thirds of the correspondents. However, there was a marked falling-off in letters from Ireland after the mid-1920s.

(iii) People living in what became Northern Ireland were much more likely to consult Stopes than those living south of the border. The North, with less than one-third of the South's population, produced one half of the Irish letters. Moreover, the Southern letters include several in 1919–21 from military gentlemen stationed in Ireland, though not necessarily of Irish birth. Censorship in the South produced no relative falling-off in letters. Most of the Irish letters came from counties Antrim, Down, and Dublin. Most of the requests, both North and South, seem to have come from non-Catholics.

(iv) Requests were by no means limited to information about family limitation. Letters of support formed a significant part of the Scottish correspondence, and in both countries many letters dealt with problems such as frigidity, impotence and premature ejaculation. Focusing on problem letters alone, Irish correspondents were more likely to be male and to seek information not necessarily entailing fertility control.

(v) The letters provide evidence of both the 'spacing' and the 'stopping' behaviour discussed in the previous section. In both Scotland and Ireland between one quarter and one third of the inquiries about contraception show a clear desire for 'spacing'. Most of the 'spacers' sought to avert births in the first year or two of marriage. Typical is the Scots woman who had read *Married Love* before marriage and 'decided upon contraception for at least a year, wishing to be fully adjusted to each other before bringing a new life into being'. Of course, Marie Stopes herself was a strong advocate of contraception in the early stages of marriage. Whether 'stopping' or 'spacing' was intended is unclear in some cases; thus the range reported above is a lower-bound estimate of 'spacing'.

(vi) Twenty-eight correspondents, twenty-five of them from Scotland, nearly all women, sought information about abortion. It is evident from Claire Davey's analysis of letters from English correspondents that their demand for such information was far greater than from the Irish or Scots. Significantly, nine of the Scottish inquiries came from identifiably poor households, versus six from middle-class households. One of the Irish requests came in 1923 from a frustrated Englishwoman married to a Corkman. 'Cork,' she complained, 'is such an old-fashioned goody-goody place that they would not sell you what you wanted if they thought it was for a wrong purpose.' Her potential source of 'a bottle of Black Mischief' had unfortunately left Cork. Stopes resolutely refused to help in such cases, with two exceptions. In one case, which turned out to be a false alarm, a wealthy Scottish knight, 'old enough to be her grandfather', sought help for a friend in distress. Stopes suggested that with luck he might find an Edinburgh consultant willing to operate on the premise that the woman's health was in danger. In the other, the request came from a Belfast couple infected with syphilis and declaring a history of defective births.

CPA WITH THREE IRISH MICRO DATA-SETS

Open access to the Irish manuscript census forms of 1901 and 1911 has prompted several social and economic historians to construct micro data-bases.[30] The present exercise, which applies C.P.A. methodology to local data, is very much in this tradition. We selected three areas, composed of clusters of District Electoral Divisions (D.E.D.s) in very different areas within Ireland. We required, first, a traditional rural area where farming predominated. For this we selected D.E.D.s in County Clare. The choice of Clare was guided in part by its placing near the top of the I_g league in 1911. Clare was also the locus for Conrad Arensberg's classic anthropological study a few decades later.[31] In the Clare D.E.D.s selected here, the great majority of women were married either to farmers or farm labourers, but a smattering had married teachers, policemen, and so on. Our second area includes mainly rural parts of Tyrone, a northern, religiously-mixed county. Again the husbands' occupations were mainly agricultural, but a minority of the men were engaged in the textile industry. Thirdly, we required an urban middle-class area, and for this we chose the comfortable Dublin suburb of Rathgar. In 1911 Rathgar had a large non-Catholic population. Clusters of D.E.D.s large enough to yield a population of about 600 were collected in each case. The size of the clusters was constrained by our research budget; women marrying before the age of 20 were too few in the selected areas to justify subjecting them to cohort parity analysis, and the same applied to those marrying in the 30–34 bracket in Tyrone and Rathgar.

The Clare set was used as the model population. In broad outline, the results (Table 5) were straightforward enough. Most important is that, by the Clare 'standard' substantial fertility control in the other areas is indicated, though the patterns in them differ. Measuring 'Rural Ireland' against the standard, significant control is implied except for one category, marriages of 30–34 year-olds of 0–4 years duration. On first examination, it was thought that this may have been due to differing intra-group distributions in the groups being compared. However, weighting the Clare data by the national weights made little difference. Another

---

[30] Compare David Fitzpatrick, 'Irish Farming Families Before the First World War', *Comparative Studies in History and Society*, XXV (1984), pp. 339–74; Ó Gráda, 'Did Irish Catholics Always Have Larger Families?'; Timothy Guinnane, 'Migration, Marriage and Household Formation: The Irish at the Turn of the Century' (unpublished Ph.D. dissertation, Stanford University, 1988).

[31] Conrad Arensberg, *The Irish Countryman* (London, 1937).

possibility, that newly-wed mothers were over-represented in Clare, prompted us to look at marriages of 1–4 years' duration. The breakdown here is as follows:

Parity	Rural Ireland	Clare
0	0.3139	0.2779
1	0.3499	0.3290
2	0.2495	0.3179
3	0.0867	0.0751

Proportionately fewer Clare women had zero or one child, substantially more had two children, while fewer had three. These last probabilities are enough to produce the result indicated.

Table 5: C.P.A. measures using Irish manuscript censal data, 1911

Duration of Marriage (Years)	Age at marriage					
	20–4		25–9		30–4	
	c_L	c_U	c_L	c_U	c_L	c_U
A. Model: Clare Target: Rathgar						
0– 4	31.8	26.4	45.1	72.5	–	–
5– 9	43.5	51.1	67.5	87.4	–	–
B: Model: Clare Target: Tyrone						
0– 4	47.3	55.6	26.3	59.0	–	–
5– 9	35.6	51.9	33.3	41.4	–	–
c. Model: Clare Target: 'Rural Ireland'						
0– 4	28.0	26.4	20.1	38.4	-1.3	-20.7
5– 9	25.9	36.5	24.4	35.0	16.7	19.9

The contrast between the Clare and Tyrone populations, both rural, is striking. It surely again raises a question about the 'rural' Ireland chosen by David et al. Taking 'rural Ireland' as target against Clare suggests that over one fifth of rural Irishwomen who married in their twenties were 'controllers' by Clare standards. Curiously, however, Clare women who married in their early thirties apparently 'controlled' less in the first five years of marriage.

CONCLUSION

One of the current controversies in historical demography concerns the fertility transition in nineteenth-century Europe and America. Prior to the transition, a variety of practices such as variation in coital frequency, withdrawal, breastfeeding, and abortion produced some variation in marital fertility across space and time. However, such practices do not seem to have been used to limit family size. Susan

Watkins's summary statement of the 'Princeton' view of the fertility transition in Europe holds that:[32]

> During the initial stages of the demographic transition this diversity of behaviour was replaced by a single approach, the earlier termination of childbearing. Only later, it would appear from what is known so far, did the deliberate spacing of children within marriage become important.

Strong support for this approach is provided in Knodel's study of German villages. In none of the eight villages surveyed did the mean interval between births—an obvious measure of spacing—rise between 1700 and 1900. Equally striking in their support for the rival 'spacing' approach are the findings of Lachiver for the Paris region.[33] These show mean birth-intervals in the mid-eighteenth century, before the transition, reflecting the traditional 'bi-annual rhythm of births'. However, from the 1760s on, the percentage of birth-intervals in the 31–48 month range increased in all areas. By the 1820s and 1830s intervals of four years or more accounted for over one half of the total.[34]

Neither the Irish nor the Scottish data examined above support the Princeton view of a European fertility transition marked by parity-specific control. Even within 'rural' Ireland, hitherto presumed innocent of spacing in the rival 'Stanford view' (associated with Paul David and his collaborators), micro census data show evidence consistent with some spacing behaviour early in marriage. C.P.A. analysis of aggregate data suggests that birth spacing was an important feature of the fertility transition, indicated by the preferred Princeton measure (I_g) at a more disaggregated level, in both Ireland and Scotland.

---

[32] Coale and Watkins, *The Fertility Transition*, p. 434.

[33] John Knodel, 'Demographic Transitions in German Villages', in Coale and Watkins, *European Fertility Decline*, pp. 376–80; Marcel Lachiver, 'Fécondité légitime et contraception dans la région parisienne', in Société de Demographie Historique, ed., *Sur la Population Française au XVIIIe et au XIXe Siècles: Hommage à Marcel Reinhard* (Paris, 1973).

[34] Lachiver, 'Fécondité légitime', pp. 395–7; see also Coale and Watkins, *Fertility Decline*, pp. 14–17, on nineteenth-century Hungary.

8

Popular culture: patterns of change and adaptation

S. J. Connolly

'IRISH AND SCOTTISH HISTORY ALIKE,' it was memorably stated at an earlier conference in this series, 'have been obscured in whiskey, mist and misery.'[1] To this evocative trinity may be added a fourth element; cultural decline. For social historians of both countries the progressive erosion of cultural distinctiveness, reflected in customs, manners, beliefs, and most of all in language, has been a central focus of interest. Similar concerns have been prominent in the work of historians of Wales. This paper considers some comparisons between the processes of cultural change in Ireland and in the other two major regions of Britain's Celtic periphery. At the same time it questions whether a preoccupation with decline, and especially linguistic decline, is in any of these three cases the best approach to the complex and varied picture that confronts the historian of popular culture.

* * *

One immediate parallel linking the histories of Ireland, Scotland and Wales is provided by the suspicion and distaste with which, up to the late eighteenth century, the language and civilisation of the common people were viewed by their social superiors. The Welsh antiquarian Edward Lhuyd commented in 1701, of the Scottish Highlanders:

> The main cause of their being reputed barbarous, I take to be no other than the roughness of their country, as consisting very much of barren mountains and loughs and their retaining their ancient habits, custom and language, on which very account many gentleman of good sense in England esteem the Welsh at this day barbarous and talk so much of wild Irish in this kingdom.[2]

---

[1] L. M. Cullen, 'Incomes, Social Classes and Economic Growth in Ireland and Scotland 1600–1900', in Devine and Dickson, p. 248.
[2] Trinity College, Dublin MS 883/2, pp. 284–5, Edward Lhuyd to —, 29 January 1701.

The Cromwellian Major General Fleetwood, complaining in 1654 that the people of Wales 'have envenomed hearts against the ways of God', described them as 'little better than the Irish'. In Scotland one of the signs of the decline in status that affected Gaelic in the later Middle Ages was its redesignation as 'Irish'.[3]

At the same time, it is necessary to note the differences as well as the similarities between the three cases. Wales, despite the complaints of Lhuyd and the disdain of Fleetwood, was from an early stage seen in a more benign light than either of the other two. Its population was small (less than half a million in the mid-eighteenth century), it had not been a centre of significant political resistance since the late Middle Ages, and it had been administratively absorbed into the English state in the early sixteenth century. Welsh language and culture may have been perceived as inferior, but they were not a political problem. As a result the eighteenth-century pioneers of Welsh elementary education, concerned with saving souls rather than with social control, were able to make free use of the Welsh language, laying the foundations for levels of literacy in the mother tongue that were never to be achieved in either Ireland or Scotland.[4] In the Scottish Lowlands, equally, powerful religious influences had, already by the end of the seventeenth century, produced a popular culture that was relatively tame—possibly more so than that of contemporary England. Here too cultural distinctions, even when heightened by the further anglicisation in the early eighteenth century of the language and manners of the gentry and middle classes, did not give rise to significant antagonisms.[5] In the Highlands, on the other hand, centuries of conflict had established the view that native barbarity was a direct threat to political order. There the late seventeenth and eighteenth centuries saw the application of a distinctive ideology of improvement, in which cultural change—to be achieved by education, religious missions and, where necessary, coercion—was seen as an essential prerequisite of economic progress and political stability.[6]

Ireland occupied a position midway between those of Wales and Highland Scotland. As long as Gaelic Ireland had remained a real political threat, there had been legislation against Gaelic bards and minstrels, and the use of Irish dress and language. By the mid-seventeenth century, however, direct cultural repression had ceased to be a priority. Elements of the older hostility to indigenous language and culture survived. As late as 1712 proposals to print prayer books and other texts in Irish in preparation for a missionary drive among the Catholic lower classes were opposed, on the grounds that this would be to perpetuate the language at a time

---

[3] Geraint Jenkins, *The Foundations of Modern Wales: Wales 1642–1780* (Oxford, 1987), p. 81; C. W. J. Withers, *Gaelic in Scotland 1698–1981: The Geographical History of a Language* (Edinburgh, 1984), pp. 22–4.

[4] V. E. Durkacz, *The Decline of the Celtic Languages* (Edinburgh, 1983), esp. chap. 2, 3.

[5] R. A. Houston and I. D. Whyte, 'Introduction', to *Scottish Society 1500–1800* (Cambridge, 1989), pp. 34–5.

[6] Nicholas Philippson, 'Politics, Politeness and the Anglicisation of Early Eighteenth-Century Scottish Culture', in R. A. Mason, ed., *Scotland and England 1286–1815* (Edinburgh, 1987); C. W. J. Withers, *Gaelic Scotland: The Transformation of a Culture Region* (London, 1988), chap. 2.

when its use should be discouraged by all means possible.⁷ The term 'Irish' itself long retained negative connotations, even in the heyday of eighteenth-century Protestant patriotism.⁸ On the other hand there was no direct attack on language and culture comparable to the body of legislation enacted in Scotland after 1745. The Irish Charter School Society, established in 1731, certainly included among its aims the promotion of English language. But this did not have the central prominence that the elimination of Gaelic had in the programme of the S.S.P.C.K.

This more relaxed attitude to native culture can in part be attributed to political change: by 1660 the social structure of Gaelic Ireland, unlike that of Gaelic Scotland, had been shattered beyond repair. But the change in elite responses also reflected recent developments in the character of popular culture itself. Here the middle decades of the seventeenth century witnessed what amounted to a revolution: the disappearance of the distinctive dress and hair style that had marked out the 'native Irish'; the diffusion among large sections of the lower class of some knowledge of English; the substantial though not complete imposition of the religious and moral discipline of the Counter-Reformation (including the apparent disappearance of the relatively free and easy sexual morality reported by Tudor and early Stuart observers); the spread of new consumer goods. All this, along with a more complete integration into the economic structures of Anglo-Ireland, made it increasingly difficult to present the Irish lower classes, as sixteenth and early seventeenth-century polemicists had done, as savages on a par with the indigenous inhabitants of north America or other overseas colonies.

Elite and popular culture cannot of course be considered in isolation. Links have been discovered, for example, between eighteenth-century writing in Scots and English, while in Ireland tenuous but suggestive correspondences have been pointed out between the work of Swift and other Anglo-Irish writers and that of their Gaelic contemporaries.⁹ In general, however, the period between the sixteenth and eighteenth centuries was to see the establishment everywhere in Europe of a more exclusive elite culture, and the progressive withdrawal of the patronage that the educated and affluent had earlier been prepared to extend to the performances and recreations of the common people.¹⁰ In Wales, Scotland and Ireland, as

---

⁷ Unless otherwise stated, comments on Ireland are documented and more fully discussed in the following: S. J. Connolly, *Priests and People in Pre-Famine Ireland 1780–1845* (Dublin, 1982); 'Popular Culture in Pre-Famine Ireland', in Cyril Byrne and Margaret Harry, eds., *Talamh an Eisc: Canadian and Irish Essays* (Halifax, Nova Scotia, 1986); *Religion, Law and Power: The Making of Protestant Ireland 1660–1760* (Oxford, 1992).

⁸ D. W. Hayton, 'Anglo-Irish Attitudes: Changing Perceptions of National Identity among the Protestant Ascendancy in Ireland c. 1690–1750', *Studies in Eighteenth-Century Culture*, XVII (1987), pp. 150–1.

⁹ Alexander Murdoch and Richard Sher, 'Literary and Learned Culture', in T. M. Devine and Rosalind Mitchison, eds., *People and Society in Scotland*, Vol. I: *1760–1830* (Edinburgh, 1988), pp. 127–8; Declan Kiberd, 'Irish Literature and Irish History', in R. F. Foster, ed., *The Oxford Illustrated History of Ireland* (Oxford, 1989), pp. 303–35.

¹⁰ Peter Burke, *Popular Culture in Early Modern Europe* (London, 1978).

in other peripheral and economically underdeveloped societies, the withdrawal came relatively late. In Wales, for example, the second half of the seventeenth century appears to have been the period of decisive change; the last household bards died out and were not replaced; the last great halls, where landlords could dine in the old fashion among their tenants and retainers, were replaced by English-style manor houses; there was a general anglicisation of manners.[11] In Scotland the early decades of the eighteenth century seem to stand out as the period that saw both the transformation of clan chiefs into landlords, and a parallel trend towards more refined—in effect more anglicised—manners among Lowland proprietors.[12]

Ireland was somewhat different. Instead of an indigenous elite abandoning its traditional role as patrons of popular culture, there was the installation of a largely new landed class. Yet this did not lead to the complete separation of elite and popular culture that is often imagined. The new proprietors established their own patterns of patronage and interaction. Robert Boyle, Earl of Cork (1566–1643), normally seen as the epitome of the new 'planter' class, kept an Irish harp among the furnishings of his house at Lismore, and had his sons taught some Irish.[13] In the early and mid-eighteenth century landlords continued to patronise harpists, bards and other performers; to watch and sometimes play the game of hurling; to support traditional festivals; to mingle with their inferiors at horse races and fairs, and in the proverbially boisterous Dublin theatre. By the end of the eighteenth century such willingness to share in popular recreations had largely disappeared. In part this reflected the intensification of sectarian and social conflict. In part, however, it can be attributed to the extension into landed society of metropolitan standards of propriety and refinement. Thus the withdrawal of support for popular performers, and a new distaste for participation in the rough and tumble of popular amusements, coincided with a marked decline in the heavy drinking and duelling that had earlier marked out the Irish gentry and aristocracy as very much a provincial elite.

At the same time that members of the Irish elite were withdrawing from practical participation in the amusements and performances of the common people, they were, like their counterparts in Scotland and Wales, developing a new interest in the promotion of a distinctive national culture. This process, as in other parts of Europe touched by the Romantic cult of ethnic and historical particularity, involved a mixture of serious intellectual enquiry and extravagant invention. Where Welsh antiquarians imagined an elaborate Druidic past, and Scots elevated the

---

[11] Prys Morgan, 'From a Death to a View: The Hunt for the Welsh Past in the Romantic Period', in E. J. Hobsbawm and Terence Ranger, eds., *The Invention of Tradition* (Cambridge, 1983), pp. 48–52; D. W. Howell, *Patriarchs and Parasites: The Gentry of South-West Wales in the Eighteenth Century* (Cardiff, 1986), pp. 194–203.

[12] T. C. Smout, *A History of the Scottish People 1560–1830* (London, 1972 edn), pp. 265–71, 315–16, 322–8.

[13] Nicholas Canny, *The Upstart Earl: A Study of the Social and Mental World of Richard Boyle, First Earl of Cork 1566–1643* (Cambridge, 1982), pp. 126–8.

previously despised Highlander into the symbol of all that was finest in their nation, antiquarians like Charles Vallancey presented pre-Christian Ireland as an outpost of Phoenician culture, and pressed the claims of Irish to have been the language spoken in the garden of Eden.[14] There was also a degree of interaction between the three regions. In the 1840s the Young Ireland movement, seeking to create a literature for an English-speaking public that would still be clearly un-English, appear to have found a model in the poetry and ballads of Lowland Scotland.[15]

* * *

Discussion of the history of Irish popular culture is all too easily overshadowed by the military defeats and confiscations that had, by the mid-seventeenth century, destroyed the old Gaelic order. But such a perspective is in many ways misleading. What was overthrown was an aristocratic culture, not a popular one. Here the replacement of Irish by English as the language of the rich and powerful is normally seen as the key to its eventual decline. Yet the experiences of Wales and Scotland provide little support for the implied conclusion that, without the dispossession of the native elite, Irish would have survived as a language of gentlemen. For the rest of the population, the loss of patronage, so much bewailed by bards and harpists, can be seen as contributing to an enrichment rather than a diminution of culture, as poets and musicians turned to simpler and less formal styles, more accessible to lower class audiences. In other respects too the revolution in popular manners and lifestyle that took place from the mid-seventeenth century should be interpreted, not in terms of surrender or conquest, but as an adaptation to changed circumstances and new possibilities.

Two examples may help to illustrate the point. The first is the development during the eighteenth century of the game of hurling. This existed across the greater part of the country as a participatory sport, played on open ground with a minimum of rules. But in Leinster and a few adjoining counties it had evolved, by the early eighteenth century, into something very different: a spectator sport, attracting audiences drawn from all levels of the social hierarchy, with important matches regularly advertised in the local press, and substantial amounts put up both in prize money and as wagers. From one point of view this development reflects the new opportunities for upper class patronage opened up by the changes in physical appearance, customs and behaviour that since the mid-seventeenth century had converted the wild Irishman into something less alien and threatening. From another it provides an Irish example of the commercialisation of leisure that

---

[14] Jenkins, *Foundations of Modern Wales*, pp. 249–51, 424–6; Hugh Trevor-Roper, 'The Invention of Tradition: The Highland Tradition of Scotland', in Hobsbawm and Ranger, eds., *The Invention of Tradition*; Norman Vance, 'Celts, Carthaginians and Constitutions: Anglo-Irish Literary Relations', *Irish Historical Studies*, XXII, 87 (1981).

[15] Graham Walker, 'Irish Nationalism and the Uses of History', *Past and Present*, 126 (1990), p. 207.

has been suggested as a central feature of eighteenth-century British culture. Hurling could develop as it did—as a spectator sport, played by skilled specialists for the benefit of an audience—only with the attainment of a denser population, better communications, larger towns, and a greater availability of cash.[16]

A similar adaptation of popular custom to new opportunities may be seen in the case of the pattern. These ceremonial and festive assemblies at wells or other sacred sites, similar in many respects to the English wake, continued up to the middle of the nineteenth century to be a central focus of popular sociability. They have generally been interpreted in one of two ways: as traditional religious festivals that over time came to be corrupted by the introduction of festive elements, or as pre-Christian survivals, their carnivalesque aspects a pagan legacy inadequately suppressed when the sites at which they were held were taken over by the new religion. An alternative perspective is suggested by one of the most important contemporary representations of what a pattern was actually like, Joseph Peacock's painting of the gathering at Glendalough in 1813. Peacock depicts the stock elements of drink, dancing and faction fight. But what emerges most forcefully from his portrayal, as W. H. Crawford has highlighted in a masterpiece of close analysis, is the commercial aspect of the pattern: the quantity and variety of consumer goods—clothing, footwear, household implements, toys—displayed on an assortment of specialised stalls.[17] To this may be added the evidence of geographical distribution. For the patterns of early nineteenth-century Ireland were not concentrated, as one might expect of survivals from either the pre-Christian or the early Christian world, in the remote and still strongly Gaelic west. Instead the majority took place, as at Glendalough, in the more commercialised (and anglicised) counties of the east. All this would suggest that the pattern, as described by observers in the late eighteenth and early nineteenth centuries, should be seen, not as a survival from 'traditional' Ireland, but rather as an adaptation of religious institutions to the new needs and opportunities opened up by commercialisation.

The effects of commercialisation on popular culture were not confined to games and festivals. Observers in the mid-eighteenth century noted, generally with disapproval, the appearance of new forms of consumption. The Reverend Samuel Madden complained in 1738 that the 'affectation of drinking wine has got even into the middle and lower ranks of our people, and the infection is become so general, that a little hedge inn would be forsaken by our drovers, horse jockeys, cadgers and carriers, if they wanted it'. A taste for tea drinking, a Dublin newspaper maintained the following year, was impoverishing the kingdom and reducing poor families to want: 'it has been frequently observed of late that several servant maids and button makers, starving in garrets, nay even dutch spinners, do pledge their

---

[16] Art Ó Maolfabhail, *Caman: Two Thousand Years of Hurling in Ireland* (Dundalk, 1973); L. P. O Caithnia, *Sceal na hIomana: O Thosach Ama go 1884* (Dublin, 1980), pp. 26–36.

[17] W. H. Crawford, 'The Patron or Festival of St Kevin at the Seven Churches, Glendalough, County Wicklow 1813', *Ulster Folklife*, XXXII (1986).

handkerchiefs and aprons for tea'. Mrs Delany, visiting County Down in 1745, commented in similar terms:

> I am very sorry to find here and everywhere people out of character, and that wine and tea should enter where they have no pretence to be, and usurp the rural food of syllabub etc. But the dairymaids wear large hoops and velvet hoods instead of the round tight petticoat and straw hat, and there is as much foppery introduced in the food as in the dress. The pure simplicity of the country is quite lost.[18]

The adaptation of popular culture to new circumstances that can thus be detected in Ireland from the mid-eighteenth century may also be seen elsewhere. In Lowland Scotland the same period saw the revival of music, dancing and song, and the growth of theatre, racing and other occasions for sociability. In Wales there was the emergence of new forms of popular theatre (the interludes), as well as a boom in cheap publications in Welsh.[19] It would be surprising to find that commercialisation in any of the three regions matched what was seen in England. But this does not mean that we should not follow the example of more recent historians of English popular culture, by paying attention to the adaptability and continuity of popular forms, as well as to their suppression or decline.[20]

* * *

At times, of course, the themes of loss and decay become impossible to avoid. In the case of Ireland the early and mid-nineteenth century stands out as one such period. By the 1820s and '30s observers were increasingly aware of the rapid decline among the rural lower classes of traditional customs and beliefs. There was also a dramatic change in language. The proportion of respondents to the census of 1881 claiming an ability to speak Irish falls from 41 per cent of those born in the decade 1801–11 to only 28 per cent of those born in the 1830s.[21] What was involved was not just a change in behaviour, but the beginnings of a revolution in mentalities. People, in the words of one antiquarian, were becoming 'too sensible etc' to believe in such things as holy wells with curative powers.[22] The transformation of outlook was also evident in the rapid politicisation of the 1820s and after. All of these changes were massively accelerated by the particular havoc which the Famine of 1845–50 wreaked on those sections

---

[18] Samuel Madden, *Reflections and Resolutions Proper for the Gentlemen of Ireland* (Dublin, 1738), p. 69; *Dublin Daily Post*, 4 June 1739; *Autobiography and Correspondence of Mary Granville, Mrs Delany*, (series 1, London, 1861), II, p. 365.
[19] Houston and Whyte, eds., *Scottish Society*, p. 34; Jenkins, *Foundations of Modern Wales*, pp. 409–17.
[20] R. D. Storch, 'Introduction: Persistence and Change in Nineteenth-Century Popular Culture', in Storch, ed., *Popular Culture and Custom in Nineteenth-Century England* (London, 1982).
[21] Garret Fitzgerald, 'Estimates for Baronies of Minimum Levels of Irish Speaking', *Proceedings of the Royal Irish Academy*, C, 84 (1984).
[22] Royal Irish Academy, Ordnance Survey Letters, King's County, I, 28.

of the population among whom traditional practices and beliefs, as well as Irish language speaking, had remained strongest. By the 1850s and '60s Irish folklorists were writing in terms of a lost world of popular custom and ritual.

These rapid changes in behaviour and outlook can be explained in a variety of ways. Improved communications and greater mobility (including the service of tens of thousands of men in the navy and army during the French wars) helped to open up hitherto isolated communities to new ideas and standards of behaviour. Involvement in a more open and sophisticated economic system diminished the appeal of customs constructed around the need to seek magical protection against a world of unseen forces, and undermined a pattern of recreation and sociability built on the alternating bouts of intense work and unrestrained festivity characteristic of a subsistence economy. Rising living standards for some sections of the population encouraged new aspirations and the adoption of new models of behaviour. Many of the same developments were at work in Wales, where accounts from the late eighteenth and early nineteenth centuries also spoke of falling support for patronal festivals, calendar customs, and customary recreations, and the decay of musical and other traditions.[23] On the other hand the Welsh language, with its greatly superior opportunities for literacy, remained considerably stronger than Irish. As late as 1879 Welsh was still spoken by 71 per cent of the population, its decline beginning in earnest only with the migration of large numbers of English speakers into the region in the last decades of the nineteenth century.[24]

Cultural discontinuities were less marked in Scotland than in either Wales or Ireland. Industrialisation in Lowland Scotland does not seem to have produced the widespread decline of popular amusements that has been suggested for contemporary England.[25] In the Highlands too changes in customs and mentality appear to have been gradual, despite the devastating effects of the economic restructuring of the region. Language change was certainly slow. The proportion of Gaelic speakers in Scotland as a whole fell from an estimated 25–30 per cent at the end of the seventeenth century to 23 per cent in the late 1760s and to 18 per cent by 1806. But this was at a time when the Highland share of total Scottish population was declining. As late as 1879 Gaelic was still spoken by 81 per cent of the population of the four main Highland counties.[26] One reason for the slower pace of cultural change may lie in the more polarised nature of Highland society. The divide between a minority of large farmers and a large majority of crofters did not offer the same opportunities for social emulation and the downward transmission of new ideas and models of

---

[23] Morgan, 'From a Death to a View', pp. 53–6.

[24] W. T. R. Pryce, 'Wales as a Culture Region: Patterns of Change 1750–1971', *Trans. of the Honourable Society of Cymmrodorion* (1978); Glanmor Williams, *Religion, Language and Nationality in Wales* (Cardiff, 1979), pp. 145–6.

[25] W. Hamish Fraser, 'Developments in Leisure', in W. Hamish Fraser and R. J. Morris, eds., *People and Society in Scotland*, Vol. II: *1830–1914* (Edinburgh, 1990), pp. 237–8.

[26] Withers, *Gaelic in Scotland*, pp. 53, 70–1, 79–83, 94–7.

behaviour as the more graduated hierarchy of large, medium and small farmers, cottiers and landless labourers, that existed in rural Ireland.

The single most important development behind the cultural and linguistic changes of the early nineteenth century was the growth of elementary education. In Ireland the number of children attending school rose from an estimated 200,000 in 1806 to more than 560,000 by 1824.[27] In Wales the circulating schools founded by Griffith Jones to teach basic literacy through Welsh attracted huge numbers: between 1731 and 1779 as many as a quarter of a million pupils may have learned to read in these schools, at a time when the total population of Wales was less than twice that number. Two-thirds of those attending were adults.[28] In the case of Scotland Rab Houston has zestfully undermined the extravagant claims once made for the educational attainments of the eighteenth century. Yet even he concludes that literacy levels in the mid-eighteenth-century Lowlands were slightly higher than those in southern England, and moved further ahead over the decades that followed. Recent work on the Highlands, suggesting that there too educational provision and attainment were expanding in the early nineteenth century, completes the picture of a Celtic periphery in which the demand for literacy was rising rapidly.[29]

Such a demand is easier to describe than to explain. Economic development brought a certain increase in the currency of banknotes, bills of exchange, and other written instruments. The widening role of government agencies and the development of popular politics further increased the utility of reading and, to a lesser extent, writing. Yet none of this seems sufficient to explain the substantial investment of money and effort by which small farmers and rural tradesmen sought to endow their children with these skills. Literacy, Houston concludes, should be seen as a cultural preference, 'a non-functional attribute associated with social prestige'.[30] But this leaves the question of why that cultural preference should have been so widely exercised, in all three regions, at this particular time. One explanation would be that the popular demand was less for literacy itself than for instruction in English, the utility of which, as the language of the law and the landlord class, of politics and trade, was obvious enough. Certainly the evidence is that Irish parents, like parents both in Wales and in the Scottish Highlands, were generally opposed to their children, when they did attend school, learning any language other than English. Alternatively, we might consider a psychological explanation: that a location on the periphery of an economically dynamic state encouraged a mentality in which people felt obliged to seize every opportunity, however slender, to improve the life-chances of their children or themselves.

---

[27] Mary Daly, 'The Development of the National School System 1831–40', in Art Cosgrove and Donal Macartney, eds., *Studies in Irish History* (Naas, 1979), p. 151.

[28] Jenkins, *Foundations of Modern Wales*, pp. 370–81.

[29] R. A. Houston, *Scottish Literacy and the Scottish Identity: Illiteracy and Society in Scotland and Northern England 1600–1800* (Cambridge, 1985), pp. 2–3, 56–7, 159–60; Donald J. Withrington, 'Schooling, Literacy and Society', in Devine and Mitchison, eds., *People and Society*, I, 164–70, 178, 181–2.

[30] Houston, *Scottish Literacy*, p. 160.

A further contrast between the experiences of Ireland, Scotland and Wales concerns the evolution of popular religion. In all three areas the first half of the nineteenth century saw major developments: the rise of Nonconformity in Wales, the explosive growth of evangelicalism in the Highlands, as well as in certain Lowland communities, a similar rise in popular evangelicalism among Irish Protestants, and the beginnings of what has been labelled a 'devotional revolution' among Irish Catholics. As in other areas of popular culture, however, the discontinuities are more apparent in Ireland than elsewhere. The new style Catholic clergy, organised into a centralised, authoritarian ecclesiastical machine devoted to the imposition of a blend of Roman orthodoxy and Victorian morality, contrast sharply with *na daoine*, the evangelical lay preachers of the north-west Highlands, whose fervent piety remained firmly rooted in the indigenous popular culture.[31] Welsh nonconformity and Scottish evangelicalism also responded to popular preferences in maintaining Welsh and Gaelic as languages of religious worship in a way that the Irish Catholic church did not.

New developments in popular religion highlight once again the inadequacy of an analysis focused solely on themes of loss and decline. In the case of Ireland, it is important to remember, in the first place, that popular culture did not consist solely of the vanishing traditions of the rural Catholic poor. There was also urban Protestant Ulster, where the political and religious traditions of Orangeism, with all the associated paraphernalia of gable wall iconography, music and procession, grew and were elaborated during the nineteenth century, adapting to the new possibilities opened up by urbanisation and the railway. For a much larger section of urban Ireland, one might point to the development of new forms of sociability linked to self help. By 1911 more than one-third of the adult male population of Dublin were members of friendly societies, including bodies like the Irish National Foresters which united the functions of their English models with a role as vehicles for popular patriotism.[32] Even in rural Catholic Ireland, furthermore, there were new developments as well as the loss of old forms. The growth of literacy may have hastened the death of Irish. But it also opened the way for the growth of a vigorous provincial press, whose content and place in popular culture have yet to be properly examined. There was also the influence of conscious cultural revivalism. The Gaelic League may be dismissed as a minority movement, appealing primarily to intellectually minded members of the urban middle classes. The Gaelic Athletic Association, on the other hand, made a real contribution to popular culture, particularly in the countryside. Once again its role, like that of the Football Association in England, was to adapt traditional sports to meet the new opportunities opened up by improved transport and rising spending power.[33]

---

[31] James Hunter, 'The Emergence of the Crofting Community: The Religious Contribution 1798–1843', *Scottish Studies*, 18 (1974).

[32] A. D. Buckley, '"On the Club": Friendly Societies in Ireland' *Ir. Econ. and Soc. Hist.* XIV (1987).

[33] W. F. Mandle, 'The Gaelic Athletic Association and Popular Culture 1884–1924', in Oliver MacDonagh *et al.*, eds., *Irish Culture and Nationalism 1750–1950* (London, 1983).

Adaptation and invention were not confined to Ireland. In Wales too the early and mid-nineteenth century saw such developments as the marking out of certain old-fashioned points of costume, originally shared with England, as a distinctive Welsh dress, and (if recent work is to be believed) the fabrication of an entire Welsh musical tradition.[34] A similar interest in national symbols can be detected in Scotland, although in this case both the mythologised Highland tradition of tartan, bagpipes and whiskey, and the idealised vision of Lowland rural life offered by Scottish novelists of the kailyard school, stand out rather more clearly as artificial constructs, appealing primarily to the exile, the tourist and the native middle classes.[35]

Technological change in the twentieth century makes it increasingly difficult to discuss the popular culture of any region in isolation. To take only the case of southern Ireland, political independence may have permitted new forms of official support for approved 'native' forms. But this was more than balanced by a new vulnerability to cultural penetration, as the printed word was joined and partly superseded by the radio and, even more, by the cinema. Here the Irish, like the Scots, quickly overtook the English as avid consumers: by 1942 there were complaints of 'Los Angelesicisation'.[36] But indigenous cultural forms could still adapt to new circumstances. In traditional music, for example, the early decades of the twentieth century saw the emergence of a wholly new grouping, the ceilidh band. This in part reflected the influence of commercial musical styles in Britain and the United States, especially as experienced by musicians within Irish immigrant communities. In part it was a response to new requirements: the need to produce a sound that would be audible as dancing moved from the farmhouse kitchen to the commercial dance hall, and also the technical demands of gramophone recording and radio.[37] Meanwhile the big bands established from the 1920s, and their successors the showbands of the 1950s and 60s, created a less original but nevertheless distinctive mix of American, English and Irish styles.[38] These, of course, are isolated examples in a field of which we know very little. The dance halls, the cinemas, or even the radio and television studios of the twentieth century, like the bull baitings and prize fights of the eighteenth, are territories into which historians, in Ireland at least, have yet to set more than a tentative foot. Yet it is surely there, rather than in the image of a 'hidden Ireland' expiring with unconscionable slowness across a period of three centuries, that the real history of popular culture remains to be written.

---

[34] Morgan, 'From a Death to a View', p. 56ff.

[35] Ian Carter, 'The Changing Image of the Scottish Peasantry 1745–1980', in Raphael Samuel, ed., *People's History and Socialist Theory* (London, 1981), p. 11.

[36] Brian Kennedy, *Dreams and Responsibilities: The State and the Arts in Independent Ireland* (Dublin, 1990), p. 35. For attendance figures see D. S. Johnson, *The Interwar Economy in Ireland* (Dundalk, 1985), p. 42; T. C. Smout, *A Century of the Scottish People 1830–1930* (London, 1986), p. 158.

[37] Barry Taylor, 'The Irish Ceilidh Band—A Break with Tradition?', *Dal gCais*, 7 (1984).

[38] Vincent Power, *Send 'em Home Sweatin': The Showbands' Story* (Dublin, 1990), pp. 22, 392–3.

9

Corporate values in Hanoverian Edinburgh and Dublin[1]

Jacqueline Hill

EIGHTEENTH-CENTURY POLITICAL HISTORY is currently in a state of flux as historians grapple with the implications of changing views of the Stuart era. In both periods, attention is shifting away from parliament towards comparatively neglected institutions, especially the monarchy, aristocracy and established church.[2] It was these institutions, according to J. C. D. Clark, which were responsible for generating the dominant political and social culture which set the terms of reference within which discussion about politics and society could take place.[3] Thus it has been claimed that eighteenth-century reformers were more commonly prompted by religious than secular considerations, their target the church, or the dynasty, rather than the extension of the franchise.[4] Such claims draw strength from the revised view of the influence of Locke on politics: his contract theory, it seems, aroused limited interest, even in America and Ireland.[5] From a somewhat different angle, J. G. A. Pocock has identified an alternative set of tensions in the early and mid-Hanoverian era: between those who still clung to the civic tradition of 'virtue', valuing the independent freeholder over the placeman or rentier and upholding the independence of monarch, lords and commons, and those who welcomed the appearance of a (paid) government bureaucracy, a professional army, and new forms of credit to fund commercial expansion and the national

---

[1] I am grateful to Rab Houston, Cadoc Leighton and David Stevenson for comments on an earlier draft of this paper.

[2] See, for instance, M. L. Bush, *The English Aristocracy* (Manchester, 1984); John Cannon, *Aristocratic Century: The Peerage of Eighteenth-Century England* (Cambridge, 1984); J. C. D. Clark, *English Society, 1688–1832* (Cambridge, 1985); Idem., *Revolution and Rebellion* (Cambridge, 1986). Forthcoming work on the established church is noted in J. C. D. Clark, 'England's Ancien Regime as a Confessional State', *Albion*, XXI (1989), p. 452, note 9.

[3] Clark, *English Society*, pp. 42–4, 77–9, 121–41.

[4] *Ibid.*, pp. 290–9.

[5] See John Dunn, 'The Politics of Locke in England and America in the Eighteenth Century', in J. Yolton, ed., *John Locke, Problems and Perspectives* (Cambridge, 1969); Patrick Kelly, 'Perceptions of Locke in Eighteenth-Century Ireland', *Royal Irish Academy Proceedings*, Sect. C, LXXXIX (1989), pp. 17–35.

debt.⁶ All this marks the return of a debate about ideology to the centre stage of eighteenth-century history, from which it was largely displaced by the work of Sir Lewis Namier published some sixty years ago.⁷

An important part of the present debate concerns the role and outlook of the electorate. For Clark, patriarchy and deference were so characteristic of social relations before the nineteenth century that the existence of any significant pressure from below to overturn oligarchy or increase 'democracy' can effectively be discounted.⁸ Others, including Nicholas Rogers and John Phillips, have taken a different view. Evidence from London and certain other towns, it is claimed, points to 'a new assertiveness' on the part of townsmen by the mid-eighteenth century, manifesting itself in campaigns against oligarchy with national as well as local dimensions.⁹

If Clark's conclusions about the nature of English society—conclusions which have already had an impact on the writing of eighteenth-century history¹⁰—have failed to convince certain leading urban historians, then this may reflect the somewhat selective use he makes of a concept borrowed from continental history: that of 'ancien regime'. In Clark's hands the concept is invoked with considerable verve to revitalise those aspects of English society, Anglican, aristocratic and monarchical, which the author believes have been underestimated. Little attention, however, is devoted to that other component of ancien regimes—the third estate, or bourgeoisie. Where mention is made in *English Society* of the bourgeoisie it is chiefly to assert that there existed in England no specialised bourgeois culture such as could be found in France; merchants as well as professional men deferred to the landed elite in manners and values.¹¹ Whether these assertions are correct or not, the third estate would benefit from a less perfunctory treatment than it receives in *English Society*. A comparative view would also be helpful. One of the features of the present debate is the willingness, even eagerness, with which the protagonists extend their arguments beyond England to other parts of the Hanoverian dominions, in a sometimes explicit rejection of Anglocentric history.¹² Accordingly, it may be asked, how did members of the bourgeoisie in Scotland and Ireland view their place in society? Is an ancien regime model helpful in understanding their views, and if so, can any light be shed on the deference/assertiveness debate? This

---

⁶ J. G. A. Pocock, 'Virtue and Commerce in the Eighteenth Century', *Journal of Interdisciplinary History*, III (1972), pp. 119–34.

⁷ Lewis Namier, *The Structure of Politics at the Accession of George III* (London, 1929).

⁸ Clark, *English Society*, pp. 17–26, 70–1, 76–8.

⁹ Nicholas Rogers, *Whigs and Cities: Popular Politics in the Age of Walpole and Pitt* (Oxford, 1989), p. 405; John A. Phillips, 'From Municipal Matters to Parliamentary Principles: Eighteenth-Century Borough Politics in Maidstone', *Jn. British Studies*, XXVII (1988), pp. 327–51.

¹⁰ See for instance the articles in *Albion*, XXI, 3 (1989).

¹¹ Clark, *English Society*, pp. 70–1.

¹² See for example, J. G. A. Pocock, 'The Limits and Divisions of British History: In Search of the Unknown Subject', *American Historical Review*, LXXXVII (1982), pp. 311–36; J. C. D. Clark, 'Revolution in the English Atlantic Empire 1660–1800', in E. Rice, ed., *Revolution and Counter Revolution* (Oxford, 1990).

paper sets out to assess the outlook of two spokesmen for urban craftsmen, Alexander Pennecuik (d. 1730)[13] of Edinburgh and Charles Lucas (1713–71) of Dublin.[14]

First, however, some points about the estates. Anglocentric historiography has commonly focused on the assembly of estates (parliament) to the neglect of the estates themselves. Whatever the merits of such an approach for English history, it appears inappropriate for Scotland and Ireland. The Scottish parliament, at least down to 1689, has been described as little more than a rubber stamp for royal policy, and it disappeared altogether with the Union of 1707.[15] The Irish parliament only gained legislative independence in 1782, and even then remained subordinate to an executive appointed by the crown.[16] But the vitality of parliaments does not necessarily reflect the vitality of the estates themselves. In France, for instance, the estates-general was moribund from the early seventeenth century until its fateful recall in 1789; but no-one would claim that the French aristocracy, church or bourgeoisie lacked identity or importance.

The idea of the state as composed of orders or estates (rather than of individuals) is central to most definitions of 'ancien regime'.[17] Georges Duby, in a brilliant account, has traced the medieval origins and evolution of the classic pattern of three orders, differentiated by function (reflected in the adage 'those who pray, those who fight, and those who work').[18] Each had its own privileges, regulated by the monarch; each was composed of smaller bodies, corporations, colleges and the like. Values of hierarchy and reciprocity permeated the system and organic metaphors were popular. The two higher orders, the aristocracy and the church, were perceived to possess noble status. The third order, which, as Duby points out, represented a better-off urban minority, was not noble (though by the 1700s some of its members had acquired noble attributes): its privileges, concerning trade and self-government, were obtained in return for royal access to its wealth and for services rendered to trade.[19] Within each order there were divisions, such as between a higher and lesser nobility. In the case of townsmen, divisions commonly

---

[13] Alexander Pennecuik, merchant and burgess of Edinburgh; author of the often reprinted *An Historical Account of the Blue Blanket, or Craftsmen's Banner* (1722) and other works; see *Dictionary of National Biography* [*D.N.B.*]

[14] Charles Lucas, freeman of the barber-surgeons' guild of Dublin; MP Dublin city, 1761–71. See *D.N.B.* and notes 42–4 below.

[15] T. C. Smout, *A History of the Scottish People 1560–1830* (Glasgow, 1972 edn), p. 201.

[16] T. W. Moody and W. E. Vaughan, eds., *A New History of Ireland*, Vol. IV: *Eighteenth-Century Ireland 1691–1800* (Oxford, 1986), pp. 265-6.

[17] For a discussion of different definitions of 'ancien regime', see Douglas A. Leighton, 'The Meaning of the Catholic Question, 1750–1790: Religious Aspects of the Irish Ancien Regime' (unpublished Ph.D. thesis, University of Cambridge, 1990), ch. 2; *idem, Catholicism in a Protestant Kingdom: A Study of the Irish Ancien Regime* (Dublin, forthcoming 1993).

[18] Georges Duby, *The Three Orders: Feudal Society Imagined* (Chicago and London, 1980). In some countries there were four estates, with a peasant elite making up the fourth; see A. R. Myers, *Parliaments and Estates in Europe to 1789* (London, 1975), p. 11.

[19] Duby, *Three Orders*, pp. 345–6, 354–5; Myers, *Parliaments and Estates*, pp. 155–6.

formed around merchant elites and guilds of craftsmen, with the latter complaining about oligarchical tendencies in the former: such tensions led to struggles in many towns and cities in Italy and northern Europe during and after the Middle Ages.[20] Finally, all the orders were anxious to defend their distinctive privileges. This might involve resistance to pressure from the monarchy or from other orders; equally, it might mean countering challenges from the 'unfree' masses, and defending monarchy as the linchpin and regulator of the existing system.[21]

At first sight, an ancien regime model appears more likely to shed light on Scotland than on Ireland. Scottish historians have been more inclined than their Irish counterparts to talk of 'estates' and to analyse the state in terms of functional groups.[22] It is worth noting that, while the Union of 1707 removed parliamentary representation to London, all the Scottish estates were confirmed in their privileges.[23] The third, or 'burgess' estate, for instance, continued to enjoy an institutional existence as an estate of the realm through the Convention of Royal Burghs. This body, representing burgesses in royal burghs, met annually and exercised considerable influence in municipal and trading matters.[24] The continued vitality of the estates after 1707 goes far to explain why the loss of the Scottish parliament turned out to be so relatively painless.

Within the royal burghs the same broad divisions were to be found as existed in many continental towns. The first of these was the fundamental one between 'freemen'—the minority who enjoyed some sort of corporate existence with attendant privileges—and the non-free. In Edinburgh, the former numbered some 1,200 out of a total population of about 36,000 in the Old Town at mid-century. The freemen, however, were themselves divided into merchants and the socially inferior craftsmen, or 'incorporated trades'.[25] The latter had begun to organise and obtain trading privileges relatively late in Scotland, at a time (the fifteenth century) when merchants had already become highly exclusive, enjoying much influence in town councils, and monopolising representation in the Convention of Royal Burghs. Hence many of the Edinburgh trades owed their original charters of incorporation ('seals of cause') to the town council rather than to royal charters or statute law. Moreover, it was the merchant-dominated town council, rather than the trades, which continued to

---

[20] Antony Black, *Guilds and Civil Society in European Political Thought from the Twelfth Century to the Present* (London, 1984), ch. 5.

[21] Duby, *Three Orders*, p. 346.

[22] James Colston, *The Incorporated Trades of Edinburgh* (Edinburgh, 1891), p. xix; George Smith Pryde, *Scotland from 1603 to the Present Day* (London and Edinburgh, 1962), pp. 12–13; John Stuart Shaw, *The Management of Scottish Society 1707–1764* (Edinburgh, 1983), pp. 2–3.

[23] Rosalind Mitchison, *A History of Scotland*, 2nd edn (London and New York, 1982), p. 309.

[24] On the activities of the Convention see Ian H. Adams, *The Making of Urban Scotland* (London and Montreal, 1978), pp. 45–6.

[25] Jane Rendall, *The Origins of the Scottish Enlightenment* (London, 1978), p. 17; Smout, *History of the Scottish People*, pp. 153–66.

regulate markets, prices and hours of sale.[26] As a result, there were periodic tensions between the town council and the trades, with a recurrent claim by the latter that they should be allowed to elect their own deacons (the equivalent of masters in English and Irish guilds) or council representatives.[27] The trades, however, were not entirely without influence in the municipality. From the sixteenth century on they had their own representative body, the convener's court, comprising the deacons of the trades; and though it lacked legal powers, the court did exercise influence over the selection of Edinburgh's civic magistrates.[28] It was the convener of trades who acted as the guardian of the banner of the trades and symbol of their privileges, the so-called 'blue blanket', around which Pennecuik was to construct his eulogy of the trades in 1722.

Pennecuik's pamphlet was written against the background of a renewed drive on the part of the Edinburgh trades in the early 1720s to extend their influence in the municipality.[29] The trades contended that the convener of trades should have a seat in the town council not simply as one of the deacons, but in his official capacity, and that he should be a member of all committees. The town council resisted, calling for the abolition of the convener's privileges. (In 1730 a compromise was reached through the earl of Islay; the convener's existing rights were confirmed, but meetings of the deacons and crafts were to be subject to the consent of the town council.)[30] In the meantime, Pennecuik, an Edinburgh burgess and freeman of the merchants' guild, had come to the defence of the trades. *An Historical Account of the Blue Blanket: or Crafts-Men's Banner* (Edinburgh, 1722) was subtitled *Containing the Fundamental Principles of the Good-Town, with the Powers and Prerogatives of the Crafts of Edinburgh*. It set out to provide a historic vindication of the Edinburgh craftsmen, and was dedicated to the deacons of the trades 'and remanent Members of the Fourteen Incorporations in the Good Town of Edinburgh'.

Study of the pamphlet reveals that the author took for granted the ancien-regime values outlined above. There was an implicit acknowledgement that tradesmen or 'Mechanicks' were of 'obscure Birth', which, in the absence of education, naturally tended to produce a 'servile' outlook.[31] Nevertheless, the defects of birth or education were no barrier to achieving distinction in the state, as long as the tradesmen remained true to their corporate identity and upheld the privileges

---

[26] W. Cunningham, 'The Guildry and Trade Incorporations in Scottish Towns', *Transactions of the Royal Historical Society*, 3rd series, VII (1913), pp. 6–7; Colston, *Incorporated Trades*, pp. xxiv–xxx; W. M. Mackenzie, *The Scottish Burghs* (Edinburgh, 1949), pp. 115–17, 126.

[27] Colston, *Incorporated Trades*, pp. xxxii–iv.

[28] *Ibid.*, pp. xliii–vii. Such courts, together with a local banner or 'blue blanket', existed in several of the leading burghs.

[29] *Ibid.*, p. xlv. A similar drive was going on in Inverness, where the trades applied for and were granted some representation on the town council in 1722: Mackenzie, *Scottish Burghs*, p. 126.

[30] Colston, *Incorporated Trades*, p. xlvi.

[31] Alexander Pennecuik, *An Historical Account of the Blue Blanket* (reproduced in Colston, *Incorporated Trades*, pp. 177–237, at pp. 182–3).

extended to them in return for service to their monarchs.[32] Thus a corporate understanding of the state—in which functional groups enjoyed appropriate privileges—was fundamental to Pennecuik's outlook.

Much of the pamphlet may be read as a confidence-building exercise, bearing in mind the lowly status traditionally accorded to trade. Wise princes, the author asserted, esteemed tradesmen and recognised their contribution to national prosperity and power. And had not Louis XIV made watches?[33] However, the main point was not that monarchs had sometimes acted like tradesmen, but that tradesmen had often acted like aristocrats, and had been rewarded for doing so. The 'blue blanket' itself, the author contended, was properly known as the 'Banner of the Holy Ghost', the name given to the standard followed by 'Vast Numbers of Scots Mechanicks' who at the onset of the crusades responded to Urban II's call for Christians to liberate Jerusalem from Islam. Furthermore, Pennecuik alleged, the banner was 'as Ancient, and more Honourable than the English Order of the Garter', for it had received royal as well as ecclesiastical sanction. Consequently, he asserted, 'The Crafts of Edinburgh having this Order of the Blanket to glory in, may justly take upon them the Title of Knights of the Blanket, or Chevaliers of Arms'.[34] And he proceeded to outline the 'extra-ordinary Proofs of Loyalty' by which the trades had won royal favour, ranging from participation in wars against Danes, Picts, Romans and English, to defending monarchs against rebellious nobles.[35] The account was laced with panegyrics on the institution of monarchy ('an Invention of Divine Wisdom'), denunciations of the 'Popish doctrine of merit', and acknowledgements of the need for 'Obedience to Superiors'.[36]

It would be hard to deny the great weight that Pennecuik attached to aristocratic and confessional values,[37] nor his dedication to the institution of monarchy. It is also worth noting that his portrayal of the trades as a plebian aristocracy was not just an affectation. In the feudal period towns had often served as royal outposts in a hostile countryside, so that freemen of towns had both then and later been required to bear arms in defence of the town and of the king. The bearing of arms, together with the fact that freemen could pass on certain privileges to their sons, served to set them apart from the mass of the population and to give them a real sense of identity with the aristocracy. Thus far there is nothing to challenge Clark's generalisations. However, it is also necessary to emphasise that the thrust of Pennecuik's recommendations to the tradesmen was that they should defend their distinctive privileges, no matter who might be inconvenienced.[38] Indeed, he was

---

[32] *Ibid.*, p. 178.
[33] *Ibid.*, p. 185.
[34] *Ibid.*, pp. 185, 188–90.
[35] *Ibid.*, pp. 187, 189–90.
[36] *Ibid.*, pp. 193–4, 203, 236–7.
[37] Note Pennecuik's praise for James VI as 'the first Protestant King of Scotland': *Ibid.*, pp. 210–11.
[38] *Ibid.*, pp. 178, 193–4.

writing at a time when the tradesmen were displaying one of their periodic bouts of assertiveness in an effort to increase their rights in what was a highly oligarchic municipality. True, they were not seeking to extend the parliamentary franchise, but the 'deference' they displayed was clearly of a qualified kind.

The value of an ancien regime model for Ireland appears, initially at least, much less promising. For one thing, other models have been strongly favoured by historians. The Protestant aristocracy and gentry, as well as the established church, have been presented as 'colonial' forces, while those with opposition or 'Patriot' tendencies are designated 'colonial nationalists', or even forerunners of liberalism.[39] As for a bourgeoisie, the lack of specific studies of Church of Ireland urban communities has promoted the erroneous view that 'nearly all' members of the trading community were Catholics or Dissenters,[40] implying that, for much of the country, there was little or nothing to constitute a third estate in ancien regime terms. As for the guilds themselves, those in Dublin (twenty five in all, including a powerful merchants' guild whose members dominated the board of aldermen) are alleged to have evolved by the mid-1700s into 'political clubs', their privileges in respect of trade falling into disuse.[41] Such a development was possible because, unlike the Edinburgh freemen, the 3,000 or so freemen of Dublin, four fifths of whom were in fact Church of Ireland members, could exercise the parliamentary franchise (out of a population of about 130,000 in 1749).[42] It is acknowledged that these freemen were politicised in the 1740s, but this politicisation has been given a nationalist gloss; their leader, Charles Lucas (a freeman of the barber-surgeon's guild), has been described as 'a colonial nationalist of a much more radical hue than Molyneux or Swift'.[43]

Lucas's criticism of the subordinate status of the Irish parliament, and of the oligarchical nature of Dublin corporation, had by 1750 incurred the condemnation of the Irish executive, parliament and Dublin corporation; he escaped arrest and imprisonment only by flight and exile abroad. In 1760, however, the accession of a new king paved the way for a royal pardon and a triumphant return to Dublin, where the corporation was reformed to give greater rights to the guilds and to the lower house in which sat the guild representatives. Lucas's own election as one of the city MPs put the seal on these achievements. The rights of the Irish parliament now came to the fore; in the winter of 1767/8 the Patriot opposition, of whom Lucas

---

[39] See for example, Moody and Vaughan eds., *New History of Ireland* IV, chs. 5 and 8; Joseph Leerssen, 'Anglo-Irish Patriotism and its European Context: Notes Towards a Reassessment', *Eighteenth-Century Ireland* III (1988), p. 15. But for a recent and illuminating application of an ancien regime model to Ireland, see S. J. Connolly, *Religion, Law and Power: The Making of Protestant Ireland 1660-1760* (Oxford, 1992).

[40] William Doyle, *The Old European Order 1660–1800* (Oxford, 1978), p. 146.

[41] John J. Webb, *The Guilds of Dublin* (Dublin, 1929), p. 242. For a different view, see Leighton, 'Meaning of the Catholic Question', ch. 4.

[42] Sean Murphy, 'Municipal Politics and Popular Disturbances: 1660–1800', in Art Cosgrove, ed., *Dublin Through the Ages* (Dublin, 1988), p. 79. In Edinburgh the parliamentary franchise was restricted to members of the town council.

[43] Murphy, 'Municipal Politics', p. 85.

was a prominent member, finally obtained the passage of legislation limiting the duration of Irish parliaments.[44] It was at this point, however, in what looks like an aberration, that Lucas published a defence of the trading privileges of the Dublin guilds.[45]

The immediate background to the publication of *The Liberties and Customs of Dublin Asserted and Demonstrated Upon the Principles of Law, Justice and Good Policy* was the so-called 'quarterage dispute', in which the Catholic merchants and craftsmen of the towns challenged the right of the guilds of Dublin and other corporate towns to compel all tradesmen who were not free of the guilds to pay a quarterly fee ('quarterage') to allow them to carry on their trade.[46] Since Restoration times Catholics had been excluded from freedom of guilds, and a quarterage system, not unlike that which existed in London, had been in operation, catering for all those who for religious or financial reasons were reluctant or unable to take out their freedom. There is little sign of outright opposition to the system in Ireland until the 1750s, when Catholics increasingly resisted the payments. When their resist-ance was upheld in the courts, the freemen of the corporate towns mounted a campaign to obtain statutory backing for the quarterage system. This campaign in turn was strongly resisted by Catholics, backed by the newly-founded Catholic Committee (1760).[47] Lucas was a leading advocate of the measure in parliament, introducing heads of a quarterage bill in November 1767. His pamphlet was thus published while debate on the question was at its height.

Lucas began his defence of the quarterage system with a eulogy on cities ('the Strength and Glory of every Nation, the Nurseries of Literature, Polity and Arts, the Seminaries of Commerce, and the Bulwarks of Liberty'). The more nations esteemed freedom, he contended, the more eager they were to build and strengthen cities:

> and in order to induce Men to inhabit, to cultivate, to improve, and to defend them, it has ever been found necessary to indue a certain Society of Men with certain Franchises, Privileges, Immunities and Pre-eminencies, superior to foreigners or extern Men, to invest them with Powers, distinct from the ordinary Subjects, particularly with a Property in the Soil, and the local Government of the City, and sometimes with an exclusive Right to Trade.[48]

---

[44] For an outline of Lucas's career in Dublin, see Sean Murphy, 'The Corporation of Dublin 1660–1760', in *Dublin Historical Record* XXXVIII (1984), pp. 22–35; Idem, 'Charles Lucas and the Dublin Election of 1748–1749', *Parliamentary History* II (1983), pp. 93–111.

[45] Charles Lucas, *The Liberties and Customs of Dublin Asserted and Demonstrated Upon the Principles of Law, Justice and Good Policy: With a Comparative View of the Constitutions of London and Dublin. And Some Considerations of the Customs of Intrusion and Quarterage* 2nd edn (Dublin, 1768) (an expanded version of a pamphlet first published in 1767).

[46] On the quarterage dispute, see Maureen McGeehin (Wall) 'The Catholics of the Towns and the Quarterage Dispute in Eighteenth-Century Ireland', *Irish Historical Studies* VIII (1952), pp. 91–114. For a reassessment, see Leighton, 'Meaning of the Catholic Question', ch. 4.

[47] McGeehin, 'Catholics of the Towns', 101–2. For London, see J. R. Kellett, 'The Breakdown of Gild and Corporation Control over the Handicraft and Retail Trade in London', *Econ. Hist. Rev.* X (1958), pp. 381–94.

[48] Lucas, *The Liberties and Customs*, p. 7.

In other words, Lucas was defending a distinctive order within the realm, enjoying privileges concerning trade and self-government: a third estate. Like Pennecuik, he was at pains to emphasise the military or 'aristocratic' role of the freemen; those of Dublin, he asserted, had distinguished themselves by defending the city 'from Traitors and Rebels, and other Enemies of the Crown, as well *English, and Scotch*, as *Irish*',[49] and this had earned the gratitude of successive kings and the issue of many charters and confirmation of privileges. Trading and other privileges, he argued, had been confirmed in recognition of the fact that those who took out their freedom served the city and crown in a double capacity, civil and military. Such men also bore substantial costs in becoming free; why should they incur these costs if they obtained no privileges? In particular, Lucas asked, why should 'Papists and other persons' who refused to take the required oaths be admitted to trading privileges? Statutory backing for the quarterage system would not only restore peace and harmony in the towns, it would 'extend and secure the established Religion'.[50]

To acknowledge that Lucas's argument was steeped with aristocratic, monarchical and confessional values is not to deny that in certain respects his case for the Dublin guilds differed from Pennecuik's on behalf of the Edinburgh trades. For one thing, while Pennecuik portrayed the trades as literally a plebeian aristocracy, Lucas preferred to align the Dublin freemen with their counterparts in London. Where Pennecuik had condemned the Edinburgh trades for their excesses in the 1640s, Lucas heaped praise on the London freemen for their role as 'the Bulwark of the Kingdom's liberties' in the same period.[51] He eulogised the Londoners for their opposition to 'the detestable Walpole', to standing armies, long parliaments and placemen (thus placing himself firmly on the side of 'virtue' in the debate identified by Pocock).[52] But according to Lucas the Londoners had also staunchly defended their trading privileges. The point of all this was to identify the Dublin freemen with a body of men who were perceived to be active in defence of their own political and trading privileges, and whose stand on these matters had apparently been recognised by the Hanoverian monarchs.[53] The similarity between the constitutions of London and Dublin, in which craftsmen as well as merchants enjoyed extensive political as well as trading rights, gave this exercise credibility; for Lucas, Dublin had as good a title to 'an exclusive Trade and every other Custom and Privilege founded upon Prescription, Charter, or Statute as *London* does or can make out'.[54]

Some differences in the outlook of Lucas and Pennecuik are also discernible in religious matters. For the latter, the Edinburgh trades from Reformation times on

---

[49] *Ibid.*, p. 43.

[50] *Ibid.*, pp. 50–5, 64.

[51] Pennecuik, *An Historical Account*, p. 237; Lucas, *The Liberties and Customs*, pp. 28–9.

[52] Lucas, *The Liberties and Customs*, pp. 31–4.

[53] *Ibid.*, pp. 34–5. Lucas pointed to the marks of favour bestowed by the Hanoverian monarchs on London corporation, and to Dublin corporation's contribution to the Hanoverian succession (pp. 31, 43).

[54] *Ibid.*, p. 48. For the efforts of the London guilds to maintain the principle of guild control, see Kellett, 'The Breakdown of Gild and Corporation Control'.

had helped to foster true religion against Popish error. Lucas had elsewhere indicated that he was reluctant to condemn men for their spiritual views: he would allow the laws denying freedom of worship to non-Anglicans to fall into disuse. However, he condemned those who submitted themselves in temporal matters to papal authority, since 'the Pope of Rome ... claims a temporal power inconsistent with the liberties to which man is heir'. For him, therefore, 'Popery and Slavery' still went hand in hand.[55] Thus, while the grounds for maintaining the penal laws had shifted, owing, no doubt, to the influence of the Enlightenment, the habit of regarding religion and politics as simply two aspects of the same thing remained intact. And while Lucas regularly insisted that the Protestant kings of Great Britain and Ireland ruled by consent, he retained a strong sense of the patriarchal nature of monarchy, and was even willing on occasion to accord the monarch a 'sacred' character.[56]

As in Edinburgh, it was recognised in Dublin that members of the third estate lacked the noble or gentle status enjoyed by the higher orders; in Lucas's newspaper the *Censor* 'the Gentleman' and 'the Citizen' (or 'Freeman') formed separate social categories.[57] If it seems odd that such perceived distinctions did not, apparently, produce any significant challenge to aristocratic values, it needs to be remembered not only that 'citizens' enjoyed privileges not shared by the masses, but also that there was a certain amount of mixing between the orders, which doubtless helped to reduce social tensions. Like the Edinburgh trades, the Dublin guilds admitted selected noblemen and gentry to honorary freedoms, and mixing also took place through such bodies as masonic lodges.[58]

In conclusion, it may be said that an ancien regime model can illuminate the urban histories of both Scotland and Ireland.[59] In many ways, the two townsmen who have been under consideration conform closely to Clark's picture of a deferential (English) bourgeoisie. They did defer to aristocratic and confessional values; they did accept a crucial monarchical role in the regulation of privilege.[60] And this

---

[55] A. F. Barber and Citizen (Charles Lucas), *A Third Letter to the Free-Citizens of Dublin* (Dublin, 1747), pp. 18–19; Idem, *Divelina Libera: An Apology for the Civil Rights and Liberties of the Commons and Citizens of Dublin* (Dublin, 1744), p. 20.

[56] Lucas portrayed England and Ireland as two sisters under the care of a common parent (*The Great Charter* (Dublin, 1749), p. xiv). For the sacred character of monarchy, see *A Second Address to the Right Hon. the Lord Mayor* ... (Dublin, 1766), pp. 22–3.

[57] See for example, 'Urbanus Vigil' to Censor; 'The Farmer' to Censor; 'Simeon Probe' to Censor, *The Censor*, I, no. iii, 10–17 June 1749; I, no. xviii, 23–30 September 1749; I, no. xxii, 21–28 October 1749.

[58] E.g, in 1746 the Edinburgh bonnet-makers presented freedom to the Duke of Cumberland (Colston, *Incorporated Trades*, p. 143); in 1766 the Dublin smiths' guild presented freedom to Henry Flood, MP (National Archives, Dublin, Transactions of the Guild of St Loy, M 2925, p. 3). See also Terence de Vere White, 'The Freemasons', in T. Desmond Williams, ed., *Secret Societies in Ireland* (Dublin, 1973), pp. 46–57.

[59] As argued (for Dublin) by Jacqueline Hill, 'The Politics of Privilege: Dublin Corporation and the Catholic Question, 1792–1823', *Maynooth Review*, VII (1982), pp. 17–36, and (in the broader Irish context) by Leighton, 'Meaning of the Catholic Question'.

[60] Note that the Patriot case for Irish parliamentary privileges depended on elevating royal authority above that of the English parliament, along the lines of William Molyneux (*The Case of Ireland Stated* (Dublin, 1977 reprint), pp. 127–8); *The Censor* I, no. xx, 7–14 October 1749.

despite (or because of) the fact that Pennecuik and Lucas were spokesmen for the lesser bourgeoisie—the 'socially inferior' craftsmen of Edinburgh, the 'minor guilds' of Dublin. But this is merely one side of the picture. They also possessed a strong sense of the corporate privileges which set such tradesmen (along with merchants) apart on the one hand from the higher orders and on the other from the unfree masses. They believed that the defence of those privileges, concerning trade and self-government, was necessary for tradesmen to preserve or perhaps improve their place in the social hierarchy and in the state. It is not surprising, therefore, to find that the tradesmen were capable of assertiveness as well as deference, and that, as the importance of trade became more widely recognised, their horizons could reach beyond the municipal level.

These conclusions will, perhaps, seem most surprising in the context of Irish history. The ubiquity of nationalist or colonial models of eighteenth-century politics; the unexamined assumption that the section of the population often described as 'the Protestant ascendancy' constituted essentially a landed community; the failure to examine in any systematic way the nature and activities of the Irish guilds—none of this prepares the ground for recognising the existence of a third estate in Ireland. Yet leaving aside Ulster altogether, there existed in the corporate towns of southern Ireland an urban, Protestant (mostly Church of Ireland) population which was quite sufficient to provide the personnel for a Protestant guild system. It was the municipal representatives of these urban Protestants who in the 1760s and 1770s showered parliament with petitions in favour of a statutory quarterage system (the last bill for this purpose was introduced into the Irish parliament in 1778).[61] By acting in this way, they were taking a broadly similar stand to that of the *Parlement de Paris* which in 1776 protested against ministerial proposals to suppress the trade guilds in the interests of free trade. Such a move, Louis XVI was warned, would jeopardise the entire structure of society:

> The clergy, the nobility, the highest courts, the lower tribunals, the officers attached to these tribunals, the universities, the academies, the financial and commercial companies, all present, in all parts of the state, living bodies which one can consider as links in a great chain of which the first link is in the hands of Your Majesty, as head and highest administrator of all that makes up the body of the nation.[62]

Both Alexander Pennecuik and Charles Lucas would have understood and approved that sentiment.

---

[61] McGeehin, 'Catholics of the Towns', pp. 107, 111. The decline of the middling ranks of Protestants from the late 1700s on has been highlighted by Kerby A. Miller, 'No Middle Ground: The Erosion of the Protestant Middle Class in Southern Ireland during the Pre-Famine Era', *Huntingdon Library Quarterly*, XLIX (1986), pp. 295–306.

[62] Quoted in Myers, *Parliaments and Estates*, p. 9.

10

Scotland, Ireland, and the antithesis of Enlightenment

Gerard O'Brien

THE OMISSION OF IRELAND, amongst other countries, from the valuable collection of studies of the Enlightenment 'in national context' in 1981, and the reasons for that omission, highlight many of the problems which this paper hopes to address.[1] If a single root (or at least a principal one) to the main difficulties can be identified, it is that the parameters of the definition of 'Enlightenment' shift according to the national context in which the movement is explored. While it tended almost everywhere to be conducted by and through an aristocratic or bourgeois elite, it operated at different levels in different types of society, through different institutions, and evoked a variety of response.

The editors of the collection referred to above stated implicitly that they had decided to use Scotland rather than Ireland as representative of the Celtic Enlightenment experience. This probably arose from the fact that historians generally have not associated eighteenth-century Ireland with the Enlightenment ethos.[2] Certainly Ireland appeared to have the trappings of Enlightenment but none of its essence. Dublin was replete with informal clubs, learned societies, professional bodies and institutions, beautiful buildings and personable characters. However the Irish governing class was clearly weak in the important Enlightenment characteristics of 'rationality, toleration, humanitarianism [and] utilitarianism'.[3] Irish philosophers of the era were few and they tended to be isolated figures rather than the centres of cliques. And even the philosophers themselves were not lacking in irrationality, intolerance and social and economic fecklessness. In general rationality failed to penetrate the culture

---

[1] Roy Porter and Mikulas Teich, eds., *The Enlightenment in National Context* (Cambridge, 1981).

[2] For a fresh look at the contribution of Irish individuals to the Enlightenment outside Ireland, see David Berman, 'Irish Philosophy and the American Enlightenment during the Eighteenth Century', *Eire-Ireland*, XXIV, 1 (1989), pp. 23–39; Berman, 'Enlightenment and Counter-Enlightenment in Irish Philosophy', *Archiv für Geschichte der Philosophie*, 64/2 (1982); Berman, 'The Culmination and Causation of Irish Philosophy', *ibid.*, 64/3 (1982); G. E. Davie, 'Berkeley's Impact on Scottish Philosophers', *Philosophy*, XL (1955).

[3] Porter and Teich, *Enlightenment*, p. 216.

of fox-pursuit, toleration had eventually to be imposed from without by a displeased London government, and humanitarianism became the victim of repeated failures to make the country economically viable. Yet for all these disadvantages the Irish had rather more control over their society than had the Scots over theirs.

With the closure of the Scottish legislature in 1707 parliamentary life had to be funnelled rather unsatisfactorily through the increasingly distant Scots minority at Westminster. The Irish not only retained their parliament and added to its political prestige as the century went on, but, through the medium of successive lords justices and undertakers, had kept a considerable amount of political power in Irish hands for much of the period. In recent years studies of the origins of the Scottish Enlightenment have led to the abandonment of the 'political vacuum' theory as even a partial explanation of the phenomenon. This would suggest an opposite effect in the Irish environment where there seems little reason to believe that the presence of parliament had any effect on Irish intellectual life.

So we come to the question as to what forces *did* affect eighteenth-century Irish intellectual life, and why so adversely? We are of course examining two societies with very different histories. It would be simple but rather unprofitable to make the rest of this paper a sketch of those differences. A more interesting line of enquiry lies in an examination of the common features of the two societies—features which in one instance were media of Enlightenment and in the other simply were not. The sterling historiographical work on the Scottish Enlightenment over the last generation has greatly mitigated problems of definition. Nothing would be easier than to 'discover' an Irish Enlightenment on the pretext that certain features of the society had been overlooked or not recognised.

For instance, but for today's Scottish historians it would be possible to represent the Irish antiquarian movement of the eighteenth century as a possible Enlightenment. However, Scotland was fortunate in having both an antiquarian movement *and* an Enlightenment, so that we are saved the error of confusing the two. Nevertheless, in the clear absence of a conventional Enlightenment the antiquarian movement had in the Irish context a position of genuine if disproportionate importance. It is worth remembering that the ascendancy's obsession with the past, expressed most visibly through its architecture and its parliamentary oratory, was a central feature of the Anglo-Irish identity with all its insecurities and its deep need to establish 'right of presence' in Ireland. The antiquarian movement, when it showed signs of proper expression during the 1730s, developed a curious defensive streak which was not only an essential part of its raison d'etre but which persisted throughout the movement's various ups and downs even into the twentieth century. One of the earliest organised expressions of the movement, the Physico-Historical Society of the 1740s, was stung into print by the need to rebut scurrilous details published in England regarding the native Irish. The Society was of course run by peers, bishops and other elements of the Anglo-Irish créme, but they felt no less threatened in that it was their tenantry rather than themselves who had been the object of the English-based attack. It was a time when the ascendancy's identity was sustained no less by the deference of its tenantry than by its own predilections.[4] In a manner not unlike that of certain Scottish Enlightenment bodies the Society was short lived (1744–52) and eventually fell victim to declining interest and poor subscriptions.[5]

Its successor, the Medico-Philosophical Society, enjoyed greater success (perhaps owing to its professional underpinnings); it lasted from 1756 to 1784 and seems to have folded only in response to the foundation of the Royal Irish Academy. By an odd irony one of the best-known of Edinburgh's Enlightenment societies, the Philosophical Society, had a similar history but in reverse, growing as it did from a Medical Society formed in 1731. Both of these Irish and Scottish societies focussed on 'medical topics, natural history and natural phenomena', in the Scottish instance taking in 'the whole of natural knowledge, and including all subjects except theology, morals and politics'.[6] Both were eventually subsumed into larger, more august bodies.[7] Notably both societies, medically based as they were, survived and possibly even flourished despite the apparent disparity in the quality and status of medical education in the two cities. This is a point to which we will return.

However, the Medico-Philosophical Society by virtue of its very endurance seems to have been one of the centres of eighteenth-century Dublin intellectual life. It was, therefore, unfortunate that it was characterised by a certain insularity. Despite the geographical proximity and common interests of Welsh and Irish scholars 'little sign' could be discovered 'of any real contact between the very vigorous literary tradition and the Irish antiquarian movement'. External influences on the Society were 'discernible' rather than obvious, though 'frequent reference' could be found to the Englishman Robert Plot.[8]

The third and supposedly final phase (for the eighteenth century) of the Irish antiquarian movement saw a qualified unification between ascendancy and Catholic bourgeoisie—the latter in the person of Charles O'Conor.[9] However, despite his 'wide general reading' and 'his awareness of European trends of thought', O'Conor was not part of any solution to the obsessive self-fascination of Dublin intellectuals, but rather represented the alternative side of the same problem.[10] Like his ascendancy opposites O'Conor was concerned to put the 'native' case in the quiet but continuing conflict between Gael and Gall. When not attempting to secure civil equality for Catholics (and therefore in real terms Protestant subordination) through his political activities, his formidable intellect

---

[4] Ann de Valera, 'Antiquarian and Historical Investigations in Ireland in the Eighteenth Century', (unpublished MA thesis, University College, Dublin, 1978), pp. 51–60, esp. pp. 54–5.
[5] de Valera, 'Antiquarian Investigations', p. 71. One Scottish example of this type of experience was the Select Society; see Davis D. McElroy, *Scotland's Age of Improvement* (Washington, 1969), pp. 59–63.
[6] de Valera, 'Antiquarian Investigations', p. 72; McElroy, *Scotland's Age of Improvement*, pp. 27–30.
[7] McElroy, *Scotland's Age of Improvement*, p. 34, referring to the merging of the Philosophical Society into the new Royal Society of Edinburgh in 1783.
[8] de Valera, 'Antiquarian Investigations', pp. 12, 93.
[9] Charles O'Conor of Belanagare (1710–91).
[10] de Valera, 'Antiquarian Investigations', pp. 108–31, esp. p. 116.

was bent on elucidating 'a mythic past which was sophisticated politically and culturally, rather than primitive'.[11]

In short the implied conclusion was the superiority of native claims of tenure to those of O'Conor's Anglo-Irish co-intellectuals.[12] The veiled political motives, therefore, which encouraged O'Conor to seek out James McLagan of the Black Watch regiment, and to correspond with the Scottish historian John Pinkerton, led inexorably to intellectual sterility. It was entirely typical of the Irish intellectual ethos of the period that the Hibernian Antiquarian Society (1779–82)—shared by ascendancy and Catholics—did not thrive on challenge and debate but merely collapsed in a welter of bitterness.[13] Their joint and separate failures to come to terms with the past had made it impossible for either ascendancy or Catholic to invest intellectually in the forward-looking and innovative ideas which characterised the Enlightenment in Scotland and elsewhere. A not-untypical example of this 'blind spot' between Irish and Scottish intellectuals was the outraged reaction of O'Conor and his colleague John Curry to David Hume's attack on the Catholic rebels of 1641. O'Conor and Curry, in their usual fashion, interpreted the assault in terms that were quintessentially Irish and Catholic. It was lost on them that Hume's vitriol had been aimed not at Catholicism *per se* but rather at religion and fanaticism in general.[14] Detachment and independence of mind, essential then as now to the prevalence of intellectual freedom, could not flourish in a society at war with itself. The primacy of political-mindedness in eighteenth-century Ireland militated against an Enlightenment led by intellectuals of whichever creed.[15] Events in the quieter and more progressive atmosphere of Edinburgh provided bleak confirmation of this view, as the years after 1770 gave rise to ultimately divisive political issues; 'politics', it has been said, 'throttled the Scottish Enlightenment'.[16]

At the centre of the Enlightenment experience in several Scottish cities were the universities. Near the centre of the Irish intellectuals' loss of direction for much of the century was Trinity College, Dublin. To some extent Trinity's failure to direct Dublin's intellectual life was as much a result of bad luck as of its regrettable tendency to reflect the paranoid state of the society in which it existed. It was a

---

[11] Clare O'Halloran, 'Irish Re-creations of the Gaelic Past: The Challenge of Macpherson's Ossian', *Past and Present*, 124 (1989), pp. 72–3 and *passim*.

[12] It should be mentioned that political motives seem not to have played any *ostensible* part in the antiquarian writings of O'Conor. Rather, as R. B. McDowell points out in *Ireland in the Age of Imperialism and Revolution 1760–1801* (Oxford, 1979), p. 185, he may genuinely have wished to 'reconcile the conquerors and the conquered'. But O'Conor's conscious desires, however laudable, could have had little impact in the political context of which he, like it or not, was a part. For a further look at 'Revivalism' see John Hutchinson, *The Dynamics of Cultural Nationalism* (London, 1987), pp. 55–71.

[13] de Valera, 'Antiquarian Investigations', pp. 130, 131, 140–3, 148.

[14] David Berman, 'David Hume on the 1641 Rebellion in Ireland', *Studies*, LXV (1976), pp. 101–12.

[15] See Hutchinson, *Cultural Nationalism*, p. 68 for comment on the non-intellectual 'liberal' view of antiquarianism.

[16] Anand Chitnis, *The Scottish Enlightenment: A Social History* (London, 1976), p. 84.

fact that Scottish universities were fortunate enough both to attract from elsewhere and to produce from within themselves the right kind of academic talent. In their seventeenth-century antecedents, it was true, Trinity and Scotland had been given a similar 'start' on which to build. The aftermath of the Restoration was 'a kind of watershed in Scottish intellectual life', a period in which the government was concerned 'less to control academic activity than to ensure that holders of university posts did not use them to undermine the existing order'.[17] The 1650s had seen the establishment in Trinity of the Chair of Mathematics for which Scottish colleges had campaigned so hard (and which they were to be denied until 1668).[18] Chairs of Law, Oratory and Physic were also established at Dublin during this time, along with more effective rules for the study of the more traditional courses of Greek and Hebrew.[19]

But Trinity lacked men of sufficient calibre to make these improvements work to their best advantage. No Gregorys and no MacLaurin emerged to fire the teaching of mathematics, nor did a Macky or Stevenson enliven the pursuit of history and logic.[20] For over forty years Trinity languished under the provostship of Richard Baldwin who, according to a recent study, 'cannot be called a philistine', but whose 'exaggerated distrust of independence of thought served to stifle such gleams of originality as may have been shown by the fellows of his time'. The almost inevitable result was the passing of a generation during which no publication of the slightest significance emerged from the lone Irish university. The importance of ill-fortune in the ordering of this malaise is further suggested by the fact that, unlike Oxford and Cambridge, new academic positions continued to be established at Trinity throughout the first half of the eighteenth century, posts which would prove to be of value in more intellectually propitious times.[21]

But the failure of Trinity to become either a lodestone or a promoter of an Enlightenment was rooted in the same socio-political factors which blighted the promise of the antiquarian movement. No serious attempt was made during the eighteenth century, until the creation of the specialised institution of Maynooth in 1795, to de-centralise Irish university education. A further half-century would pass before colleges would be established in cities other than Dublin. Scotland, a country smaller in size and population, had five universities, three of which long pre-dated Trinity. Moreover, the Scottish universities 'were regarded by parliament, by church, and by Scottish opinion in general as part of a national system

[17] Ronald G. Cant, 'Origins of the Enlightenment in Scotland: The Universities', in R. H. Campbell and A. S. Skinner, eds., *The Origins and Nature of the Scottish Enlightenment* (Edinburgh, 1982), pp. 42, 43.

[18] R. B. McDowell and D. A. Webb, *Trinity College Dublin 1592–1952: An Academic History* (Cambridge, 1982), p. 19; Cant, 'Origins', p. 45.

[19] McDowell and Webb, *Trinity College*, p. 19.

[20] Nicholas Phillipson, 'Culture and Society in the Eighteenth Century Province: The Case of Edinburgh and the Scottish Enlightenment', in Lawrence Stone, ed., *The University and Society*, Volume II (Princeton and London, 1975), p. 438.

[21] McDowell and Webb, *Trinity College*, pp. 38–41.

of education'; and within the universities specialist teachers had 'a sense of the inherent unity of the educational system in which they were comprehended'.[22] In 1696 schooling in Scotland, already on an organised footing at parish level, was given proper legislative support. At precisely the same time the Anglo-Irish victors of the Boyne were rendering impossible, among other things, the maintenance of any integrated education system. The high hopes of the same Cromwellian regime that had encouraged vocational pursuits within Trinity were finally dashed by the determination of the embryo ascendancy to exclude the bulk of the Irish population from even basic schooling. In Scotland education was not 'the preserve of an exclusive caste. Opportunities to share in its enjoyment were open, as a matter of principle, and on an extended scale, to all persons of the requisite talent'.[23] In Ireland Trinity was available only to those prepared to take an objectionable oath. Talented Catholics went to the Continent, an experience which in some cases contributed to the eventual continuance of social divisions in Ireland. Talented Dissenters went, among other places, to Scotland; Scottish students, conversely, seem not to have been attracted to Trinity in any significant number.[24]

Perhaps the aspect of Trinity most inimical to good education and to any kind of independent thought was that it was a political institution. In Scotland the universities were 'autonomous corporations' and were respected as such by establishment and society.[25] In Dublin the provost of Trinity sat in parliament. The appointment to the provostship of John Hely Hutchinson, for instance, in 1774, was announced 'to the astonishment of all Dublin' and was said to be 'the by-product of a piece of ministerial jobbery which is difficult to parallel'. Hely Hutchinson was married (this was contrary to College statutes) and moreover was a professional politician 'with no academic experience', and one who clearly regarded the provostship as another power-base from which to control individuals. He would brook no opposition and seems to have exercised his discretionary powers over fellowships, scholarships and other matters in a despotic manner, 'to reward his friends and cow his enemies'. This behaviour became particularly noticeable at election times.[26] In Scotland the absence of a parliament and the general respect long afforded the universities ensured that political influence was directed by other mechanisms and through other institutions.[27] Parliament might indeed have had its importance in Dublin academic life if only the traffic had not been so entirely 'one-way'; but Trinity refused to seize lifelines even when they

---

[22] R. G. Cant, 'The Scottish Universities and Scottish Society in the Eighteenth Century', *Studies on Voltaire and the Eighteenth Century* (1967), p. 1955; Cant, 'Origins', p. 55.
[23] Cant, 'Scottish Universities', p. 1962.
[24] W. M. Mathew, 'The Origins and Occupations of Glasgow Students, 1740–1839', *Past and Present*, 33 (1966), pp. 75–6.
[25] Cant, 'Scottish Universities', p. 1955.
[26] McDowell and Webb, *Trinity College*, pp. 53–6.
[27] For recent comment on these mechanisms see John Stuart Shaw, *The Management of Scottish Society 1707–1764* (Edinburgh, 1983), and Alexander Murdoch, *The People Above* (Edinburgh, 1980).

were offered directly to her. In 1723 parliament legislated to allow the university to use its existing surplus funds to create fresh fellowships and chairs and provided also for the publication of lectures. The most recent study of Trinity has concluded that 'some of the provisions [publication of lectures] appear to have been ignored from an early date'.[28]

The socio-political divisions which bedeviled 'outdoor' intellectual life, and which lay at the root of Trinity's malaise, are revealed yet again when one examines the study of law in the two regions. It was symptomatic of the Irish intellectual environment that the recognised 'father' of the Scottish Enlightenment, Francis Hutcheson, eventually chose to leave Dublin for Glasgow, the city where he had been educated. There, as a leading figure in moral philosophy and in civil law, he influenced both Hume and Adam Smith.[29] He was part of the 'flourishing' in Scotland of 'the philosophical study of the nature and fundamental principles of law and legality in themselves and in relation to morality, to social custom and to political economy'.[30] The connection between law and philosophy, embodied by men such as Lord Kames for instance, which made legal thought and writing an integral part of the Scottish Enlightenment, had no counterpart in Irish legal circles.[31] The law and its administration had long been an area of central importance in the Irish inter-group power-struggle and had never had the opportunity to develop apolitical philosophical underpinnings or to be moulded for the social benefit of all. This determination that the law should serve only one side of the community naturally affected the manner in which lawyers were trained and had the long-term result of curtailing the intellectual development of all but a scattered few (William Molyneux and Francis Hutcheson, for instance, who never knew each other). Recently a short but invaluable study of the training of Irish lawyers has shown how in this area, perhaps more than in any other except landownership, an institution basic to the general well-being was made a political football.[32] The admission of Catholics to the legal profession wavered and was regulated by the ebb and flow of anti-Catholic or pro-Protestant policy in London during the Tudor and Stuart periods. Were all other evidence of those times to be lost the basic political events could still be reconstructed by analysing the official attitude to the training of Irish lawyers. 'The fortunes of Catholics improved markedly' in the time of James II, only to fall victim to a series of stern restrictions enacted between 1692 and 1733. The strictures against Catholic lawyers indeed seem to have been 'consistently enforced' long after other penal laws are believed to have been relaxed. Later in the century piecemeal ameliorations of the penal statutes, such as the 1782

---

28 McDowell and Webb, *Trinity College*, p. 44.
29 T. D. Campbell, 'Francis Hutcheson: "Father" of the Scottish Enlightenment', in Campbell and Skinner, eds., *Origins and Nature*, p. 167.
30 Neil MacCormick, 'Law and Enlightenment', in *ibid.*, p. 150.
31 Chitnis, *Scottish Enlightenment*, p. 85.
32 Colm Kenny, 'The Exclusion of Catholics from the Legal Profession in Ireland, 1537–1829', *Irish Historical Studies*, XXV, 100 (1987), pp. 337–57.

act affecting Catholic education, were followed by renewed restrictions on the admission of Catholics to legal training.[33] The eventual repeal in 1792 of the bulk of the penal legislation on Catholic lawyers was conceded in Dublin only after one of the most bitter and furious parliamentary debates of the century.[34] One opponent of the London-inspired relief package stated that 'he considered a Protestant bar as necessary as a Protestant parliament'.[35] The relief measure passed but the higher positions of judge and king's counsel remained closed to Catholics until after 1829.

But in any case relief had come too late to elevate the Irish legal profession intellectually. 'This exclusiveness', it has been said, 'had "the inevitable effect of degrading" the legal profession'.[36] The creation of a Chair of Feudal and English Law at Trinity in 1761 gave rise to 'no rigorous intellectual tradition of scholarship', and even by 1830 the university played virtually no part in the training of lawyers.[37] An examination of the careers of some politicians of the later eighteenth century suggests that a parliamentary career, even in unprofitable opposition, was thought preferable to a career at the bar.[38] For some a legal qualification was clearly a means to obtaining a lucrative Castle post.[39] While less is known of audience participation in the eighteenth-century courts, the legal career of Daniel O'Connell and of some of his contemporaries suggest that trials had long been regarded in Ireland as a popular spectator sport.[40] The twin elements of dignity and respectability, which were such a marked and fundamental feature of Scottish professional law, were absent at all levels in the Irish legal world. The Georgian penal statutes had their Victorian legacy in the pervasive anti-establishment attitude in which (in the words of Maurice Walsh) 'every man was agin the government and swore accordingly'.[41]

But perhaps the missed opportunity of an Irish Enlightenment is at its most visible in the field of medicine. Dublin's College of Physicians had had a settled charter since 1692, and between 1718 and 1756 at least half a dozen hospitals were opened in the city. Given the type of urban squalor which then prevailed in Dublin the supply of patients of all varieties was reasonably assured, and conditions were on the surface ideal for the growth of a golden age of Irish medicine. Yet it was to the Scottish medical schools that Irish students resorted in large numbers throughout the eighteenth-century. To some considerable extent this was due to

---

[33] *Ibid.*, p. 355.

[34] For the full debate see *Irish Parliamentary Register*, XII (1792), pp. 24, 28–42, 57, 58–64, 116–19, 124–79, 182–231, 235–44.

[35] *Ibid.*, p. 240 (the speaker was George Ogle).

[36] Quoted in Kenny, 'Exclusion of Catholics', p. 357.

[37] J. F. McEldowney and Paul O'Higgins, 'The Common Law tradition in Irish Legal History', in McEldowney and O'Higgins, eds., *The Common Law Tradition: Essays in Irish Legal History* (Dublin, 1990), p. 15.

[38] Henry Grattan and John Forbes were prime examples.

[39] Barry Yelverton and Charles Francis Sheridan for instance.

[40] See James Comyn, *Irish at Law* (London, 1981), *passim*.

[41] For a clear-sighted view of Scottish lawyers and their role see Shaw, *Management of Scottish Society*, pp. 18–40.

the 'disputatious state' of medical training in Ireland.[42] The College of Physicians clearly suffered from its connection with Trinity College, relations being completely severed at the close of the 1750s and not resumed until 1785. Moreover, the quality of the teaching staff was uneven, one lecturer in Botany for instance presiding over a botanical garden which contained a single barren fig-tree. Even after 'a complete medical school' was legislated into existence in 1785, efforts to establish training hospital arrangements faltered and failed for a further dozen years.[43] Also, despite the fact that it had been set up to regulate the practice of medicine within a seven-mile radius of Dublin, the College of Physicians had trouble enforcing its edicts. As late as 1725 it was seeking parliamentary assistance 'to prevent illiterate persons from practising physic'.[44] The poor relationship between the College and the university was extended also to the Surgeons' Company whose proposals for co-operation with the College in 1741 apparently received no reply.[45] But it is doubtful whether such co-operation would have borne any worthwhile fruit. The records of the Surgeons' Company's dealings with its apprentices show 'no evidence that examinations were consistently carried out'. Even when the appointment of new surgeons to the new county infirmaries was put on a systematic footing after 1765 the Board 'were apparently more concerned with the correctness of candidates' indentures than with the depth of their learning'.[46] The Royal College of Surgeons was not established until 1784, and another five years were to elapse before effective teaching arrangements could be put in hand.[47]

All this compared very unfavourably with Edinburgh where 'systematic anatomical instruction began to be given' from 1697, and where from the same period hospitals were set up in direct connection with the medical schools.[48] Not surprisingly, a further explanation for the attraction of Scotland for Irish medical students is provided by the Irish socio-political situation. The effect of the religious test at Trinity is reflected in the large numbers of Presbyterian and probably Catholic students also, 'coming predominantly', it was said, 'from tenant farming families in Ulster', who went to Glasgow.[49] Of the 1,143 doctors who graduated from Edinburgh between 1726 and 1799, 280—the largest single group—were Irish. The importance for Irish students of the 'non-denominational' atmosphere created by George Drummond is indicated by the almost dramatic decline in Irish students

---

[42] Chitnis, *Scottish Enlightenment*, p. 134.
[43] John F. Fleetwood, *The History of Medicine in Ireland* (Dublin, 2nd edn, 1983), pp. 36–40.
[44] *Ibid.*, p. 67
[45] *Ibid.*, p. 68
[46] *Ibid.*, pp. 68–9.
[47] *Ibid.*, pp. 69–72.
[48] Chitnis, *Scottish Enlightenment*, pp. 130, 136. For a panoramic view of the contrast between the regions' medical training facilities see Elizabeth Malcolm, *Swift's Hospital: A History of St Patrick's Hospital, Dublin, 1746–1989* (Dublin, 1989), and Guenter B. Risse, *Hospital Life in Enlightenment Scotland: Care and Teaching at the Royal Infirmary of Edinburgh* (Cambridge, 1986).
[49] Mathew, 'Origins and Occupations', pp. 75–6.

after the establishment of Maynooth in 1795 and the Belfast Presbyterian College in 1810, and the lifting of religious restrictions at Trinity in 1793.[50]

It is true that the prospects of an Enlightenment in Ireland on the lines of the Scottish experience were retarded by the self-interestedness and insecurity of the ascendancy. But it is also true that the situation they had inherited from the Williamite wars was to a considerable extent beyond the control of even the least selfish and least insecure of their number. In the earlier eighteenth century the consequences of a successful Catholic counter-blow were obvious and terrible to contemplate. Later on the consequences of dominance by a possibly land-hungry Catholic bourgeoisie were, to say the least, uncertain. Anglo-Irish society could not reform itself without risking its own destruction. Scotland of course had its own political crises, but it was not faced with such a dilemma and so its intellectuals were not afraid to explore alternative philosophies and to contemplate different social orders. Nor was Enlightenment Scotland a perfect society. Socio-political divisions in Scotland were as deep and bitter as those in Ireland. The difference was that Irish institutions, unlike their Scottish counterparts, were built around and designed to service divisions rather than to exist in spite of or apart from them. The very institutions which in Scotland were centres of Enlightenment culture were in Ireland trapped as unwilling players in a deadlocked political conflict and so could not develop outside of that role.

Moreover, there is reason to believe that the Irish Enlightenment was postponed rather than lost. Institutions of crucial importance such as the Royal Dublin Society and the Royal Irish Academy survived the Georgian night to flourish in the Victorian day. By 1850 the medical fraternity had shed its former reputation and Dublin became one of the world's foremost centres of medical education. The growth in popularity of the Queen's Colleges during the last third of the nineteenth century provided Trinity with the competitive spur to excellence of which it had for so long been in need. The antiquarian movement advanced into the realm of language preservation and in time acquired a political relevance and significance of which Charles O'Conor could scarcely have dreamt. The Irish legal world acquired system and majesty, even if it was too late to inspire popular respect. When the Empire became recognised in its imperial reality it was Dublin rather than Edinburgh that took on the mantle of the 'second city'. In short, the reform of 1829 and the several reforms which had preceded it contributed largely to the advent of that social pacification which had in Scotland once been the seed-bed of Enlightenment.

---

[50] The figures on Edinburgh doctors are from Douglas Sloan, *The Scottish Enlightenment and the American College Ideal* (Columbia, 1971), p. 27. For Drummond see Anand Chitnis, 'Provost Drummond and the Origins of Edinburgh Medicine', in Campbell and Skinner, eds., *Origins and Nature*, pp. 86–97. For religious factors influencing students see Mathew, 'Origins and Occupations', pp. 75–6, and P. J. and R. V. Wallis, *Eighteenth-Century Medics* (Newcastle-upon-Tyne, 1988), p. xiv. It should be noted that while the numbers of Irish students did decline, a tradition of such duration was not so easily broken; when Dominic Corrigan went to Edinburgh in the mid-1820s the Irish still formed the largest group of graduates—see Eoin O'Brien, *Conscience and Conflict: A Biography of Sir Dominic Corrigan 1802–1880* (Dublin, 1983), p. 28.

The municipal corporate presence in Edinburgh was represented in a wide variety of highly structured ways. In this sketch attributed to David Allen, an element of what looks like the town guard accompanies the mace bearer of a municipal procession up the High Street in Edinburgh. (National Galleries of Scotland.)

When tourists came to Scotland between 1760 and 1830, they read tour guides which directed them to look at a wild empty landscape beyond the areas of orderly walled and 'improved' landscape. This view of Loch Tay comes from Thomas Pennant's *A Tour in Scotland* (1771) (National Library of Scotland.)

Some of the tourists made their own sketches. These extracts from a recently discovered sketch book compiled by George Goode in the 1780s show just the wild landscape with only a few isolated figures which the published tour guides had taught him to look for. (National Library of Scotland.)

Irish Famine relief in action: 'The Cork Society of Friends Soup House', *Illustrated London News*, January 1847. (Photograph reproduced with the kind permission of the Trustees of the Ulster Museum.)

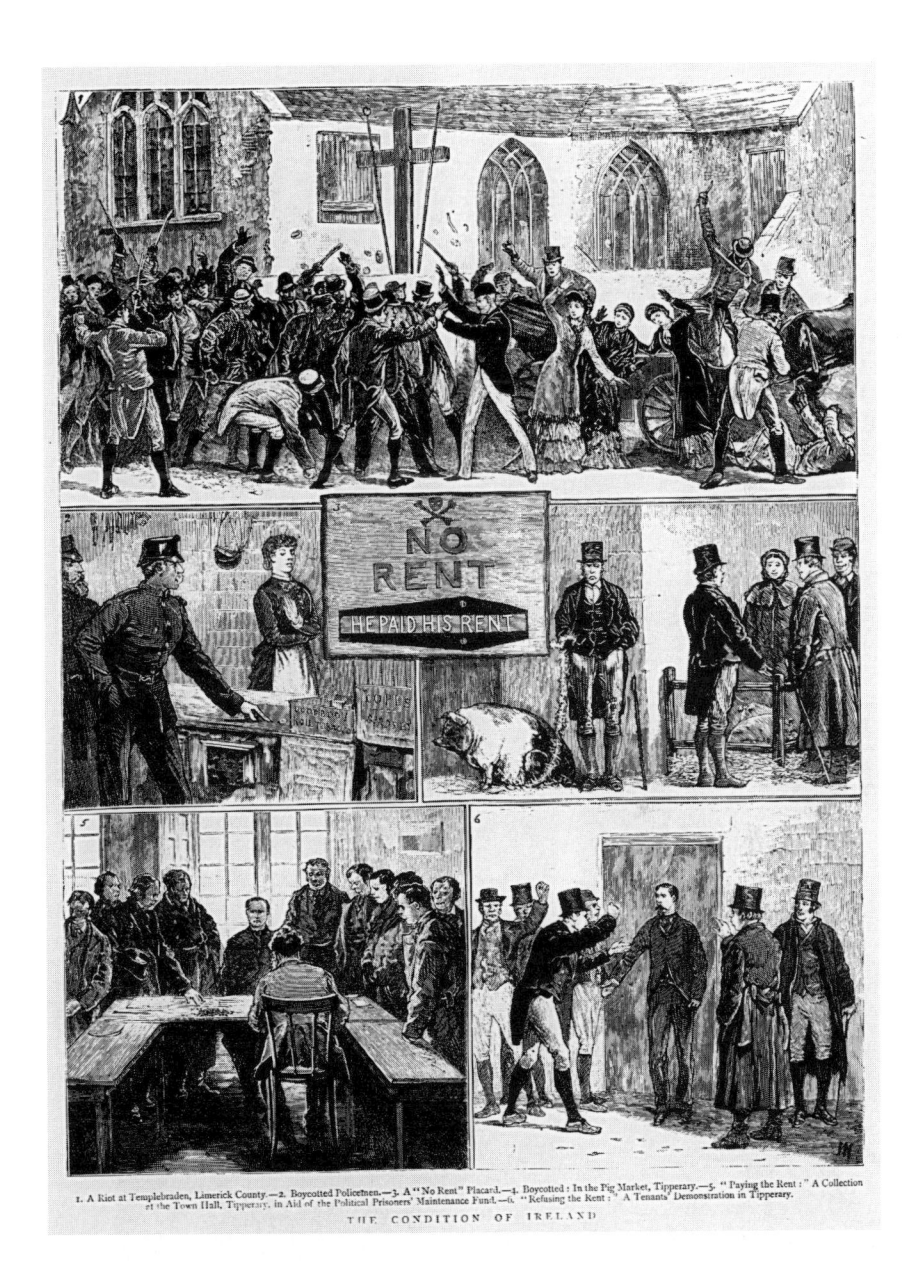

Riot, boycott and political mobilisation.
Scenes from the Irish Land War as depicted in *The Graphic*, 24 December 1881.

Part of the great turning shop in Harland and Wolff's engine works, Queen's Island, Belfast, c.1890. Note the electric overhead crane, shifting a large casing. At the sides are two fitting shops. (Welch Collection, photograph reproduced with the kind permission of the Trustees of the Ulster Museum.)

The launch of the steamship *Statendam* at the Harland and Wolff shipyard, Belfast, 1914. (Welch Collection, photograph reproduced with the kind permission of the Trustees of the Ulster Museum.)

Skilled men were paid much the same in both Scotland and Ireland. These masons are shown building the Airds Picture House in the 1930s. (National Museum of Scotland, Scottish Ethnographic Archive.)

The real difference in the Irish and Scottish labour markets was in the agricultural sector. The well organized and relatively well paid nature of Scottish agricultural labour is well illustrated by the men gathered for this ploughing match at Philiphaugh in the Scottish borders. (National Museum of Scotland, Scottish Ethnographic Archive.)

Women and children pose in front of houses in Beatty's entry, Belfast, for one of a series of photographs taken in 1912 as part of a survey of slum housing scheduled for demolition under the Belfast Improvement Order of 1910. (Photograph reproduced with the kind permission of the Trustees of the Ulster Museum.)

Johnston's Court, Belfast, 30 May 1912. Another rare image of the poorer side of Belfast's housing on the eve of the First World War. Note the wooden window shutters on the ground floor. (Photograph reproduced with the kind permission of the Trustees of the Ulster Museum.)

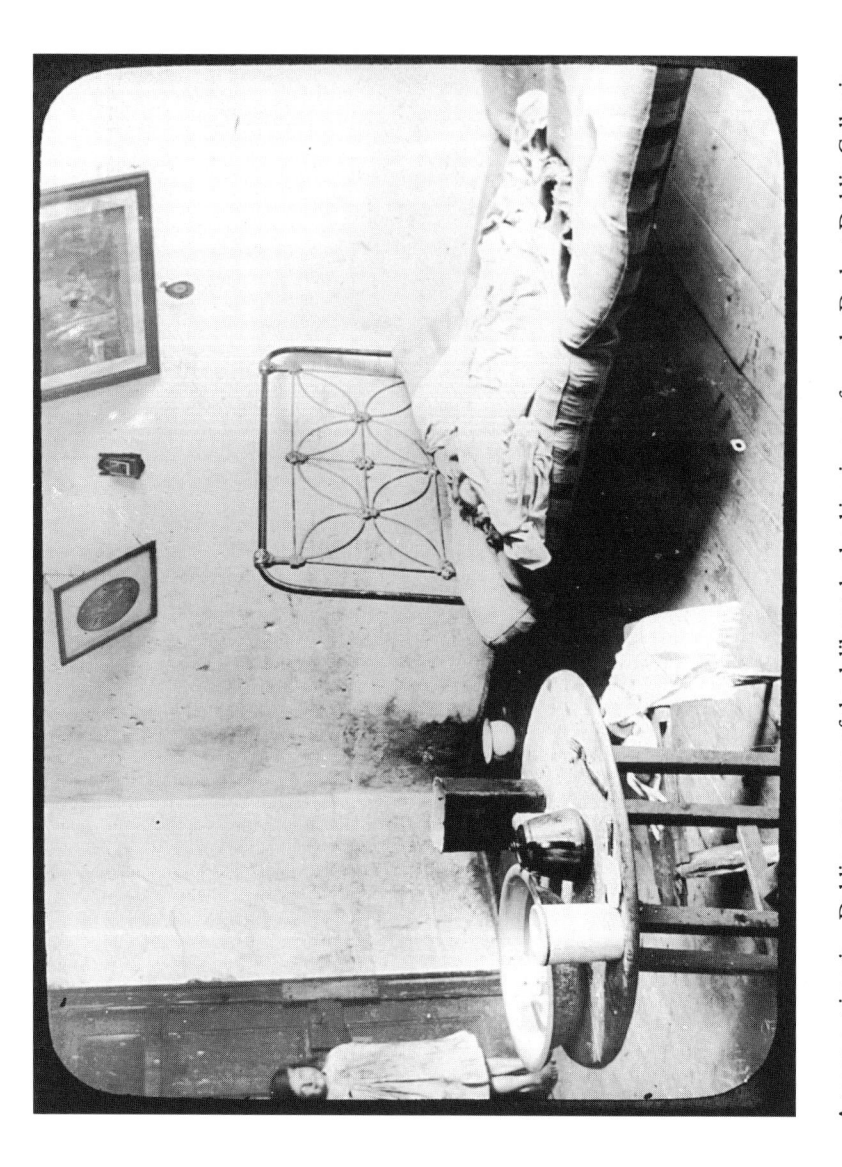

A tenement interior, Dublin, 1913; one of the deliberately shocking images from the Darkest Dublin Collection. (Royal Society of Antiquaries of Ireland.)

Aungier Place, Dublin, 1913, from the same collection.
Dublin tenements, unlike most of their Scottish counterparts, were generally older buildings, not originally intended for multiple occupancy, and often in poor structural condition.
(Royal Society of Antiquaries of Ireland.)

A lane off Townsend Street, Dublin, 1913. Conditions like these reflected both the poor state of Dublin working-class housing and the low incomes resulting from widespread dependence on unskilled, casual work. (Royal Society of Antiquaries of Ireland.)

Morgan's Cottages, Dublin, 1913. A communal pump provides what was possibly the only water supply. The hens did something to supplement low and often irregular earnings.
(Royal Society of Antiquaries of Ireland.)

The density and crowding of Scottish urban housing was seen most clearly in the Gorbals area of Glasgow. The back court (above) was taken in 1948, whilst the picture of Coburg Street (below) was taken in 1956. (National Museum of Scotland, Scottish Ethnographic Archive.)

11

Ownership of the past: antiquarian debate and ethnic identity in Scotland and Ireland

Clare O'Halloran

THE PROCESS OF IDENTITY FORMATION in pre-modern societies has been a focus of inquiry among political scientists in recent years. In his recent book, *The Ethnic Origins of Nations* (1986), Anthony D. Smith explores the development of ethnic communities, looking at the factors which seem essential for the growth of communal identity. He identifies six of these as, a collective name, a common myth of descent, a shared history, a distinctive shared culture, an association with a specific territory, and a sense of solidarity.[1] While the other elements could be present to varying degrees, Smith singles out myth and history as vital to the process of identity formation. Recent valuable surveys of the development of national identity in Ireland, by Joseph Leerssen, and in Scotland, by William Donaldson, lend support to Smith's argument.[2] When viewed together, Ireland and Scotland provide an interesting framework within which to examine the different ways in which this process could operate, for the Irish and Scottish developed their separate ethnic identities from a common pool of myth, legend and medieval pseudo-history, arising from the Gaelic culture which they had shared since the fifth century. The differing geographic, political and religious relationships of Ireland and Scotland with England often overrode the strong cultural links between the two peripheral regions, and caused a rumbling literary controversy over the centuries. The treatment of the issues of Celtic origins and the nature of Celtic society by Irish and Scottish antiquaries which forms the focus of this article also demonstrates some of the tensions involved in historical inquiry in the seventeenth and eighteenth centuries. These resulted mainly from the need to reconcile tradition and myth with changing political perspectives, as well as with new ideas about historical methodology and sources.

---

[1] Anthony D. Smith, *The Ethnic Origins of Nations* (Oxford, 1989), pp. 21-31.
[2] Joseph Th. Leerssen, *Mere Irish and Fíor-Ghael* (Amsterdam and Philadelphia, 1986); William Donaldson, *The Jacobite Song: Political Myth and National Identity* (Aberdeen, 1988).

At the centre of Hiberno-Scottish controversy from the seventeenth century onwards was the need for Scots to establish a British identity which reflected the geo-political realities of their situation. This required them at various times to adapt or even subvert the medieval Gaelic origin myth which was common to both countries. The Irish version of this origin myth also evolved in ways which reflected changing political circumstances, certain of which, especially the accession of the Stuarts to the English throne in 1603, seemed initially to create a new sense of common identity with the Scots. But native Irish identity (increasingly articulated in religious terms) was normally predicated on difference from England, and did not involve any British element. Changes in the Scottish historiographical tradition, in response to the political demands of increased integration, invariably came into conflict with the need of Irish Catholics to maintain a separate identity, even while protesting loyalism and petitioning for civil rights.

The shared history and culture of Gaelic Scotland and Ireland arose out of the fifth-century migration from the north east of Ireland into south-west Scotland, from which the Kingdom of Dalriada emerged. In the ninth century, a Dalriadan king, Kenneth MacAlpin, overcame the Picts and united the two peoples to form the kingdom of Alba north of the Forth–Clyde line. By 1034, under Malcolm Canmore, Alba comprised the territory of the Picts, Scots, Lothian Angles and Strathclyde Britons, and became known as Scotia—a Latin name which had until that time referred to Ireland.[3] The Scots and the Irish, parts of the same large state-system in the eighteenth century, yet with contrasting constitutional and political relationships to its centre, England, drew on this common past with very different political needs in mind, and there were many disputes over the ownership or interpretation of key elements of it. Some of the new historians, such as David Hume and William Robertson, dismissed these origin disputes as unimportant. Even so, in his final emendations to his *History of Great Britain*, Hume added a lengthy note on the latest stage of this controversy.[4] Similarly, Thomas Leland, who attempted, unsuccessfully, to emulate Hume by writing a 'philosophical' history of Ireland since the twelfth-century conquest, was drawn into the controversy at roughly the same time as his Scottish role model. He published an anonymous pamphlet, ostensibly taking an objective scholarly point of view, but in effect setting out the Irish case against the principal Scottish offender, James Macpherson.[5] Thus, despite the spurious scholarship of much of this polemical writing on origins, and its apparent low status in Enlightenment discourse, the

---

[3] Marjorie O. Anderson, 'Dalriada and the Creation of the Kingdom of the Scots', in Dorothy Whitelock, Rosamond McKitterick and David Dumville, eds., *Ireland in Early Medieval Europe* (Cambridge, 1982), pp. 106–32.

[4] David Hume, *The History of England*, 8 vols (London, 1778), VIII, pp. 471–3.

[5] Thomas Leland, *An Examination of the Arguments Contained in a Late Introduction to the History of the Antient Irish, and Scots* (London, 1772). On Leland as historian see Joseph Liechty, 'Testing the Depth of Catholic/Protestant Conflict: The Case of Thomas Leland's *History of Ireland*, 1773', *Archivium Hibernicum*, 42 (1987), pp. 13–28.

political as much as the intellectual importance of its subject matter ensured that it coloured changing views of the past in both countries.

Though largely discredited as an historiographical source, medieval myths of origin could still exercise a powerful appeal in the late eighteenth century. Geoffrey of Monmouth's elaborate twelfth-century Arthurian fiction had no advocates in Enlightenment England, but the origins question was still the subject of much debate by antiquaries such as William Borlase and John Whitaker.[6] It is not surprising, in the light of their recent history, that Irish writers held more tenaciously to their *Leabhar Gabhála* (the book of invasions). This twelfth-century monastic compilation of much earlier lore concerning the peopling of Ireland from the time of the Flood was based, like most medieval origin legends, on the journeys of the Children of Israel in the Old Testament. Where the Israelites were descended from Shem, one of the sons of Noah, the Gael were said to have been descended from his brother, Japhet. Their wanderings also involved a sojourn in Egypt, where their eponymous ancestor, Scota, married the pharaoh, and gave birth to Gaedheal Glas. Having spent some time in Scythia, they moved to Spain, where Míl ruled (whence Milesians) until about 1000 BC. The three sons of Míl then set out from Spain to Ireland, where they and their posterity ruled for two thousand years until vanquished by the Anglo-Normans in the late twelfth century: in other words, at just about the time this chronicle was being written. A product of political and religious upheaval, the *Leabhar Gabhála* was in part intended to give one tribe, known as the Gael, Scoti or Milesians, the strongest title to political and dynastic power in the face of new foreign invasion.[7]

If the Irish were stimulated by outside threat to produce a more elaborate version of their oral and written myths in the twelfth century, the Scots were forced into a similar exercise a century later, in the face of the threatened takeover of their vacant throne by Edward II of England. In 1299, the Anglo-Scottish dispute was brought to the court of Rome for adjudication, with English and Scottish lawyers putting forward competing accounts of the history of Scotland and of the origins of its people. Two elements of the English case were the claim of a common Trojan ancestry for all early inhabitants of the island, and that King Arthur of the Britons had conquered Scotland and made a vassal of its king. The Scots, in response, argued that they were a more ancient people than the Britons, being descended from Scota and Gathelus, who had sailed from Egypt long before Brutus arrived in Britain, and that they had always been free and independent.[8]

It was at this point that the Scottish version diverged from the last phase of the Irish myth. Under the leadership of Simon Breck, it was recounted, a group of

---

[6] William Borlase, *Antiquities, Historical and Monumental, of the County of Cornwall* (London, 1769); John Whitaker, *The Genuine History of the Britons Asserted* (London, 1773). For English antiquarianism in this period, see Stuart Piggott, *Ancient Britons and the Antiquarian Imagination* (London, 1989), pp. 123–59.

[7] R. A. S. Macalister (ed. and trans.), *Lebor Gabala Erenn*, 5 vols (Dublin, 1938–56); R. Mark Scowcroft, 'Leabhar Gabhála', *Eriu*, 38 (1987), 81–140; *ibid.*, 39 (1988), pp. 1–66.

[8] E. J. Cowan, 'Myth and Identity in Early Medieval Scotland', *The Scottish Historical Review*, LXIII (1984), pp. 111–35.

Scots migrated from Ireland to north Britain in the fourth century BC, subdued the inhabitants, and established a dynasty, beginning in 330 BC with Fergus I, which had ruled without interruption ever since. In reality, the historical Fergus Mac Erc, from whom this mythic Fergus I was cloned, established the Dalriadic dynasty nearly eight hundred years later, in AD 500.[9] This revised version of the myth interposed 45 kings between these two Ferguses, giving the Scots a far more ancient royal dynasty than the English lawyers could produce. During the course of the following centuries, this dynastic claim became central to Scottish tradition, while their Egyptian ancestry was quietly dropped.[10]

By the seventeenth century, political realignments in Scotland, and the ever closer ties with its near and powerful neighbour, England, brought on by the union of the two crowns, required the further adaptation of this national myth.[11] Concurrent political changes had an even more profound impact in Ireland, and on its historiographical tradition, but the latter was also put under strain by the evolution of the Scottish myth. In the first place, the renewed claim to an independent Scottish kingdom from 330 BC contradicted one of the factual elements of the Irish tradition, that the Scottish monarchy had been established much later by the Dalriadan colony from Ireland in the sixth century. When, in 1603, the Stuarts assumed the English throne and therefore became kings of Ireland, Irish writers such as Roderic O'Flaherty in *Ogygia* traced the 'Milesian' ancestry of the Stuarts to this event, and hence created an Irish genealogical stake in the new British monarchy.[12]

The Hiberno-Scottish dispute over the past was further intensified by the Scottish priest, Thomas Dempster, who exploited the resemblance between the Latin name for Ireland, 'Scotia', meaning the motherland of the Scoti or Gaels, and Scotland. In three works which appeared in the 1620s, Dempster inverted the historically accurate and hitherto widely accepted model of colonisation from Antrim into Argyll, and claimed Scotland as 'Scotia' and Ireland as *its* colony. Dempster's motive for this sleight of hand was to gain for the glory of Scotland any saint or scholar who had the medieval Latin label of 'Scotus'. In the process, he annexed the Irish patron saints of Patrick and Brigid, and the scholastic philosopher, John Scotus Eriugena, among many others.[13]

While Dempster's claims were energetically refuted by both Irish and English scholars, it was not until the appearance of Thomas Innes's *A Critical Essay on the*

---

[9] John Bannerman, 'The Scots of Dalriada', in Gordon Menzies, ed., *Who are the Scots?* (London, 1972), pp. 66–7.

[10] William Matthews, 'The Egyptians in Scotland: The Political History of a Myth', *Viator*, 1 (1970), pp. 289–306.

[11] Roger A. Mason, 'Scotching the Brut: Politics, History and National Myth in Sixteenth-Century Britain', in Roger A. Mason, ed., *Scotland and England 1286–1815* (Edinburgh, 1987), pp. 60–84.

[12] Roderic O'Flaherty, *Ogygia: seu Rerum Hibernicorum Chronologia* (London, 1685). Writers in Irish put forward such arguments earlier. C.f. B. Ó Buachalla, 'Na Stíobhartaigh agus an tAos Léinn: Cing Séamas', *Proceedings of the Royal Irish Academy*, C, LXXXIII (1983), pp. 81–134; Padraig Breathnach, 'Metamorphoses 1603: Dán le hEochaidh O hEoghusa', *Eigse*, 17 (1977/78), pp. 169–80.

[13] Leerssen, *Mere Irish and Fíor-Ghael*, pp. 303–5.

Ancient Inhabitants of the Northern Parts of Britain, or Scotland in 1729 that the Scottish origin myth and its more recent accretions were convincingly challenged by a Scottish writer. Innes was a Catholic priest and Stuart loyalist, based for the most part in France, and his work shows the influence of European historians. Displaying a Mabillon-like concern for documentary evidence, Innes subjected the histories of Boece and Buchanan to severe scrutiny, and particularly the latter's use of a mythic elective kingship to justify the usurpation of Mary Stuart. Armed with the Scottish kinglists, he demolished the case for the 40 odd kings before Fergus Mac Erc.[14]

However, there were interesting tensions between Innes's apparently rigorous methodology and his desire not to undermine either the Stuart pretender or the honour of Scotland, which often led to the abandonment of this enlightened historiographical approach. To give just one example, he was conscious that his demolition of the pre-sixth-century Scottish kings might have adverse implications for the Pretender's cause. In consequence, he went to considerable pains to substitute a Pictish hereditary dynasty into which the Dalriadan Kenneth MacAlpin married in the ninth century to unite the two peoples.[15] This emphasis on the Picts, whom he also called the Caledonians, was to be taken up and extended later in the century by James Macpherson and John Pinkerton.[16]

Once again, major changes in the Scottish narrative of their past had serious knock-on effects for Irish historiography. The challenge to the Milesian genealogy of the Stuarts, so important in the seventeenth century, was not in itself a great blow, and indeed could be regarded as a blessing, now that loyalty to the Hanoverian monarchy was a central issue in Irish politics. Certainly it was not dwelt on by any historian in Ireland in the eighteenth century. Innes's verdict that Irish accounts were as unhistorical as the Scottish was of more lasting significance. Irish annalists were not to be trusted on their own past, he claimed, and the only reliable material to be found in their work referred to the Pictish monarchy, because it was unrelated to their own national honour.[17] This selective scepticism, so typical of Innes, had particular implications for one of the most important Irish publications of the eighteenth century, the English translation of Geoffrey Keating's *Foras Feasa ar Eirinn* (*c.* 1634) which appeared in 1723, just six years before Innes's *Critical Essay*.

Written in part to counter the anti-Irish slurs of English writers such as Edmund Spenser and Fynes Morrison, Keating's *Foras Feasa* was arguably the

---

[14] Thomas I. Rae, 'Historical Scepticism in Scotland before David Hume' in R. F. Brissenden, ed., *Studies in the Eighteenth Century*, II (Canberra, 1973), pp. 205–21. See also Donaldson, *The Jacobite Song*, p. 14; Hector Boece, *The Chronicles of Scotland*, trans. by John Bellenden, 2 vols (Edinburgh, 1938–41); George Buchanan, *History of Scotland*, trans. by James Aikman (Edinburgh and Glasgow, 1827–30).

[15] Thomas Innes, *A Critical Essay on the Ancient Inhabitants of the Northern Parts of Britain, or Scotland*, 2 vols (London, 1729), I, pp. 134–6, 177–9.

[16] James Macpherson, *An Introduction to the History of Great Britain and Ireland* (London, 1771); John Pinkerton, *A Dissertation on the Origin of the Scythians or Goths* (London, 1787).

[17] Innes, *A Critical Essay*, I, pp. 102–4.

most significant and influential Irish narrative history of the seventeenth century. Reflecting also the trauma of new waves of foreign 'invasion', it was crucial in reviving the origin legends of the *Leabhar Gabhála* and other compilations and making them available to new audiences. In addition to his role as a populariser, Keating also contributed to the organic growth of these myths, by incorporating the Anglo-Norman colonisers of the twelfth century, who were also his own ancestors, into the medieval scheme.[18] The translation of *Foras Feasa*, under the title of *The General History of Ireland* (1723), was a handsome folio volume, containing plates of Brian Boru and the pedigrees of many 'Milesian' gentry families, such as the O'Briens, earls of Inchiquin, who had converted to Protestantism but were still proud of their native Irish ancestry. Many of these families subscribed to the volume, and the translator, Dermod O'Connor, gave some idea of its importance to them:

> [the Irish of noble birth] valued it as the choicest Collection of ancient Records that possibly can be recovered from the Ruins of Time, to support the Honour of their Ancestors, and to give the World a just Idea of the Dignity of the Country where they were born.[19]

But Innes raised doubts about the veracity of those same 'ancient Records' that Keating had drawn on, and in particular the wealth of detail which they contained about episodes in the remotest past, especially the journeying of the Milesians to Ireland.[20]

Thus, while the appearance of Keating in translation helped foster a new vogue for Milesian ancestry, it also brought to the forefront new doubts about the evidence for it. Eighteenth-century European ideas on methodology and sources were applied to the first Irish narrative history which claimed to be based on specific primary documents, and although it continued to be used in the absence of any alternative, it was generally regarded as unscholarly, and Keating was dubbed 'the Irish Geoffrey of Monmouth'.[21]

In Scotland, there was some attempt to reinstate the high antiquity of the Scottish monarchy by, among others, David Malcolme, a Presbyterian minister, who accused the Catholic Innes of putting forward 'schemes . . . hurtful to the State and the several established Churches here'.[22] But, for several decades, no

---

[18] Bernadette Cunningham, 'Seventeenth-Century Interpretation of the Past: The Case of Geoffrey Keating', *Irish Historical Studies* XXV (1986), pp. 116–28.

[19] Geoffrey Keating, *The General History of Ireland*, trans. by Dermod O'Connor (London, 1723), translator's preface, p. ii.

[20] Innes, *A Critical Essay*, II, pp. 416–18.

[21] Walter Harris, 'An Essay on the Defects in the Histories of Ireland, and Remedies proposed for the Improvement Thereof', in Walter Harris, ed., *Hibernica* (Dublin, 1747–50), part 1, p. 138.

[22] David Malcolme, *An Essay on the Antiquities of Great Britain and Ireland* (Edinburgh, 1738), item 13: 'Letter to the H.G.V.E. from C.', pp. 1–3. See also [Andrew Waddel], *Remarks on Innes' Critical Essay on the Ancient Inhabitants of Scotland* (Edinburgh, 1733), reprinted in *Scotia Rediviva: A Collection of Tracts Illustrative of the History and Antiquities of Scotland* (Edinburgh, 1826), pp. 225–56.

full-scale rebuttal of the case made by Innes emerged in either country, nor had any Scottish writer pursued the Pictish line suggested by him. However, the rise of a new political middle class in Ireland, and the complex adjustment to the final defeat of the Jacobite cause in Scotland, were soon to produce new validating or compensatory historical narratives in both countries which drew on seventeenth-century tradition. The key figures were Charles O'Conor in Ireland and James Macpherson in Scotland, who are more usually bracketed together in relation to the Ossian controversy, but whose background and work reveal some interesting general parallels as well as contrasts.[23]

Charles O'Conor was unusual, if not unique, among Irish writers and intellectuals in this period in being from a Catholic landowning family. The massive confiscations of the seventeenth century had resulted in a transformation of the landed interest in Ireland from predominantly Catholic and native Irish or Old English, to new planter stock of Presbyterian or Anglican persuasion. The small number of Catholic landowners, roughly 14 per cent in 1702, further declined through conversions to the established church, to a mere 5 per cent by 1776.[24] O'Conor farmed a remnant of his ancestral lands, which had been reduced even further in the Williamite confiscations, as his Jacobite grandfather was one of the last to surrender and was penalised accordingly. His mother retained her Jacobite sympathies until her death.[25] Charles belonged to a minor branch of a very exalted family, now in modest but comfortable circumstances. The O'Conors had been hereditary provincial kings before the twelfth-century colonisation; the last high king of Ireland, defeated by Henry II, had been Rory O'Conor. In his childhood, the family had kept up some of the customs of the almost vanished Gaelic aristocracy, such as acting as patrons to poets and musicians. Turlough O'Carolan, the blind composer, had taught the young Charles to play the harp. In addition, he learnt Gaelic as well as the classics and English literature, and copied Gaelic manuscripts under the supervision of a member of the O'Duigenan family of hereditary historians.[26] Equipped with this education, he was the only historian of the period who could read the surviving manuscripts with any facility. He felt this strongly and took on himself the role of mediating the Gaelic literary tradition to a late eighteenth-century reading public increasingly drawn to this almost lost and therefore less threatening world.

[23] Clare O'Halloran, 'Irish Re-creations of the Gaelic Past: The Challenge of Macpherson's Ossian', *Past and Present*, 124 (1989), pp. 69–95.

[24] J. G. Simms, 'The Establishment of Protestant Ascendancy, 1691–1714' in T. W. Moody and W. E. Vaughan, eds., *The New History of Ireland*, Vol. IV: *Eighteenth-Century Ireland 1691–1800* (Oxford, 1986), pp. 12–13. But see also Louis Cullen, 'Catholics under the Penal Laws', *Eighteenth-Century Ireland*, 1 (1986), pp. 23–36, for criticism of these figures.

[25] Charles Owen O'Conor, *The O'Conors of Connaught* (Dublin, 1891), pp. 284–5, 286–91; Pearse Street Public Library, Dublin, Gilbert Collection, MS 203, f. 27, Charles O'Conor to J. C. Walker, 31 January 1786.

[26] Catherine A. Sheehan, 'The Contribution of Charles O'Conor of Belanagare to Gaelic Scholarship in Eighteenth-Century Ireland', *Journal of Celtic Studies*, II (1958), p. 219.

James Macpherson also came from a Gaelic speaking background and, again like O'Conor, was born into a minor branch of a distinguished clan. While O'Conor was not yet born when his grandfather fought on the Jacobite side, the young James at 10 years of age experienced the 1745 uprising, in which his relative and clan chief, Ewan Macpherson of Cluny, played a prominent part. In the aftermath of Culloden, Badenoch, his home, swarmed with troops searching for Ewan Macpherson who hid out in the surrounding hills until 1755, when he made his escape to France. The Cluny estates, and those of 13 more rebel clan chiefs, were forfeited to the crown. Draconian laws were introduced to break up the remains of the distinctive Highland society, including the banning of the use of Gaelic in schools.[27] Thus, both O'Conor and Macpherson witnessed the breakup of the Gaelic society in which they were reared, and this is reflected in their most significant writings on the early periods of Irish and Scottish history, which were published within 5 years of each other. O'Conor's *Dissertations on the Ancient History of Ireland* first appeared in 1753, but Macpherson's Ossian poems prompted him to produce a substantially revised edition which came out in 1766 and contained the well known appendix attacking the Scot's historical arguments. Macpherson's *An Introduction to the History of Great Britain and Ireland* appeared in 1771 and went through two further editions in 1772 and 1773. It marked the beginning of his departure from Scottish poetry into historical and political writing, although he brought out a translation of *The Iliad* in 1773, and a new edition of *The Poems of Ossian* in the same year. His other books, notably *The History of Great Britain from the Restoration to the Accession of the House of Hanover* (1775) and *The History and Management of the East India Company from its Origin in 1600 to the Present Times* (1779), indicate the direction of his interests, away from the Highlands and its literature, and towards metropolitan politics and commerce.

Both O'Conor and Macpherson shared the aim of writing anew the past with little or no reference to their predecessors, or at least without acknowledging much debt to them. They also dealt with the same subject, the nature of Gaelic society in pre-Christian Ireland and in Scotland. Macpherson's portrayal of a third-century Gaelic society in the Highlands re-established at least one element of the medieval tradition, the early inhabitation of northern Britain by the Scots. He had already sketched this out in the preface and footnotes to *Temora*, the second volume of Ossianic verse which had appeared in 1763. This had enraged Irish historians with its historical scheme, which revived Dempster's seventeenth-century claim that Scotland was the motherland of the Gaels and Ireland merely a later colony.[28]

Following the suggestion of Innes, Macpherson increasingly shifted the focus onto the other tribes of North Britain, known variously as the Picts and

---

[27] Fiona J. Stafford, *The Sublime Savage: James Macpherson and the Poems of Ossian* (Edinburgh, 1988), chapter 1, *passim*.

[28] James Macpherson, *Temora* (London, 1763), pp. viii–x.

Caledonians. He subsumed both Scots and Picts into a tribe of Caledonian Celtae or 'Caël', Celts from Gaul who allegedly were the 'old Britons' and original inhabitants of the island long before the Welsh and the Anglo-Saxons.[29] In doing this, Macpherson was in a long Scottish tradition of reworking a *British* origin legend, and while concerned to highlight the recent and traumatic breakup of the Highland way of life, he was also intent on providing a reworked myth of origins to match Scotland's new position in a United Kingdom with England, and to defend Scottish identity within it.

O'Conor's treatment of Irish origins was also shaped by the disappearance of the Gaelic world. Whereas Macpherson lamented the disappearance of the customs, language and way of life of Highlanders in general, O'Conor was more exercised by the almost certain extinction of the high literary culture of the learned classes of Gaelic society. While elements of the traditional lore were still common among the Gaelic poets, he was virtually the only person in English-speaking society with even a limited competence in the archaic language of bardic literature. As he grew older he came to associate the final disappearance of that world with his own death.[30] His efforts to pass on his knowledge were not successful, and he seemed overwhelmed by the enormity of the task. In 1781 he engaged a young local boy as a scribal apprentice, but the difficulties of making a living at this kind of work were such that within two years the trainee had left to become a servant in Dublin.[31]

While O'Conor had little hope of singlehandedly creating a future for bardic learning, he could at least give it an impressive past. This may partly explain the unwavering commitment to the existence of a literate culture in pre-Christian Ireland, which was a major theme of his historical writing. He held to it despite his belief that the historian should aim to separate the factual from the fabulous in the annals and should rigidly exclude the latter.[32] He continued to make use of the Milesian tradition, because it traced the Irish back to Spain and to the Phoenicians, from whom they allegedly learnt their alphabet, and thus were able to develop such an early literate culture. His one concession to the spirit of the age was to omit the suspicious detail of the myth, for example, the eponymous ancestors, Gathelus, Scota and Míl, and the number of ships in which the Milesians sailed to Ireland.[33] He was more interested in proving Phoenician *influence* than descent; what he called, 'the Commerce of [our] Spanish Ancestors with the lettered Nations of

---

[29] Macpherson, *Introduction to the History of Great Britain and Ireland*, pp. 90–1.

[30] Charles O'Conor, 'Third letter to Colonel Vallancey', *Collectanea de Rebus Hibernicis*, IV, no. xiii (1784), p. 108; O'Conor to Hugh MacDermot, 12 June 1776, in Catherine C. Ward and Robert E. Ward, eds., *The Letters of Charles O'Conor of Belanagare*, 2 vols (Ann Arbor, 1980), II, p. 87.

[31] O'Conor to Chev. O'Gorman, 17 January 1781, 14 March 1781 and 31 May 1783, in *ibid.*, pp. 159, 162, 189–90.

[32] O'Conor, *Dissertations on the History of Ireland* (Dublin, 1766), pp. x, 11–12.

[33] *Ibid.*, p. 21.

Phenicia [sic] and Egypt'. Once settled in Ireland, however, all such contacts ceased and the Milesians became:

> a People sequestered from all the learned Nations, and indebted to their own industry for any Progress they made in the useful Arts of Life, either in bettering their Condition, or enlarging their Knowledge.[34]

While Macpherson celebrated the orality of his third-century Gaelic society, O'Conor strenuously sought to subvert such a primitivist view. Since he could not produce any actual manuscript remains of this pre-Christian culture, his case rested on Ogham writing. This was a type of runic script in which the letters of the Latin alphabet were represented by sets of parallel lines, upright or diagonal, meeting or crossing a straight baseline. It was used for commemorative inscriptions on standing stones, and is now thought to date from the early Christian period.[35] O'Conor, taking an idea from the seventeenth-century antiquary, Roderic O'Flaherty, claimed that Ogham bore no relation to the Latin or Greek alphabets and therefore pre-dated their adoption in Christian Ireland. He was even incautious enough to claim that Ogham was derived directly from the Phoenician.[36] However, the Ogham alphabet, no matter what its origins, was hardly convincing evidence of a sophisticated pagan society. In the clash with Macpherson, O'Conor's case was undermined both directly and indirectly by the former's insistence, and indeed proud boast, of a purely oral Scots Gaelic culture. It is interesting that the sceptical public reaction to O'Conor's claim of an early literate civilisation and to Macpherson's defence of the Ossian poems against forgery charges was the same: that they should produce the manuscript evidence.

In old age, while he never gave up the claim, O'Conor somewhat modified and moderated his views on the nature of this pre-Christian civilisation. The 1780s was a period of great political change in Ireland. The first Catholic Relief Act had been passed in 1778; in 1782, Poynings's Law was amended and the Declaratory Act repealed, thus seeming to give the Irish parliament more powers to regulate domestic affairs. Despite his age and ill health, O'Conor was buoyed up by these developments. He had written the *Dissertations* as part of his campaign to end the penal laws against Catholics and to counteract the negative image of the barbaric Irish which had long been used as a justification for their subordination. His vision of early Irish society was one in which learning, industry and piety predominated; characteristics which he implied would come to the fore again if religious toleration was introduced.

Political developments seemed to signal that the authorities accepted his arguments that, as he put it in a letter, 'indeed we are all become *good Protestants in politics*' and that Jacobitism was now as remote as 'the principles which animated

---

[34] *Ibid.*, pp. 27–8.
[35] Michael Richter, *Medieval Ireland* (London, 1987), pp. 30–1.
[36] O'Conor, *Dissertations*, pp. 35, 17.

the hostile parties of York and Lancaster in a former period'.[37] His late writings were, therefore, more open to the possibility that early Ireland was not the wholly polished civil society that he had once propounded. In 1784, he was prepared to admit a degree of what he called 'coarseness' among the early Irish, although he still held to their literacy, and Eastern origins:

> Though this last Colony had arrived from a country long possessed by the Phoenicians and Carthaginians, and imported hither the elements of arts and literature; yet it must not be forgot, that they also introduced the coarse manners of their Scytho-Celtic ancestors, and that on their arrival in Ireland they mixed with a still coarser people than themselves.[38]

He also conceded that unspecified 'barbarous customs' had existed among the early Irish,[39] but at no point did he come close to accepting that the history of society in Ireland fell into three distinct stages of savagery, barbarity and finally civility—a widely held theory developed most notably by Adam Ferguson in Scotland and adopted by Macpherson in his work.[40] Insofar as he had a coherent view, O'Conor seemed to adhere to the older concept of a cyclical model of historical process, put forward by, among others, Machiavelli in the *Discourses*.[41] According to O'Conor's version of this scheme, barbarism could occur at any stage of society's development and was a direct consequence of faction or corrupt government, and not of Irish national character, as English writers such as Spenser and Hume suggested.[42]

Markedly different political motives lay behind Macpherson's portrayal of third-century Scotland as a warrior society. Richard Sher has shown that the project of gathering material in the Highlands which resulted in the Ossian poems was connected with the campaign for a Scottish militia, and with the desire among the Edinburgh elite for a Scottish literature that was recognised as equal, if not superior, to that of England. A number of the Scottish literati sponsored Macpherson to produce translations of Gallic poetry which would further both ends at once.[43] Also in contrast to O'Conor, Macpherson was a thoroughgoing primitivist, in that he looked back to the third-century Fingalian society of the poems as epitomising the first or savage state in the progress to civility, when an absence of property and luxury prevented the corruption which accompanied the later phases of barbarity and civilisation. Macpherson's Caledonians 'retained the pure but

---

[37] Pearse Street Public Library, Dublin, Gilbert Collection, MS 203, f. 27, Charles O'Conor to J. C. Walker, 31 January 1786.
[38] O'Conor, 'Third Letter to Col. Vallancey', pp. 116–17.
[39] O'Conor, 'Second Letter to Col. Vallancey', *Collectanea de Rebus Hibernicis*, III, no. xii (1783), pp. 665–6.
[40] Adam Ferguson, *An Essay on the History of Civil Society* (Edinburgh, 1767); Macpherson, *Temora* (London, 1763), p. xi.
[41] Peter Burke, *The Renaissance Sense of the Past* (London, 1969), p. 87.
[42] O'Conor, *Dissertations*, p. xvi.
[43] Richard B. Sher, *Church and University in the Scottish Enlightenment* (Edinburgh, 1985), pp. 242–61.

unimproved language of their ancestors together with their rude simplicity of manners'. He gave them all the characteristics associated with the idealised savage: they were 'fierce, passionate and impetuous', 'in love with slaughter', but also 'plain and upright in their dealings, and far removed from the deceit and duplicity of modern times'.[44] His references to modern civilisation were extremely negative. On the bravery of the Celts, he wrote:

> The contempt which the Celtic nations shewed for death, is a proof that they were not anxious about possession of the conveniencies of life; and that circumstance shut up the great channel of corruption which pollutes the human mind in an advanced stage of civility.[45]

This nostalgic strain in Macpherson's work was only partly a yearning for supposedly third-century simplicities; it was also an elegy to the pre-Culloden Highlands of his childhood. He openly sought to connect these two worlds, one imagined, the other experienced, by using anecdotal evidence of allegedly strong traces of pagan superstition still in existence among what he termed 'the ancient Scots'.[46] Earlier, in the dissertation prefixed to *Fingal* (1762), Macpherson had lamented the transformation of the Highlands of his youth:

> The genius of the highlanders has suffered a great change within these few years. The communication with the rest of the island is open, and the introduction of trade and manufactures has destroyed that leisure which was formerly dedicated to hearing and repeating the poems of ancient times.

He went on to refer to those who had left the Highlands to make their careers elsewhere, as he too was in the process of doing:

> Many have now learned to leave their mountains, and seek their fortunes in a milder climate; and though a certain *amor patriae* may sometimes bring them back, they have, during their absence, imbibed enough of foreign manners to despise the customs of their ancestors. Bards have been long disused, and the spirit of genealogy has greatly subsided. Men begin to be less devoted to their chiefs, and consanguinity is not so much regarded.[47]

On one level, *An Introduction to the History of Great Britain and Ireland* can be read as a symbol of Macpherson's enduring 'devotion to his chiefs', despite his increasing involvement in English politics and commerce; its sentimentalism as much a product of the experience of self-imposed exile in the metropolis as of the literary taste of the age.

---

[44] Macpherson, *Introduction*, pp. 35, 188–9.
[45] *Ibid.*, p. 198.
[46] *Ibid.*, pp. 163–6.
[47] Macpherson, *Fingal* (London, 1762), p. xv.

Such nostalgia was entirely absent from the writings of O'Conor, in which Enlightenment perspectives predominated. When, for example, in the *Dissertations* he described the Irish climate, he emphasised, prosaically, the constant cloud and rain, instead of Ossianic-type mists, and deplored the lack of drainage schemes to improve the boggy terrain.[48] Improvement and industry were constant themes in both his books and his correspondence; in particular, the barrier to progress and prosperity in the country as a whole which the Penal Laws constituted.[49] It was essential for O'Conor to take a pragmatic attitude to his surroundings. While Macpherson had left his birth place at the age of eighteen to go to university, O'Conor stayed on in Roscommon and continued the task of consolidating the family lands begun by his father. Although he complained of his scholarly isolation and pined for Dublin and his antiquarian and political friends there, his writing was the product of that particular Catholic experience even more than of metropolitan culture.[50]

O'Conor also retained an essentially aristocratic attitude to his world. In a letter to his friend, the Catholic archbishop of Dublin, John Carpenter, without a trace of irony he compared their friendship to that of his ancestor, the high king Rory O'Conor, and the then archbishop, Laurence O'Toole.[51] In his contempt for popular literature (he dismissed the tales of Finn MacCumhal on which Macpherson drew for his Ossian as 'mere amusements for the vulgar, recited in various shapes to this day, among them'), in his oft-expressed fears for the survival of Gaelic learning, and in his regrets at not having had a patron, O'Conor echoed the earlier complaints of the bardic and post-bardic poets of the previous century.[52] His perspective on the Gaelic world was made up of both archaic and Enlightenment attitudes, which were equally derived from aristocratic notions of society and politics.

Thus, despite some shared cultural traditions and similar concerns, Irish and Scottish antiquarianism diverged in significant ways in this period. Scottish attempts to detach the Gallic language and traditions from their Irish roots did not succeed, but perhaps had to be attempted if Scotland was to develop an identity which reflected its own historical experience and contemporary political reality. Conflicts between Irish and Scottish antiquaries were inevitable, given their inheritance of the same body of myth and legend. The contrasting uses which they made of this reflect their separate political needs, but also similar cultural pressures as peripheral regions of the British state.[53]

---

[48] O'Conor, *Dissertations*, pp. 1–2.
[49] O'Conor to George Faulkner, 25 September 1767, in Ward and Ward, eds., *Letters of Charles O'Conor*, I, p. 228.
[50] O'Conor to John Curry, 23 June 1758, in *ibid.*, pp. 57–8.
[51] O'Conor to John Carpenter, 20 February 1781, in *ibid.*, II, p. 161.
[52] O'Conor, 'Second Letter to Colonel Vallancey', pp. 653–4; O'Conor to Chev. O'Gorman, 17 January 1781, in Ward and Ward, eds., *Letters of Charles O'Conor*, II, p. 158; Leerssen, *Mere Irish and Fíor-Ghael*, pp. 224–9.
[53] An earlier version of this paper was read to the Cambridge Inter-faculty Seminar. I am grateful to Tom Dunne, Brendan Bradshaw and Micheál Mc Craith for their comments and assistance.

12

Land, the landed and relationships with England: literature and perception 1760–1830

Stana Nenadic

INTRODUCTION: LITERATURE AS HISTORY

IN RECENT YEARS a number of studies have sought to establish the changing relationship between Scotland and England, and between Ireland and England.[1] The populations of Scotland and Ireland in the eighteenth and early nineteenth centuries were predominantly rural. The land was the principal source of employment for the common people, it provided a large element of the income of the professional and commercial ranks, and the wealthy and powerful of each country were mainly from a landed background. It seems reasonable to suggest that any consideration of relationships with England should give some attention to the role of land and the people and activities associated with land. This is the intention of the present essay, and since the concern is with the evolution of centre-periphery relationships as manifested within a cultural discourse, the emphasis is on perceptions—the foundation of any relationship—as revealed through a particular genre of published literature, and through a form of elite leisure activity associated with that literature.

The essay deals largely with the Scottish case, though an Irish comparative dimension is addressed in the concluding section. Its purpose is to demonstrate some of the ways whereby depictions of the land and people generated a positive and confident self-image among the Scottish elite and, for the English elite observer, a positive and acceptable image of Scotland. The study is based on contemporary accounts of pleasure tours, a source that provides detailed descriptions of the appearance of the land, of the people who owned and lived upon the

---

[1] T. C. Smout, 'Scotland and England: Is Dependency a Symptom or Cause of Underdevelopment', *Review*, III, 4 (1980), pp. 601–30; W. J. McCormack, *Ascendancy and Tradition in Anglo-Irish Literary History from 1789 to 1939* (Oxford, 1985).

land, and the purposes for which the land was employed. Travel accounts of the eighteenth and early nineteenth centuries represent a distinct and popular literary genre with precise conventions of narrative and description. The genre changed through time and was manifested in several sub-genre forms.[2] There was a close relationship between travel literature, the pursuit of pleasure travel and the fiction of the period. Many early Scottish novels, including Walter Scott's *Waverley* and more especially Smollett's *Humphrey Clinker*, have a narrative structure that is built around a tour. Galt's *The Entail* incorporates an account of a tour, the same is true of Edgeworth's Irish novel *The Absentee*. Reflecting the connection between tour literature and the novel, at certain points in the essay evidence is also drawn from fictional journeys.

Any employment of literature as historical evidence raises questions of methodology and epistemology. Such an endeavour must, of necessity, be founded on a close understanding of the nature of the source—which takes time to develop—and be sensitive to the motivations of both the producers and consumers of the genre—which are not easily discovered. Theories that refer to the 'audience in the text', or to the hermeneutic relationship between literature or art and *mentalité*, are powerful tools available to historians of past cultures, yet the marshalling of appropriate evidence is invariably problematic. Difficulties are frequently found when dealing with such issues as the treatment of reality, and it should be more widely recognised that in the use of literature as history, patterns of omission are sometimes as significant as those of inclusion. Though detailed exploration of such matters is probably inappropriate to the audience of the present text, it should be recognised, nonetheless, that this area is one of much debate.[3]

THE LITERARY TOURIST IN SCOTLAND

As noted above, the personal travel account was one of the most popular forms of published prose literature in the eighteenth and early nineteenth centuries and commanded a large audience among elite and middle class readers. The overt purpose of the genre, in common with the purpose of most types of respectable literary endeavour including early fiction, was to provide 'pleasurable instruction'.[4] Its impact on the audience was to heighten an awareness of foreign countries and cultures, both of the past and the present, and, for those who sought more than to

---

[2] See C. L. Batten, *Pleasurable Instruction: Form and Convention in Eighteenth-Century Travel Literature* (Los Angeles, 1978).

[3] A. D. Harvey, *Literature into History* (1989); T. Dunne, 'A Polemical Introduction: Literature, Literary Theory and the Historian', in T. Dunne, ed., *The Writer as Witness: Literature as Historical Evidence* (Cork, 1987); S. Nenadic, 'Illegitimacy, Insanity and Insolvency: Wilkie Collins and the Victorian Nightmares', in A. Marwick, ed., *The Arts, Literature and Society* (1990).

[4] Batten, *Pleasurable Instruction*, ch. 1.

'travel in their closets',[5] it promoted the desire to see in person the places and peoples that were described.

In the first sixty years of the eighteenth century there was a vast production of published accounts of real or fictional tours through Europe, whereas tours through Scotland or Ireland were few, and only rarely, where these did exist, were they the product of a journey undertaken for pleasure.[6] The absence of a body of Scottish travel literature reflects the fundamental want of interest in, and indeed antipathy towards, things Scottish among the English. In the words of Smollett, describing the trepidations of one fictional tourist when faced with the prospect of journeying into Scotland,

> She was so little acquainted with the geography of the island, that she imagined we could not go to Scotland but by sea; and, after we had passed through the town of Berwick, when . . . told . . . we were upon Scottish ground, she could hardly believe the assertion. If the truth must be told, the South Britons in general are woefully ignorant in this particular. What, between want of curiosity, and traditional sarcasms, the effect of ancient animosity, the people at the other end of the island know as little of Scotland as of Japan.[7]

This situation was to change in the last four decades of the eighteenth century when there developed among the English, and increasingly among Lowland Scots, a desire to know more of the different areas of 'North Britain' for both instruction and pleasure. It is impossible to quantify the numbers that toured Scotland in the eighteenth and early nineteenth centuries. Table 1 (overleaf) provides an indirect index of a significant growth in interest among English ('closet') tourists from the 1770s, Scottish tourists from the 1790s and overseas tourists, principally German and French, during the early decades of the nineteenth century.

The majority of the tourists who published accounts of their journeys were men drawn from a leisured, literary and professional elite and motivated by the desire to observe and comment on little-known antiquities and traditions, natural history, or customs and manners.[8] Scottish authors had a similar background and motivation, but frequently also sought to provide their audience with a deeper understanding of the social and economic conditions that prevailed in Scotland, especially in remote and underdeveloped areas. In several cases the aims of these tourists were tied to the interests of one or other improvement lobby, and their journeys cannot be regarded as pleasure tours as such. John Knox's *Tour through the Highlands of*

---

[5] The term is used in *A Journey to the Highlands of Scotland with Occasional Remarks on Dr Johnson's Tour—by a Lady* (London, 1777), p. 64.

[6] For example E. Burt, *Letters from a Gentleman in the North of Scotland* (1754), the account of an English soldier garrisoned in Scotland.

[7] T. Smollett, *The Expedition of Humphrey Clinker* (Oxford, 1988, first published 1771), pp. 213–14.

[8] On the different sub-genres see Batten, *Pleasurable Instruction*, ch. 3.

Scotland, published in 1787 on behalf of the British Fisheries Society—and described at the time as evidence of 'true patriotism'—is such a case.[9]

Table 1: *Number and place of publication of accounts of personal tours and travels in Scotland, published between 1730 and 1830*

	All places	England	Scotland	Europe
1730–39	0	0	0	0
1740–49	3	3	0	0
1750–59	5	5	0	0
1760–69	7	5	1	1
1770–79	14	10	2	2
1780–89	21	14	2	5
1790–99	26	10	14	2
1800–09	46	21	16	9
1810–19	37	18	14	5
1820–29	53	15	24	14

Source: A. Mitchell, 'A List of Travels, Tours etc. Relating to Scotland', *Proceedings of the Society of Antiquaries of Scotland*, XXXV (1900–1), pp. 431–638.

By the early 1790s, the rapid development of a tourist interest in Scotland could not go unremarked. Robert Heron—who published his own account of a tour through the Western Counties in 1793—attributed the phenomenon to several factors. The good roads and accommodation were one attraction,[10] and the abundance of game another.[11] The publication of Pennant's *Tour of Scotland* in 1769, and Samuel Johnson's provocative *Journey to the Western Isles* in 1775 had also, according to Heron, played a role in promoting the tourist interest.[12] Any reading of Scottish travel accounts can confirm the impact of Johnson's comments on contemporary elites. His frequent remarks on the barrenness of the land and the backwardness of the people provoked an immediate response among Scots and English eager to prove him wrong. One of the first anti-Johnson tours stated unequivocally that 'those who go the same road [as Johnson] will soon be convinced how false an account he has given of a country, to the hospitality of whose inhabitants he owns himself so much obliged'.[13] Gilpin had much to say about

---

[9] R. Heron, *Observations Made in a Journey through the Western Counties of Scotland in the Autumn of 1792* (Perth, 1793), p. 323.

[10] I. Lettice, *Letters on a Tour through Various Parts of Scotland in the Year 1792* (London, 1794), p. 235; Heron, *Observations*, pp. 41–2.

[11] Heron, *Observations*, pp. 42, 323. This source of attraction was observed as a commonplace more than ten years before the publication of Thornton's *Sporting Tour*, which Smout has described as a crucial influence. See T. C. Smout, 'Tours in the Scottish Highlands from the Eighteenth to the Twentieth Centuries', *Northern Scotland*, 5 (1983), pp. 99–121.

[12] Heron, *Observations*, p. 41.

[13] *Journey—by a Lady*, p. 65.

Johnson's choleric opinions on the want of beauty in Scotland.[14] There are frequent references to the 'deeprooted dislike of the Scotch to Dr Johnson',[15] and even as late as 1832 William Cobbett was moved to remark on the 'sententious and dogmatic lies of old Dr Johnson'.[16] Finally, in explaining the increase in tourism in Scotland, Heron refers to 'the progress of gardening and landscape painting in England' which attracted visitors seeking to observe the 'wilder scenery of nature . . . interspersed with various spots of ornament and cultivation'.[17]

BEAUTY AND UTILITY IN THE LANDSCAPE

As Smout and recently Womack have described, the interest of many tourists was founded on a correspondence between the natural terrain in Scotland and successive notions of sublime, picturesque and romantic landscape beauty.[18] The popular appeal of the Scottish landscape was stimulated by Ossianic poetry and by evocative word-pictures and engravings in certain of the travel accounts, notably Gilpin's *Observations on the Highlands of Scotland* of 1789. It was furthered in the early nineteenth century by the associations between romantic heroism or romantic love and the Highland landscape, especially in the poetry and fiction of Walter Scott. Each body of aesthetic theory—the sublime, the picturesque and the romantic—contributed to the formation of the dominant idea of the early nineteenth century, that Scotland's primary attractions were located in natural, wild, unpopulated and uncultivated landscapes or in landscapes in which human interventions and the human presence were minimal. It need hardly be stressed that the fortunate coincidence of aesthetics, landscape and literature contributed to the creation of a favourable perception of Scotland in English eyes in much the same way that seventeenth-century ideas of landscape beauty, which had not coincided with Scotland's natural terrain, had diminished the possibility of a positive view of Scotland.[19] For elites and middle ranks, fuelled by individualism and the desire to consume—states of mind that have been seen as emerging in parallel with Romanticism[20]—landscape in Scotland became a fashionable commodity to be purchased in the form of literary descriptions, as illustrations, as tour destinations or, for the wealthy few, as real estate.

Scottish observers, as with those from England and increasingly from Europe, participated in the enthusiasm for literary descriptions of the picturesque and

---

[14] W. Gilpin, *Observations Relative Chiefly to Picturesque Beauty . . . Particularly in the Highlands of Scotland* (1789), II, p. 119.

[15] J. E. Bowman, *The Highlands and Islands: A Nineteenth-Century Tour* (Gloucester, 1986), p. 187.

[16] *Cobbett's Tour in Scotland*, edited by D. Green (Aberdeen, 1984), p. 108.

[17] Heron, *Observations*, p. 41.

[18] Smout, 'Tours'; P. Womack, *Improvement and Romance: Constructing the Myth of the Highlands* (London, 1989), ch. 7.

[19] Womack, *Improvement*, p. 1.

[20] Argued in C. Campbell, *The Romantic Ethic and the Spirit of Modern Consumerism* (Oxford, 1987), ch. 1.

romantic scenes with which the Scottish landscape was endowed. But this should not cause us to forget the existence of other notions of desirable landscape, founded less on theories of aesthetics than on those of political economy, and held by many Scots and certain Englishmen during the years from 1760 to 1830. After all, the sublime, picturesque and romantic ideals, by stressing the uncultivated and the wildly natural in land and people, represented a fundamental paradox for those powerful individuals and agencies in Scotland that sought to promote the improvement and greater orderliness of Scotland's agriculture and people. There is no doubt that the landowners who dominated society and politics in Scotland had quickly recognised the benefits to be gained through facilitating tourism on their property. The investment in inns and willingness to make private parks and great houses available to elite strangers is testimony to this fact.[21] But the best interests of landowners—and these were commonly represented, by tourists who wrote on the subject, to be the best interests of Scots in general—lay in the cultivation and commercial development of the land.

Notions of the picturesque did incorporate the possibility that certain types of cultivation were capable of enhancing the landscape. Development could be consistent with aesthetics in those situations where 'nature is assisted by art, just enough to add to, not rob her of her beauties'.[22] 'Contemplating the landscape was not . . . a passive activity: it involved reconstructing the landscape in the imagination', and for those who owned the land, and had sufficient funds at their disposal, it also meant reconstructing the land in reality.[23] Landowners were enthusiastic to enhance the profits from their estates, and where this went hand-in-hand with a programme of beautification they were doubly pleased. The planting of trees, in a country criticised for a want of timber by many observers, satisfied both criteria and became a major area of landowner initiative. Other innovations may not have attracted praise in aesthetic terms, but on the issue of utility, the value placed on an orderly and, by implication, a happy population, and the overall contribution to the advance of a country conventionally perceived by all observers to be poor, development had a particular beauty of its own. Consider, for instance, the following description of Fife viewed from the Queensferry bank in the 1790s:

> The eye wandered, with delight, over one of the most populous, fertile and cultivated territories in Scotland. Its coals, its limestone, its abundant crops, its thriving manufacturing villages and the high rents which tenants are there enabled to pay to their landlords, without impoverishing themselves, occurred all together in the mind, and gave, insensibly, a new charm to the landscape.[24]

---

[21] For example see Heron's account of a visit to Lord Breadalbane's house and gardens at Taymouth. Access was via application to the game keeper on recommendation from the inn keeper. In the house he was asked to sign a visitors' book: Heron, *Observations*, pp. 237–41.
[22] *Journey—by a Lady*, p. 90.
[23] J. Barrell, *The Idea of Landscape and the Sense of Place, 1730–1840* (Cambridge, 1972), p. 6.
[24] Heron, *Observations*, p. 18.

Even Gilpin, the champion of the picturesque, presented a favourable perception of the developed landscape when he stated on visiting one of the great improved estates of the 1770s:

> Among the pleasing scenes of Drumlanrig... [is] the uncommon appearance of comfort and happiness, which reigns every where among the Duke's tenants. Contrary to the usual practice of the Scotch nobility, the Duke of Queensberry grants leases of his farms; and has built comfortable houses for his tenants, through his whole estate. Many of them are ranged within sight of his castle, at proper distances along the sides of the hills. If they are not picturesque, they have a much higher species of beauty: and adorn a country more than the most admired monuments of taste.[25]

It was recognised, of course, that change would compromise some of the natural attractions of the landscape, but this was a price that Scots were prepared to pay. As remarked by James Hogg in 1803:

> The Trossachs... have suffered severely in wild beauty by the ravages of the axe. But what they have lost in beauty they have gained in utility. They are now covered with stocks of tolerably good sheep, and there is still a sufficiency of wood to serve them for shelter in winter, which is all that is requisite for the store farmer. The lands belong most, either to the Hon. Miss Drummond, or the Earl of Moray, and are generally, though not very large, good sure farms, and will in time bring large rents.[26]

THE OWNERSHIP AND PEOPLING OF THE SCOTTISH LANDSCAPE

As the last extract suggests, tourist accounts of Scotland expended considerable efforts in describing patterns of land ownership and the peopling of the land, and also in giving precise accounts of the rising money values that were attached to land. This was especially true of those literary tours that were written by Scots who wished to convey positive perceptions of utility and development in their country. It was also characteristic of that sub-genre of tour literature of the 1770s to the early 1800s, exemplified by Johnson, that sought to portray manners and customs.[27] By the second and third decades of the nineteenth century, when the genre had shifted towards romantic accounts of uncultivated landscapes peopled with mythical or historical figures, the concern with real men (and occasionally real women) and the prosaic issue of land value and ownership was much diminished.

---

[25] Gilpin, *Observations*, II, pp. 93–4.
[26] J. Hogg, *A Tour of the Highlands in 1803* (Edinburgh, 1888), p. 13.
[27] On Johnson's intention to record customs and manners see C. Lamont, 'Dr Johnson, the Scottish Highlander, and the Scottish Enlightenment', *British Journal for Eighteenth-Century Studies*, XII, 1, (1989), pp. 47–56.

Yet it should be noted that Scottish novelists of the 1810s and 1820s—to a greater extent than English authors—were preoccupied with questions, situations and symbols arising from changes in property ownership.[28] For example, that most 'romantic' of the early Scottish romantic novels, *Waverley*, is constructed around an extended metaphor that links the history of Scotland's relationship with England to the fortunes, ownership and alliances (through marriage) of the fictional estates of Tully-Veolan in Scotland and Waverley-Honour in England.

In describing landowning, the most frequent reference is to aristocratic proprietors, their estates and their houses. The reasons for this are not hard to uncover. Much of Scotland was in the possession of a few very wealthy and powerful Anglified noblemen. In the second half of the eighteenth century several had invested considerable sums in the building and furnishing of grand new houses and gardens in the modern style, and in one case, that of the Dukes of Argyle, the complete rebuilding of the burgh that stood adjacent to the new house. Such programmes of estate development and house building commanded the attention of tourists everywhere in Britain.[29] But in Scotland they were especially striking, for as one observer stated, 'the ornamented grounds of the great proprietors appear here to extraordinary advantage ... Scenes of wild grandeur and natural magnificence are the best situations for the seats of men of great fortune. There is a sort of analogy by which all the different species of greatness are allied to each other'.[30]

Aristocratic proprietors were often acquainted with the elite tourists who visited Scotland—having met them in London while engaged in national affairs and leisure—or they were known through family connections. If the landowner was resident on his property—and by the later eighteenth century this was increasingly the case during the summer and early autumn, when most tours were made—the norms of hospitality required that such visitors be accommodated and entertained.[31] When the noble lord was not in residence, and for those tourists who had no claim to his personal attentions but were of a suitably high rank to be regarded as 'gentlemen', there were estate managers, gardeners or housekeepers instructed to act as guides to the house and its policies. Many Scottish tour accounts consist of a progress from one great house to another in a journey that took the traveller through the extensive properties of one great nobleman or another. The Dukes of Hamilton, Argyle and Queensberry, and the Earl of Breadalbane are most frequently mentioned as the builders of fine houses, as enlightened landlords and promoters of improved, capitalist farming. And if you were not privileged to be a guest of the noble proprietor, there was a fairly good chance—particularly in the

---

[28] See especially J. Galt, *The Entail* (1822); J. Galt, *The Last of the Lairds* (1826); S. Ferrier, *The Inheritance* (1824).

[29] An account of a tour incorporating some of the great estates of Derbyshire appears in chapters 42 and 43 of Jane Austen's *Pride and Prejudice* (1813).

[30] Heron, *Observations*, p. 234.

[31] See the response to Lettice's unannounced visit to the Earl of Bute at Mountstuart in 1792: Lettice, *Letters*, pp. 147–71.

southern and western Highlands, the principal tourist destination throughout the period—that you would find yourself staying at one of his inns.[32] It is not surprising, therefore, that the familiar personalities of the great aristocratic landowners should dominate the Scottish landscape when that landscape was perceived through the eyes of the literary tourist.

Lesser proprietors were also represented as a major presence, along with capitalist farmers and professionals, notably clergymen, land agents and army officers. Again the character of the average tourist accounts for this, since these were the people that visitors would meet socially, and ask for information on the areas they were visiting. The middling ranks of the Scottish countryside were described as hospitable to a remarkable degree—'so loving to strangers, that a man runs some risk of his life from their hospitality'[33]—and throughout the country were shown as possessing all the virtues of comfortable domesticity and improved understanding that were usual in England.[34] By the 1770s, literary depictions of Highland clan elites also frequently emphasised their modernised, Anglified and enlightened aspects. Though they might exhibit characteristics that were regarded as distinctly Scottish, these were commonly perceived as a colourful complement to other more important qualities that exemplified the British gentleman. The young laird of Col, Donald Maclean—who was 'so desirous of improving his inheritance, that he spent a considerable time among the farmers of Hertfordshire, and Hampshire, to learn their practice'—as described by Johnson, is a good illustration of the attractive and much promoted image of the modern Highlander, following the lifestyle of a lesser proprietor living on his own lands, observing many of the customs proper to a chieftain, such as the indulgence in hunting and maintenance of a piper—and loved by his 'subjects' in consequence—yet in all important particulars of outlook and behaviour a modernised and Anglified gentleman capitalist.[35]

By the latter part of the eighteenth century there was also a generally positive representation of that large number of lesser proprietors who had recently purchased land in Scotland, especially in areas adjacent to the great cities.[36] Travel accounts of this period, whether penned by Englishmen or Scots, promoted the advantages of landownership in Scotland in much the same way that agricultural writers, notably Sir John Sinclair, endeavoured to 'sell Scotland'.[37] As with new owners, capitalist farmers were a common feature on the landscape of the literary tourists, and accounts of new tenants were often coupled with detailed descriptions

---

[32] Bowman, *Highlands*, p. 66 states, 'the noble proprietor [Breadalbane], with a laudable attention to the wants of travellers and to his own interest, has erected suitable inns at the different stages between Kenmore and Inveraray'.

[33] Smollett, *Humphrey Clinker*, p. 239.

[34] See A. Calder, *Journal of a Tour to the North of Scotland* [1759] (Centre for Scottish Studies, Aberdeen, n.d.), p. 23.

[35] *Johnson's Journey to the Western Islands of Scotland*, edited by R. W. Chapman (Oxford, 1924), p. 68.

[36] For example, Heron, *Observations*, p. 16.

[37] See J. Sinclair, 'On the Advantages of Possessing Landed Property in Scotland', in *General Report of the Agricultural State, and Political Circumstances of Scotland* (Edinburgh, 1814), I, pp. 115–21.

of improved systems of land management and rising profits.[38] Others who peopled Scotland include the inn keepers of the major rural inns, many of whom were described as English, and other tourists, also often English and invariably members of the higher ranks. The common man, and more especially the common woman, as represented by named or identifiable individuals, were not so subject to the attentions of tour writers. This one might expect of the picturesque and romantic author, but it was true even when the purpose was to reveal customs and manners. Several factors account for the failure to represent the ordinary people. The narrative conventions of the genre were partly responsible, since they precluded details on the prosaic business of getting around the countryside, and it was here that tourists were most likely to encounter ordinary men and women.[39] Hence, it is instructive to compare published tours with private records not intended for publication. Dorothy Wordsworth's journal is a good illustration of the latter, being noteworthy for the attention that it gives to working people, especially women.[40] Most travellers were of elite status, and despite the paternal framework of social relationships, had limited contacts with the poor majority.[41] Social distance was heightened by the Gaelic spoken in so many Highland areas. When ordinary men and women do command the attention of the literary tourist, they are frequently portrayed anonymously and at a distance. Accounts of their material conditions, and of clothing and housing, stress a poverty and wretchedness in marked contrast to the favourable depictions of material conditions among individualised middle ranks. In appearance the Scottish worker bore ill comparison with those of England, even when seen through Scottish eyes.[42] But in contrast to the European peasantry, and especially in contrast to the peasants of Ireland, he showed to advantage. As suggested in the following quotation, from the 1770s onwards Scots were described as happy and peaceful, intelligent and industrious—the last two qualities usually seen as the products of parish education—despite their being so pitifully poor.[43]

> The peasants had the appearance of contentment . . . Though every habitation we passed, was as mean and almost as artless as an Indian hut, it was pleasant to see their inhabitants . . . with cheerful resignation in their looks.[44]

The poor were nowhere represented as a burden on the land; indeed, this was one of the 'advantages' of landownership in Scotland.[45] An independence of spirit was thought to prevail among the peasantry, they were strongly attached to the interests

---

[38] See Hogg, *Tour*, pp. 78, 88–9, for a good illustration with reference to farms at Letterewe and Strathinashalloch.
[39] Batten, *Pleasurable Instruction*, ch. 2.
[40] D. Wordsworth, *Recollections of a Tour Made in Scotland in 1803* (Edinburgh, 1974).
[41] For an unusual example of a tourist from a working background, see Hogg, *Tour*.
[42] See, for instance, the description in Smollett, *Humphrey Clinker*, p. 214.
[43] Womack, *Improvement and Romance*, ch. 2, has more detail on this point.
[44] Lettice, *Letters*, p. 253.
[45] Sinclair, 'Advantages', p. 117.

of their landlords, and when all else failed, and their situations were no longer compatible with the requirements of capitalist farming, they were sufficiently obliging to take themselves elsewhere, 'not like people flying from the face of poverty; but like men who were about to carry their health, their strength, and little property, to a better market'.[46] While several tourists remarked on the subject of population displacement, few regarded this as a negative phenomenon.[47] Emigration was widely represented as an unfortunate consequence of necessary development, but rendered positive when coupled to the patriotic virtue of peopling the empire. No matter how the native population was conceived by observers—and irrespective of the demographic facts of the matter—literary representations of ordinary men and women created a dominant idea of populations on the move, and of peoples leaving for distant places, with all the heroic, nationalistic and pathetic images such leavings incurred. These impressions accentuated the distance between the common people and the literary tourist, yet by being at a distance they, the common people, and also the land to which the people were native, were rendered more receptive to favourable and especially to romantic representations.

LAND AND LITERATURE IN IRELAND: SOME COMPARISONS

When viewed through the eyes of English elites, Scotland and the Scots prior to 1760 were rarely seen in a favourable light. Even among Scots themselves, 'Scottishness' was regarded at best with ambiguity and often with antipathy. But by 1830 this had changed. A pride in national identity and culture—consistent with notions of patriotic 'North Britain'—was widely manifest among Scottish elites, and though the modern commercial or intellectual Scot was occasionally an object of ridicule in England,[48] the popularity of Scotland and of things distinctly Scottish was established. This paper has argued that by informing perceptions, published literature was both an indicator and in some respects a mediator of positive relationships between Scotland and England. But what of Ireland? How were literary representations of that other peripheral country manifested during this period, and what does this imply of relationships with England? The Irish case is inevitably complex, and only a brief indication of some significant themes and contrasts can be given. But, though hardly doing justice to the subject, the following suggests a pattern of literature-born perspectives with somewhat different implications for relationships with England.

For the English tourist between 1760 and 1830, Ireland was rarely a favoured destination.[49] The country was not as accessible as Scotland (or Europe), and its

---

[46] Gilpin, *Observations*, I, p. 171.

[47] See *Johnson's Journey*, pp. 86–8.

[48] See T. L. Peacock, *Crotchet Castle* (1831) for a fictional jibe at certain types of Scot.

[49] There were some pleasure tourists, especially before the 1790s, but most tour accounts were the result of investigations of rural conditions and 'problems'. See, for instance, Arthur Young, *Tour of Ireland* (1780). This was not a publishing success.

political problems were not receptive to the kinds of romantic distancing that were possible in Scotland. The landscape did not conform to the picturesque or romantic ideals so well as the Highland landscape, and there were few grand houses and grounds to be visited. For all of these reasons, and there were others, published accounts of pleasure tours in Ireland were fewer in number than tours in Scotland. Even by the early 1840s, when the crossing to Ireland had become faster and safer, tourists were still uncommon, and Anglo-Irish authors still urged the English to abandon their prejudices. One of the best known works—*Hall's Ireland*, published in 1841—stated in the preface, 'it will be the leading object of this publication to induce the English to see and judge for themselves a country which holds out to them every temptation the traveller can need'.[50]

It is surprising that such statements should still be necessary after more than forty years of endeavours to make the English more familiar with Ireland. Though tours by pleasure tourists were relatively uncommon, there were other forms of published literature with an eye focused on an English audience that had sought to represent in a favourable light the situations and characters that were typical of Ireland. This, after all, was the primary purpose of Edgeworth's Irish novels of the first and second decades of the nineteenth century, which were popular in England, and had inspired Walter Scott to try the same for Scotland.[51] With due regard for the political and economic realities of Ireland, one cannot help but be struck by the thought that despite the best efforts of several authors they failed to generate a positive framework of English perceptions. Accounts of the land and the people on the land were in some respects at the heart of this failure.

Consider, for instance, the manner in which Edgeworth describes the ownership, transfer and tenanting of land in Ireland in *Castle Rackrent* (1800) and *The Absentee* (1812). Land is transferred mainly within families and on the basis of pre-modern systems and arrangements. When land changes hands it is more often the consequence of landowner neglect, or chicanery among the rural middle ranks, than the result of a positive operation of market capitalism. Where the market does prevail, for instance in smaller properties in the vicinity of Dublin, it serves merely to inflate the pretensions of vulgar shopkeepers.[52] The indigenous middle ranks of Ireland—the property owning *nouveau riche* and land agents in particular—are represented in a negative light that has no parallel in Scottish literature, and this must have influenced English perceptions of the nature of Ireland. Anglified elites were rarely present in the Irish landscape, and the descriptions of ordinary people were also unlikely to generate favourable perceptions. If images of Scotland stressed the absence of people—or people located at a romantic distance—images of Ireland, irrespective of realities, invariably evoked the 'teeming millions', the clamouring and unruly masses, and hordes of beggars. This was the first impression that

---

[50] *Hall's Ireland: Mr and Mrs Hall's Tour of 1840*, edited by M. Scott (1984), I, xviii.
[51] See Walter Scott's 1829 general preface to the Waverley Novels.
[52] M. Edgeworth, *The Absentee* (1812), ch. 6.

Edgeworth gave to Lord Colambre in *The Absentee*, when he stepped onto 'his mother earth', having just arrived in Dublin from England, and it is also the subject that the Halls addressed on the very first page of their tour through Ireland. It need hardly be stressed that threats of beggars and disorderly masses occupied a unique position in English perceptions of the period. One is tempted to suggest that it was almost impossible to see the Irish landscape when that landscape was viewed through the eyes of the English elite, for by comparison with Scotland the ordinary people of Ireland—by virtue of literary representations of their numbers and disposition—had an unfortunate tendency to get in the way.

13

Permissive poor laws: the Irish and Scottish systems considered together

Rosalind Mitchison

'THE FUNDAMENTAL WEAKNESS of the Irish poor laws was its permissiveness', writes Brian Jenkins with reference to the end of the eighteenth century.[1] It is the theme of this essay that the Scottish system was, for much of the time that the Old Poor Law was on the statute books, equally permissive. In particular, if we compare the situation in Scotland in 1690 with that in Ireland in 1790 there is almost no sign in either country, except in the city of Dublin, of a poor law being worked as decreed by statute. Even the important act of 1772 ordering a house of industry in every county and city was carried out eventually only in eight places. In Scotland there had been orders and statutes requiring correction houses with even less response.[2]

In making these comments on Ireland I have relied on David Dickson's brilliant paper for our last conference,[3] and on nineteenth-century parliamentary papers. For Scotland my information is mainly based on the *Acts of the Parliaments of Scotland*, the *Register of the Scottish Privy Council*, legal processes and the registers of the kirk sessions of various Lowland parishes.

The Scottish system had a clearer and more comprehensive statutory base than the Irish in the act of 1579 which, copying most of the English act of 1572, ordered all parishes to support their 'poor, aged and impotent' folk by means of a rate based on land, and to brand and imprison vagrants. But statutes in early modern Scotland were similar to pronouncements at modern party conferences, mere statements of intent, and could usually be safely ignored. The Crown had not the machinery to force policy on local magnates, whose sense of loyalty was to the person, not the policy of the monarch. The act of 1579 and supplementary ones of 1592, 1597 and 1600 leave no mark of local action. In the famine resulting from harvest failure in 1623 the privy council made desperate attempts to get the landowners of the

---

[1] Brian Jenkins, *Era of Emancipation* (Kingston and Montreal, 1988), p. 33.
[2] Rosalind Mitchison, 'North and South: The Development of the Gulf in Poor Law Practice', in R. A. Houston and I. D. Whyte, *Scottish Society 1500–1800* (Cambridge, 1989), p. 208.
[3] David Dickson, 'In Search of the Old Irish Poor Law', in Mitchison and Roebuck, pp. 149–59.

Lowland shires to organise some sort of relief, but those answers which its orders eventually drew from the shires ranged from hopelessness to defiance.[4] In 1625 Charles I put the poor law on the list of topics to be considered by his first Convention of Estates, but with no result other than a verbal reaffirmation of the statutes. Only the act of 1649, put out during the Whiggamore dominance, produced results, and even these results were not what the act ordered. The act laid the main administrative burden on presbyteries who were to 'stent' or rate their area and divide the stent between the parishes: fines were to be laid on anyone supporting beggars and on magistrates and sheriffs who failed to deal drastically with vagrants; the rating laid on landowners who dealt 'rigorously' with their tenants was to be higher than on others and there was to be a similar differential in the aid offered to those who were pious and those who were debauched.[5] The reality was that parishes ran their own relief through their kirk sessions on voluntary contributions; if these proved inadequate they passed the names of the poor for support to the landowners on whose estate they lived. In 1649, with the aristocracy in political eclipse, this method of support was the equivalent of a rate and appears to have worked in many parishes, though usually with some foot-dragging by the landowners. Religious unity made the parish a much more effective unit of government in Scotland than it was in Ireland.

Between 1649 and the famine of the 1690s the forcing of Scottish landowners to support their poor appears to have ceased. The economic climate was relatively benign and parishes, often aided by legacies from the landowning class, could manage to give minimal aid from church collections, fines, mortcloth fees and the interest on invested legacies. The only parish I have found in this period using an 'assessment system' was Gordon, Berwickshire, where the landowners had skilfully arranged that the people assessed were the tenants and cottars.[6] By contrast, in the late eighteenth century, relief in Ireland was based on a combination of rates levied on the tenantry and charitable contributions, a system less 'permissive' than that of Scotland a century earlier.

In late seventeenth-century Scotland, more neglected statutes attempted to organise relief. In 1663 vagrant labourers were to be used as a labour force in manufactories while supported by parish funds. This requirement was repeated in 1672 with the renewed demand for the setting up of correction houses. In 1696 the privy council was to see that all beggars were set to work. The Scottish parliament had not yet realised that those without an economic slot are not necessarily useful labour.

The famine in Scotland in the later 1690s brought forth a further outbreak of acts and proclamations. For the most part these had no immediate effect. Some parishes did succeed in raising funds from landowners, others tried but were

[4] *Register of the Privy Council* XIII (1622–5) (Edinburgh, 1896), pp. 257–60, 803–4, 816–38, 840.
[5] *Acts of the Parliaments of Scotland* [hereafter *A.P.S.*] (London, 1844–75), V, 178 (1625); VI, ii, 220 (1649).
[6] S.R.O. CH2/451/1, Kirk Session Register of Gordon.

frustrated. An act of 1696 and proclamation of 1693 which empowered assessed landowners to pass half the assessment on to their tenantry, and put half the money in church collections to poor relief, had little immediate effect, but were of long-term significance.[7] One proclamation did, however, produce results. In the early autumn of 1699, the privy council specifically addressed the structure of shire government, calling on sheriffs, justices of the peace and commissioners of supply to see that parishes held meetings between kirk sessions and landowners on specified dates to compile lists of the poor and to raise whatever was needed for their support from the landowners. Shire government was by then sufficiently advanced for this to be carried out in a number of parishes, and a considerable number of these can be found levying a rate with agreement of their landowners on the day specified. Altogether assessment can be found in forty-six parishes, about a fifth of those leaving records for this period. Most of these were in the south-east of Scotland, Lanarkshire or southern Perthshire, all areas where the privy council was accustomed to exercise authority not frustrated by feudal franchises. It is at this stage only that the Scottish poor law can be regarded as more than merely permissive. Even a short period of assessment would leave a record in the register of the kirk session and in the heritors' minutes.

That a fifth of the parishes obeyed means, of course, that four fifths did not. In some of these cases it can be shown that the parish had what it considered adequate voluntary funds. Bolton in East Lothian was able to come to the assistance of its neighbour, Yester, with a six-month loan made out of its reserve poor box. Not always were landowners the source of resistance. In Drainie, Moray, Gordon of Gordonstoun, main proprietor, descended on the kirk session and organised assessment of himself and the other proprietor. But for most of the unassessed we must assume that neglect of the law by the landowning class was still acceptable. In the case of South Leith, a subsidiary area of Edinburgh, the justices of the peace ordered where and when the meeting was to be held and who was to take the chair, yet the nominated chairman and most of the landowners felt free to ignore these instructions and the parish remained unassessed.[8]

In the period of restored economic tranquillity, 1700–40, when crops were on the whole adequate, there appears a change in the attitude of the leaders of the Scottish landowners. Perhaps under the influence of civic humanism, perhaps embarrassed by comments from visiting English on the prevalence of beggars, these men came to see a system of poor relief as part of the machinery of a modern society. County government which had already achieved such success as had

---

[7] *A.P.S.* VII, 485 (1663); VIII, 89 (1672); X, 64 (1696). See also A. M. Dunlop, *The Law of Scotland Regarding the Poor* (Edinburgh, 1854), pp. 21–6. The proclamations of 1692, 1693, 1694 and 1698 are printed in J. Guthrie Smith, *A Digest of the Law of Scotland Relating to the Poor* (Edinburgh, 1867), Appendix, pp. ix–xvii. For that of 1699 I am grateful to the staff of the S.R.O. for access to their typescript.

[8] S.R.O. CH2/377/2, CH2/137/3, CH2/1384/1 and CH2/716/11, Kirk Session Registers of Yester, Bolton, Drainie and South Leith respectively.

occurred in the 1690s can be seen in the shreds of record that it has left as putting pressure on parishes to participate in county schemes of relief for the poor and control of vagrancy. Usually the response of the landowning class to these schemes shows greater enthusiasm for the latter element than for the former. An instance of this is to be found in the first outbreak of such schemes, that of 1711–12 which has left traces in East Lothian, Selkirkshire, Roxburghshire and Larnarkshire: the landowners of Dirleton, East Lothian, offered to pay for extra constables to arrest vagrants while the kirk session was to support the poor.[9] Scottish justices of the peace did not have authority over the poor law, so the 'orders' in these schemes should be more truly seen as 'proposals', but they were not all without effect. The outbreak of schemes of the 1770s has left no trace in parish records or in the local newspapers in East Lothian and must be assumed to have been a failure there, yet in the Border counties the *Statistical Account* of the 1790s reveals some parishes assessed during it and still assessed.[10] This particular outbreak of schemes can be traced in fifteen counties, so it may have been of importance.

But permissiveness continued, and can even be found in parishes where assessment was established. Landowners were in a remarkably strong position if they decided to ignore the obligation to pay rates. Cases can be found of non-payment extending over a dozen years without the kirk session going to law, or even trying to extract interest. After the Court of Session decision in the case of Cambuslang, 1752, which drastically limited what a parish could do with its money, landowners could insist that any legal process brought against them be funded at the personal cost of the members of the session. Immunity from lawsuits enabled them to be dilatory in returning money borrowed. If a landowner wished to make trouble for his minister and session he could put out outrageous accusations and these would be taken very seriously by the Church's higher courts. An extreme example of this was the quarrel in Humbie, East Lothian, between the session and a minor landowner which seems to have begun in 1725 over the demand for special seating in church, became more entrenched in 1731 when the session tried to get nine years of unpaid interest on a loan, and led finally to the surprising and wide ranging decision by the Court of Session in 1751 that all money raised by a kirk session from its parish was, by natural right, under the control of the landowners.[11]

A useful mechanism devised by landowners in assessed parishes in the 1780s was to change from legal assessment to what was called 'voluntary assessment'. Under this system they agreed to pay the same amount as under legal assessment, but there would be no legal method of extracting money from defaulters. The assessment would not be seen as a permanent charge on the estate. In practice this

---

[9] S.R.O. CH2/1157/2, Kirk Session Register of Dirleton.
[10] *Statistical Account of Scotland*, (Edinburgh, 1791–9), XIV, 427 (Canonby), 468 (Ewes).
[11] Papers covering the early part of this quarrel were found in the church tower of St Mary's, Haddington and are placed in the presbytery records, S.R.O. CH2/799/19. See also Henry Home, Lord Kames, *Remarkable Decisions* (Edinburgh, 1766), p. 250; Sir James Fergusson of Kilkerran, *Decisions of the Court of Session 1738–52* (Edinburgh, 1775), p. 408, and J. Guthrie Smith, *Digest*, p. 11.

meant that absentee landowners might fail to pay and could not be brought to book. The attractions of this were reduced by the fact that the same voluntary nature extended to the part of the assessment paid by the tenantry.

The biggest element of 'permissiveness' in the Scottish system came from the structure of Scottish law and courts. Because of the widespread non-observance of statutes the Scottish courts had sensibly developed the principle of 'desuetude'. By this, if it could be shown in court that a statute had not been applied that statute lost all legal force for the future. In practice this was an invitation to create the historical past. Many features of the Scottish poor law could be argued against also from the confusions created by statutes which, while reasserting earlier statutes, at the same time created new and incompatible rulings. The proclamations of the 1690s, reaffirmed in a statute, gave a different period necessary to establish settlement from that given by another statute of the 1690s. It was thus possible to argue that three or that seven years' residence was required for eligibility. But any feature of the poor law could be argued against by a skilled lawyer on the grounds of non-observance. This is one of the reasons why what the textbooks of the nineteenth century say about the old Scottish poor law bears little relation to what was in fact operated.

A further problem comes from the readiness of the judges to invent law.[12] Such law was usually in the interest of the landed class, to which all judges and most advocates belonged. As a method of legislation this was defective for there was no adequate opportunity for consultation and the representation of alternative views. Conspicuous examples of lawmaking are the Humbie and Cambuslang decisions of the 1750s, though the latter, too sweeping to be effective, was abandoned in later cases. A judgement in 1821 destroyed the right of appeal on poor law matters to any but the Court of Session, a piece of lawmaking which set up the parish effectively as unsupervised in its decisions.[13] If a parish were to refuse relief, or to offer only a derisory allowance, the impoverished claimant had no redress unless charitably sustained by an advocate and provided with the money necessary for printed pleadings. Even if he obtained this help he still had to wait till the Court met. Not surprisingly there are few claims against parish decisions after 1821.

In abstract terms the destruction of appeals to lower courts did not affect the right to relief. Such a right was reaffirmed in a legal process with the phrase 'the pauper in Scotland is not a beggar of charity, but the creditor of a fund of which the kirk session and heritors are accountable trustees'.[14] But a right which it is almost impossible to get enforced cannot be taken as effective. According to

---

[12] Examples of judicial legislation can be found in Rosalind Mitchison, 'Patriotism and National Identity in Eighteenth-Century Scotland', in T. W. Moody, ed., *Historical Studies*, XI (Belfast, 1978), pp. 86–8.

[13] Rosalind Mitchison, 'The Creation of the Disablement Rule in the Scottish Poor Law', in T. C. Smout, ed., *The Search for Wealth and Stability* (London, 1979), pp. 208–13.

[14] P.P. 1830 VII, *Report of the Select Committee on the State of the Poor in Ireland*, p. 63, evidence of Frederick Page.

nineteenth-century legal textbooks a kirk session was obliged to weigh seriously all claims made upon it; in practice it was open to it arbitrarily to decide who should have support, and at what level, with no risk of an appeal. An instance of arbitrary allowances was noticed by the Royal Commission of 1844 in Stirling. After seeing various paupers in their houses the commissioners reported: 'Some of those who were in best circumstances had, at the same time, the highest allowances, being apparently persons of the best character and most industrious habits, while some of the others were common beggars, and, generally, persons of an inferior class'.[15]

Another aspect of permissiveness in Scotland was the semi-voluntary nature of the body administering relief, the kirk session. In the seventeenth and eighteenth centuries near uniformity in belief and the strength of the Presbyterian structure meant that the Church had a far more effective system of government than the State. The eldership was a status to be aspired to, but at the same time it was under the jurisdiction of the presbytery. The sessions' authority might be considered weakened by the Humbie and other decisions but the Church could always withdraw its administrative aid. If a session had not collected money the heritors (landowners) would be forced to levy assessment, since almost every parish had undeniable cases of need. Also the heritors would either have to appoint and pay a lay overseer to investigate claims and distribute money, or undertake this work themselves. In one parish, Auchterderran, a quarrel between session and heritors in 1757 led to the refusal of the session to act.[16] This appears to have been an unusual event, but the possibility was always there, and it was repeated at the very end of the life of the Old Poor Law. In Auldearn in 1842, at the most bitter stage of the conflict which led to the Disruption of the Church, the principal heritor had obtained an interdict against the minister holding 'non-intrusion' meetings in the church: the minister took the injunction as covering the meetings of the session, and the session supported him, with the result that no collections were taken. An indignant letter from the factor of the heritor did not change the session's mind, and the heritors had to set up their own relief system.[17]

The relief system in Scotland in parishes which had not levied assessment, the majority, was very similar to that in parts of Ireland where the churches attempted to relieve poverty but more effective because there was less destitution. The similarity is brought out in the evidence compiled by the Whately Royal Commission and the Scottish Royal Commission. It is possible indeed that charitable giving was more generous in early nineteenth-century Ireland than in Scotland, though less effective because of the vast scale of need. In both countries there were areas where there was no system of relief—in the Scottish Highlands and in parts of western Ireland. But in Scotland dissenting churches accepted, for the most part, Calvinist dogma, so there was no doctrinal gulf, as there was in Ireland, between

---

[15] P.P. 1844 XXII, *Report from Her Majesty's Commissioners for Inquiring into the Administration and Practical Operation of the Poor Laws in Scotland*, Minutes of Evidence, p. 211.

[16] Edinburgh, Signet Library, Court of Sessions papers, 32; 17 (1757).

[17] P.P. 1844 XXI, *Report . . . Poor Laws in Scotland*, Minutes of Evidence, p. 541.

the mass of the desperately poor and the possessors of property or income. It was this gulf, more than the law, which had led to differences in practice.

Both countries had suffered from a lack of legislation in the eighteenth century, a period when statutes had come to be respected. In Scotland in particular the enhanced strength of the machinery of county government, already making its mark in 1699 and gaining greater force from the encroachments on feudal franchises which followed the Act of Union, meant that neglect of recent statutes was unlikely, even though the enforcing privy council had disappeared. But the procedural rules of the imperial parliament and the mental assumptions of its members about the proper role of the legislature meant that there was very little general legislation on anything except crime before the 1830s. Such legislation as was produced for Scotland in the eighteenth century was submitted in advance to landed society at county meetings, and landowners were unlikely to press for an increase in their financial obligations. Ireland, which had the advantage of administrative centralisation, suffered from a lack of sympathy in the administration with the life of the common people. There was little impulse for major change. In the nineteenth century Ireland gave rise to numerous parliamentary commissions and occupied considerable debating time, but all this was of low productivity.

The key to differences between the two countries lies not in legislation but in the economy, social structure and local organisation. Scotland benefited by near uniformity in belief; her only non-Calvinists were a few Quakers in and around Aberdeen and some Roman Catholics in the north-east, numbering in Lowland areas, according to Webster's census, less than 4,000.[18] Episcopalianism and the later secessions from the Scottish kirk took for granted its social dominance. As in Ireland the established Church accepted the duty of supporting the poor of other communions; the difference was in the resources of cash and manpower which it could bring to bear. This is shown by the different impacts of the 1740 famine.[19]

The opinions brought before the various parliamentary commissions of the 1830s on the topic of Irish poverty made much of the lack of suitable bodies of gentry and big tenants who could be trusted to administer an English type poor law.[20] But it was not the gentry who ran the Scottish system: the bulk of elders stood socially below this level. In the towns the elders were usually merchants and craftsmen, in the country tenants and occasionally craftsmen, though resident heritors might choose to become elders if they could refrain from Episcopalianism. The move to larger farming units after 1770 and higher incomes in the urban middle class shifted the social base of the kirk sessions upwards, but it still lay below the gentry.

---

[18] J. G. Kyd, ed., *Scottish Population Statistics* (Scottish History Society, Edinburgh, 1952).

[19] J. D. Post, *Food Shortage, Climatic Variability and Epidemic Disease in Pre-Industrial Europe* (Ithaca, 1985), chapter 6.

[20] A typical statement on this theme is that by James E. Bicheno to the Select Committee of 1830 (P.P. 1830 VII, p. 382): 'There is no such class in Ireland as appears to me to be able to carry on that system of management which is absolutely essential . . .'

The sessions were capable of keeping the relief system going during vacancies in the ministry. Doctrinal unity and a social structure with a substantial middling rank enabled the Scots to develop an effective, if minimalist, system of support in the Lowland countryside. But in the growing cities from the late eighteenth century it was not possible for elders to be personally acquainted with the circumstances of a large and mobile population.

The accidents of timing also played their part in differentiating the two countries. In both the counties were relatively late constructs with little in the way of a sense of historic identity. But in Scotland the system of county government set up in the seventeenth century, culminating in 1667 with the commissioners of supply, followed the English practice of giving administrative responsibility to selected, unpaid members of the landowning class. It was this structure, sheriffs, justices of the peace and commissioners of supply, to which the 1699 proclamation was addressed, whereas the earlier proclamations about relief, those of 1692, 1693, 1694 and 1698, were issued to the world at large. The same county structure put out the county schemes of the eighteenth century.[21] The Scottish system was able to become more effective at a period relatively free of crisis. After 1745 Scotland also did not suffer from the fear of disturbance which distracted the government of Ireland in the later eighteenth century.

Ireland's main step towards a poor law, the act of 1772 setting up houses of industry, was unfortunate in two ways. Indoor relief, which it prescribed, is a relatively expensive way of using limited resources, and the inefficiency and corruption of large, residential institutions in the libertarian climate of the eighteenth century discouraged further support. By the time that the act had been partly observed and some at least of the institutions ordered set up, a change of opinion over relief had begun to operate. From 1780 onwards the English and Scottish press contains criticisms of the whole idea of a system of social welfare sustained by taxation: it was held to be an expensive way of sapping the moral fibre of the poor. This current of opinion, which became dominant after 1815, had not stopped poor relief in Britain from expanding to meet particular crises during the Napoleonic and Revolutionary wars, in England with the Speenhamland 'system' of 1795 and in Scotland the adoption of something very similar in 1800.[22] But the new and colder wind blowing made for great reluctance in starting up any system in Ireland. It is difficult not to be impressed by the enormous expenditure of time and paper on Irish social problems, the select and royal commissions of the 1830s in particular. These contain a great body of evidence of severe poverty and of lack of

---

[21] Traces of this scheme can be found in the Kirk Session Registers of Dirleton and Pencaitland, S.R.O. CH 2/1157/2 and CH2/296/2, and also in Sheriff Court records for Selkirkshire which happen to contain Justice of the Peace material for that county and for Roxburghshire, S.R.O. SC63/10/1. I owe the latter reference to John Ballantine.

[22] Graham M. Birnie, 'Tradition and Transition, the Scottish Poor Law, Harvest Failure and the Industrious Poor' (unpublished MA thesis, Department of Economic and Social History, Edinburgh University, 1976), chapter 5.

employment. They also show the influence of highly standardised social and economic theories, dogmas if you like: the stress is on the bad effects of relief systems on wage levels, population growth and family relationships.

These commissions, and the Scottish Royal Commission, also show the effects of interaction between the different systems, or rather the influence of beliefs about the systems in the British Isles. It would not be surprising if, after 1800, the imperial parliament had legislated to bring the systems together. It could even be argued that it did something of the sort in forcing a cut-down version of the English New Poor Law on Ireland in 1838. The literature of the time shows the widespread belief that the English poor law was still operating the Speenhamland system. By contrast the Scots successfully covered up the fact that many parishes had been using rates to supplement wages, and denied that anything of the sort had ever happened.[23] The commission of 1830 on the Irish poor spent three days interviewing the Reverend Thomas Chalmers, and receiving from him some erroneous history about the Scottish law, as well as the assurance that Chalmers's own system, which was designed to bring home 'the evil and disgrace of public charity' by systematically discouraging applications for relief would, even in the cities, make statutory provision unnecessary, and strengthen the principle of independence.[24] The parliamentary debate which had set up that commission had heard various current beliefs about the Scottish poor law—that absentee landowners had to pay double assessment was one—but it also heard Peel point out that the Scottish 'system' showed great differences between the Highlands and the Lowlands, and that within the Lowlands it differed between the manufacturing and the agricultural areas.[25] Peel also expressed a doubt as to whether the Scottish system, whatever it was, was in accord with its own law, a point eventually confirmed by the Royal Commission of 1843–4. It was not beyond possibility that a more effective and responsive version of a poor law might have been designed for Ireland if this could have been achieved before the outburst of anti-poor law pamphleteering which started up in 1816.

There was developing a gap in attitudes to poor laws in the churches of the two countries. In the eighteenth century churchmen of both had supported the idea of a relief system. As Dickson shows, the Church of Ireland was the most active body in Ireland on this theme, but in Ulster the Presbyterian Church had created a system similar to that of Scotland. The Irish clergy continued to press for a better system: Bishop Doyle's evidence to the 1830 commission shows that the Catholic church, though handicapped by lack of resources, shared this view.[26] In Scotland the clergy tended to follow the lead of Chalmers and argue that relief from public

---

[23] See, for instance, the Reverend Robert Burns, *Historical Dissertations on the Law and Practice of Great Britain and Particularly of Scotland with Regard to the Poor* (Edinburgh, 1819), p. 62.
[24] P.P. 1830 VII, pp. 279–397.
[25] Hansard, new series, vol. 23, 218, 11 March 1830.
[26] P.P. 1830 VII, pp. 511–63.

funds was morally corrupting. This is the common response to the answers to a questionnaire put out by Kennedy of Dunure in 1815,[27] and the same attitude dominates the parish contributions to the *New Statistical Account* some twenty years later. In practice the Church supervised the enlargement of the scale of relief and the reliance on assessment: its theoretical position was at odds with its actions.

It is clear that attempts to reform the Scottish and Irish relief systems influenced each other. The statistical material sustaining the report of the Scottish Royal Commission of 1844 is an enlarged edition of the type of material collected by the Whately Commission for Ireland in the 1830s.[28] The local investigations carried out were similar except that for Scotland the commissioners did the visiting themselves instead of sending assistants. But more significant than the cross influences was the shadow of beliefs about the English poor law and the hostility to it. In Ireland, without a general level of observance of a relief system, this attitude did much to postpone the creation of a poor law, and to restrict the scope of that which was set up in 1838. This was designed to sustain only a small proportion of the population, a much smaller part than even in prosperous times had been found in both England and Scotland to need help.[29] The commission of 1830 on Ireland produced a large amount of evidence of the need for a poor law, but the commissioners ended by sitting on the fence and making no recommendation. The Whately Commission took a wide remit, the whole topic of poverty rather than simply that of relief, but the very scale of its concern enabled a hostile London government to bypass it and impose a poor law based simply on a cut-down version of the English.

The relative immunity of Scotland to this sort of intervention is puzzling, considering that Scottish members formed a smaller proportion of the Westminster parliament than did Irish. It cannot simply be due to the Act of Union of 1707 enforcing a respect for Scottish institutions, since by the nineteenth century Ireland was also formally united with Britain at the level of parliament. It seems that London governments were unwilling to regard Ireland, whatever her formal status, as anything but a colony. The Scottish landed elite was accepted as equivalent to that of England and effectively controlled the local communities. In Ireland the elite accepted by the government was imported and cut off by its religion from the mass of society. Until 1829 the main aim of the government in Dublin had been to frustrate Catholic aspirations, and this habit died hard.[30] For Scotland throughout

---

[27] The papers survive in the keeping of Lord Moncrieff of Tulliebole at Tulliebole Castle, and I have kindly been allowed access to them.

[28] P.P. 1836 XXI–XXXIII, *Supplements to the Report from His Majesty's Commissioners for Inquiring into the Condition of the Poorer Classes in Ireland* (the Whately Commission), and P.P. 1844 XXIII–V, *Appendices to the Report . . . Poor Laws in Scotland*.

[29] The Irish Act insisted that all relief should be indoor. Workhouse accommodation by 1847 was for under 15,000 paupers in a population of over eight million, or for less than 1.5 per cent of the population. In Scotland the percentage of paupers in parishes which carried out the law varied between 2.5 and 5 according to the *New Statistical Account*, 15 vols. (Edinburgh, 1845).

[30] Jenkins, *Era of Emancipation, passim*.

the nineteenth-century parliament showed a continuation of the eighteenth-century unwillingness to provide legislation. This may have owed much to a fear that legislation was likely to end in conflict with the kirk, and that the 'anti-Erastian' views of that body were an unpredictable hazard which had in the past entrapped governments. There was also the success that Scottish propagandists had had in proclaiming the superiority of Scottish institutions to people who did not know the real facts.

In the progression from 'permissive' poor laws to enforced provision one has to see the main difference in the developments in the two countries stemming from the regard that parliament had for a Protestant and ostensibly holier-than-thou country and the habitual disregard it had for Irish opinion. This basic difference had important consequences, not merely in the suffering of the unsupported section of the poor, but in the whole structure of local government as it was built up in the nineteenth century. The Scottish 'reformed' poor law became the first element in a system of centrally supervised local government, eventually to become democratic, which created a central and local civil service. Ireland already had a powerful central administration, other parts of which were expanded to cope with the emergency of the Famine. MacDonagh has pointed out that further local government in Ireland used the local machinery of the 1838 poor law in spite of its inadequacies, but that the poor law itself became an instrument in depopulation.[31] The beliefs and preconceptions on which the early elements of the nineteenth-century transformation of government were based had a long influence.

---

[31] Oliver MacDonagh, 'The Economy and Society, 1830–45' in W. E. Vaughan, ed., *New History of Ireland*, Vol. v: *Ireland under the Union 1801–70* (Oxford, 1989), p. 228.

14

Rural protest in the Highlands of Scotland and in Ireland, 1850–1930

Charles W. J. Withers

THERE ARE SEVERAL REASONS why comparative analysis of the nature, chronology and causes of rural protest in Ireland and in Highland Scotland in this period is both valid and instructive.[1] The 'land issue' was crucial to both areas. Rural protest was often against 'loss' of land in the economic senses of estate rationalisation, holding subdivision, or eviction. Protest has also been considered culturally motivated as tenants defended 'traditional' rights to the occupation and management of land. Land was a political issue in both: the Irish National Land League (I.N.L.L.), founded in 1879, had its Highland counterpart in the Highland Land Law Reform Association (H.L.L.R.A.), begun in 1883. The 1886 Crofters Act in the Highlands was explicitly modelled on the 1881 Irish Land Act. Both Ireland and Highland Scotland had a 'Land War', in 1879–82 and 1881–6 respectively. Contemporaries saw these events as directly related. John Murdoch, a major figure behind the politicisation of the Highland crofters in the 1880s, was greatly influenced by Fintan Lalor's analysis of the Irish land question.[2] One report of 1886 to the secretary of state for Scotland considered that 'Ireland was certainly the origin of the Skye agitation', and a commentator on lawlessness in the Outer Hebrides in 1887 saw wider political implications for the agrarian outrages then occurring: 'If there is to be a little Ireland in Scotland the cause of the Union will certainly suffer. Lewis is the Connaught of Scotland and requires special treatment.'[3]

---

[1] Whilst acknowledging the helpful comments by all participants, I should particularly like to thank Tom Bartlett, Sean Connolly and David Fitzpatrick for their criticisms and guidance. I am grateful to Samuel Clark and Paul Bew for their comments on an earlier draft.

[2] J. Hunter, *The Making of the Crofting Community* (Edinburgh, 1976), p. 129; *idem, For the People's Cause: From the Writings of John Murdoch* (Edinburgh, 1986). On Highland protest more generally, see Hunter, *passim*; I. M. M. Macphail, *The Crofters' War* (Stornoway, 1989); I. F. Grigor, *Mightier than a Lord* (Stornoway, 1979); E. Richards, *A History of the Highland Clearances*, Volume 1: *Agrarian Transformation and the Evictions 1746–1886* (London, 1982), pp. 472–505; C. W. J. Withers, *Gaelic Scotland: The Transformation of a Culture Region* (London, 1988), pp. 355–91.

[3] Scottish Record Office (S.R.O.), GD 40/16/32, f.3; GD 40/16/34, ff.59–60a (R. Macleod to Rt Hon. Lord Hartington, 8 December 1887).

RURAL PROTEST   173

Both Highland Scotland and Ireland, especially the west, shared in the fluctuating fortunes of agriculture in the late 1880s: labour restructuring following the Famine, prosperity in the later 1850s and 1860s, and recession in the late 1870s and 1880s.[4] Comparison is useful, too, given the fact that whilst the old order in the Scottish Lowlands 'passed away with little dissent',[5] Highland agricultural change was marked by a 'bitter, if sporadic, protest and deep hostility'[6] akin much more to the experience of Ireland than elsewhere in Scotland. Finally, comparison is justified given the interest in rural social protest beyond these regions and for other periods.[7] As Fitzpatrick has argued of Ireland, 'there is a world of difference between

[4] W. E. Vaughan, 'Landlord and Tenant Relations in Ireland between the Famine and the Land War, 1850–78', in Cullen and Smout, pp. 216–26.
[5] T. M. Devine, 'Unrest and Stability in Rural Ireland and Scotland, 1760–1840', in Mitchison and Roebuck, p. 126.
[6] T. M. Devine, 'Social Responses to Agrarian "Improvement": The Highland and Lowland Clearances in Scotland', in R. A. Houston and I. D. Whyte, eds., *Scottish Society 1500–1800* (Cambridge, 1989), p. 158; idem, 'Social Stability and Agrarian Change in the Eastern Lowlands of Scotland 1810–40', *Social History*, III, 3 (1978), pp. 331–46; W. H. Fraser, 'Patterns of Protest', in T. M. Devine and R. Mitchison, eds., *People and Society in Scotland*, Vol. 1: *1760–1830* (Edinburgh, 1988), pp. 268–92; K. Logue, *Popular Disturbances in Scotland* (Edinburgh, 1975); R. A. Dodgshon, 'Agricultural Change and its Social Consequences in the Southern Uplands of Scotland, 1600–1780', in Devine and Dickson, pp. 46–59.
[7] On this theme in European and British rural history, see for example, J. Bohstedt, *Riots and Community Politics in England and Wales 1790–1810* (Harvard, 1983); J. Bohstedt and D. E. Williams, 'The Diffusion of Riots: The Patterns of 1766, 1795, and 1801 in Derbyshire', *Journal of Interdisciplinary History*, XIX, 1 (1988), pp. 1–24; A. Charlesworth, 'The Development of the English Rural Proletariat and Social Protest 1780–1850', *Journal of Peasant Studies*, VIII, 1 (1980), pp. 101–11; idem, 'The Spatial Diffusion of Rural Protest', *Environment and Planning D: Society and Space 1* (1983), pp. 251–63; idem, *An Atlas of Rural Protest in Britain 1548–1900* (London, 1983); idem, 'A Comparative Study of the Agricultural Disturbances of 1816, 1822 and 1830 in England', *Peasant Studies*, XI, 2 (1984), pp. 91–110; J. P. D. Dunbabin, *Rural Discontent in Nineteenth-Century Britain* (London, 1971); D. Geary, *European Labour Protest 1848–1939* (London, 1981); T. Herbert and G. E. Jones, eds., *People and Protest: Wales 1815–1880* (Cardiff, 1988); A. Howkins, *Poor Labouring Men: Rural Radicalism in Norfolk 1870–1923* (London, 1985); F. E. Huggett, *The Land Question and European Society* (London, 1975); D. J. V. Jones, *Before Rebecca: Popular Protests in Wales 1793–1835* (Harmondsworth, 1973); H. J. Kaye, ed., *The Face of the Crowd: Studies in Revolution, Ideology and Popular Protest* (London, 1988); K. Lindley, *Fenland Riots and the English Revolution* (London, 1982); R. B. Manning, *Village Revolts: Social Protest and Popular Disturbances in England 1509–1640* (Oxford, 1988); G. E. Mingay, ed., *The Unquiet Countryside* (London, 1989); M. Mullett, *Popular Culture and Popular Protest in Late Medieval and Early Modern Europe* (London, 1987); D. Pretty, *The Rural Revolt that Failed: Farm Workers' Trades Unions in Wales 1889–1950* (Cardiff, 1989); A. Randall, 'The Gloucestershire Food Riots of 1766', *Midland History*, X (1985), pp. 72–93; B. Reay, 'The Last Rising of the Agricultural Labourers: The Battle of Bossenden Wood, 1838', *History Workshop*, 26 (1988), pp. 79–101; B. Sharp, *In Contempt of all Authority: Rural Artisans and Riot in the West of England, 1586–1660* (London, 1980); F. Snowden, *Violence and Great Estates in the South of Italy: Apulia 1900–1922* (Cambridge, 1986); J. Stevenson, *Popular Disturbances in England 1700–1870* (London, 1979); J. Stevenson and R. Quinault, eds., *Popular Protest and Public Order 1780–1820* (London, 1974); R. A. E. Wells, 'The Development of the English Rural Proletariat and Social Protest, 1700–1850', *Journal of Peasant Studies*, 6 (1978–79), pp. 115–39; G. A. Williams, *The Welsh in their History* (London, 1982); D. Williams, *The Rebecca Riots* (Cardiff, 1986); M. Reed and R. Wells, eds., *Class, Conflict and Protest in the English Countryside 1700–1870* (London, 1990).

assertions of Irish uniqueness derived from rigorous model-testing, and assertions reflecting ignorance or heedlessness of the history of the rural world outside Ireland'.[8] The same is true for Highland Scotland. What follows is a partial move towards this wider understanding of protest in the rural world.

Irish sources are both richer and more diverse than those for Highland Scotland. Official statistics in Ireland of agrarian protest were first systematically collected from 1844, although isolated official records exist for earlier dates.[9] For Ireland it is possible for the period 1844 to 1900 to document the number of agrarian offences by county and province and to know the form taken by protest since events were enumerated under one of three headings: agrarian outrages 'against the person', 'against property', and 'against the public peace'.[10] For Highland Scotland, official statistics are few but extensive manuscript evidence does permit analysis of single events and assessment of general causes of protest.[11] Even with this evidence, assessing 'the *anatomy* of unrest: when and where did who do what to whom',[12] is not straightforward. Several difficulties may be identified. The first is terminological. 'Riot', 'disturbance', 'affray', 'land raid', 'outrage' were all terms used (amongst others) to record protest. The use by contemporaries of several general terms to describe particular incidents or protest as a whole means we must be careful in ascribing events to 'simple' typological categories and cautious about treating events as single phenomena when they may have been compounded, as many were, of personal assault, killing of livestock and destruction of property. Secondly, there is evidence that the civil authorities over-represented the extent of unrest in order to legitimise their reaction to it. In this sense, sources documenting protest are a function both of administrative efficiency and of authorities' perceptions of the

[8] D. Fitzpatrick, 'Unrest in Rural Ireland', *Ir. Econ. and Soc. Hist.* XII (1985), pp. 98–105; on the call for comparison, see also S. Clark and J. S. Donnelly Jr., eds., *Irish Peasants: Violence and Political Unrest 1780–1914* (Madison, 1983), pp. 20–1.

[9] The record of outrages for 1844 to the 1880s is contained in *Return of Outrages Reported to the Royal Irish Constabulary Office from 1 January 1844 to 31 December 1880*, P.P. LXXVII 1881, pp. 1–24; on pre-Famine official records, see, for example, *A Return of the Outrages Reported by the Constabulary in Ireland during the years 1837, 1838, 1839, 1840 and 1841: A Like Return of Outrages during each Month of the Year 1842; and for the months of January, February and March 1843*, P.P. LI 1843, p. 149; *Number of Agrarian Outrages* [1845 and 1846], P.P. LVI 1847, p. 231; *Minutes of Evidence taken before Select Committee Appointed to Enquire into the Disturbances in Ireland, in the Last Session of Parliament 13 May–18 June 1824*, P.P. VII 1825; see also G. Broeker, *Rural Disorder and Police Reform in Ireland 1812–1836* (London, 1970), and G. C. Lewis, *Local Disturbances in Ireland* (London, 1836). This paper is based on detailed analysis of the following P.P.: LV 1882, p. 17; LVI 1883, pp. 2–3, LXIV 1884, pp. 2–3; LXV 1885, pp. 2–3; LIV 1886, pp. 2–3; LXVIII 1887, pp. 2–3; LXXXIII 1888, pp. 400–1; LXI 1889, pp. 522–3; LIX 1890, pp. 796–7; LXIV 1890–1, p. 807; LXV 1892 pp. 450–1; LXXIV 1893–94, Part II, pp. 416–17; LXXII 1894, pp. 44–5; LXXXII 1895, pp. 102–3; LXIX 1896, pp. 582–3; LXXIII 1897, pp. 288–9; LXXIV 1898, pp. 144–5; LXXIX 1899, pp. 648–9; LXIX 1900, pp. 629, 645, 649, 653.

[10] Agrarian outrages were distinguished from non-agrarian protest events. For a list of categories used, see P.P. LXXIII 1909, p. 2.

[11] These sources are discussed in detail in the works listed in note 2 above.

[12] Fitzgerald, 'Unrest in Rural Ireland', p. 98.

scale of unrest as much as a record of real events.[13] Further difficulties concern assessing the relationship between 'overt' and 'covert' events and the problem of knowing if 'local' events were just that— particular and local expressions of dissent with unique causes and outcomes at given moments—or were, rather, expressions in a certain place and time of a more widely-occurring context of unrest that transcended county, provincial or even national boundaries.

* * *

The chronology of officially-recorded protest in Ireland from c. 1850 to 1900 suggests a record of varying levels of unrest punctuated by periods of considerable agitation (Figure 1). This picture obscures, however, variation in the type of protest as well as geographical and structural variations in terms of the classes involved. The 'peak' of 1869–70 is misleading; the result of a short-lived system of enumerating protest which, in having 'the effect of apparently increasing the number of outrages' was swiftly abandoned. Further, annual numbers disguise seasonality of protest within years, a seasonality linked to labour demands and the rhythms of the agricultural year.

For some commentators, the Famine was a watershed in terms of Irish protest. For Winstanley, 'the Famine, by wiping out a significant portion of the smallholding class, effectively curtailed wholesale rural protest and agrarian outrages'. Beames considers that 'the Famine quite clearly resolved the conflict between the interests of the poorer peasantry and those of the commercially minded rural classes firmly in favour of the latter'. For Knott, however, the relative lack of agitation in the Famine may be explained in that the Famine itself did not directly challenge established patterns of land-holding: 'It was not until 1849, when owners of encumbered estates started evicting tenants wholesale to obtain a better price when their land was sold, that the incidence of agrarian violence escalated dramatically'.[14]

The role of the famine in Highland protest is less clear. Food riots aimed at stopping out-movement of grain at times of shortage were numerous in 1847 but chiefly occurred in the north-eastern Highlands where dearth was less severe.[15]

---

[13] Hunter, *The Making of the Crofting Community*, p. 137; A. C. Murray, 'Agrarian Violence and Nationalism in Nineteenth-Century Ireland: The Myth of Ribbonism', *Ir. Econ. and Soc. Hist.*, XIII (1986), pp. 71–2.

[14] M. J. Winstanley, *Ireland and the Land Question 1800–1922* (London, 1984), p. 24; M. Beames, *Peasants and Power: the Whiteboy Movements and Their Control in Pre-Famine Ireland* (Brighton, 1983), p. 217; J. W. Knott, 'Land Kinship and Identity: The Cultural Roots of Agrarian Agitation in Eighteenth-Century Ireland', *Journal of Peasant Studies*, XII, 1 (1984), pp. 102–3; K. T. Hoppen, *Elections, Politics and Society in Ireland 1832–1886* (Oxford, 1984), pp. 362–8 argues there is no clear decline in violence after the Famine.

[15] T. M. Devine, *The Great Highland Famine* (Edinburgh, 1988) is the best guide to the famine in the Highlands; on food riots in the Highlands, see E. Richards, 'The Last Scottish Food Riots', *Past and Present*, Supplement 6 (1982); idem, 'Food Riots in 1847', in Charlesworth, ed., *An Atlas of Rural Protest*, pp. 108–11.

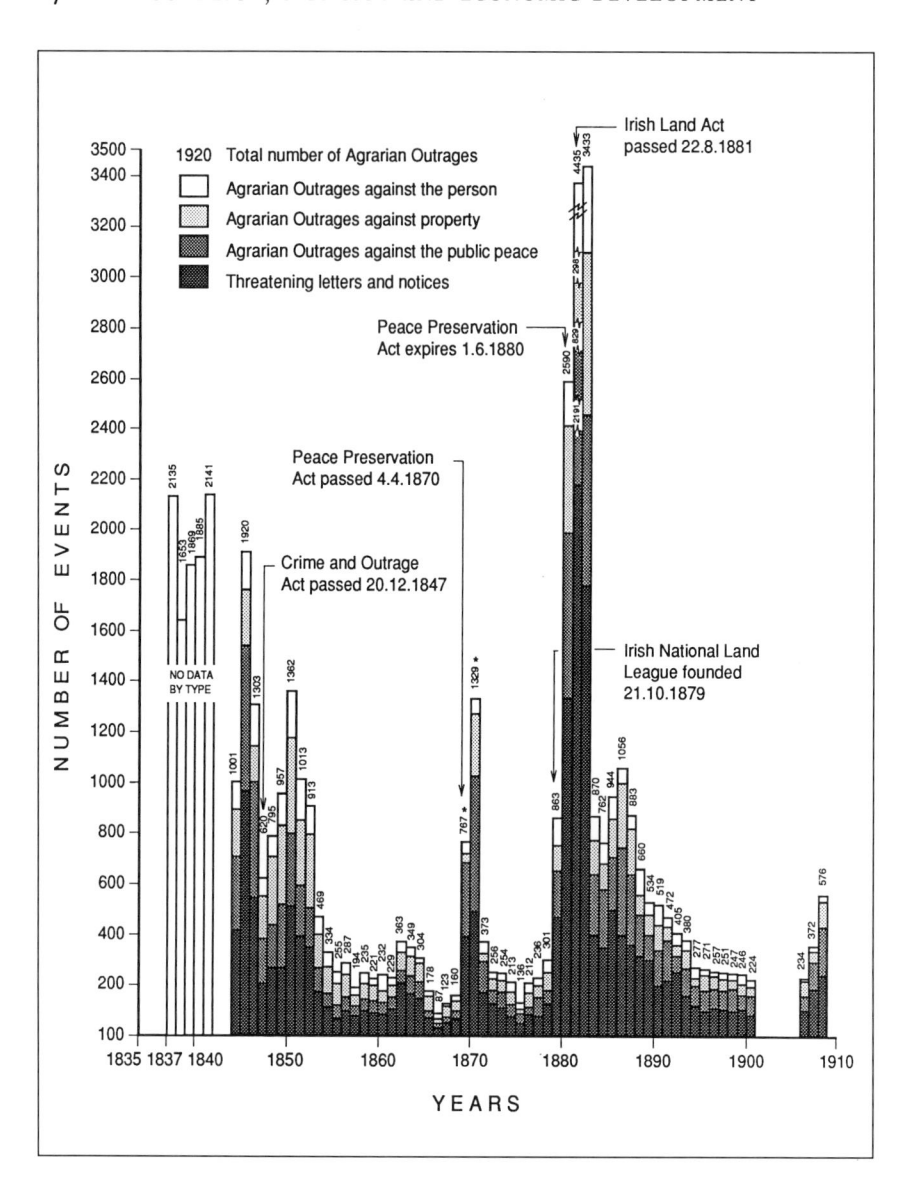

Figure 1

Sources: Return of Agrarian Outrages, P.P. *1881 LXXVII; 1843 LI; 1882 LV; 1883 LVI; 1884 LXIV; 1885 LXV; 1886 LIV; 1887 LXVIII; 1888 LXXXIII; 1889 LXI; 1890 LIX; 1890–1 LXIV; 1892 LXV; 1893–4 LXXIV (part II); 1894 LXXII; 1895 LXXXII; 1896 LXIX; 1897 LXXIII; 1898 LXXIV; 1899 LXXIX; 1900 LXIX; 1909 LXXIII.*

* *For these two years, the number of individuals participating in outrages was considered to be the total number of outrages: e.g., twenty-two threatening letters posted on twenty-two houses in the same townland in Mayo on 13 January 1870 were recorded as twenty-two outrages. In 1871, the old system was re-introduced: 'to record similar cases as only one of each kind, when the outrages are perpetrated by the same party on the one occasion'.*

In some of the thirteen recorded events of protest in the Highlands between 1849 and 1857, protest which took the form of opposition to the *then* fact of eviction and clearance was also prompted by concern at the *future* reallocation of tenants' holdings.[16] But there is no direct evidence in the Highlands of protest as a result of famine.

The chronology of a downturn in protest between c. 1853 and 1879 in Ireland is repeated in the Highlands. Between the clearance protests of 1857 at Treshnish and Bernera in 1874, no major disturbances have been enumerated in the Highlands.[17] Patial explanation of the decline in protest may lie in the relative economic recovery of the two areas between c. 1850 and c. 1880. In the Highlands price trends for wool and cattle favoured producers and whilst crofters' rents rose against a background of land shortage, they did not do so as steeply as in other periods or for sheep farms or sporting estates.[18] The fact that Irish agriculture shared the prosperity of this period and that tenants may have enjoyed some redistribution of total agricultural income may similarly explain the relative decline in Irish agitation.

Protest in Highland Scotland by the later nineteenth and early twentieth centuries was largely confined to the north-west crofting districts and the Outer Isles (Figure 2). Protest in Ireland between 1844 and 1900 was nation-wide but with differing regional emphasis by type and causes. Deforcement of civil officers and assault were common in the Highlands, but personal violence was never as widespread as in Ireland and many counties there never reached the levels of violence in, for example, Tipperary both before and after 1847.[19] Threatening letters were, numerically, the most important outrage in Ireland between 1844 and 1900. Threats and intimidation took various forms there and in the Highlands. Threats worked both ways. In Ireland, the notice to quit 'was the estate agent's maid-of-all-work, being used to collect arrears, to force tenants to pay increases of rent, to settle quarrels between tenants and to discourage bad farming'.[20] More common was the tenants' declared threat of a future protest: covert expressions warning of future overt consequences. Threatening letters were often decorated with a coffin or a gun as are many, for example, of those surviving from the 1868–71 agrarian protests in Westmeath.[21] On Lewis in 1888, Lady

---

[16] Richards, *A History of the Highland Clearances*, Volume 1, pp. 363–472.

[17] Withers, *Gaelic Scotland*, pp. 359–62.

[18] T. M. Devine, 'The Emergence of the New Elite in the Western Highlands and Islands, 1800–1860', in T. M. Devine, ed., *Improvement and Enlightenment* (Edinburgh, 1988), pp. 108–35; Hunter, *Crofting Community*, pp. 107–30; Richards, *A History of the Highland Clearances*, Volume 2: *Emigration, Protest, Reasons*, p. 485; Withers, *Gaelic Scotland*, pp. 246–55.

[19] M. Beames, 'Rural Conflict in Pre-Famine Ireland: Peasant Assassinations in Tipperary, 1837–1847', in C. H. E. Philpin, ed., *Nationalism and Popular Protest in Ireland* (Cambridge, 1987), pp. 264–83; see also M. Thuente, 'Violence in Pre-Famine Ireland: The Testimony of Irish Folk-lore and Fiction', *Irish University Review*, XV, 2 (1985), pp. 129–47; E. Richards, 'How Tame were the Highlanders during the Clearances?', *Scottish Studies*, 17 (1973), pp. 35–50.

[20] Vaughan, 'Landlord and Tenant Relations', p. 221.

[21] Murray, 'Agrarian Violence and Nationalism in Nineteenth-Century Ireland', pp. 58–60; C. Townshend, *Political Violence in Ireland: Government and Resistance since 1848* (Oxford, 1983), makes the point (p. 9) that levels of actual violence reveal little of the efficacy of threatened violence as a sanction.

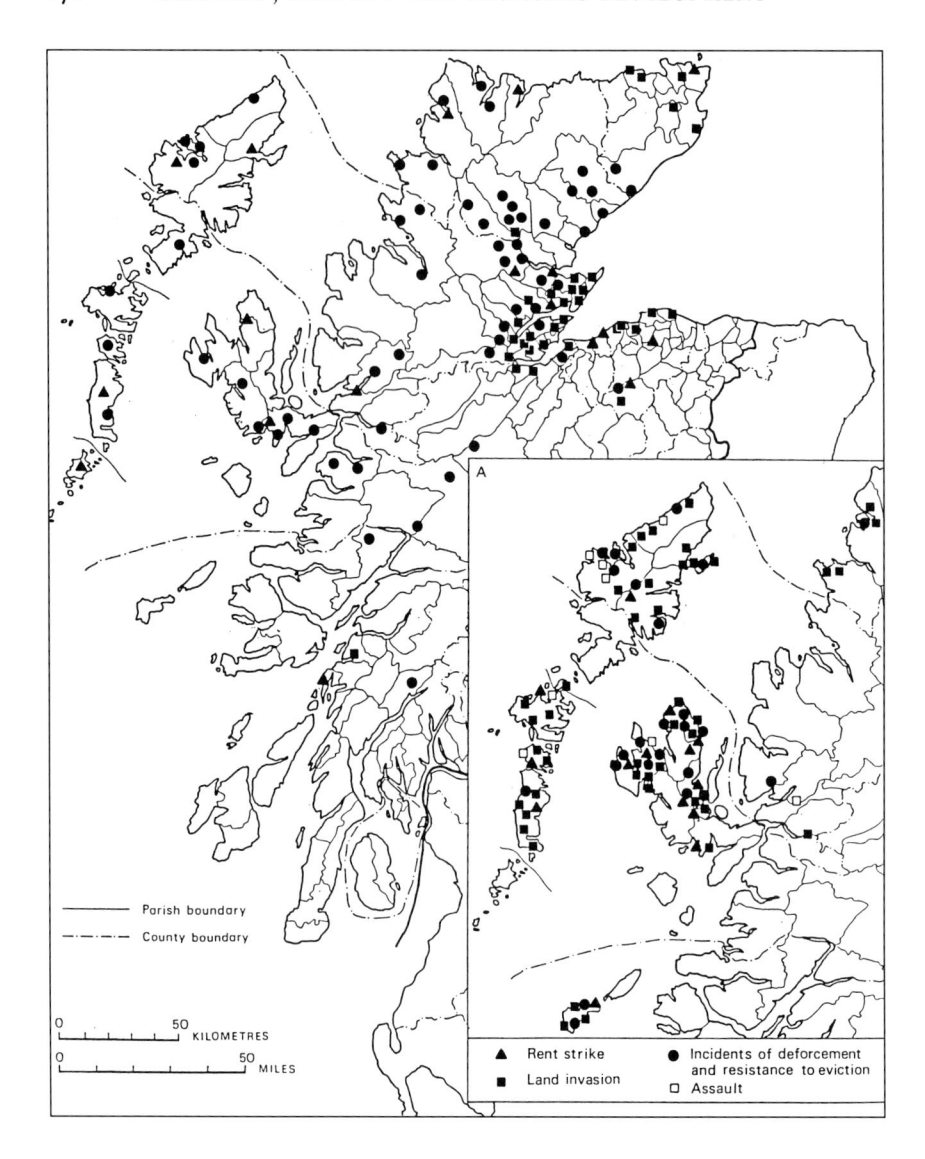

178 CONFLICT, IDENTITY AND ECONOMIC DEVELOPMENT

Figure 2.

Sources: Richards *(1974)*; Hunter *(1976)*; Charlesworth *(1983)*; Logue *(1975)*; S.R.O. GD *40*; GD *1/36*;

● *Protests concerned with enclosure or clearance, 1782–1874*

▲ *Other incidents of protest, disorder or deforcement, 1777–c.1956*

■ *Food riot, 1793–1796, 1847.*

Matheson (the wife of the landowner) received a letter with a picture of a coffin and the words 'the shape of your Coffin that will carry you to hell'.[22] Tenants in Skye in 1886 who were paying rents and were not Land League members during periods of no-rent policy led by H.L.L.R.A. members were threatened with retribution by fellow crofters. The widespread nature of what the procurator fiscal in Portree called 'these fearful threats used towards non-leaguers'[23] illustrates that protest in the form of intimida-tion was often between tenants as well as between landlords and tenants (a fact disguised by official statistics).

In typological terms, neither the dramatic increase in Irish protest represented by the Land War of 1879–82 nor the renewal of Highland protest signalled by the 1874 Bernera riot and the Leckmelm evictions of 1879 represented new departures. Rent strikes were common to both regions, and part of widespread covert protest in Ireland (Figure 3). Irish no-rent tactics were copied by Highland tenants. Civil and military force was used in both areas, either in burning out evicted tenants, or in preventing access to landlord's property. The firing of landlords' property was more common in Ireland than in Highland Scotland as was the use of trees to obstruct eviction parties. By the early twentieth century, however, there were several important structural differences in the nature of protest between Ireland and Highland Scotland. Many recorded events in Ireland between 1905 and 1910 were 'cattle drives' where tenants drove off landlords' livestock. These events were principally located in Clare, Galway, Meath, and Westmeath.[24] In the Highlands by then, protest which may have *begun* with driving off landlords' cattle chiefly took the form of land 'raids' in which 'ancestral lands' occupied by large tenants or landlords' livestock were reclaimed as arable by tenants after forcible seizure. Many such raids were preceded by a veiled threat or formal declaration to raid: the re-occupation of ancestral holdings was, indeed, almost ceremonial.[25] In the forty-two Highland land raids recorded between 1914 and 1929 and in contemporary Ireland, where agrarian unrest was caught up then with Home Rule and trade unionism,[26] access to land was the principal motivation.

---

[22] S.R.O. AD 56/5, 7 February 1888.

[23] S.R.O. GD 40/16/3, f.3, 16 August 1886.

[24] P. Bew, *Conflict and Conciliation in Ireland 1890–1910* (Oxford, 1987), p. 142.

[25] The Aignish land raid in 1888 was formally begun in an almost military style and the agitators marched to their conflict behind a piper and in columns of two. At Portskerra in Sutherland in May–June 1920, raiding was begun with a piper 'leading in' and concluded with a celebratory dance (S.R.O. AF 67/65, 28 May, 14 June 1920).

[26] E. O'Connor, 'Agrarian Unrest and the Labour Movement in County Waterford 1917–1923', *Saothar*, 6 (1980), pp. 40–58; P. Alter, 'Traditions of Violence in the Irish National Movement', in W. J. Mummsen and G. Hirschfield, eds., *Social Protest, Violence and Terror in Nineteenth- and Twentieth-Century Europe* (London, 1982), pp. 137–54; Winstanley, *Ireland and the Land Question*, p. 130; J. Lee, 'Patterns of Rural Unrest in Nineteenth-Century Ireland: A Preliminary Survey', in L. M. Cullen and F. Furet, eds., *Ireland and France, Seventeenth–Twentieth Centuries: Towards a Comparative Study of Rural History* (Paris, 1980), pp. 223–30.

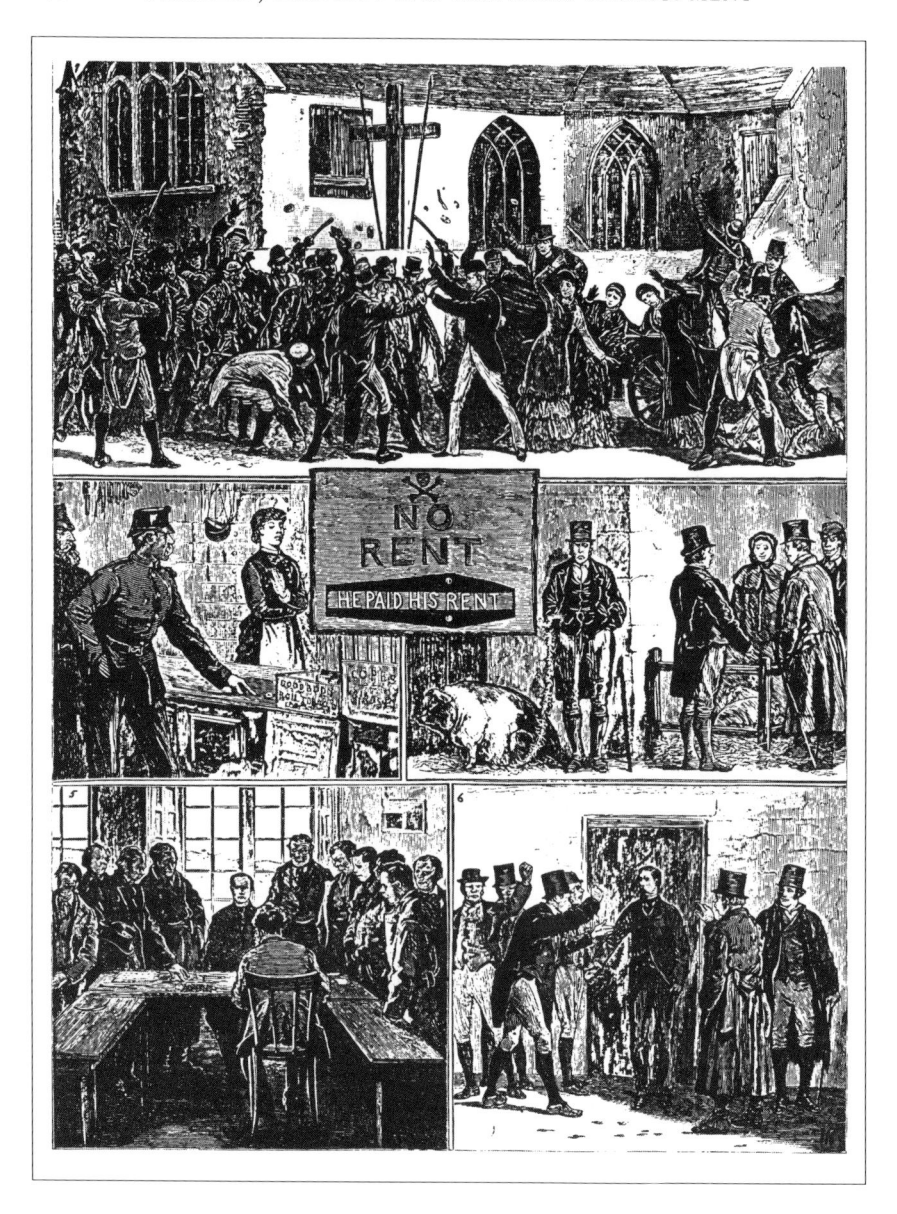

Figure 3.
'The Condition of Ireland'
1. A Riot at Templebraden, Limerick County. —2. Boycotted Policemen. —3. A 'No Rent' Placard. —4. Boycotted: In the Pig Market, Tipperary. —5. 'Paying the Rent': A Collection at the Town Hall, Tipperary, in Aid of the Political Prisoners' Maintenance Fund. —6. 'Refusing the Rent': A Tenants' Demonstration in Tipperary.

* * *

In explanation of post-1850 protest in both Ireland and the Highlands most attention has been paid to the respective 'Land Wars'. Yet it is clear that the Land War in both areas was rooted in earlier structural and economic changes. Clark has emphasised shifts in economy and rural class structure after the Famine: a decline after 1845 in the practice of subletting land and in population (and in numbers of labourers specifically) took place alongside a dramatic increase in Irish livestock numbers. The result, in class terms, was the emergence in Ireland during the second half of the nineteenth century of a three-fold rural class structure of landowners, tenant farmers, and labourers. Protest during the later 1800s and in the Land War especially was the result of earlier processes of structural change in Irish agriculture and of collective action from tenant farmers, not a sudden conflict between landlords and the mass of the rural population. The unity of tenants' identity centred upon three claims: fair rents, fixity of tenure (in the sense of legal recognition of a tenant's right to occupy a holding subject to regular payment of rent and to the fulfilment of any reasonable conditions laid down by landlords), and free sale (the right of an out-going tenant to sell his claim to the holding on quitting a farm). The Irish Land War for Clark was, then, the result of struggle between a 'challenging collectivity' of large and small independent landholders and non-farming elites.[27]

Bew has argued, however, that there was 'a considerable degree of peasant disunity within the overall anti-landlord unity of the Land League framework', and that the tactics, intent and geography of protest varied according to the prevalence and interests of different tenant groups. Indeed, the Land League served as an arena for conflict between the larger bourgeois tenant farmers and the poorer, smaller, farmers concentrated in west Ireland. Class conflict as a cause of protest occurred within tenants' movements as well as between farmer and landowner.[28]

Irish protest may also be explained by often small-scale geographical variations in the alignment of rural classes and in the local agricultural economy. In Mayo, for example, expansion of a live-stock-based market-led economy in the 1850s and 1860s not only created socio-economic tensions conducive to radical political activity but did so particularly in the fertile central districts of the county. Large areas of this rich heartland had been cleared during and immediately after the

---

[27] S. Clark, 'The Importance of Agrarian Classes: Agrarian Class Structure and Collective Action in Nineteenth-Century Ireland', *British Journal of Sociology*, XXIX, 1 (1978), pp. 22–40; idem, *Social Origins of the Irish Land War* (Princeton, 1979); Winstanley, *Ireland and the Land Question*, p. 27.

[28] P. Bew, *Land and the National Question in Ireland, 1858–1882* (Dublin, 1978); idem, *Conflict and Conciliation in Ireland*; on earlier views of the Irish Land Wars, see J. Pomfret, *The Struggle for Land in Ireland, 1800–1923* (Princeton, 1930); N. D. Palmer, *The Irish Land League Crisis* (New Haven, 1940); for a good review of Bew (1978) and Clark (1979) and their contrasting perspectives see L. P. Curtis, 'On Class and Class Conflict in the Land War', *Ir. Econ. and Soc. Hist.*, VIII (1981–2), pp. 86–94.

Famine (a cause of agitation in the early 1850s). The intensification of agrarian disorder in the late 1860s centred in this rich core where divisions between wealthy graziers on the one hand and small farmers, urban traders, and the mass of tenants on the other were most marked. In Mayo, the agitation that culminated in the Land War between 1879–82 was the result of pre- and post-Famine consolidation of arable smallholdings into grazing farms as well as of contemporary external agencies. Moreover, protest in Mayo was influenced by an alliance between political nationalists and small and large arable farmers in opposition to capitalist graziers and landlords. It was divisions within this alliance rather than a reduction of tension between large landlord and small tenant that led to a decline in agitation.[29]

In County Cork, alliances between townsmen dependent upon agricultural produce and small farmers against landlords underlay agitation during the 1860s and 1870s. Outrages there were also directed at those who co-operated with landlords: caretakers of evicted farms, land grabbers and 'grazing grabbers' (persons who hired grazing land on evicted farms). For Jones and others, explanation of the conflict between graziers and peasants between 1890 and 1910 and of the cattle 'drives' and the 'Ranch Wars' of 1906–9 lies in the graziers' land-acquisitiveness, the disruption of the status order in the countryside, and the failure of graziers to bolster the welfare of the peasant community.[30]

Class conflict was likewise a cause of protest in the Highlands. But there unrest was the more direct result of opposition from tenants to the rent levels, land acquisitiveness and eviction policies of landlords. Holding size varied but there was no significant stratification within crofting. The Highlands were virtually without a middle class and there is no evidence to suggest, as for Ireland, that protest initiated by crofters was supported by loose confederations of urban merchants or others who perceived their interests to lie with the peasantry. Highland rural society was not, however, simply a crofting community. The creation of the crofting community was paralleled by the growth of two essentially landless groups, cottars and squatters. Cottars occasionally paid rent and usually cultivated part of the croft; squatters did not pay rent although they may have cultivated part of the common pastures.

If we follow Clark's model for Ireland and distinguish rural classes one from another 'in terms of their relationship to the principal means of production, i.e. land',[31] then Highland protest may be interpreted as a tripartite affiliation of landworking classes who collectively perceived their respective interests in

---

[29] This description of Mayo is taken from D. Jordan, 'Merchants, "Strong Farmers" and Fenians: the Post-Famine Political Elite and the Irish Land War' in Philpin, ed., *Nationalism and Popular Protest in Ireland*, pp. 320–48.

[30] J. S. Donnelly, *The Land and People of Nineteenth-Century Cork* (London, 1975), pp. 251–307, 308–77; D. S. Jones, 'The Cleavage between Graziers and Peasants in the Land Struggle, 1890–1910', in Clark and Donnelly, *Irish Peasants*, pp. 374–413; Bew, *Conflict and Conciliation*, pp. 142–9; K. T. Hoppen, *Ireland since 1800: Conflict and Conformity* (London, 1989), p. 99

[31] Clark, 'The Importance of Agrarian Classes', p. 26.

opposition to landlords. In explanation of protest before c. 1874–9 and for the recorded lack of unrest between 1857 and 1874, this model of class allegiance has some appeal. But during the Land War and after the 1886 Crofters Act, conflict was for several reasons the result of more complex class issues.

Firstly, the 1886 Act, whilst guaranteeing crofters' security of tenure and their right to claim compensation for improvements, made no legislative provision for cottars or squatters. Secondly, the Act contained no provision for making more land available. The result was that from 1886 Highland agitation, in the over-crowded and 'landless' Outer Isles especially, was directed almost entirely at regaining access to land. Cottars and squatters played a leading rôle in many land raids. Thirdly, the fact that several protest events in the Highlands in the mid-1880s and the 1920s were the result of conflict *between* groups of crofters and on occasion between cottars and crofters, and that threats were made (and action taken) against anyone occupying holdings of evicted tenants, may suggest that protest was the result of disunity within the land-working classes as well as of tenants' collective action in opposition to landowners.

Protest, perhaps particularly the increased agitation of the early 1880s, is partly to be explained in economic terms. The agricultural economy of both regions shared in the increase in tenants' rent levels during the 1870s and both suffered the effects of harvest failure and widespread livestock disease following the bad weather of 1879–89.[32] In County Cork in the late 1870s, landlords precipitated conflict by insisting on rents during periods of depression and renewed agitation then was an attempt to defend the relative material prosperity of the previous two decades. The fact that increased Land League activity in Cork in 1880 took place against a background of increasing economic improvement lends weight to the claim that protest there was rooted in rising economic expectations.[33] But protest was also rooted in future protection of past gain: 'The background to the Land War of 1879–82 was not, therefore, a "revolution of rising expectations" . . . but a state of deep anxiety that the economic roller-coaster was once again heading in a downward direction'.[34]

Contemporary comment on the Highlands would support this view. One observer of the 1880s noted how 'the irritating struggle to keep up the expensive tastes of prosperous times on the diminished income of the days of agricultural depression explains a good deal of the murmuring discontent heard among crofters and others during the recent, and to some extent still enduring, "agitation" '.[35]

Others, then and now, have pointed to the failure of fishing, ruined harvests and livestock disease as one cause of the agitation of the 1880s in the Highlands.[36]

---

[32] Hunter, *Crofting Community*, pp. 132–3; Richards, *A History of the Highland Clearances*, Volume II, pp. 477–503, esp. 485–91.

[33] Donnelly, *The Land and People of Nineteenth-Century Cork*, pp. 265–6; Clark and Donnelly, eds., *Irish Peasants*, pp. 9–10.

[34] Hoppen, *Ireland since 1800*, pp. 94–5.

[35] Quoted in Richards, *A History of the Highland Clearances*, Volume II, p. 490.

[36] Hunter, *Crofting Community*, pp. 132–3; Richards, *Highland Clearances*, Volume II, pp. 477–503.

Economic considerations affected the seasonality of protest. The temporary absence of crofters at the east coast fishing often signalled a seasonal respite in Highland protest: as one police officer wrote to his chief constable in 1884, 'I expect things will be quiet now, until they return again in harvest time'.[37] Where temporary employment of Highland labour involved travel to Irish fishing grounds, the authorities were doubly alarmed by the prospect of Highlanders learning directly from the Irish experience: 'I am confident that all is quiet till winter [wrote an observer of protest on Skye in May 1882] when the men will return from the Irish fishings—what will be done then depends on the state of Ireland.'[38] Protest was predominantly a winter event. Twenty-one of the thirty-five principal land raids enumerated in the Outer Isles between 1913 and 1922 took place between November and March.[39] The evidence for Ireland between 1884 and 1900 suggests a similar seasonality of protest: 1,427 of the 2,590 recorded outrages in 1880, for example, occurred in November and December, but in many earlier years the seasonal incidence is much less marked. Whilst it is possible for Ireland that the seasonality of outrages hints at causal links between the cycle of the peasant economy and rural custom,[40] the evidence of the later nineteenth-century Highlands suggests that periodicity of protest was more the result of Highlanders' dependence upon economic returns from beyond the Highlands.

The political bases to rural protest are directly comparable and have been the focus of much attention.[41] The Irish National Land League continued on a national scale the agrarian activism of earlier secret societies. In part, it did so because in bringing together local and national dissent amongst tenant farmers, rural labourers and small-holders in opposition to graziers and large landowners, the League politicised tenant consciousness and provided effective political leadership.[42] In part, too, the Land League linked local agrarian issues with national political ones. Michael Davitt, the principal motivator behind the creation of the Land League in 1879, hoped to link 'the land or social question

---

[37] S.R.O. GD 1/36/2/1, f.1, 3 May 1884.

[38] S.R.O. GD 1/36/1/Box 1, 21 May 1882, N. Macpherson to Sheriff Ivory.

[39] S.R.O. AF 67/61–5; AF 67/143–54; 157–60; 292; 299; 324; 325; 326; 328; 329; 331; 345; 348; 370–1; 389.

[40] *Return of Outrages . . . 1844 . . . 1880*, P.P. LXXVII 1881, p. 24; J. W. O'Neill, 'A Look at Captain Rock: Agrarian Rebellion in Ireland 1815–45', *Eire–Ireland*, XVII, 3 (1982) pp. 29–30; Beames, 'Rural Conflict in Pre-Famine Ireland'; on this seasonality in records of English protest, see Bohstedt, *Riots and Community Politics*, pp. 20–1, 221; Charlesworth, 'Spatial Diffusion of Rural Protest', pp. 258–9; Howkins, *Poor Labouring Men*, p. 38.

[41] For Ireland, in addition to those works cited in note 28 above, see Alter, 'Traditions of Violence in the Irish National Movement', M. Davitt, *The Fall of Feudalism in Ireland* (London, 1904); B. L. Solow, *The Land Question and the Irish Economy* (Cambridge, Mass., 1971); Hunter, *Crofting Community*, pp. 129, 132–5, 149, 162–4, 182–5, 187; idem, 'The Gaelic Connection: The Highlands, Ireland and Nationalism, 1873–1922', *Scottish Historical Review*, LIV, 2 (1975), pp. 178–204; S. Warwick-Haller, *William O'Brien and the Irish Land War* (Dublin, 1990).

[42] Hoppen, *Ireland since 1800*, pp. 94–6.

to that of Home Rule, by making the ownership of the soil the basis of a fight for self-government'.[43] Although the Kilmainham treaty of April 1882 effectively ended the Land League as a national force, issues of conflict over land remained and connections between national politics and agrarian dissent were stressed again in the United Irish League in 1898, in the growth of labour militancy, and in the land seizures that accompanied the political upheavals of 1918–23.[44]

In the Highlands, the Highland Land Law Reform Association followed the example of the Irish National Land League in working for fair rents and tenants' rights, and, like Ireland, gave Highland tenants a national political voice. Rural agitation in both areas was often directly linked through men like John Murdoch and Michael Davitt. Murdoch, editor of the *Highlander*, used his journal to support and campaign for Irish Home Rule; Davitt's Highland speeches urged crofters to 'organise and agitate until they had overthrown the whole fabric of the landlord system'.[45] In 1886, Skye crofters not only mirrored in their protests contemporary agitation in Ireland but petitioned Gladstone in support of Irish Home Rule: 'to put an end to centuries of oppression and misrule in Ireland by granting to the Irish people the fullest possible measure of self-government'.[46] Even by 1921, when a South Uist factor wrote to the Board of Agriculture stating that 'the Sinn-Fein element is pretty strong'[47] (amongst cottars engaged in land raids that January), the connections were evident and have been seen as part of moves towards national political identity, even an emergent Pan-Celticism between Ireland and Scotland despite differences in political background.

If, then, protest was rooted in issues of 'access to land', one motivating factor in both areas was the claim by agitators to be defending traditional rights and customs in relation to ownership, occupation, and management of land. This claim was not confined to those outrages committed in relation to eviction or possible future occupation of small-holdings. Some assaults were motivated by a claim to maintain customary practices of land inheritance and were perpetrated in the knowledge that 'the community' would remain silent when challenged by authority.[48] There is clear evidence among the peasantry in Highland Scotland and Ireland that they felt themselves entitled to a plot of land, however small, and that such entitlement was based in customary obligations. Established methods of land holding involved much more, however, than the maintenance of an 'unofficial

---

[43] Davitt, *The Fall of Feudalism in Ireland*, p. 121.
[44] Alter, 'Traditions of Violence in the Irish National Movement'; Hunter, 'The Gaelic Connection', pp. 193–204.
[45] *Oban Times*, 30 April, 7 May 1887: quoted in Hunter 'The Gaelic Connection', p. 187.
[46] *Oban Times*, 20 March 1886: quoted in Hunter 'The Gaelic Connection', p. 187.
[47] S.R.O. AF 67/152, 27 January 1921, John MacDonald to Board of Agriculture for Scotland.
[48] Beames, 'Rural Conflict in Pre-Famine Ireland', p. 278; *Report from the Select Committee on Outrages (Ireland)*, P.P. XIV 1852, has numerous references to the way the local population refused to answer questions relating to protest and would 'shelter' the offenders of even murderous protest; this point is made for English agrarian protest in East Anglia in 1816 and 1822 by Charlesworth, 'Spatial Diffusion of Rural Protest', and Howkins, *Poor Labouring Men*.

contract' between landlord and tenant. Land itself had a cultural significance over and above economic returns and beyond even geopolitical connotations. In 1847, one witness in Ireland noted how, upon eviction, 'they [the peasants] get demoralised, and frantic, and savage, and wild; and they go idle about, and congregate together and meet at wakes, and combine; and then such a person's destruction is determined on'.[49] In the Highlands, tenants claimed the *duthchas* of a holding, the term for a traditional belief, that, if they and their ancestors occupied a piece of land for four generations or more, it was theirs in perpetuity. This agreed code was without legal foundation no matter the strength of customary belief.

It is, in this sense, possible to consider agrarian protest as an ideological clash, an unequal conflict between the practices of custom and the imperatives of capital.[50] Certainly, legitimising notions of entitlement to land underlay the reclamation of what were widely recognised as ancestral holdings in the 'land raids' in the Outer Isles. The claim of Alexander Macdonald of Paiblesgarry, North Uist, who noted in March 1920 that 'we are convinced that we are acting right when we take possession of the land from which our ancestors were wrongfully driven',[51] is typical of many then in the Highlands and finds direct equivalents in earlier periods and in Ireland. It is possible to suggest that, in both regions, this persisting moral claim to land was bolstered by the politicisation of agrarian conflict in the Land Wars and, indeed, even to argue that this ideological attachment to land represented by rural protest directly influenced national politics. As one agrarian radical noted in Ireland in 1907, 'the land is what most concerns the country people and a splendid substantial thing it is to fight for'.[52]

* * *

This comparative paper has not been exhaustive: issues not covered include the role of religion in protest, or the place of women in protest. No particular events have been anatomised in the detailed ways sometimes necessary for more complete general understanding and no direct comparative analysis has been attempted of protest in Ireland and in Highland Scotland in relation to other parts of the British Isles.

---

[49] *Digest of Evidence taken before Her Majesty's Commissioners of Inquiry into the State of the Law and Practice in Respect of the Occupation of Land in Ireland* (Dublin, 1847), Part I, pp. 361–2; quoted in Knott, 'Land, Kinship and Identity', p. 95.

[50] The term *duthchas* has been treated elsewhere in explanation of the Highlanders' ideological commitment to land: see R. A. Dodgshon, *Land and Society in Early Scotland* (Oxford, 1981), pp. 110–13; Hunter, *Crofting Community*, pp. 56–7; Withers, *Gaelic Scotland*, pp. 77–8, 177, 205, 213, 318–19, 331–2, 350, 370, 389, 414–15; idem, '"Give Us Land and Plenty of It": The Ideological Basis to Land and Landscape in the Scottish Highlands', *Landscape History*, 1990, pp. 45–54.

[51] S.R.O. AF 67/152, 2 March 1920, Alexander Macdonald to Board of Agriculture for Scotland.

[52] The words are those of Laurence Ginnell, much involved with agrarian radicalism in early twentieth-century Ireland; Bew, *Conflict and Conciliation*, p. 148.

Irish and Highland Scottish protest shared the same general characteristics in terms of the nature of events. Agitation was a process of opposition compounded of numerous events and particular individual typologies: personal violence, rent strike, covert threat, arson, maiming livestock. All these forms of protest (and others) were apparent in both regions. The fact that they were widely known before the Famine would suggest some continuity over time in the ways that underlying tensions in rural society were made 'real' as events. The particular place of the rent strike in the 1870s and 1880s (though not unique to that period) was closely linked to the increased national and political attention being given to agrarian unrest. The 'land raids' in the early twentieth-century Highlands had no direct equivalent in contemporary Ireland. To Highland land raiders, this re-appropriation of ancestral land may have been a formal breach of the law, but was legitimated in their eyes by customary beliefs attaching to land: 'Cottars in Skye and other parts of the Highlands have never considered themselves as being in breach of any moral law in laying claim to cultivate some of the lands held by their forefathers for centuries'.[53] The land question in Ireland has similarly been seen as an attempt to redress through morally justifiable action past political and historical grievances.[54] Post-Famine protest in both areas was as much rooted in moral outrage as events before 1845. What distinguished later protest was the increasingly national political context in which these essentially cultural claims to land as propriety *and* property were implicated.

Protest in both areas was closely related to structural change in rural society particularly within those groups we may collectively term the 'tenantry'. In Ireland, however, divisions by class within the land-working sectors of the rural population were more important as a cause of protest than in Highland Scotland. There was conflict between crofters in the Highlands but such intra-class conflict was never on the Irish scale. Since protest in both areas took the form of conflict within classes and, on occasion, between members of the same family or non-collateral individuals working the same holding, it is possible to suggest that strict adherence to notions of class defined in terms of landworkers' relationships to land may not be nuanced enough to explain in detail the causes of protest. This claim would find support in an Irish context in Fitzpatrick's assessment of rural protest as a struggle between and within families, not classes.[55] Protest was the result of perceived and real threats to personal standing and familial or community standing as well as to more generally-agreed customary practices relating to access to land. What may be needed, then, is further attention to issues of class consciousness and the often local and familial origins of that sense of opposition underlying the inherent ideology of the groups involved.

[53] S.R.O. AF 67/158 and *Dundee Advertiser*, 28 February 1923.
[54] This is a point made by Bew in *Conflict and Conciliation*, pp. 148–51.
[55] D. Fitzpatrick, 'Class, Family and Rural Unrest in Nineteenth-Century Ireland', in P. J. Drudy, ed., *Ireland: Land, Politics and People* (Cambridge, 1982), pp. 37–75.

In both regions, the Land Wars were largely economically motivated (by agricultural depression) and part, too, of a contemporary wider politicisation of agrarian dissent. The relative cessation of protest in the preceding twenty years may also be explained by the comparative economic prosperity of the period. Given this wider political and economic context in which rural protest was set, full explanation of the timing, geographical scale and intensity of the essentially local phenomena of protest demands attention to external circumstances. Attention to unitary and immediate causes not only neglects the particular evidence that contemporaries saw to connect rural protest in late nineteenth-century Ireland and Highland Scotland, but also makes difficult any comparison with events elsewhere and at other times.

15

Inequality, social structure and the market in Belfast and Glasgow, 1830–1914

R. J. Morris

ACCOUNTS OF THE DISTINCTIVE NATURE of Belfast give wide ranging attention to the violence and conflict endemic in the city. This paper will look at the relationships between these factors and the wage and employment structure of the city. It will do so in the light of comparison with Glasgow and the Clydeside economy. This is designed to supplement rather than replace existing explanations. Many histories consider the conflicts of Belfast as the product of Irish history over a long period.[1] Others have offered a variety of explanations for the sustained nature of the conflict. Baker saw Catholic migration as the initial trigger for a conflict which was then sustained by the Home Rule crisis.[2] For Boyd the late eighteenth century was a period in which radical and liberal Protestant elements were building the possibility of stable relationships with the Catholic population, but this was brought to an end by the activities of bigoted and fanatical preacher politicians like Hanna and Drew.[3] Again the Home Rule crisis of the 1880s intensified conflict by drawing a wide range of Protestant middle class people into the conflict. Bew, Patterson and Gibbon added the diverging economic structure of Belfast and the rest of Ireland as a motive for Unionism amongst the capital owning and professional classes of the city.[4]

At other levels Belfast's history is characteristic of dozens of large industrial towns-cum-regional service centres which were growing up all over Europe. The

---

[1] A. T. Q. Stewart, *The Narrow Ground: The Roots of Conflict in Ulster* (London, 1977), provides the most subtle and thoughtful version of this position.
[2] Sybil E. Baker, 'Orange and Green', in H. J. Dyos and Michael Wolff, eds., *The Victorian City: Images and Realities* (London, 1973), II, pp. 789–814.
[3] Andrew Boyd, *Holy War in Belfast* (3rd edition, Belfast, 1987).
[4] Paul Bew, Peter Gibbon and Henry Patterson, *The State in Northern Ireland, 1921–72* (Manchester, 1979); Peter Gibbon, *The Origins of Ulster Unionism* (Manchester, 1975); Henry Patterson, *Class Conflict and Sectarianism: The Protestant Working Class and the Belfast Labour Movement, 1868–1920* (Belfast, 1980).

process began with the slow growth of a port. The building of the Brown, then White Linen Halls in the 1740s and 1780s marked Belfast's function as the marketing and financing centre for the linen industry of the surrounding countryside. The intensification of capitalist relationships and the changes in the technology and organisation of production in the early nineteenth century drew industry in from the countryside. By the late 1830s, the linen industry was well established in Belfast through the intermediate period of cotton spinning in the 1820s.[5] In the second half of the century major shipbuilding and engineering units were added to the city's economy. In Glasgow, the early dominance of cotton was replaced after mid-century by engineering and related trades. Shipbuilding, though important for the Clydeside economy, does not directly enter the economy of Glasgow until early twentieth-century boundary extensions. The early growth produced periods of social and political violence before 1850. By the 1860s, like most urban societies, Glasgow had found ways of resolving or at least negotiating and controlling social conflict. This did not happen in Belfast. The objective in this paper is to outline some of the economic and market structures involved in the growth of Belfast and Glasgow and to examine the potential interaction of these structures with the major source of conflict in Belfast.

POPULATION

In Belfast, rapid growth took place in the second half of the century when political events in Ireland as a whole placed maximum strain on social relationships. Belfast had little time to create the institutions of conciliation and bargaining which were characteristic of other cities. This growth took place in a period of rapid change in the religious composition of the Belfast population. The proportion of Catholics fell from a peak of around 40 per cent in the 1840s to around 25 per cent by 1900.[6] Conflict in Glasgow over the control of space and work did take place, notably in the period of rapid growth in the first half of the century, but was rapidly institutionalized in the trades union movement and the politics of the Liberal hegemony of urban Scotland.[7]

---

[5] Jonathan Bardon, *Belfast* (Belfast, 1982), pp. 31–121; J. C. Beckett and Emily Boyle in J. C. Beckett, *et al*, *Belfast: The Making of the City, 1800–1914* (Belfast, 1983).

[6] I. Budge and C. O'Leary, *Belfast: Approach to Crisis* (London 1973), p. 32; the 1848 figure (43 per cent) is an estimate from Baker, 'Orange and Green', p. 793. It seems to have come from a street directory, *Henderson's Belfast Street Directory 1850* (Belfast, 1850).

[7] W. Knox, 'The Political and Workplace Culture of the Scottish Working Class, 1832–1914', in Hamish Fraser and R. J. Morris, eds., *People and Society in Scotland*, Vol. II: *1830–1914* (Edinburgh, 1990); G. C. Hutchison, *A Political History of Scotland* (Edinburgh, 1986).

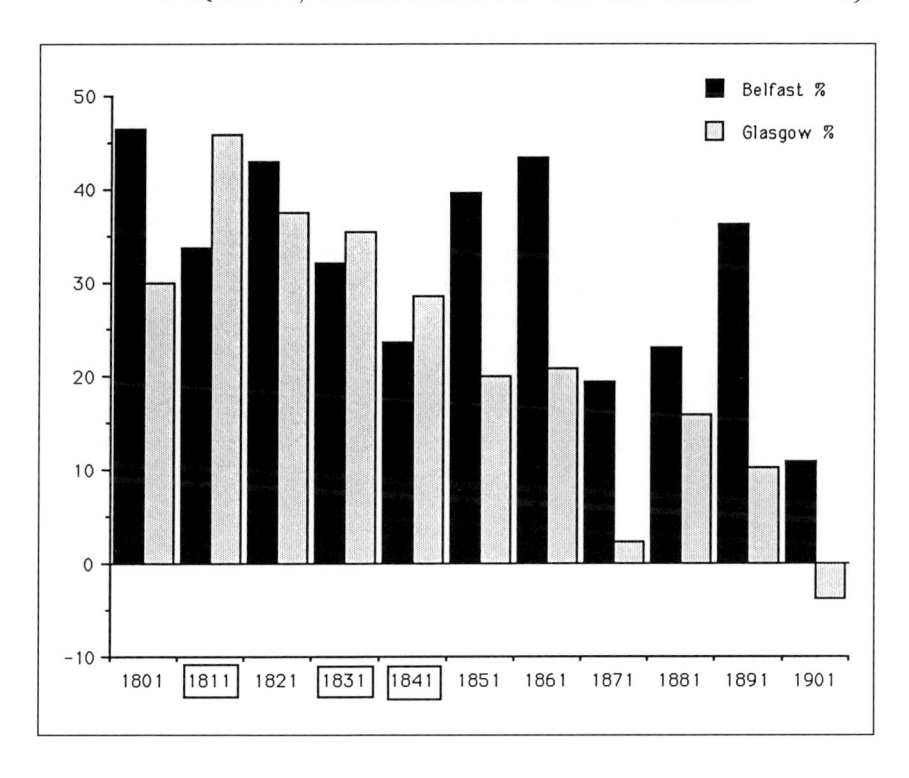

INEQUALITY, SOCIAL STRUCTURE AND THE MARKET 191

Figure 1: Growth rates of populations of Belfast and Glasgow, 1801–1911. (Boxed decades are those in which Glasgow grew more rapidly than Belfast.)

Belfast figures:
1831–1911 from *Census of Ireland, 1911*, relate to town and suburbs for 1831, and to the borough as constituted for each of the subsequent census dates; 1801–1821 relate to the 'town' of Belfast apparently as constituted under the Police Acts; see Ian Budge and Cornelius O'Leary, *Belfast: Approach to Crisis: A Study of Belfast Politics 1613–1970*, p. 28

Glasgow figures:
1801–1831 city and suburbs; 1841–1911 relate to the parliamentary burgh. The figures are taken from the *Census of Scotland, 1911*. If the boundary extension which took place in 1896 is taken into account, then the figures for the 1890s were 35 per cent higher and for the 1900s 3 per cent higher.

ECONOMIC OPPORTUNITIES AND STRUCTURES

The printed census remains the most accessible source of comparable information on the economic structure of Belfast and Glasgow. As a source it is a powerful distorting lens but can be used with care to show the general shape of the economic opportunities available in the two cities.

The figures for 1891 and 1901 are fairly consistent and comparable. The categories do not separate labour and capital or industrial sectors in any meaningful way, but they do separate six very different sets of relationships with capital. The two economies were very much the same in their reliance on industrial activity. Two differences do emerge. Belfast had a higher professional sector suggesting that it was more important as a service centre for Ulster and the north of Ireland than Glasgow was for west and central Scotland. This relationship had existed for some time. In 1831, the census category 'capitalists, bankers, professional and other educated men' contained 5. 9 per cent of the males over 20 in the city and suburbs of Glasgow and 11. 2 per cent of those in the town and suburbs of Belfast. On the other hand, Glasgow was a port with a richer hinterland than Belfast and a more extensive international trading function; hence commercial activity was much more important. A third important difference involved women's relationship to the economy. A larger portion of Belfast women worked in the industrial sector, with a consequence that fewer were placed in the category 'indefinite and non-productive class'.

Table 1: Occupational structure, males over twenty years of age.

	Glasgow		Belfast	
	1891	1901	1891	1901
Professional	5.0	4.6	7.8	6.6
Domestic	2.0	0.8	1.8	1.8
Commercial	19.3	21.6	15.9	16.5
Agricultural	0.5	0.4	1.3	1.5
Industrial	70.9	69.9	69.3	69.3
No occupation	2.2	2.8	3.9	4.4

Source:
Printed census of Ireland and Scotland, 1891 and 1901. The figures give each occupational group as a percentage of the total male population over twenty years of age.

Table 2: Occupational structure, females over twenty years of age.

	Glasgow		Belfast	
	1891	1901	1891	1901
Professional	1.5	2.3	1.8	2.0
Domestic	8.8	8.4	8.8	7.8
Commercial	0.8	1.6	0.4	0.8
Agricultural	0.1	0.1	0.1	0.1
Industrial	24.0	20.7	35.1	29.8
No occupation	64.8	67.0	53.9	59.5

Source:
Printed census of Ireland and Scotland, 1891 and 1901. The figures give each occupational group as a percentage of the total female population over twenty years of age.

The occupational titles in the printed census indicate further differences in the economic opportunities in the two cities towards the end of the century.

Table 3: Major occupational groups in Belfast and Glasgow, 1891

Belfast 1891			Glasgow 1891		
Labourer	10,304	13.3	Labourer	12,841	6.1
Flax/linen	6,751	8.7	Iron manufacturer	12,040	5.7
Clerk	3,269	4.2	Clerk	11,456	5.4
Iron manufacturer	2,803	3.6	Carter	7,551	3.6
Carpenter	2,669	3.5	Porter	6,046	2.9
Shipbuilder	2,076	2.7	Fitter	5,956	2.8
Porter	1,945	2.5	Machine maker	5,530	2.6
Carter	1,584	2.0	Carpenter	5,106	2.4
Grocer	1,559	2.0	Blacksmith	4,817	2.3
Soldier	1,550	2.0	Tailor	4,294	2.0
Shoes	1,263	1.6	Shoemaker	3,674	1.7
Seaman	1,249	1.6	Grocer	3,638	1.7
Docks	1,224	1.6	Boiler maker	3,233	1.5
Tailor	1,222	1.6	Inns/hotels	3,085	1.5
Bricklayer	1,211	1.6	Seaman	3,043	1.4

The male labour force of Glasgow was faced with a greater choice than that of Belfast. In Belfast, 50 per cent of the male labour force came from fourteen titles and 70 per cent from thirty-two. The numbers for Glasgow were twenty and forty-five. Much of the difference came from the greater differentiation of labour in Glasgow. 'General Labourers' were 13. 4 per cent of Belfast males but only 6. 1 per cent of Glasgow's.

The leading sectors of the external income earning economy of the two cities were very different. Glasgow was dominated by engineering, machine makers, boiler makers, blacksmiths and iron manufacturers. In Belfast, the textile sector was still very much more important, even for males. In Glasgow, cotton manufacture and weaving each had only 0. 5 per cent of the male labour force. In the internal urban economy, differences were slight. Two items were significant for Belfast. It was a brickbuilt city, hence the bricklayers. It was an insecure city, hence the soldiers. The figures for 1901 confirmed the major features and indicated the increased importance of shipbuilding in Belfast.

The printed census of Ireland gave the religious composition of the occupational groups. The shipbuilders were, as expected, Protestant dominated, but the path of change showed the importance of the 1886 riots. The rapid expansion of the last 30 years of the century drew many Catholics into the yards. Although the percentage fell, the numbers of Catholics in the yards still doubled during the 1880s. The battle between sectarian and market forces was very uneven in the yards, but one system was still not able to dominate totally the other.

Table 4: Proportion of shipbuilders in the main religious denominations

	Total	Catholics per cent	Episcopalian per cent	Presbyterian per cent
1871	758*	9.4	28.0	57.6
1881	557	13.5	35.7	43.8
1891	2,076	7.9	40.1	42.8
1901	4,040	7.5	38.8	41.4

* In 1871 shipwrights were included in the total. In 1881, there were 670 shipwrights recorded, of whom 64 were Catholic, so this should not affect the percentages very much.

Although the Protestant-dominated areas of the Belfast economy are the best known and were clearly defended with success and often violence, the Catholic population was also able to carve out niches in the economy and defend these with varying degrees of success. The clearest group were the publicans. Again the effect of the Home Rule riots appears as a massive shift in an already dominant position. The same position existed amongst wine and spirit merchants. Little seems to be known of the processes by which this dominance was achieved or the motivations for entering these trades. Indeed, as rioting was often punctuated by the destruction of Catholic-run public houses, it was at first sight a paradoxical choice.[8] The likeliest explanation lies in some sort of response to blocked aspirations either in capital accumulation or in the skilled labour market. Little more can be said until we know more about the three hundred or so net increase in Catholic publicans which came about in the 1880s and 1890s.

Table 5: Proportion of innkeepers, hotel keepers and publicans in the main religious denominations

	Total	Catholics per cent	Episcopalian per cent	Presbyterian per cent
1871	446	52.2	18.2	28.2
1881	484	55.6	16.9	24.6
1891	598	70.9	13.0	14.0
1901	714	80.1	7.8	10.1

Some of these specialised sectarian niches were defended with less success. The Catholics had dominated the butcher trade since the 1830s. The clashes between the butchers of Hercules Street and the Orange marches had been a constant hazard since the election of 1832.[9] Here the majority change appeared in the 1870s, when the area of Hercules Street was being cleared for the building of Royal Avenue

---

[8] Evidence of John Riordan and Bernard Duffy in QQ 14041 to 14106, *Report of the Belfast Riots Commission*, P.P. 1887 XVII.

[9] Baker, 'Orange and Green'.

which began in 1880.[10] It can have been no coincidence that the Unionist-dominated town council used its powers of urban reconstruction to undermine the Catholic domination of territory near to one of the key marching routes.

Table 6: Proportion of butchers in the main religious denominations

	Total	Catholics per cent	Episcopalian per cent	Presbyterian per cent
1871	361	65.4	18.0	15.5
1881	435	52.2	22.8	21.6
1891	553	51.0	19.5	24.8
1901	803	41.1	23.0	27.9

This was part of a more general movement in which retail occupations lost some of their sectarian bias. The grocers became slightly less Presbyterian between 1871 and 1901, whilst the general shopkeepers became slightly less Catholic. In part this was a matter of economic status. Catholics in general had less capital and hence took the lower status positions in retailing. As time went on, the rate of separate community development was increased by the politics and conflict of the last 40 years of the century. This would explain some of the change, as each group shopped increasingly with retailers from their own denomination.[11] In addition, a portion of the Catholic population may have increased in wealth to a point where they could, as customers, support the more specialist retailing of the grocer.

Table 7: Proportion of grocers in the main religious denominations

	Total	Catholics per cent	Episcopalian per cent	Presbyterian per cent
1871	782	12.4	19.4	55.9
1881	1,303	17.3	18.3	53.9
1891	1,559	16.1	18.3	52.6
1901	2,186	18.6	17.9	50.9

Table 8: Proportion of general shopkeepers in the main religious denominations

	Total	Catholics per cent	Episcopalian per cent	Presbyterian per cent
1871	593	64.4	16.5	17.2
1881	665	52.3	20.1	23.3
1891	589	51.1	19.9	20.2
1901	895	51.4	19.3	21.6

[10] Bardon, *Belfast*, p. 142.
[11] F. W. Boal, 'Territoriality on the Shankill–Falls Divide', *Irish Geography*, VI (1969), pp. 30–50.

There were many other parts of the economy which were staked out as niches for one group or another and became part of the battle between market and sectarian forces.[12]

WAGES [13]

An indication of the rewards offered in the economies of the two cities can be gathered from the wage returns of the Labour Department of the Board of Trade and by the various statistical collections which preceded that body. These returns are often as distorted and structured as the printed census returns but they do tell a coherent story.

The material on the shipyards which were so important to Belfast was even more distorted and opaque than the figures for other trades. The comparison has to be with the Clyde region as there were no shipyards in Glasgow before the boundary extension which took in Govan. The wage range entailed by any one job description was even greater than with other industries. In addition, the method of payment was usually to the work gang which then divided earnings according to a variety of market and customary rules.[14] The figures offered in the wage returns must have covered a variety of conventional and customary expectations.

Table 9: Wages for iron shipbuilding

	Glasgow area (1880) shillings per week	Belfast (1883) shillings per day
Riveters	25.5	5.75
Platers	30.5	6.0
Angle iron smiths	24.7	5.0
Holders up	16.7	3.9
Labourers	16.3	2.4
Differentials: holders up to platers	54.9 per cent	65.3 per cent
Differentials: labourers to platers	53.4 per cent	40.3 per cent

There seems to be no consistent hierarchy of payments amongst the skilled men. This may be due to the range of payments made to each group. The general

---

[12] A. C. Hepburn, 'Work, Class and Religion in Belfast, 1871–1911', *Ir. Econ. and Soc. Hist.*, X (1983), pp. 33–50, especially table III, hints at many of these.

[13] Unless otherwise stated all wages data were drawn from the following sources, *General Report on the Wages of the Manual Labour Classes in the United Kingdom, 1886 and 1891*, P.P. 1893–94, LXXXIII, Part 2, and *Report on the Standard Time Rates of Wages in the United Kingdom in 1900*, P.P. 1900, LXXXII. All the rates quoted were time rates and are given in shillings with the pence reduced to decimals. All data on occupational structure are taken from the printed census returns for Scotland and for Ireland 1861–1911.

[14] Sylvia Price, 'Rivetters' Earnings in Clyde Shipbuilding, 1889–1913', *Scot. Econ. and Soc. Hist.*, I (1981), pp. 42–65.

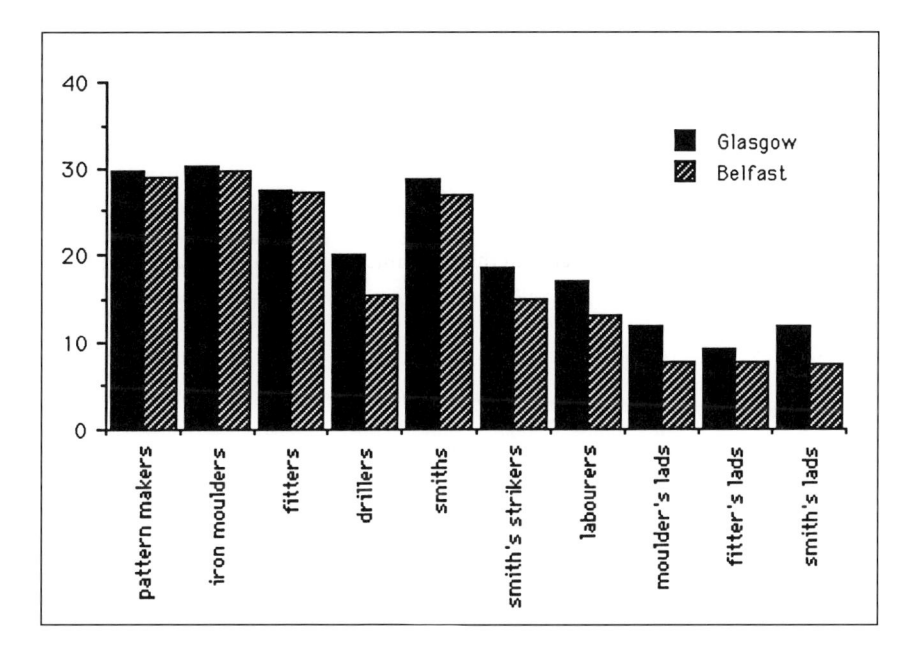

Figure 2: Wages in engineering and machine making (shillings per week), 1885.

Table 10: Average weekly rate of wages, 1885 (shillings per week)		
	Glasgow	Belfast
Pattern makers	29.8	29.1
Iron moulders	30.3	29.8
Fitters	27.5	27.1
Drillers	20.0	15.3
Smiths	28.7	26.8
Smith's strikers	18.5	14.9
Labourers	17.0	13.0
Moulder's lads	11.9	7.7
Fitter's lads	9.3	7.8
Smith's lads	11.8	7.4
Differentials:		
Moulders to labourers	56.0	43.6
Moulders to lads	39.3	26.0
Fitters to lads	33.9	28.3
Smiths to strikers	64.3	55.6
Smiths to lads	41.1	27.7

level of skilled wages was equal with perhaps a slight advantage to Belfast. The semi-skilled holders up also seem to have had an advantage in Belfast, but the labourers differential was vastly inferior.

In the engineering trades the pattern was the same. The level of skilled wages was more or less even. The slight advantage to Glasgow disappeared in the 1900 figures.[15] The figures for the unskilled and the lads confirmed that Belfast differentials were much greater. The census category 'engine and machine makers' shows that engineering, like shipbuilding, was a sector in which Catholics began the 1880s under represented and finished the century even more marginalized in this expanding industry.

Table 11: Proportion of engine and machine makers in the main religious denominations, Belfast 1881–1901

	Total	Catholics per cent	Episcopalian per cent	Presbyterian per cent
1881	284	19.7	31.3	39.1
1891	539	14.8	32.7	34.1
1901	631	10.0	32.1	39.1

The much wider differentials of Belfast may have influenced and provided additional motivation for the sectarian defence of certain areas of work, but these differentials were not a simple result of the sectarian segmentation of the labour market. The existence of this structure of differentials in the Belfast labour market independent of sectarian segmentation was clear in the building industry. The building trades were clearly separated in the printed census and wages were offered in a reasonably consistent fashion.

Table 12a: Wages in the building industry of Glasgow 1885–6, 1890–91

	Summer 1886	Winter 1885–6	Summer 1891	Winter 1890–1
Masons	29.7	24.5	29.7	25.11
Bricklayers	29.7	26.2	36.2	31.9
Carpenters	31.9	28.2	34.0	30.0
Slaters	29.7	26.2	31.9	28.2
Plasterers	29.7	26.2	31.9	28.2
Painters	32.8	22.7	35.0	24.4
Mason's labourers	19.2	15.7	21.2	18.7
Bricklayer's labourers	19.2	16.9	23.4	20.8
Mason's differential per cent	64.4	64.3	71.4	74.8
Bricklayer's differential per cent	64.4	64.5	64.8	64.8

[15] *Report on the Standard Time Rates of Wages in the United Kingdom in 1900*, P.P. 1900, LXXXII.

Table 12b: Wages in the building industry of Belfast 1885–6, 1890–91

	Summer 1886	Winter 1885–6	Summer 1891	Winter 1890–1
Masons	30.4	25.9	36.0	30.0
Bricklayers	33.7	28.7	36.0	31.0
Carpenters	31.5	31.5	33.7	33.7
Slaters	30.0	28.0	30.0	30.0
Plasterers	30.0	30.0	33.7	33.7
Painters	31.5	27.2	33.7	28.2
Mason's labourers	15.0	14.0	16.0	14.5
Bricklayer's labourers	15.0	14.0	16.0	14.5
Mason's differential per cent	49.3	54.0	44.4	48.3
Bricklayer's differential per cent	44.4	48.7	44.4	46.8

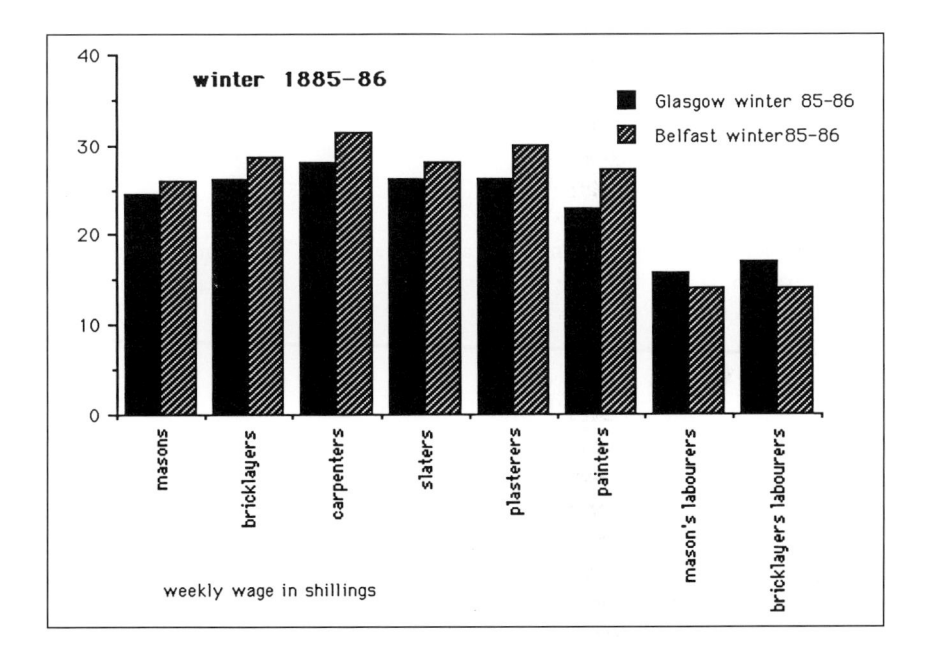

Figure 3: Wages in the building industry of Glasgow and Belfast, 1885–6

The religious composition of the building trades was not as one-sided as the metal trades. The table for 1901 (table 13) was typical of those constructed for the period 1871–1911.

The Presbyterians were over-represented amongst the 'builders'. These were the entrepreneurs who co-ordinated construction. They were also important amongst the carpenters and plumbers, but Catholics were over represented amongst the masons, slaters and tilers and plasterers. As Belfast was a brick built town the Catholic importance amongst the masons was probably due to the Catholic dominance of

Table 13: Religious structure of the building trades in Belfast, 1901

	Total	Catholic	Episcopalian	Presbyterian	Methodist	Others
Builder	391	63	94	174	22	38
Carpenter	3,947	614	895	1,967	244	227
Bricklayer	1,336	357	319	529	69	62
Mason	177	63	40	51	12	11
Slater, tiler	139	86	24	19	5	5
Plasterer	477	172	114	152	23	16
Plumber	830	96	241	376	65	52
Painter, glazier	1,589	340	482	528	135	104
			per cent			
Builder	100	16	24	44	5	9
Carpenter	100	15	22	49	6	5
Bricklayer	100	26	23	39	5	4
Mason	100	35	22	28	6	6
Slater, tiler	100	61	17	13	3	3
Plasterer	100	36	23	31	4	3
Plumber	100	11	29	45	7	6
Painter, glazier	100	21	30	33	8	6
Total male population	100	23	30	35	6	6

civil engineering. The importance of Catholics amongst slaters and tilers is less easy to explain. It may be some supply side relationship. In any case none of this affected differentials.

EXPLANATION

The major features were clear. Skilled wages were equal or slightly higher in Belfast. Unskilled wages were much lower. Belfast was a much more unequal society than Glasgow as a result of its labour market. Explanations are less easy to come by. There was no simple link of this structure to Protestant power in the labour market for the same inequality existed in trades with a Catholic 'bias'.

The easier feature to explain is the inequality of the unskilled wage. The concept of a reservation wage is hard to apply in late nineteenth-century society, where any support for the 'unemployed' was lacking or minimal. However, given that in migration from the countryside was the major source of supply of labour, it seems reasonable to use agricultural wages as a proxy for such a reservation wage. A detailed survey of agricultural wages for the United Kingdom was made in 1900. In Scotland, the dominant form of agricultural labour was the horseman. They were 60 per cent of those for whom wage returns were obtained. This job title implies both skill and status, so the wage returns for the orraman were also examined. Although only 11 per cent of the returns, their job description was much closer to that of the general labourer category favoured in the Irish figures. In both cases figures have been taken from the four largest counties close to the urban centre concerned. In both cases two sets of figures have been given. The first is cash wages and the second an estimate of the total value of returns to labour. Payment in kind was especially important in Scotland, and the returns make some heroic assumptions about the value of these payments. For example, a tied cottage provided for married farm servants was held to be worth £4 per year; as there was no market in such property it is hard to know what the figure means, except that it is just below the minimum value at which the occupier gained a vote.

Table 14: Weekly earnings (shillings and pence) of farm labour in four counties of Scotland contributing labour to Glasgow, 1898

	Horseman				Orraman			
	cash		total		cash		total	
	s.	d.	s.	d.	s.	d.	s.	d.
Ayrshire	15	6	19	2	no data			
Lanarkshire	17	9	21	5	16	1	20	2
Argyllshire	13	2	17	10	12	3	16	5
Stirlingshire	17	8	21	2	17	9	20	3

In both Ayrshire and Lanarkshire, the figures were influenced by the demand from the coal mines and in Lanarkshire also by the demand from the cotton mills.

In Ulster, there was the same system of hiring fairs, although the half year contract rather than the year contract as in Scotland was important. A true cash market in agriculture labour really only operated in the counties of Antrim, Down and Armagh. Payments in kind were less important and the sub division of labour obtaining in Scotland did not apply.

Table 15: Predominant weekly wage rates (in shillings and pence) for agricultural labour in four counties of Ireland contributing labour to Belfast, 1898

	cash		total	
	s.	d.	s.	d.
Antrim	12	0	12	4
Down	12	0	12	5
Armagh	10	0	10	11
Tyrone	9	0	9	10

Source: *Return of the Wages and Earnings of Agricultural Labourers in the United Kingdom*, P.P. 1900 LXXXII.

The explanation for the level of skilled wages is harder to find. Three suggest themselves. Supply may have been limited by the sectarian segmentation of the market, especially in the machine and shipbuilding industries. This cannot be a complete explanation as the same differentials obtained in areas of the building industry with a high Catholic representation. Secondly wages may have been set by the need to attract labour from Scotland; hence the marginal supply price of skilled labour was set by the cost of moving from Scotland to Belfast. Again this explanation can only be partial, but once labour market segmentation and the need to pull labour from Scotland had set wages in some industries, social factors such as the notion of a customary wage may have set levels in other trades like the tilers and slaters.

However, once the links with the Scottish market have been accepted as an account of the general equality of skilled wages, explanations must be sought for the failure of this market link to lead to the eventual equality of unskilled wages. The undoubted flow of unskilled labour from Ireland to Scotland should have led to convergence of the two rates of wages. On the supply side, the costs of the reproduction of labour seem to be equal in both cities. The Board of Trade enquiry into the cost of living in the United Kingdom in October 1905 showed that Belfast had cheaper beef but costlier coal and tea.

Table 16: Living costs in Belfast and Glasgow, October 1905

a) Food costs

	Glasgow	Belfast
Bread per 4lbs.	5s 5d.	5s. 5d.
Coal per cwt.	8½d. to 9½d.	1s.
Potatoes per 7lbs.	3d.	3d.
Tea per lb.	1s. 4d. to 2s.	2s.
Eggs	10–15 per 1s.	8–10 per 1s.
Beef ribs per lb.	9d. to 10d.	8d. to 9d.
Beef thick flank	8d.	6d.
Mutton leg	9d. to 10d.	9d. to 10d.

b) Housing costs

	Housing rent		Proportion of population occupying such houses	
	Glasgow	Belfast	Glasgow	Belfast
one-room	2s 4d. to 2s. 10d		16.2	0.4
two-room	3s. 11d. to 4s. 5d.		38.9	4.7
three-room	6s. to 7s. 4d.	2s. 6d. to 3s. 6d.	19.0	6.4
four-room		3s. to 4s. (kitchen) 4s. 6d. to 5s. (parlour)	6.8	29.1
five rooms		5s. to 6s. 3d.	19.1	59.4

Note: 12d. (old pence) = 1s. (one shilling).

Housing is harder to compare. Room for room Glasgow was more expensive, but rooms were bigger and the bulk of the population lived in one or two roomed houses. In Belfast most lived in four roomed houses of the kitchen or parlour type.[16] The Scots paid less and got much less, so that on low incomes quality of housing

[16] *Report of an Inquiry by the Board of Trade into Working Class Rents, Housing and Retail Prices in the United Kingdom*, 1908, CVII.

provided one motive for staying in the low wage environment of Belfast. In Belfast, another motive was provided by the availability of work for women in the cash economy. The earnings of wives, daughters and lodgers were more likely to enable a family to avoid poverty in Belfast than in Glasgow.

It remains to explain why these factors did not result in lower prices for skilled labour. On the supply side attention must turn to restrictions on entry to the trade. Craft union restrictions on apprenticeship and learnerships were familiar right across the British economy. Here sectarian divisions could be effective, although this would not explain why Catholic dominated trades had equal advantage. It has already been shown that the riots of 1885, when sectarian divisions were at their most effective and violent, provided a break in continuity in the sectarian structure of key occupations. Little seems to be known of the demand side for labour in Belfast. In terms of raw material and semi-processed inputs Belfast had a disadvantage because of transport costs. These showed clearly in domestic coal prices. Given this, Belfast employers may have sought a high quality and more stable craft labour force and hence were unwilling to bid down the wage price set when marginal labour was pulled across from Glasgow during expansion. In other words, Belfast employers paid an efficiency wage for skilled labour but a market clearing wage for unskilled labour.[17] An efficiency wage is set more by the relationships of factors within the production function of the firm or industry, whilst the market clearing wage is determined more by the relationships of demand and supply within the labour market. The result was to tie Belfast skilled labour more to Glasgow conditions and unskilled labour to conditions within the Ulster countryside, thus producing a dual economy within the Belfast labour market. This division did not coincide with the religious structuring of the Belfast labour market, but it did increase the stakes of any conflict over access to skilled positions.

This paper then presents evidence on the distinctive nature of the labour market in Belfast in comparison to Glasgow, as well as some evidence on the conditions affecting the distribution of petty capitalists in Belfast. It suggests that the nature of that market was structured by the growth of the economy as a whole, by supply conditions in Ireland, for production, for the reproduction of labour and for rural urban migration, by the proximity to the Glasgow market for skilled labour and by the impact of the sectarian structuring of the Belfast labour market.

---

[17] Janet L. Yellin, 'Efficiency Wage Models of Unemployment', *American Economic Review, Papers and Proceedings*, LXXIV (1984), pp. 200–5. My thanks to Richard Anthony for help with this section.

16

Irish Catholics in Belfast and Glasgow in the early twentieth century: connections and comparisons

A. C. Hepburn

THE HALF-CENTURY BEFORE 1914 witnessed a massive migration of non-dominant ethnic groups, mainly from agrarian backgrounds, to cities dominated by other cultures. The last years of that period, when population movement was less apparent than it had been in the immediate past, saw important changes within those relatively new ethnic communities—changes in occupational structure and, most important, in group social and political organisation. Changes of this type occurred, for instance, among the Prague Czechs, the Trieste Slovenes and the Black communities of north American cities such as Cleveland and Detroit.[1] Developments in literacy and education, and in journalism and sport, the emergence of new elite groups within minorities, the increasing democratisation of central and local politics, and the growth of mass trade unionism and the challenge of multi-ethnic class-based labour politics, all played their part in these changes.

Irish Catholics were amongst the earliest of European ethnic minorities to take to the road in the industrial era. The development of their communities across three continents has been the subject of massive study. It is not inconceivable that the Belfast nationalist Joe Devlin (1871–1934) may have visited all of these communities in the course of his work for the United Irish League and as Irish parliamentary nationalism's envoy to America and Australasia. From Kalgoorlie and Rotorua to Boston, Massachusetts and Butte, Montana, Irish communities were canvassed by Joe for funds to support Home Rule.[2] Devlin was able to put

---

[1] E. J. Hobsbawm, *Nations and Nationalism since 1780: Programme, Myth, Reality* (Cambridge, 1990), p. 109. For examples see G. B. Cohen, *The Politics of Ethnic Survival: Germans in Prague, 1861–1914* (Princeton, 1981); M. C. Cattaruzza and A. C. Hepburn, 'Minorities and Economic Development on the Ethnic Frontier: The Cases of Belfast and Trieste, 1850–1920', in E. Aerts and F. M. L. Thompson, eds., *Ethnic Minority Groups in Town and Countryside and their Effects on Economic Development, 1850–1940* (Leuven, 1990), pp. 68–84; D. Katzman, *Before the Ghetto: Black Detroit in the Nineteenth Century* (Illinois, 1975); K. L. Kusmer, *A Ghetto takes Shape: Cleveland 1870–1930* (Illinois, 1978).

[2] See Devlin's correspondence with John Dillon (Trinity College, Dublin, Dillon Papers MS 6729, 6730) and John Redmond (National Library of Ireland, Redmond Papers MS 15181).

remarkable oratorical and organisational abilities at the service of expatriate nationalism, skills developed in his native Belfast and exported initially to Glasgow. This paper was prompted initially by curiosity about the personal links between the Irish Catholic minorities of the two cities which Devlin helped to forge. The exploration of these links, however, has suggested a number of more general questions.

To what extent were the characteristic features of Catholic Belfast in the generation before the First World War—residential, cultural and recreational segregation; skewed occupational and industrial structure; tensions within the ethnic elite as to both aims and personnel; the predominance of nationalist politics; and an uneasy relationship with the 'labour movement'—found also in Glasgow? To what extent was ethnic rivalry in Belfast a 'peculiar institution', its character moulded by the local majority's perception of the minority as an actual or potential force for irredentism? Or was the Belfast Catholic experience in this period in fact little different from that of minority Irish Catholic communities in cities outside Ireland? Glasgow is particularly appropriate for comparison in view of its comparably large Catholic community, its proximity to the Belfast region, and the cultural, regional and personal links with Belfast of both its minority and its 'host' community. Exploration of these issues will also permit an examination of the interplay of personnel and political ideas between the Irish nationalist movements of Belfast and Glasgow.

How should we define the Irish Catholic community? The cumbersome name indicates a combination of ethnic origin and religious observance. At the level of mentality, membership of the community required a linking of these concepts, demonstrated at the behavioural level by personal contact through residence in a predominantly ethnic neighbourhood or participation in the activities of ethnic associations. Attendance at Mass was not enough: a small proportion of the upper middle class who lived, worked, relaxed, voted and perhaps married among Protestants (sometimes identified, in Dublin especially, by the abusive term 'Castle Catholic') were not members; neither were English Catholics of the recusant tradition nor Catholic Scottish Highlanders, necessarily members. Membership of the Catholic church nonetheless constitutes a useful objective measure, albeit an approximate one, of the community's size. In the case of Belfast this was 84,992 or 24 per cent of the total population in 1901. Glasgow's Catholic population in the 1890s is estimated at 92,000, or about 15 per cent of the city's 1901 population.[3] These migrant populations had come, predominantly, from rural areas in the north of Ireland. A few, no doubt, had come to Belfast via the small textile towns of eastern Ulster. Glasgow, however, had a much larger industrial hinterland, including the north Lanarkshire coalfield, where some of the centres were predominantly

---

[3] The Irish-born percentage of the Glasgow population declined from 13 per cent in 1881 to 7 per cent in 1911, and is not a useful measure of the community's size. J. Cunnison and J. B. S. Gilfillan, eds., *The Third Statistical Account of Glasgow* (Glasgow, 1958), pp. 67, 799; J. F. McCaffrey, 'Politics and the Catholic Community since 1878', in D. McRoberts, ed., *Modern Scottish Catholicism* (Glasgow, 1979), p. 154.

Irish and Catholic.⁴ It is likely therefore that a significant proportion of Glasgow's 'Irish' Catholics, like the labour leaders John Wheatley and Patrick Dollan, came into Glasgow from this background, rather than directly from Ireland.

The industrial structure of the two cities was similar. Both had been amongst the most rapidly-growing United Kingdom cities, with especially strong economic spurts towards the end of the nineteenth century. Glasgow's main strengths were in steel, engineering and shipbuilding, and while Belfast lacked steel its world textile predominance (in linen) had been confirmed during the years when Glasgow was losing its position (in cotton) to Lancashire. In both cities the proportion of working females was above the national average, although the proportion in Belfast was significantly higher. The patterns of ethnic differentiation in the Belfast labour market have been analysed elsewhere. The most pronounced difference was in engineering and shipbuilding, where one in four Protestant males were employed, but only one in fourteen Catholic males; about one half of Catholic males were semi- or unskilled workers, compared with little over one third of Protestants. Although broad occupational status differences in the non-manual sector appear on the face of it to have been slighter, the cross tabulation of householders' occupational status with residential property valuations shows, for instance, a mean valuation of £15.27 for Catholics in business and the professions, as against £24.47 for Protestants.⁵

About Glasgow we can quantify relatively little in this way. It is widely accepted, however, that the Clyde shipyards were predominantly Protestant, with one contemporary alleging that 'it was next to impossible for anyone of Irish descent to secure an apprenticeship'.⁶ In John Brown's Admiralty Yard, where work was steady, Protestants were said to have a near-exclusive position; whereas in the East Yard the work was less regular and Catholics were found in some numbers, especially among the rivetters.⁷ We know in general terms that the group described by witnesses as 'the Irish' were believed to predominate among the less skilled classes in the city at the time of the Royal Commission on the Poor Law in 1909.⁸ Similarly, we have testimony that the early National Union of Dock Labourers in

---

⁴ Forty-nine per cent of Coatbridge miners in 1851 were Irish-born. See A. B. Campbell, *The Lanarkshire Miners: A Social History of their Trade Unions, 1775–1874* (Edinburgh, 1979), p. 178.

⁵ A. C. Hepburn, 'Work, Class and Religion in Belfast, 1871–1911', in *Ir. Econ. and Soc. Hist.*, X (1983), pp. 33–50; A. C. Hepburn, 'Employment and Religion in Belfast, 1901–51', in R. J. Cormack and R. D. Osborne, eds., *Religion, Education and Employment: Aspects of Equal Opportunity in Northern Ireland* (Belfast, 1983), pp. 42–63.

⁶ Taped reminiscences of Harry McShane, cited in I. McLean, *The Legend of Red Clydeside* (Edinburgh, 1983), p. 181.

⁷ A. McKinlay, 'Employers and Skilled Workers in the Interwar Depression: Engineering and Shipbuilding on Clydeside, 1919–39' (Oxford Univ. DPhil thesis, 1986) p. 281; see also A. McKinlay, 'Making Ships, Making Men: Working for John Brown's between the Wars' (Clydebank Public Library pamphlet, 1992).

⁸ J. H. Treble, 'The Market for Unskilled Male Labour in Glasgow 1891–1914', in I. McDougal, ed., *Essays in Scottish Labour History* (Edinburgh, 1979), p. 122.

Glasgow in the 1890s drew its strength mainly from the unskilled categories of dock work, which were said to be predominantly Irish, just as in Belfast we know that the Catholics of the deep-sea docks enjoyed less regular and remunerative work than the Protestants who controlled the cross-channel docks.[9]

This similarity in minority circumstances in the two cities was also apparent in the non-manual sector of the labour market. Leaving aside shopkeepers, who are not distinguishable from shop assistants in the published census reports, an analysis of Belfast in 1901 gives us the following middle-class numbers in a Catholic workforce of 23,592 males:

Clergy and professionals	160
Big merchants, accountants, etc.	155
Publicans, wine merchants, etc.	898
Managers and clerks	1,038
Teachers, journalists, the arts	261

The preponderance of publicans (more than one in three of the above list; one in twenty-five of the entire male Catholic workforce) is striking. It would probably not be wide of the mark to say that they accounted for at least one-half of all Belfast Catholics with money to spare. Unlike Catholic lawyers, doctors and shopkeepers, whose potential in Belfast was limited mainly to meeting the needs of their own community, publicans were unique among Catholic occupational groups in operating within a relatively open market.

The *retail* liquor trade was an ethnic niche for Catholics in Belfast, providing a much-needed, if inadequate, avenue of upward economic mobility.[10] Protestants in contrast inhabited a world where the range of career choices was far wider and where the prevalent religious ethos had become permeated by the temperance movement: increasingly they shunned the retail sale of drink, if not its manufacture and consumption. In 1871 Belfast Catholics were one-and-a-half times more likely to be publicans than population proportions would suggest, whereas by 1911 this figure has risen to three-and-a-half times.[11] We do not know what the position was in Glasgow. But we shall see later that the leaderships of the small Catholic political elites in the two cities were very similar, suggesting that the predominance of the Catholic minority in the Belfast liquor trade may well have been reflected in the Scottish city.

Although limitations of the Glasgow data prevent precise comparisons, the available evidence suggests that similar patterns of limited opportunity and relative

---

[9] *Ibid.*, p. 121; D. P. Barritt and C. F. Carter, *The Northern Ireland Problem* (Oxford, 1962), p. 103.

[10] For the concept of the ethnic niche, see F. Barth, *Ethnic Groups and Boundaries: The Social Organisation of Cultural Difference* (Oslo, 1969), pp. 19–20.

[11] A. C. Hepburn, 'The Catholic Community of Belfast, 1850–1940', in M. Engman, F. W. Carter, A. C. Hepburn and C. G. Pooley, eds., *Ethnic Identity in Urban Europe* (Aldershot, 1992), p. 64.

deprivation afflicted the minority communities in both cities in the Edwardian era. The pathological aspects of the Belfast labour market, which have become an object of statutory and international concern in recent years, may not have been so unique or distinctive a phenomenon eighty years ago.

If the structure of the labour market is to some extent an indicator of ethnic relations in the two cities, the nature of residential patterns is another even more obvious guide to levels of ethnic consciousness. In Belfast almost 70 per cent of Catholics lived in seven distinctly and exclusively Catholic neighbourhoods, including 40 per cent in the Falls area and a further 14 per cent in the north of the city around New Lodge.[12] The Falls concentration was sufficiently strong to permit the nationalists, with probably less than 20 per cent of the city's electorate, to hold one of the city's four parliamentary seats for much of this period. In local elections, however, the pre-1896 ward boundaries cut across the major Catholic concentration, the political impact of which was that no nationalist, and only on three isolated occasions a Catholic of any political persuasion, was ever elected to the city council. The redistribution of local government boundaries after 1896 to reflect ethnic patterns guaranteed eight seats (out of sixty) for the Catholic community.

In Glasgow the position is less clear. We have no statistical data other than election results. Unlike Belfast (or indeed Liverpool, which returned an Irish nationalist MP with more regularity than Belfast after 1885, and where nationalists constituted an important group on the city council) Glasgow never returned an Irish nationalist as such to parliament or to the city council, and no Catholic was ever returned to the council until 1897 when the businessman Patrick O'Hare was elected in the not particularly Irish or Catholic neighbourhood of Springburn. Tom Gallagher argues that Glasgow was in fact a less thoroughly segregated city than Liverpool and that 'no districts were exclusively populated by Catholic immigrants'.[13] Ian McLean, though stressing the importance of the separate organisation of the Irish in the development of Labour politics in Glasgow after 1918, does not suggest that Irish/Catholic districts as intensely segregated as the Falls or as Liverpool's Scotland Road existed in Glasgow. Neighbourhood divides could be much more readily associated with class and with skill than with ethnicity. The main unskilled districts like Gorbals, Hutchesonstown, Anderston and Cowcaddens included many Catholic Irish, but there was no large neighbourhood which was regarded as specifically Catholic, or which could provide an electoral platform capable of sustaining nationalist politics.[14] McCaffrey's analysis of Glasgow's seven parliamentary constituencies suggests that every seat had a Catholic population

---

[12] *Ibid* pp. 62, 69.

[13] T. Gallagher, 'Communal Strife in Glasgow and Liverpool before 1914', in R. Swift and S. Gilley, eds., *The Irish in the Victorian City* (London, 1985), pp. 114, 117.

[14] I. McLean, *Red Clydeside*, pp. 176–7. In 1891 each of Glasgow's ten central districts included an Irish-born population of between 7 and 23 per cent. See D. W. Lamont, 'Population, Migration and Social Area Change in Central Glasgow, 1871–91', (unpublished Ph.D thesis, University of Glasgow, 1976), p. 136.

within the range 8–20 per cent and an estimated 'Irish vote' in the range 10–20 per cent.[15]

The political culture of a minority community is perhaps the best indicator of its sense of ethnic identity. In Belfast, as in all Ireland, British political parties failed to survive the second and third reform acts. Catholics progressed from Liberal voting fodder to independent nationalist politics, while Orange Unionism gave Conservatism an ethos distinct from British Conservatism, which none but a tiny minority of upper middle-class Catholics could find palatable. Glasgow retained the British party model, in a local context where Liberalism was the dominant orthodoxy. Gladstone's identification of the Liberal party with Home Rule in 1885 drew Irish Catholic communities in Britain into British politics, in a way which permitted communal unity to be maintained. In Glasgow, Irish Catholic support was won for the Liberals without losing the support of Protestant workers. In Belfast (and to an extent in Liverpool) this did not happen: Liberalism expired.

Only a carefully moderated emphasis on the national question could serve to maintain the communal unity of Irish Catholics. Temperance reform, control of schools, and the role of the clergy in politics generally were all potentially divisive. In Belfast the creation of eight local council seats for the Catholic Falls in 1897 resulted in a decade of bitter internal feuding. Until 1905 local political predominance was not in the hands of Joe Devlin and the local representatives of the nationalist movement, but under the direct control of the Bishop of Down and Connor, Henry Henry (1895–1908), and his Belfast Catholic Association. The C.A. was nominally nationalist, but maintained that such wider concerns should be excluded from local politics. In so far as it had an ideological position, the C.A. view was that the legitimate local concerns of the Catholic community were to do with the access of Catholics to the benefits of Belfast's economic success and to status and recognition in local society: drawing attention to national aspirations, or suggesting that only the attainment of power nationally could achieve advances locally, was to be eschewed.[16]

To an extent the origin of the C.A. lay in Henry's eccentric and autocratic personality, reinforced by the existence of a small renegade faction of clerical nationalists in Ireland, led by T. M. Healy MP, with the tacit support of Cardinal Logue. But the C.A. also had a social base: it returned to the council a predominantly upper-middle-class elite, Catholic in religious observance but integrated socially and residentially into the wider elite of the city. Seven of the eight C.A. councillors lived outside the Falls area which they represented, whereas the majority of the defeated Nationalist candidates lived within the community. The C.A. included representatives like the surgeon Dr Peter O'Connell (later High Sheriff of Belfast

---

[15] J. F. McCaffrey, 'Politics and the Catholic Community', p. 154.

[16] For the Catholic Association see the files of the *Irish News* and the *Northern Star*, especially October–November 1897.

1907, and knighted 1908) and the city centre estate agent William McCormick, both of whom lived in Malone Road mansions and were caricatured for years in the local Nationalist press as 'red robers', following their participation in civic receptions for members of the royal family.

Opposed to this leadership was a newer, *parvenu* elite: middle class, but mainly of humble origins; with a secondary education provided by the Christian Brothers rather than the more prestigious diocesan colleges; still likely to be living in the Falls area. Joe Devlin, son of a jarvey from Hamill Street was one; his schoolmate John T. Donovan, son of a storekeeper and later editor of the *Northern Star*, solicitor, barrister, and MP for West Wicklow (1914–18) was another. Publicans and grocers, schoolteachers and 'the betting men' were the core of the Nationalist party's support in Belfast during these years.[17] As early as 1895 Devlin could offer the wider nationalist movement a group of young schoolteachers who were willing to spend their vacation in 'any part of Ireland where fight and work is to be done'.[18] National schoolteachers were an assertive bunch in these years: Cardinal Logue feared 'an active agitation among the schoolmasters to get rid of their clerical managers . . . [as] one of the first fruits of the Compulsory Attendance Act'.[19] Within the publican class, whose financial importance to Catholic politics, journalism and sport was even greater than its numerical significance, there was also a divergence between the majority of publicans and the biggest traders, who sought to control the Ulster Licensed Victuallers' Association on behalf of the Catholic Association.[20] Efforts were made by the Nationalists to win mass working-class support, notably by bringing the veteran 'labour' nationalist Michael Davitt to speak in Belfast as often as he could be prevailed upon to do so, but, as the journalist Tim McCarthy commented privately, the audience attracted by Davitt bore little resemblance to 'the poor creatures who were marched into booths like sheep by the Bishop's domineering force of curates. In my experience of elections I never saw anything like it'.[21] Catholic politics in Belfast in these years was in effect a struggle between two petty elites for the leadership of the Catholic working class, an unskilled and economically depressed group with little experience of political or industrial organisation outside the structure of the church.

The Devlinites were ultimately successful in Belfast because the wider national organisation, of which Devlin quickly became an important part, was able to use its achievements to wear the C.A. down. Clerical leadership in the political life of the Catholic community came to an end. But Devlin and his friends also compromised.

---

[17] Devlin to John Dillon, 29 July 1897 (T.C.D. Dillon MSS, 6729/40).
[18] Devlin to Dillon, 10 July 1895 (T.C.D. Dillon MSS, 6729/23).
[19] Logue to Archbishop Tobias Kirby, 5 March 1894 (Irish College, Rome, Archives, Kirby MSS, 1894/39).
[20] *Northern Star*, 19 March 1898.
[21] T. McCarthy to W. O'Brien MP, 29 November 1897 (University College, Cork, O'Brien MSS, AH.94).

Their change in style is most clearly visible in the changing character of the *Northern Star*, a weekly paper founded by Devlin in 1897 to counter the *Irish News*, which had become the bishop's mouthpiece. Characterised by one (sympathetic) Nationalist MP as 'a national labour and publicans' paper', it began operating under the banner 'A Nationalist Democratic Weekly' which Devlin hoped would be 'read in the houses of our people and in the houses of the Protestant working men'.[22] Its name, of course, was designed to indicate links with the Presbyterian revolutionary tradition of 1798. Its early editorials declared strongly in favour of the rights of labour, and denounced capitalist efforts to smash the overwhelmingly Protestant engineering unions.

But notwithstanding Henry's view of him and his associates as dedicated anticlericals, Devlin had a clear understanding from the beginning of the central importance of the clergy in Ulster Catholic politics.[23] Time and again his youthful reports to John Dillon on prospects in the various districts were based entirely on the attitude to the Nationalist party taken by local priests. The *Star*'s banner was changed in 1899 from 'A Nationalist Democratic Weekly', to 'Ulster's Nationalist Weekly'. By 1904, in its chronicle of Devlin's developing career with the United Irish League of Great Britain, it could report earnestly to its Belfast readers that 'Mr Devlin is constantly presiding and speaking at purely Catholic functions, and of course the clergy gladly reciprocate by co-operating in the work of strengthening the National organisation as a powerful factor working for the twin causes of Faith and Fatherland'.[24] This formulation became the basis of Devlin's later career, a position that he evolved less through ideological conviction (though his views on these matters were not cynically held) than out of pragmatism: priests and publicans, properly managed, proved invaluable to the organisation of the nationalist cause. In contrast, appeals to Protestant working men and trade unionists appeared to achieve little. Devlin's early difficulties with the church thus centred on opposition not to Catholicism but to the view that effective politics in the Catholic community could be articulated through Catholicism rather than nationalism. In order to win lay control of politics from the traditional clerical leaders he had in fact to demonstrate both his own unimpeachable Catholicity and his ability to advance Catholic interests.

After 1900 Devlin's career outgrew the narrow lanes off Royal Avenue which were the locus of Catholic politics and journalism in Belfast, as he travelled on behalf of the party first to Glasgow, and subsequently as a paid official throughout Britain, and to north America and Australasia. Unlike the other major leaders of Irish Nationalism, Devlin's entire political apprenticeship had been served in organising and sustaining ethnic consciousness among minority communities. For

---

[22] R. McGhee to Dillon, 30 April 1897 (T.C.D. Dillon MSS, 6757/1017); Devlin to Dillon, 29 July 1897 (T.C.D. Dillon MSS, 6729/40).
[23] Henry Henry to Mgr M. Kelly, 14 November 1897 (Ir. Coll. Rome Archives, Kelly MSS, 1897/504).
[24] *Northern Star*, 2 January 1904.

some years it seemed that his only reward might be a late opportunity to attain some of the upward social mobility which so many of his regular associates had achieved: still earning his living at the age of thirty as the manager of a dingy back-street bar, he had achieved little material recognition for his manifest talents. Several times he asked John Dillon to use his influence to help set him up as a publican in London or Glasgow, and in 1901 Glasgow friends were apparently ready to put up the enormous sum of £7,000 to help him. His friend and patron Patrick Flanagan (owner of the still-famous Crown Liquor Saloon) described this offer to what must have been a slightly bemused John Dillon as 'the great chance of his life'.[25] Only a large testimonial organised privately for him within the nationalist movement, followed by a lengthy American political tour and a seat in parliament, diverted him from these humdrum aspirations.[26]

Devlin's development of the Ancient Order of Hibernians as a nationalist political organisation in Belfast and elsewhere arose from his work in emigrant nationalist politics and his early clashes with the Down and Connor clergy. In 1896 the A.O.H. in Belfast was very small, 'of a very low class' and 'no respectable nationalist appears to sympathise with the movement'.[27] Although Devlin later claimed to have become a member in 1893 he paid little attention to the movement until his links with Scotland and his visits to America made him aware of the association's potential. As an organisation providing welfare benefits and support it had a special urban appeal in a nationalist movement which was predominantly rural in focus. Its slogan 'For Faith and Fatherland' encapsulated the mixture of patriotism and religiosity which constituted the ethnic identity of the Irish community outside its southern Irish heartlands. Strictly speaking the A.O.H. was not a political movement at all, but simply the world's largest Irish ethnic association. Devlin steered it in the interests of constitutional nationalism for many years, with mixed success in America, but with less difficulty in Ireland and Scotland.

The links between Belfast and Glasgow, mainly implemented by Devlin and the veteran Glasgow Protestant nationalist from County Armagh John Ferguson (1836–1906), were a feature of nationalist politics during the Edwardian decade. The money and the talent of Irish/Catholic Glasgow was drawn on to reinforce the struggling Belfast nationalist movement, opposed as it was not only by Unionism and Orangeism but until Bishop Henry's death in 1908 by many of its own Catholic clergy. William McKillop (1860–1909), one of Glasgow's largest restaurateurs and wine merchants, became MP for North Sligo, and later for South Armagh; Dr Charles O'Neill (1849–1918) of Coatbridge succeeded him in the latter seat in 1909; in the same year Thomas Scanlan, a Glasgow barrister, succeeded to the North Sligo seat (though he had actually been born in that constituency); Patrick

[25] P. Flanagan to Dillon, 9 January 1901 (T.C.D. Dillon MSS, 6781/1011).
[26] J. Rooney to W. O'Brien, 26 March 1901 (Univ. Coll. Cork, O'Brien MSS, AL.51).
[27] Police report, cited in S. E. Baker, 'Orange and Green: Belfast 1832–1912', in H. J. Dyos and M. Wolff, eds., *The Victorian City: Image and Reality* (London, 1973), II, p. 808.

O'Hare sat more briefly for North Monaghan. Carpet-baggers though these Scotsmen were in Irish politics, it must be remembered that their chances of election to British constituencies, where the number of Catholics among the 567 MPs rose in the 1906 parliament to a total of four, would not have been good. The *Northern Star* was always a highly precarious financial enterprise, and would have collapsed within a year or two of its foundation had not the Catholic press baron Charles Diamond, himself an Ulster Catholic immigrant to Britain, taken over the printing of it in Glasgow, safe from the anathemas of the Bishop of Down and Connor.[28] In 1903 the publicans of Glasgow's Home Government Branch of the U.I.L. bought the *Glasgow Examiner* and ran it jointly with the *Star* as regional editions of effectively the same paper, thereby subsidising it. After Devlin had wrested from the bishop control of Catholic Belfast's daily, the *Irish News*, the *Star and Examiner* was bought by Diamond and subsumed into his *Glasgow Observer*.

Catholic and nationalist politics in Glasgow reflected some of the issues that divided Belfast. Although the bitter conflicts of the 1860s between the Highland-dominated Catholic Church and the small minority of Irish Catholic priests in Scotland had been resolved by the restoration of the Scottish Catholic hierarchy and some new appointments in 1878, there were still tensions within the leadership of the Catholic community in the city. There was no Henry Henry, but there was a very powerful Home Government Branch of the United Irish League in Glasgow, with 1,500 members, to a considerable extent under the leadership of the liquor interest. This group gave strong support to the Irish Parliamentary Party, and was the focus of Devlin's operations in Glasgow. Temperance advocates in the community attempted sporadically to counter this interest through support for rival U.I.L. branches, and through the activities of individual priests. *The Glasgow Observer*, the leading paper of the Catholic community (if only for its superior coverage of Celtic Football Club's activities through its 'Man in the Know' column), articulated the views of this second group. The paper's editor, Mitchel Quin, and its owner, Charles Diamond, were both temperance advocates. One of the objectives of the H.G.B. in setting up the *Star and Examiner* was to have an alternative voice to the *Observer*.[29] But the most vivid example of this particular struggle was the battle for control of Celtic Football Club, founded in 1887 by priests as a charitable/fund-raising organisation, but converted a decade later, after considerable in-fighting, into a limited liability company with shareholders and a board of directors consisting of six publicans and a building contractor (all Catholics). Both William McKillop and Tom White (who succeeded Devlin as chairman of the Star) became members of the Celtic board, and Diamond's *Observer* lost the club's advertising business through its opposition to limited liability.[30] The Celtic team became regular Easter

---

[28] Diamond had no role in the ownership or editorship of the *Northern Star*, which was 'printed for the proprietors by a limited liability company, of which I am the chairman, just as we print a great many publications of all kinds'. Correction published in *Northern Star*, 9 September 1905.

[29] J. E. Handley, *The Irish in Modern Scotland* (Cork, 1947), p. 288.

[30] B. Murray, *The Old Firm: Sectarianism, Sport and Society in Modern Scotland* (Edinburgh, 1984), pp. 24–5, 72.

guests-of-honour at Belfast's National Club (established by Devlin in 1899 in opposition to the bishop's Central Catholic Club).

The decade prior to the First World War also marked the beginnings of the serious emergence of labour and socialist politics in Britain. Frank Wright has offered an interesting general assessment of the potential of internationalist socialism for diverting ethnic confrontations in a number of European states during these years.[31] But the injection of socialist or labour politics into the Irish Catholic communities of Belfast and Glasgow was not a simple matter in this period, consisting as they did of clerical and petty bourgeois leaderships and largely unskilled and non-unionised working classes. It would be a mistake, nonetheless, to regard the urban politics of nationalism as anti-labour in the way that writers in the James Connolly tradition have tended to suggest.

Irish nationalism had a strong radical tinge based, not always wittingly, on the ideas of the American economist Henry George (1839–97), who took a close interest in the Irish and the Scottish land questions. George believed that the problems of both capital and labour were rooted in the problem of rising land values. The landlord or rentier was cast as villain of the piece. The solution was a tax on land values, and politicians who advocated George's ideas were known as 'single-taxers'. These ideas held wide currency in both British and Irish radical political circles at the turn of the century, Michael Davitt and Glasgow's John Ferguson being among the leading advocates.[32] Popularised versions of such views had a particular attraction for urban ethnic communities consisting mainly of rural migrants, linking as they did animosity towards landlords, which was well understood in such circles, with an explanation of urban poverty. A U.I.L. organiser told a Belfast audience in 1899 that 'the policy of driving people from the country filled the towns with unskilled labour and kept wages down'.[33] Many Georgeites later moved on to a socialist form of labour politics but the Nationalist MP Richard McGhee (1851–1930), like Ferguson a County Armagh Protestant who spent much of his adult life in Glasgow, was a labour activist who remained a committed Georgeite. He was co-founder of the National Union of Dock Labourers in 1889, the union which was later responsible for sending Jim Larkin on his first trip to Belfast.[34] Devlin regarded Pope Leo XIII as 'the greatest friend of the workers', but argued that his ideas could only achieved by combination: 'every worker should join a trade union. He is powerless as an individual . . .'[35]

---

[31] F. Wright, *Northern Ireland: A Comparative Analysis* (Dublin, 1987), pp. 75–86.

[32] See for example, Ferguson's speech to the Belfast U.I.L., *Northern Star*, 19 August 1899. The Henry George Foundation of Great Britain was established as late as 1929. See H. George, *Progress and Poverty* (51st anniversary edition, London, 1930).

[33] *Northern Star*, 29 July 1899. The speaker, Michael McKeown, later became a Labour organiser.

[34] For McGhee's career see J. Bellamy and J. Saville, eds., *Dictionary of Labour Biography*, vol. 7 (London, 1984). His son, Henry George McGhee, became Labour MP for Yorkshire Penistone, 1935–59.

[35] Devlin, lecture to Belfast branch, Irish National Foresters, *Northern Star*, 1 February, 1908. See also *Northern Star*, 2 May 1908, for Devlin's views on the Belfast housing problem.

Few Irish nationalists were also socialists in this era, but it would be a mistake to regard the movement as anti-labour or anti-union in principle. The A.O.H. was itself 'essentially a workingman's organisation', primarily concerned with welfare issues.[36] The Catholic church was anti-socialist in many ways before 1914, though this was mainly a matter of concern over the future of Catholic schools. Essentially for Irish nationalists like Devlin the problem with labour in Ireland was simply that it was either ideologically opposed to the nationalist cause like the pro-British socialism of William Walker and the skilled Protestant working class of Belfast, or it was an electoral rival for 'nationalist' votes, like the Irish Labour party after 1912. Comparison with the Irish nationalist experience in Glasgow points this up. Leading nationalists in the city like Ferguson, Hugh Murphy, and McGhee were trades unionists and trades councillors and Lib-Labs on the city council from the late 1880s onwards, and found no difficulty in combining these positions with membership of Irish nationalist bodies.

One who found it less easy was the future Labour cabinet minister John Wheatley (1869–1930), once chairman of Shettleston U.I.L., who transferred his energies after 1906 to British concerns and to socialist politics. Wheatley was born in County Waterford, but grew up in the North Lanarkshire coalfield. The son of a miner whose early years were lived in 'bleak poverty', he ran a printing business for most of his adult life.[37] Through his development of a Catholic Socialist Society in Glasgow in the years after 1906, when so many Catholic clergy read 'socialism' as 'secularism', he provided for the Irish Catholic community of Glasgow an ideological route for integration into the mainstream of British political life. But only once the Irish question was removed from the centre of the British political stage between 1918 and 1922, as Ian McLean and Graham Walker have demonstrated, was the way cleared for the mass translation of the Glasgow Irish community into support for the Labour Party.[38] A Labour party which had been Protestant, skilled, secular, and temperance was able to secure its political future in Glasgow by taking on board the Glasgow Irish community, with its local political elite, its publicans and its Ancient Order of Hibernians intact. Ethnic conflict was bitter amidst the unemployment and bad housing of inter-war Glasgow. But it was contained within British party political culture, aided only by the controlled ethnic violence of Rangers v. Celtic, the 'old firm'.

In Belfast by contrast, after the traumas of 1920–2 Labour was forced steadily back into its ethnic components, a process which was concealed somewhat, but not reversed, by the Northern Ireland Labour Party. One outcome was the break-up of the communal solidarity that Devlin had engineered: unlike in Glasgow, the remnants of the U.I.L./A.O.H. machine in Belfast became characterised in due course as 'green Tory', challenged and in 1946 finally removed from Belfast politics by

---

[36] *Northern Star*, 9 May 1908.

[37] For Wheatley's career see W. Knox, ed., *Scottish Labour Leaders, 1918–39* (Edinburgh, 1984), pp. 274–84.

[38] McLean, *Red Clydeside*, ch. 14; G. Walker, 'Labour in Scotland and Northern Ireland: The Inter-war Experience', in Mitchison and Roebuck, pp. 267–76.

Republican Labour. Devlin would have hated the 'green Tory' sobriquet, but at the by-election following his death in 1934, his heir-apparent was characterised in precisely this way. Had he succeeded in making the transfer into British politics which he attempted at Liverpool Exchange in the general election of 1922, he would conversely have become, as William O'Brien predicted that he would, 'a mere English Labourite with a Belfast accent'.[39] Relations between urban Irish nationalism and labour in the early twentieth century were determined more by circumstance than by ideology.

[39] W. O'Brien MP to T. M. Healy, MP, 18 September 1918 (N.L.I. O'Brien MSS, 8556/20).

17

Working-class housing in Scottish and Irish cities on the eve of World War I

M. E. Daly

ONE OF THE MAIN PROBLEMS associated with urban history is the apparent uniqueness of every city. Only by comparative analysis is it possible to distinguish between local factors and broader phenomena. A comparative study of housing conditions in Belfast, Dublin, Edinburgh and Glasgow on the eve of World War One offers the possibility of differentiating between the general and the particular. All four cities operated within a common economic environment and shared a broadly similar political, legislative and administrative context.[1] Both Scottish and Irish housing were subject to lengthy inquiries in the second decade of the twentieth century: the *Royal Commission* on Scottish Housing appointed in 1912,[2] and the departmental inquiry into Dublin housing,[3] which also contained information on Belfast and other Irish towns. Both inquiries took place at a time when the question of working class housing was receiving increasing political attention at Westminster,[4] yet no official inquiry was launched into English housing.[5] This prompts a query whether Scottish and Irish housing conditions differed significantly from those in England.

All Scottish towns and cities, and Dublin, though not Belfast or other Irish towns, were dominated by tenement housing, though in Dublin, unlike Scotland, tenements were exclusively working class dwellings.[6] Dublin, Edinburgh and

---

[1] There were administrative and legal differences between Scotland and Ireland and England, some of importance for housing and social policy. For Scotland see R. G. Rodger, 'The Law and Urban Change: Some Nineteenth-Century Scottish Evidence', *Urban History Yearbook* (1979), pp. 79–91.

[2] R.C. *Housing of the Industrial Population of Scotland*, 1917, 1917–18, Cmd. 8731, XIV, para. 11; Laurence F. Orbach, *Homes for Heroes: A Study of the Evolution of British Public Housing, 1915–1921* (London, 1977), pp. 20, 56.

[3] *Report of the Departmental Committee Appointed to Inquire into the Housing Conditions of the Working Class in Dublin*, 1914, Cmd. 7317, XIX; evidence, 1914, Cmd. 7273, XIX.

[4] Orbach, *Homes for Heroes*, pp. 39–42.

[5] The Land Enquiry Committee established by Lloyd George in 1912. It published in 1913.

[6] J. G. Robb, 'Suburb and Slum in Gorbals: Social and Residential Change 1800–1900', in G. Gordon and Brian Dicks eds., *Scottish Urban History* (Aberdeen, 1983), p. 131.

Glasgow, tenement cities, suffered high rents and overcrowding. In Glasgow, 16 per cent of the population lived in one-room units, 61.7 per cent in two-room; for Edinburgh the corresponding figures were 5.7 per cent and 32.3 per cent; for Dublin, 26.4 per cent and 24.7 per cent. Belfast had minimal overcrowding; 0.33 per cent of its population lived in one-roomed units, 2.6 per cent in two rooms. While most tenement rooms were more spacious than those in cottages, tenements posed severe problems of sanitation, cleansing and water supply, reinforcing the image of a housing crisis.

The factors responsible for inferior housing in three of our four cities are complex. On the demand side, population growth appears of little relevance. Belfast grew (with boundary alterations) from 37,000 in 1821 to 386,000 by 1911, Edinburgh from 82,000 in 1801 to 320,000 by 1911, Glasgow from 77,000 (with suburbs) in 1801 to 784,000 by 1911. Dublin with an estimated population of 182,000 in 1800 had a population of 304,000 by 1911, or 404,000 if we include the most generous suburban estimate. Belfast, the most rapidly growing city in the British Isles in the period 1841–1901,[7] suffered minimal overcrowding, though the concentration of growth at a time when housing regulations had been strengthened may have spared it some of the worst horrors of working class housing.

Occupational patterns were of greater significance.[8]

Table 1: Occupational structures 1911 (%)

	Belfast		Dublin		Glasgow		Edinburgh	
	M	F	M	F	M	F	M	F
Professional/public service	6.6	4.9	9.2	10.0	5.8	7.0	13.9	8.9
Domestic service	2.1	14.7	3.7	38.7	1.8	21.0	3.9	39.5
Manufacturing	36.2	70.0	20.4	31.7	43.7	47.4	30.6	28.6
Dealing	12.6	5.9	12.9	13.9	12.9	14.4	14.5	13.4
Service industries	5.7	3.9	6.3	4.4	6.2	7.9	6.4	8.2
Transport	10.3	0.2	15.5	0.4	17.0	2.5	15.0	1.1
Building	7.7	–	9.8	–	7.7	–	10.4	–
General labour	17.0	–	19.5	–	2.9	–	2.5	–

The predominance of professional and public service employment in Edinburgh and Dublin accounts for the importance of domestic service in both cities. The

---

[7] A. C. Hepburn, 'Belfast 1871–91: Work Class and Religion', *Irish Economic and Social History*, X (1983), p. 33.

[8] Occupations in Table 1 are grouped according to the categories used by W. A. Armstrong, 'The Use of Information about Occupation, I: As a Basis for Social Stratification', E. A. Wrigley, ed., *Nineteenth-Century Society* (Cambridge, 1972), pp. 296–310. There are certain problems in comparing Scottish and Irish statistics: the census categories are not identical; the Scottish census is more careful at distinguishing between dealers and manufacturers; the Irish figures may slightly overstate the percentage of workers in manufacturing with a consequent understatement for dealing. The totals do not add up to 100 as minor sources of employment such as agriculture and mining have been excluded.

industrial cities of Belfast and Glasgow shared a common pattern of substantial employment in shipbuilding and engineering: almost 48 per cent of Belfast and 57 per cent of Glasgow male manufacturing workers were engaged in metal, engineering and shipbuilding. While Glasgow's textile industry declined in the second half of the nineteenth century,[9] the Belfast linen industry employed 5.6 per cent of occupied males and 36.6 per cent of occupied females.[10] Dublin and Edinburgh shared a common strength in brewing and printing but printing employed significantly more workers in Edinburgh and that city boasted substantial employment in rubber, chemicals and metals. While Glasgow and Edinburgh employed more women in industry than Dublin—Glasgow in cotton textiles and thread, Edinburgh in printing, rubber and dressmaking—Belfast alone offered substantial factory employment for both sexes.

Table 2: Participation rates 1911 (%)

	Belfast	Dublin	Edinburgh	Glasgow
Male – all	61.6	63.8	65.3	66.4
Male <20	21.6	20.2	23.0	23.9
Male >20	94.0	92.9	93.2	96.9
Female – all	31.1	26.0	31.2	27.7
Female <20	21.5	13.8	22.4	20.7
Female >20	37.5	33.4	35.6	32.3
% male pop <20	44.8	40.0	39.8	41.8
%female pop <20	39.9	37.8	51.3	40.2

Dublin records the lowest participation for those under twenty and for adult males, reflecting a shortage of employment opportunities. The participation of adult Dublin women exceeds Glasgow's, suggesting that they were forced into the labour force, as charwomen or dealers, to compensate for poor earning possibilities for men and children.

Employment of young men in Belfast was below Scottish levels—perhaps because of a shortage of unskilled jobs—and, while the participation of adult males appears high, there was a low percentage of adult males in the population, suggesting some employment problems. In contrast Belfast had the highest participation rate for adult women. The differences in female employment between Glasgow and Edinburgh were due to better opportunities in Edinburgh for single women working as domestic servants: Glasgow had a marginally higher employment rate among married women than Edinburgh, 5.5 per cent as against 5.1 per cent. At 105 females per 100 men, Glasgow had the lowest proportion of excess women. Dublin was next with 106, followed by Belfast (113) and Edinburgh (123).

---

[9] A. Gibb, *Glasgow* (London, 1983), pp. 114–15.
[10] Hepburn, 'Work, Class and Religion', pp. 39, 42.

The published census returns do not permit precise comparison of skilled and unskilled employment proportions. However Collins and Hepburn show the Belfast workforce, and specifically the Protestant workforce, as having a privileged socio-economic structure.[11] Glasgow offered significant male skilled employment in shipbuilding and metalworking. While Edinburgh's artisan elite was less homogeneous,[12] the high representation of professional and public service employees must be taken into account.

Unskilled, casual work was not unknown in Scottish cities: both Glasgow and Edinburgh had substantial male employment in transport. However 19.5 per cent of occupied males in Dublin and 17 per cent in Belfast were returned as unskilled labourers, compared with less than 3 per cent in Edinburgh and Glasgow, suggesting either an Irish problem in defining occupation or, more probably, a surplus of unskilled, casual labour. Transport and general labouring employed 35 per cent of male workers in Dublin and 27.3 per cent in Belfast, compared with 17.5 per cent in Edinburgh and 20 per cent in Glasgow. The existence of a casual labour surplus is repeatedly documented for Dublin; Gray confirms a similar pattern among Belfast dockers.[13] Collins and Hepburn show a high level of absentee husbands in Belfast and suggest that this was due to lack of employment for unskilled males, especially Catholics.[14] However Belfast labouring families could boost family income via wage-earning wives, raising the question whether Belfast's higher participation of adult women was driven by supply-side factors, or by the demand for female workers. In his study of Victorian Edinburgh, Robert Gray noted that 'casual labour is the key factor distinguishing the prosperous from the poverty-stricken occupations'.[15] Given the higher proportion of casual labourers, Irish cities faced greater poverty.

While census data do not reveal an apparent surplus of unskilled labour in either Glasgow or Edinburgh, Board of Trade figures collected in 1905[16] suggest that Scotland, like Ireland, recorded a higher skilled/unskilled wages differential than England. London unskilled wages were approximately two-thirds of skilled rates. In Ireland the figure was closer to 50 per cent; Scotland came in-between. The London ratio was the norm throughout England and Wales: in Northern England, building craftsmen and building labourers earned 88 per cent of London skilled and labouring rates respectively; skilled engineering workers and labourers 89 and 86 per cent. For Scotland and Ireland wider differentials prevailed with skilled rates much closer to London rates (Table 3).

Skilled wages in Irish and Scottish cities were similar to, and frequently in excess of, those paid in England and Wales outside London; Belfast engineering wages were

---

[11] A. C. Hepburn and B. Collins, 'Industrial Society: The Structure of Belfast, 1901', in P. Roebuck, ed., *Plantation to Partition* (Belfast, 1981), pp. 225–6.
[12] R. Q. Gray, *The Labour Aristocracy in Victorian Edinburgh* (Oxford, 1976), especially ch. 4.
[13] John Gray, *City in Revolt: James Larkin and the Belfast Dock Strike of 1907* (Belfast, 1985), pp. 4–8.
[14] Collins and Hepburn, 'Belfast 1901', pp. 217–18.
[15] Gray, *Labour Aristocracy*, p. 88.
[16] *Board of Trade: Cost of Living of the Working Classes*, 1908, Cmd. 3864, CVII, p. xxxix.

the highest outside London. However Scottish labouring rates fell below English and Welsh rates, and the divergence between skilled and unskilled was greater in Ireland, with the widest gap in Belfast. Figures for 1912 show similar trends (Table 4).

Table 3: Wages of skilled and unskilled labour, 1905

	Building		Engineering		Furnishings	Printing
	Skilled	Labourers	Skilled	Labourers		
London	100	100	100	100	100	100
Edinburgh and Leith	88	80	86	81	84	83
Glasgow	91	83	86	81	84	83
Belfast	88	60	94	69	87	87
Dublin	84	68	88	67	82	90

Table 4: Relative wages for 1912 (London = 100)

	Building		Engineering		Printing
	Skilled	Labourers	Skilled	Labourers	Compositors
Edinburgh and Leith	88	79	93	81	87
Glasgow	92	81	96	79	92
Belfast	81	56	98	73	90
Dublin	79	66	–	–	90

Source: *Board of Trade: Cost of Living of the Working Classes*, 1913, Cmd. 6955, LXVI, p. 37

This disparity in relative wages is not implausible. While pockets of labour surplus existed throughout the British Isles, the surplus was greater in Ireland and Scotland, as the threatened inflow of unskilled workers from rural areas depressed unskilled wages. In contrast high skilled wages were maintained by less elastic supply, restrictions on admission, and the existence of UK-wide trade unions which disseminated information on wage rates and facilitated equalising labour flows. Differentials may have been increased by educational problems among the unskilled or by restrictions on access to apprenticeships, reinforced in the case of Belfast by discrimination on religious grounds.[17] Ireland seems to have suffered from a shortage of skilled labour: a significant proportion of the skilled workforce in both Dublin and Belfast consisted of English migrants.[18]

The wider gap between skilled and unskilled wages had a major impact on living standards. In both Scotland and Ireland prices of essential commodities were equal to or in excess of London levels (Edinburgh 102, Glasgow 99, Belfast 101, Dublin 100); prices in provincial England ranged from 2 to 8 per cent less.[19] Scottish and

---

[17] On Dublin apprenticeships, Mary E. Daly, *Dublin: The Deposed Capital: A Social and Economic History 1860–1914* (Cork, 1984), ch. 5 and especially p. 137. On Belfast, Collins and Hepburn, 'Belfast 1901', and Hepburn, 'Work, Class and Religion'.

[18] Information on the background of the Belfast shipyard skilled workforce supplied by Frank Geary, and for Dublin skilled workforce by Martin Maguire.

[19] *Board of Trade 1908*, p. XXXVIII.

Dublin rents, though lower than London (Edinburgh 81, Glasgow 76, Dublin 71) were significantly above those in provincial England, which varied from 50 to 62 per cent of London rates. Belfast rents averaged 46 per cent of London levels, the lowest for any major city in the British Isles. The combined rent/price index left the cost of living in Edinburgh at 98 per cent of the London level, Glasgow and Dublin at 94 per cent. Even Belfast at 90 per cent was exceeded only by the south of England.

A comparison of the rent/price and wage indices suggests that all workers in the four cities, with the exception of Belfast engineering craftsmen, had lower real wages than their English counterparts. It is not altogether surprising that Campbell shows that around the turn of the century many Scottish wage rates had become the highest in the UK.[20] However the convergence was at the level of skilled rather than unskilled rates. Belfast engineering workers had extremely high wages, as had Dublin craftsmen in industries less exposed to competition such as printing.[21] While high wages eroded competitiveness, higher living costs must have contributed to this trend.

The Scottish and Irish working classes, particularly unskilled workers, experienced significantly lower living standards than their English counterparts, irrespective of greater vulnerability to unemployment or casual working. This impacted on expenditure patterns and on standards of nutrition and housing. The high level of overcrowding can be explained by relative wages, rents and living costs. High prices and lower wages forced families, particularly unskilled, to devote a higher proportion of income to food, leaving less money for rent. Butt has suggested an unwillingness on the part of the Scottish working class to spend as much in rent as its English counterpart;[22] this may be explained by income and substitution effects, with lower real incomes reducing expenditure on rent[23] and the high cost of housing encouraging workers to substitute other forms of expenditure. Sutcliffe has suggested that, 'offered such unfavourable terms, the poor town-dweller might quite reasonably have given up any efforts to secure a more pleasant urban environment, choosing instead to devote his meagre resources to the purchase of goods or services available on more favourable terms', such as food, clothing, entertainment, or alcohol 'to limit his perception of the unfavourable environment'.[24] Dublin and

---

[20] R. H. Campbell, *The Rise and Fall of Scottish Industry 1707–1939* (Edinburgh, 1980), pp. 84–9.

[21] In addition to newspapers, Dublin printing concentrated on producing works of Irish nationalist or historic interest and Catholic devotional literature, areas where it was less likely to suffer direct competition from British publishers. See Daly, *Dublin*, pp. 45–7.

[22] John Butt, 'Working Class Housing in Glasgow, 1851–1914', in Stanley D. Chapman, ed., *The History of Working Class Housing: A Symposium* (Newton Abbot, 1971), p. 82. This was also stated in evidence to the Hunter inquiry into Scottish rentals; Orbach, *Homes for Heroes*, p. 14.

[23] A point made by Richard G. Rodger, 'The Invisible Hand: Market Forces, Housing and the Urban Form in Victorian Cities', in Derek Fraser and A. Sutcliffe, eds., *The Pursuit of Urban History* (Leicester, 1983), p. 197.[23]

[24] Anthony Sutcliffe, 'The Growth of Public Intervention in the British Urban Environment during the Nineteenth Century: A Structural Approach', in James H. Johnson and Colin G. Pooley, eds., *The Structure of Nineteenth-Century Cities* (London, 1982), p. 119.

Scottish labouring families devoted a lower proportion of income to rent than their English counterparts. Dublin labouring families in 1904 spent over 63 per cent of income on food, compared with 51 per cent in York and a maximum of 45 per cent in London. Rents accounted for 14.5 per cent of income in Dublin, 18 per cent in York, and 21 to 35 per cent (commonly in excess of 30 per cent) for London labouring families. Glasgow labourers and carters paid 11–12 per cent of income in rent, though Edinburgh Trades Council allocated 19.7 per cent of its minimum household budget to rent in 1914.[25] Belfast workers got significantly better value for money; a three-, four- or five-roomed house for the cost of one or two rooms in Dublin, Glasgow or Edinburgh.[26]

High rents were the primary cause of overcrowding. Glasgow census figures for 1911 show acute overcrowding combined with a vacancy rate of almost 11 per cent.[27] However we must explain the high rents. The three high-rent cities were tenement cities, which marks them out from the English norm where, as in Belfast and other Irish towns, cottages predominated. In Scotland tenements were found in small towns, and even in underpopulated crofting counties.[28] It hardly seems coincidental that the north-east of England, another high-rent area, also contained tenements. In *Multi-Storey Living*, Sutcliffe suggested that pressure resulting from socio-economic differentiation within a town's population, which may force some groups to compete for restricted space, or external restrictions on a growing town's outward extension, whether natural or manmade, accounted for this phenomenon.[29]

Unlike the other three cities, Belfast, the city without tenements, was a relatively new city with a plentiful supply of undeveloped land. Roebuck has suggested that the bankruptcy of the Donegall estate, by freeing an almost unlimited supply of land in the first half of the nineteenth century, was a key factor in Belfast's success.[30] The 1914 Dublin Housing Inquiry referred to Belfast's cheap land and locally available bricks.[31] We need, however, to know more about the Belfast house-building industry It seems possible that the more limited market for middle class housing forced builders to concentrate on the working class market. In many cities, middle class villa building was better able to take advantage of cheaper land during down-turns in the building cycle, effectively preventing working-class

---

[25] For a comparison between Dublin and York, *Deposed Capital*, p. 111; Glasgow, Butt, 'Working-Class Housing', p. 82; London, Maud, Pember Reeves, *Round About a Pound a Week* (London, 1980 edn), pp. 80–7; Edinburgh, John Holford, *Reshaping Labour: Organisation, Work and Politics—Edinburgh in the Great War and After* (London, 1988), p. 46.

[26] *Board of Trade 1908*, pp. 506–34.

[27] M. J. Daunton, *A Property-Owning Democracy? Housing in Britain* (London, 1987), p. 25.

[28] Roger Smith, 'Multi-Dwelling Buildings in Scotland, 1750–1970', in A. Sutcliffe, ed., *Multi-Storey Living: The British Working-Class Experience* (London, 1974), p. 210.

[29] Introduction in *Multi-Storey Living*, p. 4.

[30] Peter Roebuck, 'The Donegall Family and the Development of Belfast, 1600–1850', in P. Butel and L. M. Cullen, eds., *Cities and Merchants* (Dublin, 1986), pp. 125–38.

[31] *Dublin Housing: Evidence*, appendix.

housing from spreading into certain areas.[32] The high proportion of well-paid craftsmen and the strength of supplemental female earnings may have bolstered working class housing demand. The role of industrialists in providing housing for textile workers may also be of relevance.

Scottish housing costs were adversely affected by both demand and supply factors. Weak working class demand meant an absence of speculative building, except for short periods when higher real incomes and housing shortages persuaded builders to enter this market, while the small size of firms precluded economies of scale.[33] More rigorous building regulations meant higher costs despite lower wages.[34]

Building land was more expensive as a consequence of the Scottish practice of feuing, under which land was leased in perpetuity subject to an annual rent, and, until 1914, to regular special imposts or casualties which could double or triple the annual charge. It has been argued that Scottish landlords, lacking the property reversion open to their English and Irish equivalents, were forced to maximise ground-rent income and to anticipate future development and inflation by charging higher land prices, and that owners were reluctant to dispose of land until maximum feuing rates could be obtained. High-priced land appears to have been found both in the centre and on the outskirts of Scottish cities.[35] The *Royal Commission* suggested that feuing reduced the supply and increased the cost of land, leaving some working-class tenements in Edinburgh carrying annual feuing rates of £150 to £250 per acre, in one quoted case a capital charge of £13,120 per acre.[36] High land prices acted as an incentive to build tenements rather than cottages, spreading the land cost as widely as possible. The problem was intensified by the rating system, which encouraged the withholding of land from development by charging low agricultural rates, where development land was highly taxed. Sub-infeudation brought increased impositions as successive owners and developers imposed their feuing charge. In consequence land prices were high: £40 per acre for land used for working-class housing in Edinburgh and Glasgow, compared with £3,850 in London and £2,730 in provincial England.[37] Glasgow Corporation aggravated the problem by reducing the supply of land. The City Improvement Trust acquired 90 acres in the city centre for urban improvements in 1866, but kept it under-developed for decades, because the 1878 commercial crisis and the collapse of the City of Glasgow bank made it impossible to dispose of the land to private enterprise 'at prices that would largely recoup the ratepayer', and trustees were unwilling to develop the land lest they be forced to increase rate

---

[32] R. G. Rodger, 'Rents and Ground Rents: Housing and the Land Market in Nineteenth-Century Britain', in Johnson and Pooley, *Structure of Nineteenth-Century Cities*, p. 67.
[33] R. G. Rodger, 'Speculative Builders and the Structure of the Scottish Building Industry, 1860–1914', *Business History* (1979), p. 291.
[34] Rodger, 'Invisible Hand', p. 204.
[35] Rodger, 'Rents and Ground Rents, p. 54.
[36] *R.C. Scottish Housing*, paras. 1513–77.
[37] Rodger, 'Rents and Ground Rents', pp. 50, 54, 65–6.

demands.[38] Many workers employed outside Glasgow were forced to live in the city, indicating further supply problems.

Institutional barriers also impeded the working class housing market, with most housing rented by the year and only becoming available during two short periods, as opposed to being rented by the week or month in England or Ireland. Workers were frequently forced to commit themselves to a yearly lease some months in advance. The fact that most rates in Scotland were paid by the occupier in two half-yearly moieties, as opposed to being compounded with the rent, as in Ireland and England, added a further financial handicap; short rentals and the payment of rates by instalments were introduced in 1911 in response to recommendations from an official inquiry.[39]

Unlike Scotland where many nineteenth-century tenements were built for working class occupation, most Dublin tenements dated from an older era, though Dublin-style subdivisions of older houses were common in Edinburgh.[40] Many Dublin tenements had formerly housed the city's elite, particularly those on the north side, which found limited alternative uses. Their availability acted as a disincentive towards new construction as aspiring landlords could invest in existing properties. As older tenements were located convenient to docks, markets, coal yards, railway terminals—the main sources of casual employment—this enhanced their attractiveness. However tenement rents were relatively high: the rent of a one-roomed tenement in Dublin was equal to a three-roomed cottage in Belfast and the cost of alternative accommodation was high. As in Scotland, part of the problem related to land supply. Most Dublin labouring families could not move to the suburbs because of uncertain employment, the concentration of employment in the centre city, and high tram fares on the privately-owned system. Building cottages, or purpose-built tenements, on cleared land in the city was extremely expensive, as Dublin Corporation discovered; costs per acre were on a par with Scottish figures because of middlemen interests. Site acquisition and clearance by Dublin Corporation for Artisans Dwellings Company housing in the Coombe and Plunkett Street cost £5,500 and over £6,700 per acre respectively; the site for Foley Street flats, built in the city's notorious 'night-town' district, cost almost £5,700 per acre,[41] though in Edinburgh municipal housing was built on cleared areas which cost an average of £15,359 per acre.[42] Private schemes within the city concentrated on infill houses and cottages to the rear of older tenements. While vacant land was available various obstacles precluded its use for working class housing. Legal problems relating to the Blessington-Gardiner estate[43] removed an

---

[38] Glasgow City Corporation, *Municipal Glasgow: Its Evolution and Enterprises* (1915, reprinted Glasgow, 1985), pp. 48–56.
[39] *Municipal Glasgow*, p. 325.
[40] R.C. *Housing Scotland*, para. 404.
[41] Calculations from Appendices III and VI, *Dublin Housing Inquiry*.
[42] R.C. *Housing Scotland*, para. 193.
[43] Daly, *Deposed Capital*, p. 120.

extensive north-city area from the land market until the 1870s when it was devoted to small houses for mostly clerical workers. Land adjoining the docks suffered problems of drainage and access, though working class housing eventually emerged there. South of the River Liffey, the dominant position of the Pembroke estate ensured high residential standards.

Lack of cheap convenient land plus the competing attractions of tenement investment acted as supply-side restrictions, while population stagnation and the uncertain, casual employment of much of the working class weakened demand for new housing. The Dublin working class was anchored to the city centre by the proximity to jobs, and access to old clothes markets, street food markets and pawnbrokers. Families paid the lowest possible rents because of uncertain employment. In later years, as in Glasgow, bye-law and sanitary regulations deterred housing investment; most new private housing affordable to the labouring class was in breach of sanitary regulations. The middle class suburban housing market was more profitable and more secure and had access to cheaper land. While the 1914 Dublin housing inquiry argued that firmer administration resulting in tenement closures would have generated a market for working class housing,[44] their figures showing that Corporation housing would require a substantial subsidy from the rates, amounting to more than one third of rent,[45] negated that argument.

Both Dublin and Glasgow were pioneers in local authority housing prior to 1914, though both contributions were insignificant; Glasgow Improvement Trust built a total of 2,199 units, accommodating 10,000 people or 1 per cent of the population; Dublin Corporation's 1,385 units housed 7,500 people or 2.5 per cent, possibly the highest percentage in the United Kingdom;[46] an alternative candidate is Cork with 515 houses.[47] Belfast had yet to embark on municipal housing.[48] Dublin and Glasgow local authority housing reveal common problems: a failure to house the poorest section of the community,[49] though both implemented schemes specifically for that group;[50] the high cost of slum clearance; excessive compensation awards to property interests particularly when public houses had to be closed.[51] In Dublin such costs were attributed to administrative shortcomings or corruption on the part of Dublin Corporation. Such allegations were not made against Scottish local authorities and it would appear that the problems related to administrative norms rather than corruption or incompetence. Glasgow Corporation faced fewer difficulties in extending its supervisory powers than Dublin. Its authority to ticket tenement

---

[44] *Dublin Housing*, para. 51.

[45] The break-even rent was deemed to be 5s. 5d. and it was believed that tenants could afford to pay 3s. 7d., though only 28 per cent of tenement dwellers paid in excess of 3s. in rent.

[46] For Glasgow, Butt, 'Working Class Housing in Glasgow', p. 63; for Dublin, Daly, *Dublin*, p. 318.

[47] Michael Gough, 'Socio-economic Conditions and the Genesis of Planning in Cork', in Michael Bannon, ed., *The Emergence of Irish Planning, 1880–1920* (Dublin 1985), pp. 309–14.

[48] Sybil Gribbon, *Edwardian Belfast: A Social Profile* (Belfast, 1982), p. 30.

[49] *R.C. Housing Scotland*, minority report, para. 187.

[50] Daly, *Dublin*, p. 304, and Daunton, *Property-owning Democracy*, p. 19.

[51] Dublin, Daly, *Dublin*, ch. 9; Scotland, *R.C. Housing Scotland*, paras. 1643–68.

houses with rights of inspection during the night exceeded the powers of Dublin Corporation; whether it alleviated housing problems is questionable.

Glasgow, unlike Dublin, benefited from a rapidly rising rateable valuation which permitted the borrowing of £1.25m in the 1860s for the Glasgow Improvement Commission and the financing of this scheme at a cost of less than sixpence in the pound.[52] Dublin housing schemes consisted of small piece-meal sites, in part because borrowing restrictions would not permit more ambitious proposals. While the buoyancy of Glasgow's rateable valuation permitted art galleries, libraries and new municipal buildings, not available in revenue-starved Dublin, the similarity in housing problems suggests that these could not be resolved by revenue buoyancy, given the institutional and ideological constraints applying to local authority spending at this time.

---

[52] *Municipal Glasgow*, p. 49. The maximum rate was set at sixpence for the first five years and threepence for a further ten years; after 1880 the maximum was set at twopence in the pound.

18

Financial institutions and the Scottish financial centre in the inter-war years

C. W. Munn

STUDENTS OF ECONOMIC HISTORY who wish to know about the evolution of Scotland's highly successful financial services sector have a much harder task facing them than those who wish to know about the manufacturing sector or the extractive industries or agriculture. General textbooks tend to say very little about financial services. Where these are mentioned at all it is usually to say something about the structure of banking but very little about banking services and nothing at all about insurance. None of them attempts to analyse, or criticise, the contribution which this sector made to the development of the economy. This generalisation is especially true of the inter-war period when the Scottish economy was struggling with regional and structural difficulties and with demand deficiencies. In short, the staple diet for students of economic history gives them no insight into how this important sector of the economy coped with the inter-war period in terms either of its structure or profitability or of its contribution to the development of the economy.[1]

It also seems strange that nothing should be said about financial centres as such. The location of an industry is usually the subject of attention by commentators who make much of the economies enjoyed by virtue of its location in a particular place, or places. If any impression at all is created by text books it is that financial services are provided in limbo, that the place where they are concentrated, and they are often highly concentrated, is irrelevant to their existence.

This is a matter of contemporary relevance, for there are many countries throughout the world whose current economic development strategies give prominence to the creation and development of financial centres. Most notably this is the case in Ireland where Dublin city centre has recently seen the building of a series of office blocks designed for the purpose of attracting financial institutions. Other examples of this strategy being followed are to be found in Vancouver, Lyon and

---

[1] This comment refers only to under-graduate textbooks.

Singapore.² Other countries, fortunate enough to possess established financial centres, are taking advantage of their position to develop this type of business. In particular the Scottish financial community set up Scottish Financial Enterprise in 1986. The purpose of S.F.E. is to promote Scotland, not just Edinburgh, as a financial centre and, in so doing, to encourage financial organisations to set up operations.

This type of exercise must be seen as part of a wider programme of economic development, but where it differs from earlier strategies is in the recognition that financial services have a substantial role to play. It is certainly the case that the major policy objective is the creation of jobs, but there is also the consideration that a financial centre's strength lies in the diversity of organisations which operate within it. For this reason development programmes for financial centres nearly always stress the international nature of the business.

In part the recognition of the potential of financial services in the UK in general and Scotland in particular arose out of the experience of the sector in the early 1980s when it exhibited healthy growth at a time when almost every other sector of the economy was experiencing the opposite. It remains to be seen, however, why this potential was not recognised in an earlier age. In particular, the inter-war years were a period when economists and politicians began to think about, and to implement, development strategies to solve the problems of a beleaguered economy. Was the potential of the financial services sector ignored and, if so, what were the consequences for the economy. Would Scotland's strengths as a financial centre in the 1990s be even greater if the growth potential of the financial services sector had been recognised in the inter-war years?

* * *

Rationalisation was the key word on the minds of many of Britain's industrialists in the inter-war years. It also occupied the thoughts of government policy makers. It is not surprising therefore that much time and attention was given to the problem of how to make Britain's manufacturing industry efficient and profitable once more. When the financial services sector was investigated to see if it could make a greater contribution to the recovery process it was found to be, on the whole, efficient at its chosen tasks.³

There does not appear to have been anyone giving thought to the possibility of financial services *per se* contributing to the recovery process by expanding their business. Such thought as was given to the sector was entirely in terms of the provision of funds for manufacturing industry. The creation of the Bankers Industrial Development Company in 1930 must be seen in this light.⁴

---

² See Scottish Financial Enterprise publicity booklets.
³ Report of the Committee on Finance and Industry (The Macmillan Committee), 1931, Cmd. 3897.
⁴ A. R. Holmes and Edwin Green, *Midland: 150 Years of Banking Business* (London, 1986), pp. 181–2.

Clearly financial services did not enter public thinking in terms of their ability to contribute directly to the growth of the economy or to help to solve the problem of unemployment. When the Board of Trade commissioned an industrial survey of the south-west of Scotland from the Department of Political Economy in the University of Glasgow the terms of reference were strictly in terms of manufacturing industry.[5] Similarly the Scottish Economic Committee's thinking was largely in terms of manufacturing industry although they had the foresight to look beyond heavy industry to the potential of light industry.[6] This type of mind-set can also be seen in the revolutionary Special Areas legislation which was largely concerned with the needs of manufacturers for suitable accommodation.[7]

This type of thinking was also to be found in the private sector, even within financial services. From 1934 until 1960, with a break for the war years, the Clydesdale Bank published an annual *Survey of Economic Conditions in Scotland*.[8] Some service sector industries were analysed in this publication. Retailing was usually covered and there was a more extensive coverage of tourism and transport. Yet there was never any mention of the financial services sector.

To the modern eye this seems rather strange. Could it be that financial services were not seen as part of the 'real economy'? This seems unlikely given their importance and the boardroom links between financial institutions and manufacturing industry.[9] More likely this state of affairs arose simply because the financial services sector was not seen as a problem area in the economy. Much of the public debate at the time was concerned with unemployment and most of the major financial institutions were to be found in Edinburgh where the unemployment problem was a good deal less severe than it was in other parts of the country. Moreover financial institutions did not have large administrative units, as they do now, where many of the 'back-office' processing functions are carried out. Most of the administrative functions were carried out in the branches, especially in the banks. Financial institutions were not therefore like manufacturing industry where the opening of a new factory or yard could make a sizeable impact upon local unemployment. The opening of a new branch, which might employ between five and ten people, would have little impact on a large scale unemployment problem. Moreover, financial institutions were unlikely to be able to provide employment for the types of people who were becoming unemployed. Unskilled and semi-skilled manual workers were unlikely to make good bank clerks.

This argument is given some plausibility by the fact that even as late as the 1960s economists, writing about strategies for regional development, ignored any possibility that financial services might contribute to economic regeneration.[10] It

---

[5] Board of Trade, *An Industrial Survey of the South West of Scotland* (1932).
[6] Scottish Economic Committee, *Light Industries in Scotland* (1938).
[7] R. H. Campbell, *The Rise and Fall of Scottish Industry, 1707–1939* (Edinburgh, 1980), p. 180.
[8] The Clydesdale Bank Ltd, *Survey of Economic Conditions in Scotland* (Glasgow, 1934–60).
[9] John Scott and Michael Hughes, *The Anatomy of Scottish Capital* (London, 1980), chap. 2.
[10] T. Wilson, *Strategies for Economic Development* (Edinburgh, 1964), and G. C. Cameron and G. L. Reid, *Scottish Economic Planning and the Attraction of Industry* (Edinburgh, 1966).

was not until the 1970s and the 1980s, when financial institutions greatly increased their range of services and re-organised their administration to create very large administrative offices, that they began to enter into the reckoning of development economists and others concerned with growth.

Economic historians have simply followed the economists in their pre-occupations. The result of this has been almost to ignore a large and vital element of the economy in the inter-war years. It has not been possible to disentangle the various elements of the Commerce and Finance sector as defined in the Standard Industrial Classification, but in 1931 this sector employed 16.36 per cent of the workforce.[11] This was more than the mining and quarrying; textiles; chemicals; gas, water and electricity; and bricks and pottery sections combined. It was the largest sector in terms of employment. The next largest was metals and machinery with 12.62 per cent.

It is also interesting to compare these figures over time, particularly in the four Scottish cities. Table 1[12] sets out the changing employment patterns between 1911 and 1931 for metals and machinery and for commerce and finance.

Table 1: Employment patterns in Scottish cities 1911 and 1931

% by sector	Edinburgh		Glasgow		Aberdeen		Dundee	
	1911	1931	1911	1931	1911	1931	1911	1931
Metals etc.	5.2	6.1	18.5	20.1	8.3	6.9	7.3	7.6
Finance etc.	4.5	21.6	4.1	21.0	3.7	26.3	2.2	15.2

Perhaps the most surprising element in these figures is the enormous growth in the employment contribution of the Commerce and Finance sector. Clearly there were significant changes taking place in this sector. The figures represent real increases in jobs amounting to 40,563 in Edinburgh; 94,705 in Glasgow; 18,137 in Aberdeen and 12,614 in Dundee. Thus the four cities enjoyed an increase in employment of 166,019 jobs in this sector. The figures are all the more surprising, in view of the traditional way of looking at things, in Glasgow where, in 1931, Commerce and Finance employed more people than Metals and Machinery. What is also particularly surprising is the strength of the growth of employment in this sector between 1911 and 1931.

So far as banking is concerned its contribution to this growth can be explained largely by the increase in the number of branches. In 1919 there were 1264 branches of Scottish banks and this number climbed steadily to a peak of 1,900 in 1938; this is an increase of 50.3 per cent. Of the new branches some 395 were created before the end of 1930 with a further 241 added in the 1930s.[13] The year 1932 showed the only decrease in the period but the increase in 1933 more than compensated for this.

---

[11] *Census of Scotland 1931.*
[12] *Census of Scotland 1911* and *1931.*
[13] S. G. Checkland, *Scottish Banking: A History 1695–1973* (Glasgow, 1975), table 44, pp. 743–5, and E. Murphy, 'Banking and the Inter-War Economy as Viewed by the Chairmen and Governors of the Scottish Banks' (undergraduate dissertation, Department of Economic History, University of Glasgow, 1986), p. 16.

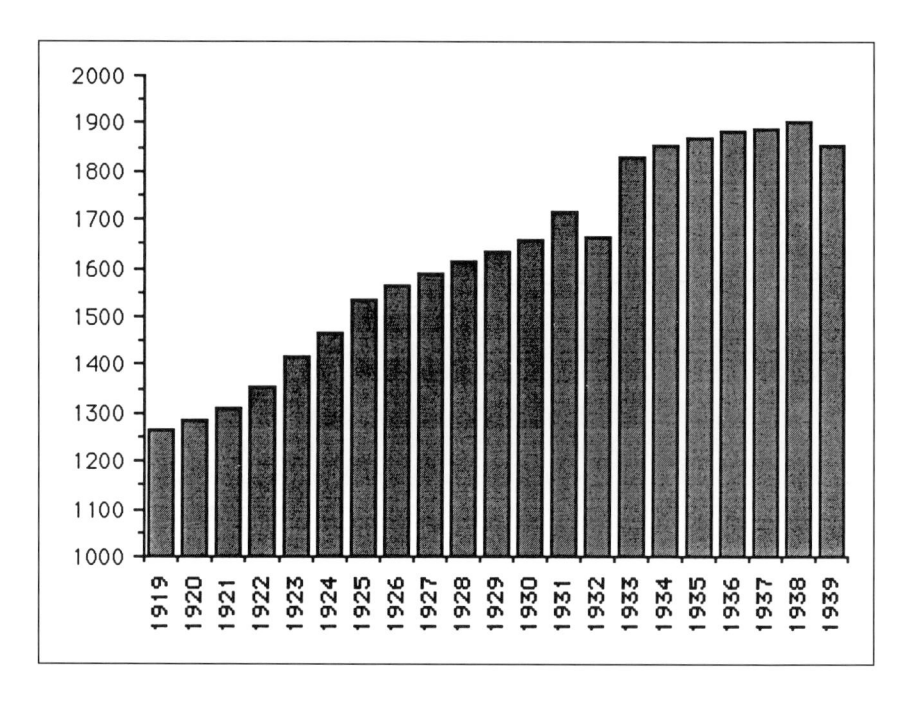

Figure 1: Number of Scottish bank branches, 1919–39.
(Source: Checkland, Scottish Banking, Table 44.)

Branches varied quite considerably in the numbers of staff which they employed but five would be an average for small branches with ten in the larger offices. The other important element here is that the creation of all of these new branches created demand, and therefore employment, in the building and construction sector. Much of the demand ran counter to the trade cycle. Figure 1 depicts the annual formation of branches over this period.[14]

Not surprisingly most of the new branches were set up in areas of urban growth where new suburbs were being created. The primary function of these would be deposit gathering rather than lending. 'Few of these [branches] were set up in areas dominated by the traditional export industries, for these were the trades most adversely affected by the depression. Instead, the new branches tended to be in farming areas such as Ayrshire, or in places enjoying a substantial growth in population because of new housing developments such as Anniesland and King's Park in Glasgow'.[15]

In view of the paucity of research which has been done on the insurance (including life assurance) industry, banking must stand as a proxy for the whole of the financial services sector. There is, however, some evidence to show that life

---

[14] Murphy, 'Banking and the Inter-War Economy'.
[15] C. W. Munn, *Clydesdale Bank: The First 150 Years* (Glasgow, 1988), pp. 206–15.

assurance was enjoying a growth phase every bit as dramatic as banking. Table 2 shows some figures for the Scottish Amicable Life Assurance Society which indicate that this society enjoyed a period of considerable growth.[16]

No figures are available for the numbers of people employed by the Society but the increase in business indicated in the table suggests an appreciable growth rate. Furthermore the number of branches increased from ten in 1919 to twenty by 1936 although there was some retrenchment in 1937–8. If this sort of experience was repeated by the other life assurance offices then it represents a very substantial accretion of business. Figures from the *Insurance Directory and Year Book* show that United Kingdom premium income for ordinary life assurance grew, in a relatively steady fashion, from £37.8m in 1919 to £84.1m in 1939. Industrial life assurance premiums exhibited a similar rise from £35.3m to £59.8m over the same period. The implications of these figures are such as to suggest that life assurance enjoyed a period of growth which was every bit as dramatic as that enjoyed by banking.

Table 2: Scottish Amicable Life Assurance Society Statistics for inter-war period (all figures in £000s)

Year	Premium revenue	Interest revenue	Payments to policyholders	Total fund	Bonus rate
1920	536	351	389	7,105	1.5
1925	771	469	579	8,948	2.0
1930	689	584	692	10,507	2.175
1935	796	569	763	12,087	2.0

Table 3: Investment trusts in Scottish cities

Period	Edinburgh	Glasgow	Aberdeen	Dundee
Pre 1914	25	2	4	9
Inter-war additions	7	10	3	1
Total	32	12	7	10

Information about the investment trust movement is even harder to find but the little which is available suggests that this too was a dynamic part of the commerce and finance sector. There were many formations of new trusts in this period but a number seem to have been conceived as short term ventures and the figures given here include only those which enjoyed a long life-span and survived into the 1960s. The impact on the unemployment problem was negligible as trusts employed tiny numbers of people and were often run as adjuncts to accountancy firms or lawyers' practices. Table 3 shows the number of trusts in each Scottish city in 1914 and the numbers of new formations in the inter-war years.[17]

---

[16] Anon., *A History of Scottish Amicable Life Assurance Society 1826–1976* (Glasgow, 1976), appendices 3–5, pp. 124–6.
[17] D. C. Corner and H. Burton, *Investment and Unit Trusts in Britain and America* (London, 1968), table A4, pp. 344–7.

All but one of the inter-war formations came in the 1920s. Despite a very strong showing in Dundee the table clearly indicates Edinburgh's dominance in the investment trust movement.

* * *

The factors which determine the physical location of an industry are usually of major importance in any historical or economic analysis of that industry. Yet this is a subject which has been almost entirely ignored by modern commentators on the development of financial institutions. In the introduction to his 1974 study on the location of financial centres Charles Kindleberger argued that his subject fell between urban and regional economics on the one hand and financial economics on the other.[18] It has been claimed by neither.

The 'geography of finance' is of contemporary relevance for developing countries, as many development economists place the growth of a financial centre further up in the list of desiderata than foreign aid or even export expansion.[19] Such is the importance they attach to the contribution of financial institutions to the process of growth. In developed countries the question to be addressed is: what sustains financial centres and how do they relate to one another?

An older generation of economic historians took an interest in financial centre location. For example Gras in 1922 outlined a stage theory of development in which the growth of specialised financial institutions was one stage. This development was clearly a metropolitan function.[20] From Gras in the 1920s to Kindleberger in the 1970s little further thought seems to have been given to the subject.

Historically the location and composition of financial centres is of interest because of the central role of money in the process of economic growth. There is also the question of whether or not the location of a financial centre is of importance in relation to the centre of industry. It is certainly remarkable that the main financial centres in Scotland, Ireland and England, based as they are in Edinburgh, Dublin and London, should be geographically separate from the main industrial centres of Glasgow, Belfast and Lancashire. But does it matter? Does it have implications for the efficiency of financial institutions and the ways in which they meet the needs of their customers? Why were there lesser financial centres in the industrial centres? Were the major financial centres to be found in capital cities rather than industrial centres for political rather than economic reasons? There are many such questions which can be asked, but not answered, in an article of this length, but it is possible, however briefly, to identify the factors which contribute

---

[18] C. P. Kindleberger, *The Formation of Financial Centres: A Study in Comparative Economic History* (Cambridge, Mass., 1974), and *Keynesianism vs Monetarism and Other Essays in Financial History* (London 1985), pp. 155–67.

[19] Kindleberger, *Formation of Financial Centres*, p. 1.

[20] N. S. B. Gras, *An Introduction to Economic History* (New York, 1922).

to the location of a financial centre. Indeed the thrust of Kindleberger's argument is, once having identified the factors which are important, to show how their relative importance has varied throughout the world.

The major variable has been political considerations but this was more often the case in countries where economic development came late and growth was a feature of governments' agendas. In countries where economic development came earlier, before the days of planned economies, economic factors were of greater importance, although even here political factors were not without significance. It must be remembered too that a certain amount of financial centre evolution took place in Edinburgh, Dublin and London before major industrial developments came to their countries.

In addition to political considerations the factors which Kindleberger identified as being potentially important to the evolution of a financial centre (to which I have added a few of my own) were location on a trade route, a developed legal system, currency stability, local demand, culture, good communications, tradition, skills, savings accumulation, economic information, head offices of other businesses, central bank activities and economies of scale. Clearly such complexity defies compression into an economic equation or even a short historical article.

* * *

Significantly all factors, with the exception of central bank activities, were present in some degree in eighteenth and nineteenth-century Scotland. For much of the nineteenth century Edinburgh and Glasgow vied with one another for supremacy in financial markets. It is doubtful if Glasgow ever came close to overtaking Edinburgh but the failure of the Western Bank in 1857 and the City of Glasgow Bank in 1878 put an end to any aspirations which Glasgow might have had to be the financial capital of Scotland.

Before the middle of the nineteenth century Scotland had a homogeneous banking structure which had been created, for the most part, by market forces. Large scale joint-stock banks, with branch networks and independent note-issues, were the only type of commercial bank operating in Scotland. (Three of the seventeen banks operating in 1850 were incorporated by Act of Parliament or Royal Charter but the others were co-partneries, although they eventually took advantage of the Companies Acts). Several takeovers of the smaller banks, together with the failures of the Western Bank in 1857 and the City of Glasgow Bank in 1878, reduced the numbers to ten by 1880. From that time until 1914 there were only two changes, when the Inverness-based Caledonian Bank was taken over by the Bank of Scotland in 1907 and the two Aberdeen banks merged in the same year. Five of the eight banks had their head offices in Edinburgh, two in Glasgow and one in Aberdeen.[21]

In England, by contrast, the years between 1880 and the First World War saw enormous changes in the structure of banking. This period witnessed the emergence

[21] Checkland, *Scottish Banking*, *passim*.

of the Big Five banks, the largest of which was Midland Bank. Most of these had their origins in the English provinces but all were head-quartered in London. By processes of acquisition of other banks and branch extension the Midland increased its branch network from ten in 1885 to more than one thousand by 1914. By that time it was the largest bank in the world.[22] One of the great 'might have beens' of banking history is to speculate what might have happened to the structure of British banking if the Scots had not been stopped from opening branches in England in the 1870s.[23] It is feasible that they would have come to dominate the weak English banking system and might have forestalled the emergence of the Big Five by means of their own acquisition policy. By 1914, however, the Scots had lost whatever initiative they might have had and the large English banks were, for the most part, much larger than their Scottish counterparts. There was an understanding, although not a law, that the Scots and English banks should confine their activities in the UK to their own territories. The Scottish bank offices in London and a few Clydesdale branches in the north of England were the only permissible exceptions to this understanding. The problem with this arrangement was that it had no foundation in law and when the English banks began to outgrow their own country's potential for further growth they soon turned their sights on Scotland and Ireland.

The consequence of this was that by 1920 the position of Scottish banking was radically different from what it had been in 1914 and the next few years were to see further change. The numbers of banks had not altered but several had been taken over by English banks.

Table 4: Scottish banks taken over by English banks

Scottish bank	Rank in 1920	English bank	Date
National Bank of Scotland	5	Lloyds	1918
British Linen	7	Barclays	1919
Clydesdale	3	Midland	1920
North of Scotland	8	Midland	1924

Note: Ranking is by total liabilities.

These takeovers were never described as such. They were called 'affiliations' and they were different from the type of amalgamation which had taken place in England because the Scottish banks kept their separate identities, note issues and boards of directors.[24] Similar tactics were adopted for the Irish banks which were taken over by English banks. These affiliations did nothing to diminish Edinburgh's importance as a financial centre.

The main purpose in maintaining the separate identities of the Scottish banks which had English affiliations was to preserve the profitable right to issue bank-notes.

---

[22] Holmes and Green, *Midland*, chap. 3–6.
[23] Munn, *Clydesdale*, pp. 96–8.
[24] Checkland, *Scottish Banking*, pp. 576–81, and Munn, *Clydesdale*, pp. 155–62.

Recent research on the history of the Clydesdale Bank and the North of Scotland Bank[25] has shown that English ownership of Scottish banks was unobtrusive and, occasionally, helpful; as when the Midland Bank encouraged the North of Scotland Bank to open a London office. There is certainly no evidence to show that, in the inter-war years, English ownership of a large part of the Scottish banking system in any way inhibited developments north of the border.

The traffic of takeovers was not all one-way. In 1924 the Royal Bank of Scotland acquired Drummonds, a private London bank, and in 1930 the Manchester-based Williams Deacons was purchased. This was followed in 1939 by Glyn, Mills and Company, a small London clearing bank.[26] Nevertheless, on balance, the traffic was very much in one direction and it is difficult to escape the conclusion that if the Scots had not been prevented from extending further into England in the 1870s then they would have achieved a very substantial penetration of the English market, much as the Scottish Life Offices had done.

Figures discussed earlier showed that the inter-war period was one of great activity for the Scottish banks in their branch expansion policies, with an increase of 50 per cent in the number of branches. Amongst themselves the number of branches which each bank maintained was the most important measure of status in the Scottish banking world. More conventional measures, such as profitability, level of deposits or advances, were treated with scant regard by the bankers themselves because banks were not obliged under the Companies Act to declare their true profits. The result of this was that they tended to declare what they felt the market expected of them and transferred the remainder to their hidden reserves. Moreover they tended to indulge in window dressing their balance sheets so that the amount of deposits in particular was enhanced. The effect of this was to reduce their lending ratios to a figure which they felt interested parties might find more acceptable. Not that lending was particularly high. Indeed the almost constant cry of Scottish bankers in this period was that they were under-lent and would have liked to be lending more to their customers.[27]

Published figures confirm Edinburgh's dominance over Glasgow as a financial centre. Figure 2 (overleaf)[28] shows the percentage share of bank liabilities held by Edinburgh, Glasgow and Aberdeen banks. Quite apart from the evident dominance of the Edinburgh banks it is also noteworthy that the relative shares of the three cities changed very little over this period. This is not in itself very surprising given that all banks had a good spread of business throughout the country and, with the possible exception of the North of Scotland Bank, none was dependent for its business on only one region of Scotland. The importance of Edinburgh therefore lies in the domicile of the banks. Many modern analysts argue that the location of

---

[25] Munn, *Clydesdale*, pp. 155–62.
[26] Checkland, *Scottish Banking*, pp. 578–80.
[27] F. Capie and A. Webber, *A Monetary History of the United Kingdom 1870–1982*, Vol. 1 (London, 1985), chap. 10, and evidence of Scottish bankers to the Macmillan Committee, 1931, Cmd. 3897.
[28] Murphy, 'Banking and the Inter-War Economy', p. 15.

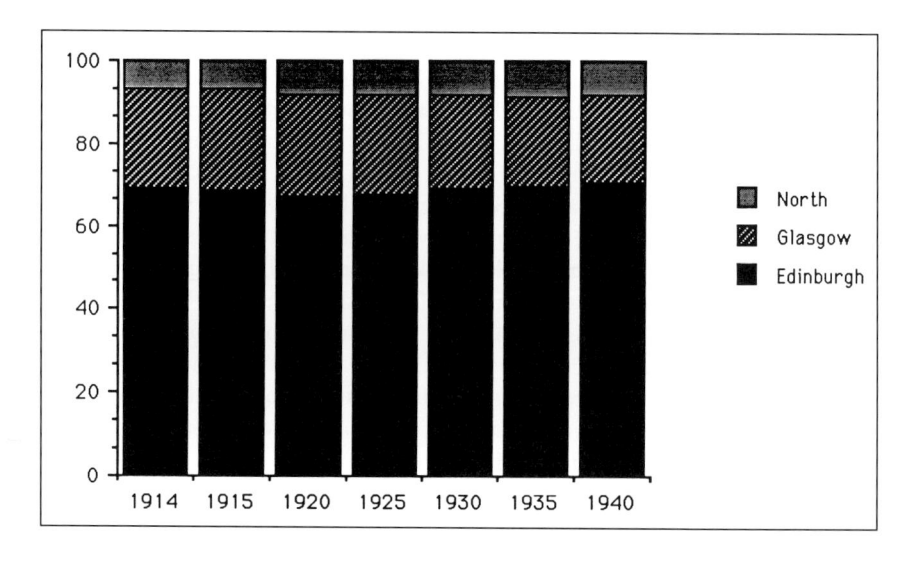

Figure 2: Bank liabilities, Edinburgh, Glasgow and northern based banks, percentage shares, 1914–1940.
(Source: Checkland, Scottish Banking, Table 48.)

a group of head offices is essential to the definition of a financial centre. Given that Edinburgh boasted the head offices of five banks, several large life assurance offices, one large composite insurance office and a substantial number of investment trusts, its claim to be a large financial centre is assured.

* * *

In view of the size of the financial services sector and the central role of money in the capitalist system, it seems strange that economists and economic historians have not, hitherto, given more attention to the role and evolution of this sector of the economy. Given the growing realisation of the important part which financial institutions and financial centres can play in the process of economic growth it seems likely that academic interest in this subject will increase. There are clearly a large number of questions to be addressed and this article has identified a number of them. Most notably it has identified the very large role played by financial and other service industries in the growth of the inter-war years and in the maintenance of employment. If there had not been such healthy growth in these areas then the depression would have been very much worse. Yet it also seems unlikely that very much could have been done, given the economic development framework at the time, to encourage further growth in financial services. The potential for contributing to the economy's growth may well have been as fully realised as possible. There is a need for further research in this area but until the over-emphasis on the study of heavy industry is corrected it seems unlikely that much will be done.

19

Wages and employment in Northern Ireland and Scotland between the wars: the case of shipbuilding

F. Geary and W. Johnson

RECENT DISCUSSION of inter-war employment and unemployment has been at the level of the macro-economy. However it is widely recognised that there was a strong structural component to the problem of unemployment in its industrial and regional incidence. For example, both Northern Ireland and Scotland were characterised as high unemployment regions and both regions contained heavy concentrations of the so-called 'declining' industries. In the case of Scotland these are identified as mechanical engineering, shipbuilding, coal, and iron and steel; in the case of Northern Ireland they may be identified as mechanical engineering, shipbuilding, textiles and clothing.[1] The 1924 Census of Production shows just over 40 per cent of all workers in Scotland occupied in its declining industries, against an average in Britain of 25 per cent.[2] Similarly in Northern Ireland the Census of 1926 shows around 28 per cent of all workers engaged in its declining industries compared to a Great Britain (1921) average of 20 per cent.[3]

Since Champernowne and Beveridge[4] a number of writers have drawn attention to the impact of the decline of the staple industries on regional employment. Glynn has recently argued that

> these industries may have contributed *directly* at least one-third and up to one-half of total unemployment in the best years of the interwar period.

---

[1] D. H. Aldcroft, *The Inter-War Economy: Britain, 1919–1939* (London, 1970), pp. 91–2; K. S. Isles and N. Cuthbert, *An Economic Survey of Northern Ireland* (Belfast, 1957), Statistical Appendix, Tables 3, 9, 11–17.

[2] Aldcroft, *Inter-War Economy*, pp. 91–2.

[3] *Ulster Year Book 1929* (Belfast 1929), pp. 19 and 63; C. H. Lee, *British Regional Employment Statistics, 1841–1971* (Cambridge, 1979).

[4] D. G. Champernowne, 'The Uneven Distribution of Unemployment in the United Kingdom, 1929–36, I, II', *Review of Economic Studies*, 5 (1937–8), pp. 93–106; 6 (1938–9), pp. 111–29; Sir William Beveridge, 'An Analysis of Unemployment, I, II, III', *Economica*, n.s. 3 (1936), pp. 357–86; 4 (1937), pp. 1–17, 168–83.

Indirectly, of course, employment decline in the staples influenced other industries and regions and the national economy. The traditional industrial areas with high concentrations of staples experienced higher average levels of unemployment overall and in all industries. Clearly there were important links between structural and regional problems in the economy.[5]

It is to one aspect of these links that this paper is addressed. Specifically it examines the link between the real wage and employment in one of the staple industries, shipbuilding. Beenstock and Warburton have recently found a negative relationship between own-product real wage and manufacturing employment for the interwar period,[6] and Beenstock, Capie and Griffiths have attributed the increase in unemployment between 1929 and 1932 to a rise in real wages.[7] Casson finds support for the view that between the wars real wages and employment were inversely related.[8] Dealing with the staple industries Glynn and Booth argue that

> The traditional British industrial economy, based on the staple export industries, faced a severe cost problem resulting in classical unemployment which could be solved unilaterally only by deflation and wage reductions...[9]

If it is indeed the case that the staple industries were suffering from classical, i.e. real-wage, unemployment and if, as we have seen, the concentration of staple industries in certain regions contributed heavily to their poor employment record between the wars, then it follows that the labour force in these regions was pricing itself out of employment.

This paper examines the relationship between wages and employment in Northern Ireland and Scotland in the case of one of the staples, shipbuilding. Its main aim is to present evidence that employment in this industry was not related to the real wage. Consequently, the decline in employment in shipbuilding in these two regions is not attributable to excessive real wages.

* * *

---

[5] S. Glynn, 'The Scale and Nature of the Problem', in S. Glynn and A. Booth, eds., *The Road to Full Employment* (London, 1987), p. 14.

[6] M. Beenstock and P. Warburton, 'Wages and Unemployment in Interwar Britain', *Explorations in Economic History*, 23 (1986), pp. 153–72.

[7] M. Beenstock, F. Capie and B. Griffiths, 'Economic Recovery in the United Kingdom in the 1930s', in *The UK Economic Recovery in the 1930s*, Bank of England Panel of Academic Consultants Panel Paper no. 23 (London, 1984).

[8] M. Casson, *Economics of Unemployment: An Historical Perspective* (Oxford, 1983), p. 179.

[9] S. Glynn and A. Booth, 'Unemployment in Interwar Britain: A Case for Re-learning the Lessons of the 1930s?' *Econ. Hist. Rev.*, 2nd ser., XXXVI (1983), p. 337.

Shipbuilding was clearly an industry in trouble between the wars. Beveridge, in examining the manufacturing sector between 1924 and 1937, identified seventeen industries with employment growing at twice the national average rate, twelve growing at more than the national average rate, twenty-five growing at less than the national average rate, and nineteen declining industries. Shipbuilding fell into this last category, losing about 25 per cent of its 1924 employment total by 1937. Of these nineteen declining industries only four—cotton, jute, pig-iron, and carriage and cart making—fared worse.[10] In Scotland shipbuilding lost about 42 per cent of all jobs between 1924 and 1937, employment falling from 53,740 to 31,390;[11] in Northern Ireland the loss was about 41 per cent of all jobs, with employment falling from 12,300 to 7,200 in the same period.[12]

These job losses, as we have seen, have been attributed to a negative relationship between employment and real wages. A wage cut may be seen to have two effects. The direct effect is to make labour relatively cheaper causing the firm to substitute labour for capital (substitution effect); the indirect effect is to lower costs enabling price cuts and thereby inducing an increase in the quantity demanded of the product (output effect). The substitution effect arises from the assumption that the marginal product of labour declines as employment rises. This follows from the assumption that the capital stock is fully employed, so that producing more output with more labour lowers the capital-labour ratio and hence reduces the productivity of labour, necessitating then a fall in wages if more labour is to be employed. These assumptions, however, may well be inappropriate for modelling the production process in the case of the shipbuilding industry between the wars.

Consider the case of a production process in which the capital to labour ratio is fixed. This may arise either because of the prevailing technology or because, even though capital and labour are substitutes in the planning stage, the capital to labour ratio becomes fixed in the planned proportions once the capacity is installed and operating.[13] Under these circumstances changes in the relative prices of factors will not induce changes in the employment of one factor or the other. This implies that demand for labour and hence employment will depend only on the amount of output that is demanded and will not be directly related to the real wage. This is an extreme example. Yet, given the importance of labour—skilled and unskilled—in the production process which characterised UK shipbuilding between the wars, it may have some relevance for our discussion.[14]

---

[10] Sir William Beveridge, *Full Employment in a Free Society* (London, 1944), Appendix B, Table 33.
[11] N. K. Buxton 'The Scottish Shipbuilding Industry Between the Wars: A Comparative Study', *Business History*, 10 (1968), Appendix I.
[12] *Ministry of Labour Gazette*, 1923; Isles and Cuthbert, *Economic Survey of Northern Ireland*, Statistical Appendix, Tables 9 and 13.
[13] The discussion which follows may be encountered in more detail in T. F. Dernburg, *Global Macroeconomics* (New York, 1989), pp. 169-77.
[14] See below pp. 243-4

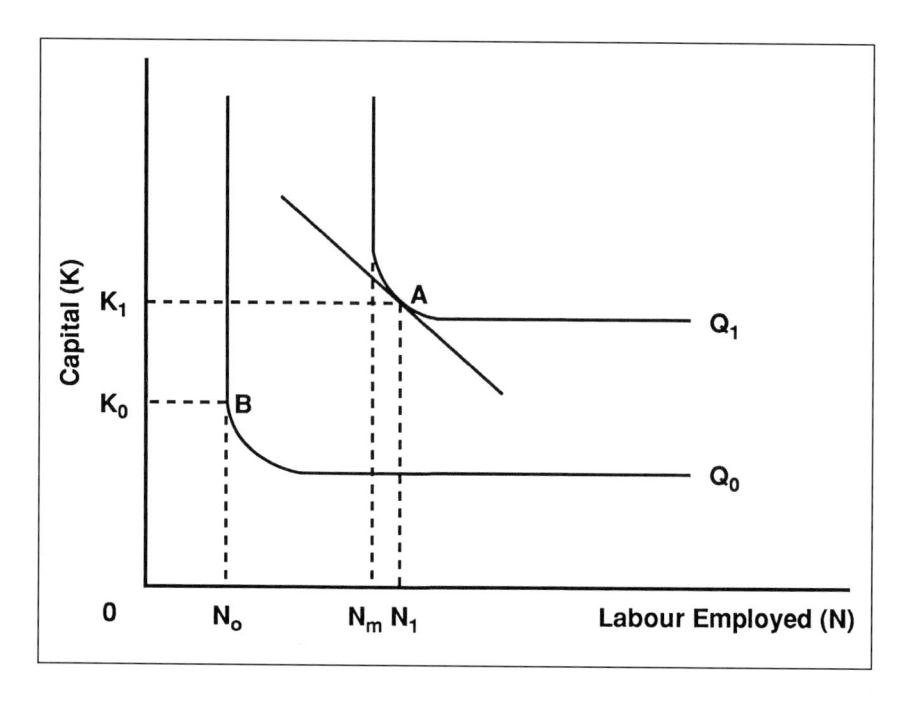

Figure 1: Production isoquants for an individual firm.

Alternatively consider the possibility of a technology which permits limited substitution of factors. Figure 1 shows production isoquants for an individual firm operating under such conditions.[15]

The curved part of the isoquant indicates the region over which capital and labour may be substituted for each other to produce a given level of output, say Q_1. The vertical part of the isoquant shows the minimum amount of labour, N_m, that is necessary to produce output Q_1. No further reductions in employment can take place if Q_1 is to be produced. Similarly the addition of more capital to N_m units of labour will yield no additional output. At this point the marginal productivity of capital is zero.

Suppose an industry or firm has estimated future demand to be the quantity Q_1 and, given relative factor prices, it selects a capital-labour combination at point A, with K_1 units of capital and N_1 units of labour. Now suppose a slump in demand occurs. It already has K_1 units of capital installed on which the rental costs—interest and depreciation—cannot be avoided. Since it is incurring these costs come what may, the firm might as well use as much of its capital stock as possible. It can economise by using as little labour as possible, since labour costs are substantially

---

[15] An isoquant is a curve that shows the different combinations of labour and capital required to produce a given quantity of output.

variable costs. Thus the firm, in seeking to minimise costs associated with the new smaller level of demand Q_0, selects the factor combination at point B, using as little labour as is technically possible, namely N_0 units. The amount of capital K_1—K_0 is mothballed. Since the firm has this amount of capital and is forced to bear the rental costs associated with it whether it is used or not, then the effective price of using the additional capital K_1–K_0 if required is zero. Therefore any positive wage produces an incentive to economise on the use of labour as far as is technically possible. The wage is irrelevant to the determination of the factor combination. The implication of this is that demand for labour or employment depends simply on which production isoquant the industry or firm wishes to produce on, i.e. on the level of demand for the industry's output.

There is evidence to suggest that this last case approximates to the situation in which the UK shipbuilding industry found itself in the period between the wars. By the end of the postwar boom in 1921 berth capacity had been expanded to more than 4 million gross tons, to a level of between 30 per cent and 40 per cent greater than it was in 1913.[16] Since the average annual world output between 1920 and 1938 was only 2.3 million gross tons, the UK could have satisfied total world demand in these years and still have had excess capacity.

This excess capacity persisted throughout the interwar period. In the seven years 1923–9 about one third of the industry's capacity was sufficient to meet the demand for its output.[17] In Scotland about 50 per cent of capacity could have satisfied demand. Over 80 per cent of all berths were unoccupied between 1931 and 1933, and not less than 44 per cent were unused between 1934 and 1938.[18] As Slaven has observed, 'such a degree of unused capacity involved a high cost in establishment charges for facilities that could not be employed. The burden was estimated at up to £1 million per year in the 1920s'.[19] Clearly, then, firms were carrying unutilised capital stocks. These represented not inconsiderable investments undertaken towards the end of the war and during the short-lived postwar boom. For example, between 1919 and 1921 Harland and Wolff made gross additions to its fixed assets totalling in excess of £6 million.[20]

Now consider the production process. It has been graphically observed that 'the metallic din which characterised pre-1940 shipyards was the sound of manual rather than mechanised work, of hand- rather than power-driven tools. Mechanisation played a secondary and subordinate role to the physical work of the skilled trade

---

[16] L. Jones, *Shipbuilding in Britain: Mainly between the Two World Wars* (Cardiff, 1957), p. 124.

[17] *Ibid.*, p. 128.

[18] A. Slaven, 'Growth and Stagnation in British/Scottish Shipbuilding, 1913–1977', in J. Kuuse and A. Slaven, eds., *Scottish and Scandinavian Shipbuilding Seminar: Development Problems in Historical Perspective* (Glasgow, 1980), p. 22.

[19] *Ibid.*, p. 22.

[20] M. Moss and J. R. Hume, *Shipbuilders to the World: 125 Years of Harland and Wolff, Belfast 1861–1986* (Belfast, 1986), p. 215.

gangs and their associated helpers.'[21] Indeed the success of UK shipbuilders before the Great War has been attributed to the importance of skilled labour inputs in the production process.[22] This preponderance of skilled labour which went into the assembling of a ship from its different parts limited the possibilities—at least in the short run—for the substitution of capital for labour. Given this limited possibility of substitution of capital for labour and the presence of excess capacity relative to demand for output, it may be argued that British shipbuilders found themselves in the theoretical situation outlined above.

Cutting wages will have no effect on employment except in terms of the indirect (output) effects. These operate through lower unit costs acting to increase the quantity demanded of the final product, and will depend crucially on its price elasticity of demand. Estimation of a price elasticity for UK ships between the wars is complex. An estimate of demand for UK ships would have to take into consideration not only the prices of domestic and foreign vessels but also the likely response of foreign governments, which were heavily subsidising their own shipbuilding industries, to UK price reductions. A crude estimate of demand for UK ships between the wars suggests that the price elasticity was low.[23] A low price elasticity of demand curtails the possibility of increasing employment through the indirect effect of wage cuts on unit costs. For example, wages represented about 30 per cent of the total costs of constructing a vessel.[24] This means a 10 per cent cut in wages would enable a 3 per cent cut in prices. Assuming a price elasticity of -0.5 this would generate a 1.5 per cent increase in quantity demanded. In terms of UK output for 1921–38 this would represent an average increase of 14,000 tons per annum.[25]

---

[21] A. McKinley, 'The Inter-War Depression and the Effort Bargain: Shipyard Riveters and the "Workman's Foreman"', 1919–1939', *Scot. Econ. and Soc. Hist.*, 9 (1989), p. 55.

[22] E. Lorenz and F. Wilkinson, 'The Shipbuilding Industry 1880–1965', in B. Elbaum and W. Lazonick, eds., *The Decline of the British Economy* (Oxford, 1986), p. 116.

[23] Estimating $\ln Q = \ln A + \alpha \ln P + \beta \ln GDP$ for 1920–38 (where α is an estimator of the price elasticity of demand) the result (adjusted for serial correlation) was (t-statistics in parentheses):

$\widehat{\ln Q} = -16.362 - 0.206 \ln P + 4.071 \ln GDP$
            (2.188)   (0.403)   (2.922)
$R^2 = 0.656$

(Data from C. H. Feinstein, *National Income, Expenditure and Output of the United Kingdom, 1855–1965* (Cambridge, 1972), Tables 3, 52 and 63.)

On the low price elasticity of demand for British exports between the wars see also B. W. E. Alford, *Depression and Recovery? British Economic Growth 1918-1939* (London, 1972), pp. 35-6 and N. H. Dimsdale, 'British Monetary Policy and the Exchange Rate 1920-1938', *Oxford Economic Papers*, new series 33 (1981 Supplement), 322.

[24] A. Slaven, 'A Shipyard in Depression: John Browns of Clydebank 1919–1938', *Business History*, 19 (1977), p. 203; J. R. Parkinson, 'Shipbuilding', in N. K. Buxton and D. H. Aldcroft, eds., *British Industry between the Wars* (London, 1979), p. 88.

[25] See F. Geary and W. Johnson, 'Shipbuilding in Belfast, 1861–1986', *Ir. Econ. and Soc. Hist.*, XVI (1989), p. 55.

If, as outlined above, the possibility of using wage cuts to increase employment was limited by both the excess accumulation of capital stock relative to demand and the low price elasticity of demand, then employment should prove insensitive to real wages and be positively related to the level of output demanded. This hypothesis is tested in the following section for the Northern Ireland and Scottish regions and for the UK as a whole.

* * *

Some support for this hypothesis is in fact provided by case studies of individual yards, which indicate that overcapacity encouraged shipbuilders to reduce prices to the level of variable costs. John Browns of Clydebank, for example, made 23 successful tenders for merchant vessels between 1922 and 1928 but, in contrast to the pre-1921 position, all were at fixed price and 17 covered just material and labour costs with no provision for overhead charges.[26] Similarly in 1922 Harland and Wolff started to abandon its commission system and to build vessels at fixed prices which were almost at cost.[27]

More formally the hypothesis relates employment to output and to own-product real wage. Given the peculiar conditions between the wars of depressed demand and excess capacity, the model predicts a positive relationship between employment and output and no relationship between employment and own-product real wage. The demand for labour relationship estimated for each of Northern Ireland (1926–38), Scotland (1924–38) and the UK (1920–38) was log-linear with annual employment a function of annual current output and annual current own-product real wage:

$$\ln E_t = \ln A + \alpha \ln Q_t + \beta \ln W_t$$

where E_t is the number of persons employed at time t, Q_t is output measured in number of gross tons launched, and W_t is own-product real wage measured as a ratio of the current wage rate and the price of ships.[28] As there were no separate wage indices or prices of ships available for Northern Ireland and Scotland UK indices were used as proxies. Given the movement between the wars towards nationally agreed wage rates in shipbuilding and the competitive pricing of ships, these serve as satisfactory alternatives to regional wage and

---

[26] Slaven, 'A Shipyard in Depression', pp. 197, 201. For indications that this pattern was more widespread see Slaven, 'Growth and Stagnation', p. 23; J. M. Reid, *James Lithgow : Master of Work* (London, 1964), p. 103; Jones, *Shipbuilding in Britain*, pp. 73, 99, 103.

[27] Moss and Hume, *Shipbuilders to the World*, pp. 234, 239, 262, 267. For details of the commission system of building at cost plus builder's commission see Geary and Johnson, 'Shipbuilding in Belfast', pp. 50–2, 56. The system was finally abandoned in 1930.

[28] For further discussion of this type of employment function see Casson, *Economics of Unemployment*, pp. 166–77, and Beenstock and Warburton, 'Wages and Unemployment', pp. 156–7.

price data and should not significantly distort the results for Northern Ireland and Scotland. For purposes of estimation all data are expressed in terms of indices with 1926 = 100.[29]

The results were as follows (with t-statistics in parenthesis):

Northern Ireland, 1926–38:

$$\hat{\ln E_t} = -5.308 + 0.369 \ln Q_t + 1.693 \ln W_t$$
$$(-0.570) \quad (3.602) \quad\quad (0.848)$$
$$R^2 = 0.583; DW = 1.855$$

Scotland, 1924–38:

$$\hat{\ln E_t} = 3.521 + 0.643 \ln Q_t - 0.465 \ln W_t$$
$$(1.548) \quad (11.740) \quad\quad (-0.964)$$
$$R^2 = 0.922; DW = 1.504$$

UK, 1920–38:

$$\hat{\ln E_t} = 3.074 + 0.300 \ln Q_t + 0.062 \ln W_t$$
$$(4.943) \quad (5.533) \quad\quad (0.510)$$
$$R^2 = 0.946$$

Adjusted for serial correlation.

For Northern Ireland, Scotland and the UK as a whole the co-efficient for output was significantly different from zero at the 1 per cent level, while the co-efficient for own-product real wage was insignificantly different from zero. Explained variation (R^2) was particularly high in the case of Scotland and the UK, and there was no problem of serial correlation. The results therefore indicate that while output was an important determinant of the level of employment in interwar shipbuilding in the two regions and in the UK as a whole, the level of own-product real wage was not,[30] and so support the hypothesis outlined above.

* * *

Labour supply at the economy-wide level is given by the labour force participation rate. Traditionally aggregate labour supply is positively related to the real wage. For an industry the labour force is more difficult to define. One obvious definition

---

[29] For details see Appendix 1.
[30] While the R^2 value for Northern Ireland is lower than the values for Scotland and the UK, the DW value indicates the absence of serial correlation. With Scotland the DW value indicates the absence of serial correlation at the 1 per cent level of significance. Adjustment for serial correlation was necessary in the case of the UK.

is insured labour force in the industry.[31] Unemployment is given by the difference between labour supply and labour demand. Tables 1 and 2 indicate the relationship between labour supply, employment and unemployment in shipbuilding in the two regions in the period 1924–38.

Table 1: Numbers of insured workers, employed and unemployed, in Northern Ireland shipbuilding, 1924–38 (in thousands)

Year	Insured workers	Employed	Unemployed	Change in employed from previous year	Change in unemployed from previous year
1924	21.5	12.3	9.2		
1925	18.5	n.a.	n.a.		
1926	14.6	8.2	6.4		
1927	12.8	9.6	3.2	+0.6	-3.2
1928	11.1	6.9	4.2	-2.7	+1.0
1929	12.0	8.8	3.2	+1.9	-1.0
1930	12.4	9.2	3.2	+0.4	0.0
1931	11.6	5.1	6.5	-4.1	+3.3
1932	10.5	2.4	8.1	-2.7	+1.6
1933	8.5	1.3	7.2	-1.1	-0.9
1934	8.1	4.2	3.9	+2.9	-3.3
1935	9.2	5.1	4.1	+0.9	+0.2
1936	11.1	8.0	3.1	+2.9	-1.0
1937	9.6	7.2	2.4	-0.8	-0.7
1938	9.5	7.1	2.4	-0.1	0.0

Sources:

Isles and Cuthbert, *Economic Survey*, Statistical Appendix, Tables 9 and 13 (July figures); *Ministry of Labour Gazette*.

The fall in employment was more than matched by a fall in the labour force. In Northern Ireland between 1924 and 1937 some 5,100 jobs were lost and the labour force fell by 11,900. In Scotland a loss of 22,300 jobs was more than matched by a fall of 29,400 in the labour force. In percentage terms a 41 per cent fall in demand for labour in Northern Ireland was associated with a 55 per cent fall in the supply of labour. In Scotland a 42 per cent fall in demand for labour was associated with a 41 per cent fall in the supply of labour.

This decline in the shipbuilding labour force occurred despite a relative rise in the shipbuilding wage.[32] Figures 2 and 3 illustrate the relationship between the size

---

[31] In using figures on the insured labour force it is important to note that workers are recorded as unemployed in a particular industry only if they were last employed in it, not if they are seeking work in it for the first time (Isles and Cuthbert, *Economic Survey of Northern Ireland*, p. 236).

[32] This should not be allowed to obscure the absolute fall in shipbuilding wages, which in 1938 were 29 per cent below their 1920 level (B. R. Mitchell, *British Historical Statistics* (Cambridge, 1988), p. 160). See also Slaven, 'A Shipyard in Depression', p. 205.

of the insured labour force and the shipbuilding wage rate relative to the average wage in each region.[33] Despite an increase in the relative shipbuilding wage in each region the labour force unequivocally declined. Diminished probability of employment therefore appears to have outweighed remuneration in consideration of labour supply to shipbuilding. Similarly, given the elastic response of labour supply to the fall in demand for labour, it seems unlikely that the payment of unemployment benefit substantially discouraged the mobility of the shipbuilding labour force.

Table 2: Numbers of insured workers, employed and unemployed, in Scottish shipbuilding, 1924–38 (in thousands)

Year	Insured workers	Employed	Unemployed	Change in employed from previous year	Change in unemployed from previous year
1924	71.6	53.7	17.9		
1925	63.5	41.4	22.1	-12.3	+4.2
1926	64.6	36.7	27.9	-4.7	+5.8
1927	57.5	46.2	11.3	+9.5	-16.6
1928	57.4	42.9	14.5	-3.3	+3.2
1929	55.8	43.9	11.9	+1.0	-2.6
1930	56.4	39.0	17.4	-4.9	+5.5
1931	54.4	18.5	35.9	-20.5	+18.5
1932	49.9	12.1	37.8	-6.4	+1.9
1933	45.1	11.4	33.7	-0.7	-4.1
1934	42.0	19.1	22.9	+7.7	-10.8
1935	41.0	21.2	19.8	+2.1	-3.1
1936	42.3	28.5	13.8	+7.3	-6.0
1937	42.2	31.4	10.8	+2.9	-3.0
1938	46.7	36.8	9.9	+5.4	-0.9

Source:
Buxton, 'Scottish Shipbuilding', Appendix I.

This lack of attachment of its labour force meant that despite the decline in demand for labour in the shipbuilding industry, unemployment in shipbuilding fell over the period from a collective rate in the two regions of 29 per cent in 1924 to 25 per cent in 1937. In the absence of this flexibility in the labour force unemployment rates would have been much higher: 66 per cent in Northern Ireland and 56 per cent in Scotland. Thus the relatively high unemployment in shipbuilding should not be allowed to obscure the mobility of the labour

---

[33] As there were no separate wage rate data for Scotland, UK data were used for both shipbuilding and general wage rates. Given the increase in nationally negotiated wage rates since 1900, it is unlikely that there would have been much divergence between Scottish and UK general rates, while wage rates in Scottish shipbuilding corresponded fairly closely to those for the UK as a whole. (See D. J. Robertson, 'Wages', in A. K. Cairncross, ed., *The Scottish Economy* (Cambridge, 1954), pp. 149–51 and 163–4).

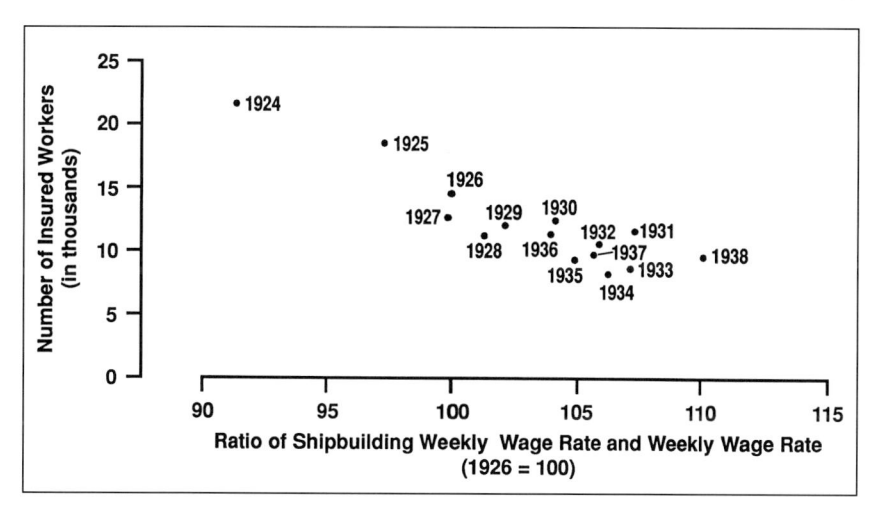

Figure 2: Northern Ireland shipbuilding: number of insured workers and ratio of shipbuilding weekly wage rate and weekly wage rate, 1924–38.

Sources: Mitchell, British Historical Statistics, p. 160; Isles and Cuthbert, Economic Survey, Statistical Appendix, table 36; table 1 above.

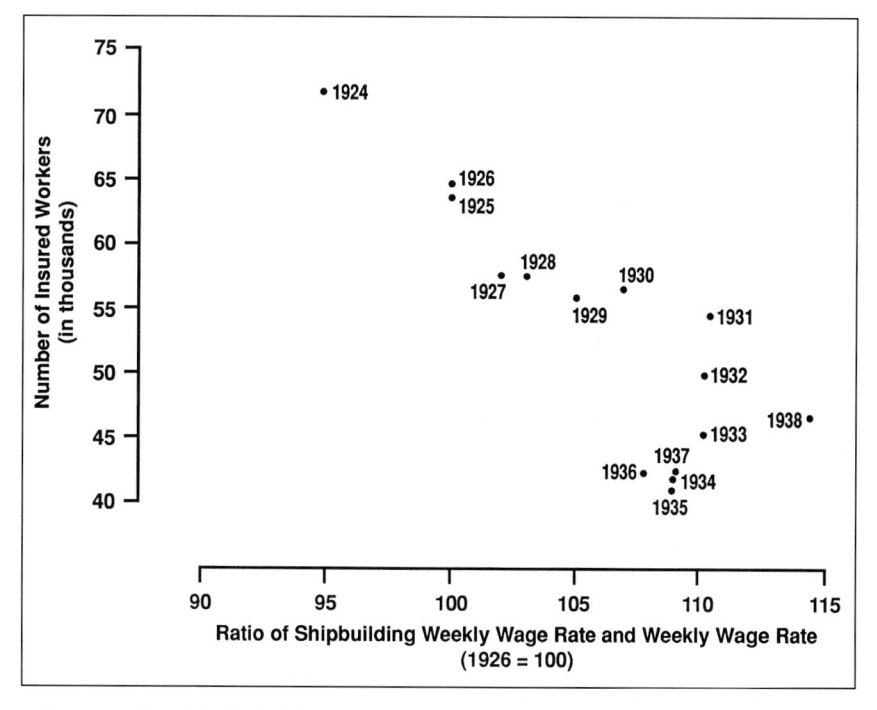

Figure 3: Scottish shipbuilding: number of insured workers and ratio of shipbuilding weekly wage rate and weekly wage rate, 1924–38.

Sources: Mitchell, British Historical Statistics, p. 160; Isles and Cuthbert, Economic Survey, Statistical Appendix, table 36; table 2 above.

force. This mobility occurred as we have seen despite a relative improvement in shipbuilding wages. An explanation then may be sought in the collapse in demand for shipbuilding labour. Of the 40 or so trades in the shipbuilding labour force only the shipwrights and the five trades of the 'black squad' had skills peculiar to shipbuilding. One estimate puts them at 50 per cent of the labour force in any yard.[34] The remainder had readily transferable skills and 'when activity declined in the shipyards, these particular craftsmen looked for work in those industries which had previously given them employment'.[35] In the long run as this decline in activity persisted the insured labour force fell. This process is illustrated in Tables 1 and 2. In the short run changes in employment were accompanied by corresponding changes in unemployment.[36] That they were not exactly corresponding arises from the fact that yards were drawing on labour from other insured populations, and other industries were drawing on the insured shipyard labour force. So, for example, in 1925, when Scottish shipbuilding employment fell by 12.3 thousand, shipbuilding unemployment rose by only 4.2 thousand, and in 1927, when employment rose by 9.5 thousand, unemployment fell by 16.6 thousand. Thus in the short run a fall in employment led to a rise in unemployment and vice versa. However in the long run a fall in employment led to a greater fall in the insured labour force and hence to a fall in unemployment. Changes in unemployment resulted then from changes in both employment and the insured labour force. Employment we have argued was determined by demand for ships. Thus in the short run changes in unemployment in shipbuilding resulted primarily from changes in demand. In the long run changes in demand for ships decreased both employment and the size of the insured labour force.

* * *

The negative relationship between real wage and employment, found by some writers for manufacturing and for the economy as a whole in the interwar years, was not found in the case of shipbuilding for Northern Ireland, Scotland or the UK. We found that the excess capacity relative to demand which existed in the British shipbuilding industry after 1920 meant that there was a limited possibility for the substitution of labour for capital in the interwar period, and that wage cuts would have had little impact on the demand for ships and hence for labour. Given these peculiar conditions, we found a significant positive relationship between employment and output, and a zero relationship between employment and own-product

---

[34] S. Price, 'Rivetters' Earnings in Clyde Shipbuilding, 1889–1913', *Scot. Econ. and Soc. Hist.*, 1 (1981), p. 43.

[35] Jones, *Shipbuilding in Britain*, p. 161.

[36] The co-efficient of correlation between annual changes in employment and annual changes in unemployment was -0.800 in the case of Northern Ireland (1926–38) and -0.913 for Scotland (1924–38). Each of these co-efficients was significantly different from zero at the 1 per cent level.

real wage. Consequently the argument that unemployment in shipbuilding was classical in nature and was 'caused' by costs and real wages being too high was not supported by the evidence. As workers were not therefore pricing themselves out of employment, the classical solution to this unemployment of reducing costs by cutting wages was not an option for British shipbuilding firms in Northern Ireland, Scotland or the UK as a whole.

In the long run, however, total unemployment in shipbuilding in Northern Ireland and Scotland did decline. Despite a relative rise in the shipbuilding wage, the fall in employment was more than matched by a fall in the total labour force, which reflected the diminished probability of obtaining work in the industry. Although these transfers of labour from shipbuilding did occur 'naturally', Booth and Glynn have argued that what was required in the case of Britain's interwar unemployment problem was

> a comprehensive regional policy promoted by the central government in order to ease the transfer of resources from the export-oriented industries.[37]

However, this transfer would not have been so necessary in the case of shipbuilding had it not been for the drastic reduction in demand. General or indiscriminate reflation of the economy would not have helped. Even Keynes in 1937 argued that rigidities in the economy meant that

> building activity in the home counties is less effective than one might have hoped in decreasing unemployment in the distressed areas. It follows that the later stages of recovery require a different technique. To remedy the condition of the distressed areas, *ad hoc* measures are necessary. The Jarrow marchers were, so to speak, theoretically correct. The Government have been wrong in their reluctance to accept the strenuous *ad hoc* measures recommended by those in close touch with the problem.[38]

Among these *ad hoc* measures in the case of shipbuilding and shipping services might have been those pursued by Britain's rivals, namely, 'national and municipal subsidies, operational subsidies, mail contracts, grants in aid for the replacement of obsolete tonnage, relief from the burden of rates and taxes, loans for the modernisation of plant, and differential building subsidies'.[39] Instead of facilitating the transfer of resources out of shipbuilding and shipping services, these would have promoted demand and provided a measure of protection for the British maritime industries on which employment in Northern Ireland and Scotland was so heavily dependent.

---

[37] A. E. Booth and S. Glynn, 'Unemployment in the Interwar Period: A Multiple Problem', *Journal of Contemporary History*, 10 (1975), p. 625.

[38] J. M. Keynes, 'How to Avoid a Slump', *The Times*, 12 January 1937, in D. M. Moggridge, ed., *The Collected Writings of John Maynard Keynes*, Vol. XXI (London, 1982), p. 385.

[39] Jones, *Shipbuilding in Britain*, p. 63.

APPENDIX I

The index for Northern Ireland shipbuilding employment is from K. S. Isles and N. Cuthbert, *An Economic Survey of Northern Ireland* (Belfast, 1957), Statistical Appendix, Table 22, using the July figure for each of the years 1926–38, where July 1926 = 100. The index for Scottish shipbuilding employment for 1924–38 has been compiled from N. K. Buxton, 'The Scottish Shipbuilding Industry Between the Wars: A Comparative Study', *Business History*, 10 (1968), Appendix I, and for the UK 1920–38 from A. L. Chapman and R. Knight, *Wages and Salaries in the United Kingdom* (Cambridge, 1953), Table 44.

The index for Northern Ireland output has been compiled from data in Appendix II. The index for Scottish output has been compiled from Buxton, 'Scottish Shipbuilding Industry', Appendix I, Mercantile Tonnage, and that for the UK from C. H. Feinstein, *National Income, Expenditure and Output of the United Kingdom, 1855–1965* (Cambridge, 1972), Table 52.

The index of own-product real wage has been compiled from the shipbuilding and repairing weekly wage rates in B. R. Mitchell, *British Historical Statistics* (Cambridge, 1988), p. 160, Table B, and from the index of the price of ships in Feinstein, *National Income, Expenditure and Output*, Table 63.

As regional data are not available for weekly wage rates and the price of ships, national data were used to estimate the own-product real wage for Northern Ireland and for Scotland. The weekly wage rates in Mitchell cover time workers only, as there is insufficient information for the piece workers who played an important role in the shipbuilding iron and steel trades. Although there were regional differences in time rates for skilled men and labourers, these were reduced in 1930 when the National Uniform Wage Scheme came into operation (Jones, *Shipbuilding in Britain*, p. 177). In the case of Northern Ireland the rates for the skilled shipwrights and joiners, which had been respectively 4. 4 per cent and 4. 9 per cent above the average UK rates in 1923, had become uniform throughout the country for shipwrights in 1931 and for joiners in 1936; while labourers in Northern Ireland shipyards actually received the same rates of pay as in the UK as a whole in 1923, 1924 and 1936 (Isles and Cuthbert, *Economic Survey of Northern Ireland*, pp. 217–18).

APPENDIX II

Belfast shipbuilding, output, 1926–38 (in thousands of gross tons launched)

Year	Harland & Wolff	Workman Clark	Total*
1926	65.7	26.6	92.3
1927	62.4	49.2	111.6
1928	75.4	0.4	75.7
1929	91.3	52.9	144.1
1930	117.8	54.9	172.7
1931	62.0	33.2	95.2
1932	nil	5.7	5.7
1933	nil	13.8	13.8
1934	54.4	29.0	83.4
1935	102.1		102.1
1936	62.5		62.5
1937	74.4		74.4
1938	79.8		79.8

* The combined output of the two firms may not sum to the total because of rounding.

Sources: M. Moss and J. R. Hume, *Shipbuilders to the World: 125 Years of Harland and Wolff, Belfast 1861–1986* (Belfast, 1986), Ship List; Workman Clark (1928) Ltd., *Shipbuilding at Belfast 1880–1933* (London, n.d.).

20

Employers and policymaking: Scotland and Northern Ireland, c.1880–1939

Eleanor Gordon and Richard Trainor

IN CONTRAST TO THE VIEW which dominated academic literature and popular consciousness for much of this century, recent analyses have stressed the relative political impotence of 'provincial' industrial employers in comparison with the leverage exercised by metropolitan financial and commercial elites and their landed allies.[1] Despite different causal emphases, the confluence of opinion is that the British state pursued policies, particularly those of free trade and sound money, which favoured the economic interests of internationally-oriented finance and commerce and disadvantaged industrial employers, thereby damaging the long-term interests of the economy as a whole.[2] Even those who accept that within their own localities industrial manufacturers had considerable political influence argue that from the end of the nineteenth century the locus of political power was increasingly concentrated in Westminster.[3] These views dovetail with the widely

---

[1] P. Anderson, 'Origins of the Present Crisis', *New Left Review*, XXIII (1964); B. Elbaum and W. Lazonick, *The Decline of the British Economy: An Institutional Perspective* (Oxford, 1986); G. Ingham, *Capitalism Divided? The City and Industry in British Social Development* (London, 1984); F. Longstreth, 'The City, Industry and the State', in C. Crouch, ed., *State and Economy in Contemporary Capitalism* (London, 1979); W. D. Rubinstein, *Elites and the Wealthy in Modern British History: Essays in Social and Economic History* (Brighton, 1987); M. J. Wiener, *English Culture and the Decline of the Industrial Spirit 1850–1980* (Cambridge, 1981).

[2] W. L. Guttsman, *The British Political Elite* (London, 1963); S. Pollard, ed., *The Gold Standard and Employment Policies between the Wars* (London, 1970), introduction; E. J. Hobsbawm, *Industry and Empire* (Harmondsworth, 1968); Longstreth, 'The City, Industry and the State'; Ingham, *Capitalism Divided*; P. J. Cain and A. G. Hopkins, 'Gentlemanly Capitalism and British Expansion Overseas, II: New Imperialism 1850–1945', *Econ. Hist. Rev.*, 2nd ser., XL (1987); Elbaum and Lazonick,*The Decline of the British Economy*; Rubinstein, 'Cultural Explanations for Britain's Economic Decline: How True?', in B. Collins and K. Robbins, eds., *British Culture and Economic Decline* (London, 1990).

[3] A. Briggs, *Victorian Cities* (London, 1963); D. Fraser, *Power and Authority in the Victorian City* (Oxford, 1979). For the argument that manufacturers had little impact even in industrial towns see J. A. Garrard, *Leadership in Victorian Industrial Towns 1830–1880* (Manchester, 1983).

held assumption that in the regions, as in the metropolis, finance and commerce held the upper hand economically.[4]

This analysis is doubly distorted, first because it is based largely on evidence drawn from London-centred national studies, and second by its origins in a debate about Britain's relative economic decline.[5] Both of these distortions entail neglect of the regional dimension. Britain's economic development involved a high level of regional specialisation, paralleled by significant regional variations in political cultures and social structures.[6] Thus a regional perspective is required in order to give a more rounded and fuller picture of the nature and extent of industrial employers' influence on policy during the period between the late nineteenth century and the outbreak of the Second World War.[7]

As 'peripheral' regions containing significant shares of UK industry, especially of heavy industries which grew rapidly and then faced drastic contraction during the period,[8] Scotland and Northern Ireland are highly relevant to these debates. Although from 1885 Scotland, and from 1921 Northern Ireland, enjoyed measures of devolution, the latter's significant limits—confined to London-based administration in Scotland's case before 1939, and hedged in with 'reservations' to Westminster of power over wide areas of Northern Irish policy[9]—ensure that a study of these two major parts of the United Kingdom has considerable relevance to other regions. This paper, like the project out of which it has grown,[10] will concentrate on

---

[4] W. D. Rubinstein, 'Wealth, Elites and the Class Structure of Modern Britain', *Past and Present*, 76 (1977); 'The Victorian Middle Classes: Wealth, Occupation and Geography', *Econ. Hist. Rev.*, 2nd ser., XXX (1977).

[5] This interpretation currently holds sway, but is not uncontested. Certain works attempt to reinsert industrial employers into the nexus of social and political power, such as: D. Nicholls, 'Fractions of Capital: The Aristocracy, City and Industry and the Development of Modern British Capitalism', *Social History*, XIII (1988); M. J. Daunton, '"Gentlemanly Capitalism" and British Industry 1820–1914', *Past and Present*, 122 (1989), p. 134; S. Gunn, 'The Failure of the Victorian Middle Class: a Critique', in J. Wolff and J. Seed, eds., *The Culture of Capital: Art, Power and the Nineteenth-Century Middle Class* (Manchester, 1988); A. Howe, *The Cotton Masters 1820–1860* (Oxford, 1984); R. H. Trainor, 'Urban Elites in Victorian Britain', *Urban History Yearbook* (1985), and 'The Gentrification of Victorian and Edwardian Industrialists', in A. L. Beier et al, eds., *The First Modern Society: Essays in Honour of Lawrence Stone* (Cambridge, 1989).

[6] P. Hudson, ed., *Regions and Industries: A Perspective on the Industrial Revolution in Britain* (Cambridge, 1989); K. Burgess, 'Authority Relations and the Division of Labour in British Industry, with Special Reference to Clydeside, 1860–1930', *Social History*, XI (1986).

[7] For a pioneering collection of essays (tending to emphasise business disunity and impotence) on the relations between business and government see J. Turner, ed., *Businessmen and Politics* (London, 1984).

[8] D. S. Johnson, 'The Northern Ireland Economy, 1914–39', in L. Kennedy and P. Ollerenshaw, eds., *An Economic History of Ulster 1820–1940* (Manchester, 1985), p. 208; R. B. Weir, 'Structural Change and Diversification in Ireland and Scotland', in Mitchison and Roebuck, p. 299.

[9] P. Buckland, *The Factory of Grievances: Devolved Government in Northern Ireland 1921–39* (Dublin, 1979); Weir, 'Structural Change', p. 299.

[10] 'The Role of Employers in Economic and Social Policy Formation 1880–1939: A Regional Perspective', *Business History Newsletter*, 20 (1990), pp. 3–4, outlining the preliminary findings of a research project supported by the Economic and Social Research Council.

Scotland, using Northern Ireland as a comparator. Within Scotland the focus will be on west central Scotland, the most significant industrial region and the source both of the majority of Scotland's MPs and of many of its leading businessmen-politicians.

As office is not synonymous with influence and power, this article will be less concerned with positional analysis than with scrutiny of the role played by employers in policy formation. In examining this role the chapter is particularly concerned to establish employers' policy preferences, which are often assumed rather than systematically explored. In looking at the tactics and influence as well as the views of industrial employers in policy formation the paper is primarily interested in economic policy,[11] especially protective tariffs and the gold standard, key issues which supposedly were decided against the interests of provincial industry. Exploration of the role played by provincial employers in policy will be pursued not only in their own organisations such as employers' associations and chambers of commerce, but also in local and national politics. In order to take account of influence behind the scenes, the paper will also look at informal channels of communication and influence between industrialists and government.

* * *

Most industry-based employers' associations were only infrequently concerned with national economic policy; their agendas were largely concerned with labour questions. The exception was the Federation of British Industries (FBI), a national employers' organisation whose primary role was to represent to government employers' views on all aspects of finance, commerce and trade.[12] Consequently in order to focus on regions the emphasis here is on chambers of commerce, local organisations which, in addition to providing services to individual members, were advocates to governmental bodies of the interests of the entire business community, including manufacturing industry.[13]

---

[11] The project from which this article arises also deals with social policy, especially education. For recent indications that industrial employers influenced social legislation, see: S. Blackburn, 'Employers and Social Policy: Black Country Chain-Masters, the Minimum Wage Campaign and the Cradley Heath Strike of 1910', *Midland History*, XII (1987); R. Fitzgerald, *British Labour Management and Industrial Welfare 1846–1939* (Beckenham, 1988), pp. 212–48. For an emphasis on the industrialists' lack of influence, see for example (with particular reference to labour policy) A. J. Reid, 'The Division of Labour and Politics in Britain, 1880–1920', in W. J. Mommsen, and H. G. Husung, eds., *The Development of Trade Unionism in Great Britain and Germany, 1880–1914* (London, 1985), pp. 162–3.

[12] T. Rogers, 'Employers' Organisations, Unemployment and Social Politics in Britain during the Interwar Period', *Social History*, XIII (1988). For an emphasis on the weakness of the FBI before 1939, see S. Blank, *Industry and Government in Britain: The Federation of British Industries in Politics, 1945–65*, ch. 2.

[13] See for example: G. Chambers, *Faces of Change: The Belfast and Northern Ireland Chambers of Commerce and Industry 1783–1983* (Belfast, 1983); C. A. Oakley, *Our Illustrious Forbears* [Glasgow Chamber of Commerce] (Glasgow, 1980); G. H. Wright, *Chronicles of the Birmingham Commercial Society and Chamber of Commerce AD 1783–1913* (Birmingham, 1913).

The standard conception of chambers of commerce is that they represented the interests of merchants, traders and small scale or minor manufacturers.[14] Undoubtedly the numerous ordinary members of the Glasgow chamber, like their counterparts in Belfast, stretched across a broad range of size as well as type of business.[15] However, an analysis of the office-bearers (presidents, directors and convenors of committees) of Glasgow Chamber of Commerce reveals that manufacturers were numerous and influential in these leadership roles, which attracted such major employers as Michael Connal, Charles Tennant, Sir Samuel Beale, Lord Weir, Sir Steven Bilsland and Colonel John Colville.[16] Likewise many industrial employers' organisations were affiliated to the chamber and nominated representatives on the board of directors, notably the Clyde Shipbuilders Association, the Lanarkshire Coalmasters Association and the North-West Engineering Trades Association.[17] Similarly, the Belfast chamber of commerce attracted an increasing number of major industrialists during the later nineteenth century.[18]

Well represented in the chambers as industrialists were, they did not sit there as members of discrete industrial groups. Indeed one of the most significant points to emerge from the scrutiny of membership rolls and the biographical details of office-bearers is the difficulty of categorising individuals into neatly bounded occupational categories. A striking feature of leading members of the chambers is the diversity of their business interests, cutting across the sectors which in the literature are usually presented as distinct. For instance, Glasgow's Sir Samuel Beale sat on the board of nineteen different companies, including the engineers Mavor and Coulson, the Bank of Scotland and Scottish Amicable Life Assurance. More generally, this diversity is reflected in respondents to the questionnaire sent out to Glasgow chamber members in 1904, thirty-nine of whom described their business activity as a combination of two or more of the designated categories of importer, exporter, manufacturer, shipowner and dealer.[19]

The confluence of different types of business activity evident in these chamber leaders is paralleled in the relationship between the two sectors most often portrayed as conflictual, industry and finance. The supposed separation of industry and finance has frequently been cited as *prima facie* evidence of the dualism in

---

[14] A. R. Illersic and P. F. B. Liddle, *Parliament of Commerce: The Story of the Association of British Chambers of Commerce 1896–1960* (London, 1960).

[15] P. Ollerenshaw, 'Industry 1820–1914', in Kennedy and Ollerenshaw, eds., *An Economic History of Ulster*, pp. 65–6.

[16] Mitchell Library Glasgow and Glasgow Chamber of Commerce, Minutes and Annual Reports of the Glasgow Chamber of Commerce; biographical information from: A. Slaven and S. G. Checkland, eds., *Dictionary of Scottish Business Biography*, 2 vols (Aberdeen, 1986, 1990); *Post Office Directories*; *Scottish Biographies 1938*; *Glasgow Contemporaries* (1901); *Who Was Who*; *Who's Who in Glasgow* (1909); *Lanarkshire Leaders* (1908); *The Baillie*.

[17] Annual Reports of Glasgow Chamber of Commerce.

[18] Chambers, *Faces of Change*.

[19] Glasgow Chamber of Commerce Annual Report 1904, p. 502. In addition, twenty-one of the 'manufacturers' were also 'directly interested' in exporting, importing or both.

Britain between industrial capitalism on the one hand, and financial and commercial capitalism on the other, a dualism which, it is claimed, has worked to the disadvantage of industry. However, in Scotland the connection between industry and banks was close; *de facto* long-term loans at short-term interest rates were prevalent throughout the period.[20] Industry and finance were also tightly linked in Northern Ireland. As Ollerenshaw has shown, in the nineteenth century Irish banks in general and Belfast banks in particular were more responsive to the credit requirements of industry than has usually been understood.[21] In the period after partition links between industry and finance were even closer because of the 1922 Loans Guarantee Act whereby the government guaranteed and negotiated loans made by banks and insurance companies for capital projects. As the shipbuilding industry was the prime beneficiary of this policy, the banks were significantly represented on the boards of shipbuilding and shipping companies such as Harland and Wolff.[22] Likewise, the economic leaders of these regions had links to the City itself, notably in the case of the shipbuilder Sir James Lithgow, who played a key role, in alliance with City bankers, in the reorganisation of the Scottish steel industry in the 1930s.[23] Recent research suggests that close Scottish and Northern Irish links between banks and industry applied to some extent in England as well.[24] While in Britain these sectors were not so close as in the European system of investment banks, they were by no means discrete and separate.

The policy viewpoints of Scottish and Northern Irish chambers reflected not only the strength of industrialists but also their integration with other leading business interests. For example, the Glasgow chamber was unanimous in its adherence to the Stop-Spending Movement after the First World War, aimed at curbing government expenditure, particularly on the civil service, and so reducing the burden of income tax.[25] On more controversial issues, divisions within the chambers did not coincide with neat occupational categories, as illustrated by the tariff issue.

---

[20] S. G. Checkland, *Scottish Banking: A History 1695–1973* (London, 1975); C. W. Munn, 'Aspects of Bank Finance for Industry: Scotland 1845–1914', in Mitchison and Roebuck; *idem, Clydesdale Bank: The First One Hundred and Fifty Years* (London, 1988).

[21] P. Ollerenshaw, *Banking in Nineteenth-Century Ireland* (London, 1987).

[22] P. Bew et al, *The State in Northern Ireland 1921–72: Political Forces and Social Classes* (Manchester, 1979), p. 91; Buckland, *The Factory of Grievances*, p. 116.

[23] S. Tolliday, *Business, Banking and Politics: The Case of British Steel* (London 1987), p. 81 and *passim*; A. Slaven, 'Sir James Lithgow', in *Dictionary of Scottish Business Biography*, I, pp. 222–7.

[24] Cf. Daunton, 'Gentlemanly Capitalism', p. 134; S. Diaper, 'The Sterling Combine and the Shipbuilding Industry: Merchant banking and Industrial Finance in the 1920s'; D. Ross, 'The Clearing Banks and Industry: New Perspectives on the Inter-War Years', in J. J. Van Helten and Y. Cassis, eds., *Capitalism in a Mature Economy: Financial Institutions, Capital Exports and British Industry 1870–1939* (Aldershot, 1990).

[25] *Glasgow Chamber of Commerce Journal*, 1920. This was the one issue which united the FBI, which consistently spoke out against government extravagance and interference (L. J. Hume, 'The Gold Standard and Deflation: Issues and Attitudes in the 1920s', in Pollard, ed., *Gold Standard*, p. 139).

One of the key arguments adduced to illustrate the precedence of financial and commercial interests over industrial interests is the failure of successive governments to introduce protective tariffs. It has tended to be asserted rather than proven that industry favoured tariffs, perceiving a clear economic advantage.

With regard to contemporary regional views on the issue, neither consensus nor conflict was based in disagreements between industrialists and other major business sectors. Before the First World War the Glasgow chamber generally maintained an anti-tariff position which embraced industrialists as well as financiers and merchants. This was not surprising as west central Scotland's economy pivoted on the staple export industries which are generally thought to have benefited from unrestricted free trade.[26] Yet when unflinching commitment to free trade began to weaken at the turn of the century, one of the first leading members to question the sanctity of the principle was George Handasyde Dick, an East India merchant whose business interests were exclusively concerned with trade and commerce. In his presidential address to the chamber in 1901 he espoused the somewhat heretical viewpoint that 'Neither Free Trade nor Protection are axiomatic principles. They are but questions of expediency.'[27] Nonetheless, further movement on the issue did not result in vigorous promotion of protectionism: at a special meeting of the chamber in 1904 a motion calling for a royal commission on fiscal policy was passed in preference to a stronger one which favoured a retaliatory policy, the halfway house position advocated by Balfour.[28] Support for protective tariffs gained ground during the war, when there was great concern about the prospect of intense post-war economic rivalry. However, a 1916 survey attracted only a small response which, in favouring by four to one a variety of tariff measures, revealed no significant split even between merchants and the membership at large.[29] The defeat of Germany pushed the tariff question into the background and it did not predominate in chamber discussions in the 1920s.

Patterns and trends on the issue were similar in Northern Ireland, though in Ulster concern with tariffs was often subsumed into the Belfast chamber's obsession with Home Rule, a policy which the chamber felt would destroy its effective representational role in relation to commercial and industrial questions.[30] In the Belfast chamber enthusiasm for tariffs gained more ground than in Glasgow between the 1880s and 1914, but occasional disagreements on the issue evidently did not coincide with any fissure between industrialists and other members.[31]

---

[26] A. Slaven, *The Development of the West of Scotland 1750–1960* (London, 1975), ch. 7.

[27] Glasgow Chamber of Commerce Annual Report 1901.

[28] Glasgow Chamber of Commerce Annual Report 1904.

[29] Appendix to Glasgow Chamber of Commerce Annual Report 1916.

[30] On these preoccupations see: Chambers, *Faces of Change*, pp. 193–4, 197ff, 223ff, 234ff, 237; *Mr Gladstone and the Belfast Chamber of Commerce* (Belfast, 1893). We are grateful to Dr P. Ollerenshaw for the latter reference.

[31] Chambers, *Faces of Change*, pp. 173, 191–2, 220, 249.

Beyond these regions, as well as within them, the complex pattern of opinion on tariffs did not coincide with sectoral boundaries. In Birmingham, a stronghold of the protectionist movement from an early date, where support for tariff reform was less equivocal than in Glasgow and Belfast, backing for tariffs straddled economic interests, encompassing significant segments of the mercantile community.[32] In Britain as a whole the tariff question also divided individual industries, even iron and steel; there were also disagreements between heavy steelmakers and those industrialists whose production costs would rise if steel obtained protective tariffs.[33] Similarly, organisations such as the FBI had difficulty sustaining a consensus on the issue.[34] So it cannot be concluded that a united front by industry regarding tariffs was frustrated by the City and the politicians.

Only after the war, and then gradually and incompletely, did a general industrial consensus develop in favour of protection, as reflected for example in the stance of the Glasgow chamber and the FBI. This delay is not surprising. The economic case for protectionism had not been irrefutably demonstrated and, like present-day cliometricians, many early twentieth-century businessmen remained to be convinced. It seems implausible to conclude that the protracted and patchy emergence of a coherent strategy about tariffs by industrialists demonstrates their political impotence, especially when the benefits of such a strategy were at best uncertain and might actually have been negative for important sections of industry.[35]

Nor did industry have particular difficulty making up its mind about tariffs. There were disagreements on the issue even within the City, where some merchants with imperial interests had supported tariff reform as early as the 1880s.[36] In addition to the interlocking of financial with industrial interests, such diversity stemmed from the fact that, as Marrison has argued, positions on the tariff question were not always determined by narrowly defined economic interests but often reflected views on the long-term development of the economy and broader political positions.[37] Thus tariffs were as likely to be difficult issues for politicians as they were for manufacturers and financiers.

---

[32] B. H. Brown, *The Tariff Reform Movement in Great Britain 1881–1895* (New York, 1943), pp. 16–17, 19, 72, 135, 140; Wright, *Chronicles*, passim.

[33] S. Tolliday, *Business, Banking and Politics*, ch. 12; F. Capie, 'The Pressure for Tariff Protection in Britain, 1917–31', *Journal of European Economic History*, IX (1980), pp. 435–6.

[34] R. F. Holland, 'The Federation of British Industries and the International Economy, 1929–39', *Econ. Hist. Rev.*, 2nd ser., XXXIV (1981), p. 228.

[35] See for example: F. Capie, 'The British Tariff and Industrial Protection in the 1930s', *Econ. Hist. Rev.*, 2nd ser., XXXI (1978); M. Kitson and S. Solomou, *Protectionism and Economic Revival: The British Interwar Economy* (Cambridge, 1990); and debate in *Econ. Hist. Rev.*, 2nd ser., XLIV (1991).

[36] Daunton, '"Gentlemanly Capitalism"'; P. Thane, 'Financiers and the British State: The Case of Sir Ernest Cassell', *Business History*, XXVIII (1986); J. Harris and P. Thane, 'British and European Bankers, 1880–1914', in Thane and G. Crossick, eds., *The Power of the Past* (Cambridge 1984); Brown, *Tariff Reform Movement*, p. 91.

[37] A. J. Marrison, 'Businessmen, Industries and Tariff Reform in Great Britain, 1903–1930', *Business History*, XXV (1983).

Another common misconception in the 'hegemony of finance' argument is that the decision to return to the gold standard in 1925 was taken over the vigorous objections of British industry. However, the evidence from the Glasgow chamber, the Association of Chambers of Commerce and the FBI confounds this position. Ever since Britain had gone off the gold standard, the Glasgow chamber, echoing the position of the 1919 Cunliffe Committee, adopted the policy of a return to gold at the appropriate time as the best strategy to boost economic prosperity.[38] When in 1925 Britain returned to the gold standard at prewar parity, the decision was applauded by the chamber with the observation that

> it should not be assumed by the most fervent advocate that the re-opening of the gold market for international payments will be all plain sailing and entirely without drawbacks, but long and broad views must be taken, and it will be surprising if the ultimate result is not entirely beneficial to British industry and commerce.[39]

Although there was some opposition within the FBI to economic orthodoxy as embodied in the Cunliffe Committee, criticism centred more on general deflationary policies than on the return to gold, to which the Federation gave a qualified welcome. Moreover, the return to gold had its critics within the City itself.[40] More generally, the Glasgow chamber, in common with the Belfast chamber,[41] the UK Association and the FBI, generally adhered to the major economic orthodoxies of the time: sound money and balanced budgets. Thus their views on economic issues tended to be in harmony with the governments of the day rather than in opposition to them.

Having established that manufacturers played a significant role, in alliance with leaders from overlapping sectors, in developing policy viewpoints within the key business organisations of two major regions, it is now necessary to examine how far such provincial opinions on public policy were successfully transmitted outside business organisations—that is, to politicians at local and national level.

* * *

Quite apart from their continuing substantial presence in the still highly significant sphere of local government institutions such as Glasgow Corporation,[42] employers played a prominent role in the west of Scotland's parliamentary politics. For

---

[38] Glasgow Chamber of Commerce Annual Reports and *Glasgow Chamber of Commerce Journal, passim.*
[39] *Glasgow Chamber of Commerce Journal*, May 1925.
[40] Hume, 'The Gold Standard', pp. 139, 142–4 and *passim.*
[41] For its support for cuts in government spending see Ollerenshaw, 'Textiles and Regional Economic Decline: Northern Ireland 1914–1970' (unpublished paper).
[42] N. Morgan and R. Trainor, 'The Dominant Classes', in W. H. Fraser and R. J. Morris, eds., *People and Society in Scotland*, Volume II: *1830–1914* (Edinburgh, 1990), pp. 128–9; Strathclyde Regional Archives and Paisley Public Library, Minutes and Annual Reports of Glasgow and Paisley School Boards, 1872–1926. For similar trends in Belfast see Chambers, *Faces of Change*, p. 171.

example, in 1886–7 Glasgow Conservative Association numbered at least eight manufacturers among its twenty-two officebearers with traceable occupations. Similarly, of the fifteen officebearers of the Western Organising Committee of the Scottish Liberal Federation in 1913 whose occupations are known, thirteen were businessmen, at least five of whom were primarily manufacturers.[43] Such well placed businessmen were likely to obtain a sympathetic hearing for business interests, whatever the occupations of the MPs themselves. Nonetheless, their task was easier in the substantial number of Scottish constituencies represented by businessmen, especially in urban areas before the interwar advance of Labour.[44]

Contrary to existing views about Scottish MPs, they attained office frequently.[45] Of the Scottish members of parliament serving between 1868 and 1945, just over a quarter held ministerial office or served as parliamentary private secretaries; of this group, more than half held at least one UK rather than Scottish post.[46] These MPs were useful conduits, though not cyphers, for the views of industrialists. Glasgow chamber of commerce frequently and often successfully lobbied MPs to persuade them to argue their case in parliament, notably with regard to commercial treaties. Similarly the mediations of the chamber on occasion provided individual firms with a sympathetic MP to lobby on their behalf.[47] Reliance on MPs to represent the interests of industrialists was facilitated by the fact that a significant number of western Scotland's parliamentarians had been or were members of the chamber, were businessmen themselves, or had significant local ties. Almost two thirds of west of Scotland MPs had such local connections, and more than a quarter of those with known occupations were themselves businessmen on a strict definition which excludes the professions and those with industrial investments only. The looser criterion of business interests embraces eighteen (at least five of whom were primarily manufacturers) of twenty-five west of Scotland MPs in 1900 for whom information is available.

It was not only backbench MPs to whom the chamber had access. A number of former chamber luminaries went on to occupy high government office and play a prominent role in national politics. Bonar Law was still a chamber member when he was deputy prime minister to Lloyd George; Joseph Maclay, a shipowner and a chamber member, became minister of shipping in 1916; William Weir, a chamber director, was secretary of state and president of the Air Council in 1918. Robert Horne, who became minister of labour immediately after the First World War and

---

[43] Edinburgh University Library, Scottish Liberal Association General Minutes 1908–25; Catriona Levy, 'Conservatism and Liberal Unionism in Glasgow, 1874–1912' (unpublished Dundee University Ph.D. thesis, 1983), Appendix.

[44] Morgan and Trainor, 'The Dominant Classes', p. 127.

[45] Cf. K. Robbins, *Nineteenth-Century Britain: Integration and Diversity* (Oxford, 1988), pp. 102–7.

[46] This information, and that given below about the MPs' local ties and occupations, is derived from a database whose principal sources are the entries in M. Stenton and S. Lees, *Who's Who of British Members of Parliament*, vols. 2–4 (Hassocks, 1978–81), compiled from the annual *Dod's Parliamentary Companion*.

[47] Glasgow Chamber of Commerce Annual Reports and Minutes, *passim*.

chancellor of the exchequer in 1921, was 'frequently consulted by the Glasgow chamber when advice or help was needed'.[48] Such contacts gave key Scottish businessmen widespread informal access to policymakers which Scottish businessmen such as Lithgow, Sir Steven Bilsland, and Andrew McCance used in the 1930s to advance initiatives designed to promote regional and social development. Through the establishment of a number of quasi-official organisations such as the Scottish Economic Committee, leading employers, in concert with local government leaders, trade unionists and important figures in the Scottish Office, sought to develop long-term solutions to Scotland's economic problems.[49] These organisations, which gained the support of the Scottish Office, provided bridges linking industrialists, the Scottish political elite and the mandarins of the Scottish Office, and were an invaluable means of exerting influence on official thinking.[50]

Businessmen were also very well placed for the exercise of political influence in Northern Ireland. Retailers, professional men and the province's large number of small-and medium-scale manufacturers were well represented in the province's local authorities and in the constituency associations of the dominant Unionist Party. Moreover, through the latter, whose emergence between 1886 and 1914 had transcended previous divisions between Liberals and Conservatives, these minor worthies were allied to the large, Belfast-based linen and ship manufacturers whose membership of the Belfast Reform Club and of the Belfast chamber of commerce gave them privileged access after 1921 to Northern Ireland ministers with special responsibility for economic and financial matters. Indeed, on two occasions in the interwar period serving Northern Ireland ministers held the presidency of the Belfast chamber.[51]

Moreover, most Northern Irish ministers in the interwar years had significant business ties which often bridged the distinctions both between land and industry, and between industry and finance. As Patrick Buckland observes, the list of ministers at Stormont 'read like an executive committee of Northern industry and commerce'.[52] For example John Andrews, the minister of labour for much of the 1920s and 1930s, and his contemporary John Milne Barbour, minister of finance, were directors of linen companies, posts which they were not required to surrender when they took up government office.[53] The relatively small area and size of population of Northern Ireland, and the exclusion of a significant part of the

[48] Oakley, *Our Illustrious Forbears*.
[49] R. Saville, ed., *The Economic Development of Modern Scotland 1950–1980* (Edinburgh, 1985); R. H. Campbell, 'The Scottish Office and the Special Areas in the 1930s', *Historical Journal*, XXII (1979).
[50] The interaction of businessmen, politicians and civil servants in developing a Scottish perspective on economic problems will be examined in more detail by us and by Dr James Smyth in a project supported by the Leverhulme Trust on 'Politicians, Businessmen and Public Policy 1931–59: The Scottish Dimension'.
[51] J. F. Harbinson, *The Ulster Unionist Party 1882–1973* (Belfast, 1973) pp. 69–70, 125; Chambers, *Faces of Change*, pp. 239, 241, 249, 252; Buckland, *Factory of Grievances*.
[52] Quoted in *ibid.*, p. 12.
[53] Bew *et al.*, *The State in Northern Ireland*, p. 84.

population from the political process, meant that contacts among well-to-do Unionists were even closer than among their Scottish counterparts, though the tendency to fragment into a large number of employers' organisations was also greater.[54] In addition, Northern Irish employers figured prominently among MPs both at Stormont and in the Ulster delegation at Westminster.[55]

As has been acknowledged, occupancy of ministerial and other elite positions does not automatically mean power. It is therefore necessary to examine how successfully the views of industrial employers were reflected in the formal political process, that is in the views of political parties and in the decisions of government.

Nationally, of course, the political parties paid considerable attention to 'industrial' questions, especially tariff reform. The latter was the focal point of arguments amongst Unionists in the decade before 1914 and, having attracted the official backing of the party, the issue played a large role in leading it to defeat in 1923.[56] In the west of Scotland, too, the question had considerable impact on the views and fortunes of politicians. Before 1914 the influence of the free trade lobby (which included most employers) is evident in the stance of the local Unionist parties which refused to endorse the full-blown protectionist position of Chamberlain; they opted until the eve of the 1906 election for the more anodyne position that the government should reconsider fiscal policy.[57] In 1906, none of the Unionist candidates endorsed Chamberlain's position, most supported Balfour's compromise of negotiation and retaliation, and some remained staunch supporters of free trade.[58] Indeed of the seven Unionist candidates standing at the 1906 election for Glasgow constituencies, four were free traders, including the only Unionist to be returned.[59] Sensitivity to the complex views of the western Scottish electorate on the issue continued after the First World War: local Unionists played down their party's commitment to tariff reform in a successful effort to win over former Liberal voters.[60] Scottish politicians' commitment to protection, like that of many industrialists, emerged only at the end of the decade under the impact of the Depression.[61]

Even if Scottish parties and politicians were sensitive to the views of the country's businessmen on such issues, did the governments of the day act in

---

[54] Buckland, *Factory of Grievances*, p. 63.
[55] Harbinson, *The Ulster Unionist Party*, pp. 99, 100; Buckland, *Factory of Grievances*, pp. 27, 33–4, 44.
[56] A. Sykes, *Tariff Reform in British Politics 1903–14* (Oxford, 1979); E. H. H. Green, 'Radical Conservatism: The Electoral Genesis of Tariff Reform', *Historical Journal*, XXVIII (1985); P. Cain, 'Political Economy in Edwardian England: The Tariff-Reform Controversy', in A. O'Day, ed., *The Edwardian Age: Conflict and Stability 1900–1914* (London, 1979).
[57] Levy, 'Conservatism and Liberal Unionism'.
[58] Scottish Liberal Association Records, book of newspaper cuttings.
[59] Levy, 'Conservatism and Liberal Unionism'.
[60] I. G. C. Hutchison, *A Political History of Scotland 1832–1924: Parties, Elections and Issues* (Edinburgh, 1986), pp. 322, 325, 327.
[61] On Scotland's lingering economic vulnerability to protection see M. Daly, 'Industrial Policy in Scotland and Ireland in the Inter-War Years', in Mitchison and Roebuck, p. 291.

accordance with these opinions or at least pay attention to them? The linchpin of the case that employers were politically impotent is the supposed lack of responsiveness of successive governments to their claims, in particular the delay in introducing tariffs and the reintroduction of the gold standard at pre-war levels of parity. Both of these issues have been interpreted as evidence that governments were more sympathetic to the claims of the City.[62]

How unsympathetic were governments? Although it is difficult to demonstrate that the politicians of a specific region such as Scotland had direct impact on key economic decisions, the policymaking process indicates that Whitehall politicians' perception of the needs of industry, a perception that regionally-based agitation no doubt helped to form, played a significant part in their deliberations. The long delay in introducing tariffs after they became a major political issue had little to do with politicians' favouring the interests of finance and commerce over those of industry; more important was the fear, on the part of governments who wished to help key industries, that tariffs were not electorally acceptable, especially in the years between the electoral fiasco of 1923 and the economic crisis of 1931.[63] Also, when tariffs came in 1932, as Capie argues, long-run industrial pressure was as important as the short-term economic crisis in bringing about the decision.[64] Likewise, the decision to return to gold in 1925 was taken on the assumption, fortified by the views of provincial employers such as those in the Glasgow chamber, that the policy would favour long-term prosperity in industry as well as in finance and commerce.[65] Moreover, to the extent that the return to gold and other key decisions reflected the 'Treasury' or 'Bank' view, the input of those institutions represented their own broad views of economic policy rather than the opinions of the City.[66]

Within the devolved framework of government in Northern Ireland employers obtained many concessions from the government which, as the minister of labour said, 'was always ready ... to remedy their grievances if possible and to do anything in our power to help them'.[67] Indeed, Sir James Craig, the prime minister, favoured industry over finance, despite the Midland Bank's great power.[68] Likewise, farmers (more numerous in Ulster than in any other UK region) found Stormont very

---

[62] Cf. for example: (on tariffs) Rubinstein, 'Cultural Explanations', and Longstreth, 'The City, Industry and the State'; (on the gold standard) Pollard, *The Gold Standard*, introduction, and the debate summarised in M. Collins, *Banks and Industrial Finance in Britain 1800–1939* (Basingstoke, 1991), pp. 86–91.

[63] J. Ramsden, *The Age of Balfour and Baldwin 1902–1940* (London, 1978), pp. 177–83, 298; P.R.O. Cab. 58/1, Committee of Civil Research, Minutes of Fifteenth Meeting, 19 November 1925.

[64] Capie, 'Pressure', pp. 431–2, 437, 447; *idem, Depression and Protectionism: Britain Between the Wars* (London, 1983), *passim*.

[65] P.R.O. T. 175/9, 175/11, Papers of Sir Richard Hopkins; cf. P. Williamson, 'Financiers, the Gold Standard and British Politics, 1925–1931', in Turner, *Businessmen and Politics*.

[66] Cf. G. C. Peden, *British Economic and Social Policy: Lloyd George to Margaret Thatcher* (Deddington, 1985), pp. 62–3.

[67] John Andrews, quoted in Buckland, *Factory of Grievances*, p. 105.

[68] Bew *et al, The State in Northern Ireland*, pp. 90–2.

responsive. Admittedly there was greater difficulty in implementing Ulster's wishes at Westminster. For example, Northern Irish farmers were often stymied by Whitehall's inability and, occasionally, its refusal to prevail over the Irish Free State's protective tariffs.[69] Nevertheless, Northern Ireland's industry had many policy successes during the interwar period. For example, the Belfast shipbuilders obtained prolonged government guarantees for loans which were substantial enough to alarm their Scottish colleagues.[70] Similarly, although frustrated in the 1920s, Ulster's linen manufacturers obtained large returns for their lobbying in the following decade, especially through the Anglo-American Trade Agreement of 1938. Ulster milling and baking interests had comparable triumphs.[71]

In any event, insofar as Northern Ireland's industrialists experienced frustration in their attempts to influence policy at Westminster, their difficulties stemmed far more from the restrictive nature of Northern Ireland's devolution than from any lack of sympathy on the part of the province's leading politicians.[72] The ability of Northern Ireland's employers to exert leverage within this limited framework, despite the considerable distractions posed by constant disputes about Partition itself, supports the argument for the influence on policymaking of provincial employers far more than it detracts from it.

* * *

Thus the supposed political predominance of metropolitan finance over provincial industry looks increasingly suspect when examined from a regional perspective. A central tenet of the orthodox view is the separation of economic interests into three distinct categories. Yet leading businessmen in the west of Scotland and in Northern Ireland displayed a diverse range of business interests which meant that beyond their primary occupation of merchant, manufacturer or financier they had varied interests which did much to integrate the business community. These linkages between industry, commerce and finance were extended and complemented by links between each region and the City itself. With regard to views on policy, clearly there were differences among leading businessmen, but rival viewpoints did not coincide, as the literature supposes, with industry, finance and commerce. Thus the adherents of particular controversial views were drawn from all three of these sectors. Still, far from being constantly entangled in disagreements, the business communities of western Scotland and Northern Ireland displayed considerable coherence on policy, cutting across tidy occupational distinctions. Frequently these coherent viewpoints found sympathetic echoes in the national as well as the regional political process. This harmony reflected not only the prominence of businessmen

---

[69] Ibid., p. 77.
[70] Ibid., pp. 116–18.
[71] Ibid., pp. 108–10.
[72] Ibid., pp. 1–6 and *passim*.

in politics but also the sympathy toward provincial interests shown by Westminster politicians. The economic orthodoxy of government policies on subjects such as free trade and the gold standard indicated a consensus of opinion, which included industrialists, rather than indicating any political impotence of industry. Insofar as the state had its own interests and opinions, remaining above the pressures of lobbying forces,[73] those interests were as likely to favour the preferences of industrialists as to oppose them.

The proposition that the different economic sectors were integrated regionally and nationally, and that there were shifting alliances which cut across sectors, requires some modification of the prevalent view that industry's interests were subordinated in the policymaking process. The representation of interests is clearly an important, though not the only, component in the formulation of public policy, and the evidence of this study suggests that industrialists were well integrated into the ranks of the business leaders who exerted influence in this process. Yet, in dissenting from the current orthodoxy of financial supremacy, the intention is not to attempt to resurrect an older consensus about the 'hegemony' of industrialist interests.[74] Instead this article suggests that, in formulating a more nuanced interpretation of modern British elites and their decisions, historians should incorporate a robust role for provincial industrialists and for provincial regions generally.

---

[73] On the nature of the state with regard to policymaking see: J. Tomlinson, *Problems of British Economic Policy 1870–1945* (London, 1981); S. Tolliday and J. Zeitlin, eds., *Shopfloor Bargaining and the State* (Cambridge, 1985), introduction.

[74] Nor is it intended to subscribe to the 'corporatist' thesis of influence broadly shared among government, employers and trade unions, as developed with particular reference to industrial relations (cf. K. Middlemas, *Politics in Industrial Society: The Experience of the British System Since 1911*, London, 1979).

Index

Aberdeen 23, 24, 26, 64, 65, 67, 71–5, 231, 233, 235, 237
abortion 98, 99, 101
Absentee 149, 159, 160
agrarian protest 8, 9, 172–88
agriculture 1, 27, 73, 75, 76, 82, 153, 228
ale 48, 52, 54, 57, 58
America 37, 74, 101, 105, 114, 204, 212
Amsterdam 38
Ancient Order of Hibernians 212, 214, 215
Anglican 115, 123, 141
anglicization 104, 106, 155, 156, 159
Anglo-Irish 126, 128, 130, 134, 159
antiquarians 107, 109, 126, 127, 135, 144, 147
Argyll, duke of 85, 155
Argyllshire 65, 70, 71, 73, 138, 201
aristocracy 106, 114, 115, 116, 119, 120, 122, 125, 141
Armagh (county) 201, 212, 214
army (British) 82, 114, 120, 193
Arnot, H. 56, 59, 60
artisans 45–63, 117, 118, 121, 122, 220
Australia 9, 85, 94, 204, 211
authority 2, 3, 123
Ayr 24, 38, 39, 44, 65

ballads 107
Bank of Scotland 235, 257
bankruptcy 62, 84, 85
banks, banking 7, 29, 30, 31, 36, 37, 38, 39, 44, 111, 228–38, 258, 266
Bartlett, T. 9

Belfast 4, 11, 12, 32, 98, 100, 189–203, 204–15, 217–26, 234, 257, 259, 260, 261, 263, 266
Beveridge, Sir W. 239, 241
bills (of exchange) 30–44, 111
birth—
  control 94, 96–9
  intervals 72, 102
  rate 69–72, 76, 89–91, 93–4, 96–102
bourgeoisie 9, 11, 115, 116, 120, 123, 124, 125, 127, 134
brandy 58
Breadalbane 39, 48, 155
breast feeding 101
brewers 48, 57–8
bribery 52
British Isles 4, 11, 39, 79, 81, 103, 136, 137, 142, 150
building 54, 56, 58, 60–2, 193, 198–200, 223–4, 251
bullion 32, 34
burgesses 46, 48, 50, 118
Burke, E. 10
Burke, P. 9

Caithness 65, 93
Caledonians 139, 143, 145
Cambridge 10, 129
Canada 82, 85, 94
Canongate 52, 54
Catholic Association 209–10
Catholic Relief act 144
Catholics 4, 9–12, 87, 89, 92, 99, 100, 104, 112, 120, 121, 127, 128, 130, 131–4, 136, 139–41, 144, 147, 167, 189, 190, 193, 194, 195,

269

198, 199–200, 201, 203, 204–15, 220
celibacy 7, 8, 69, 71, 89
Celtic football club (Glasgow) 213, 215
Celtic 103, 111, 125, 146
census 14, 15, 17, 18, 21, 26, 64, 67, 90, 93, 96, 100, 102, 109, 191–3, 196, 198, 207, 218, 220, 223, 231, 239
chambers of commerce 256, 257, 258, 259, 261, 262, 263, 265
charities 77, 80, 85, 86
Charter School Society 105
children 71, 89, 93, 94, 98, 99, 101, 102, 111
church 52, 62, 72, 114, 116, 120, 125, 140, 141
City of Glasgow Bank 224, 235
civility 5
Clare, county 100, 101
Clark, J. C. D. 114, 115, 119, 123
class(es) 1, 2, 4–11, 60, 182, 183–7, 210, 222–5
clearances 77, 82, 83
clergy 12, 112, 156, 207, 209, 211, 212, 213, 214, 215
clientism 3
Clyde (river) 12, 136, 189, 196, 206
Clydesdale Bank 230, 236, 237
cohort-parity analysis 90, 94, 95, 97, 100, 102
coinage 32–4
Coleraine 99
College of Physicians 132–3
colonies 8, 10
commercialisation 6, 12, 73, 107, 108, 109
Common Good 46, 50, 51, 59, 61, 62
communicants 48
community 5, 50, 205, 208, 211, 213, 256, 259
conflict 5, 9, 104, 106, 190, 203
Connell, K. H. 16, 64
Connolly, S. J. 9, 10, 12, 103

constitution 13
consumption 10, 28, 45, 47, 48, 49, 52, 58, 60
Convention of Royal Burghs 117
Cork 22, 23, 24, 25, 68, 99, 182, 183, 226
corporatism 13
cottars 8, 74, 80, 82, 85, 111, 182, 183, 187
Court of Sessions 54, 57, 58, 60
Coutts (Edinburgh family of) 30, 41, 43
crofts and crofters 75, 80, 82, 83, 85, 86, 110, 172–88
Cromwellian era 22, 26, 27, 104, 130
Cullen, Louis 6, 7, 10, 15, 16, 17, 29
culture 1, 3, 5, 8, 9, 12, 29, 103–14, 125, 135, 148, 149
customs 49, 50, 52, 57, 58, 59, 61, 103, 108, 150, 154

Dalkeith 43, 56
Daly, M. 4, 11
Darien 27, 30, 53, 62
David, P. A. 93, 94, 95, 96, 101, 102
Davitt, Michael 210, 214
de Vries, J. 14, 15, 19
death rate 69, 70, 71, 72, 76
debt 46, 50, 53
defence 13
deference 9, 115, 120, 124
demography 1, 4–8, 14, 15, 16, 19, 27, 28, 48, 64–9, 72, 73, 75, 76, 81, 82, 87, 101, 102, 148, 158, 191, 218
Dempster, Thomas 138, 142
Devine, T. 4, 7, 8, 77
Devlin, Joe 11, 204–5, 209, 210–15
diaries 10
Dickson, D. 8, 45
diet 47, 48, 52, 56, 60, 61, 202, 222
dissenters 120, 130
distillers 58
Donegal 92

Drogheda 24, 26
drovers 56
Dublin 1, 7, 9, 10, 11, 13, 22–7, 32, 38, 62, 68, 91, 92, 98, 100, 106, 108, 112, 114, 116, 120–34, 143, 147, 159–61, 205, 217–27, 228, 234, 235
duelling 106
Dumfries 24, 65
Dundee 22, 24, 26, 52, 56, 231, 233–4

economy 1, 2, 5, 6, 7, 8, 11, 12, 13, 14, 17, 19, 26, 27, 29, 94
Edgeworth, M. 149, 159, 160
Edinburgh 2, 7, 9, 10, 11, 15, 19, 22–6, 30–43, 45–63, 64, 65, 68, 84, 100, 114, 116–18, 120, 122–4, 127, 128, 133, 134, 145, 163, 217–26, 229, 230, 231, 233–4, 235, 236, 237, 238
education 97, 104, 111, 113, 127, 130, 132, 133, 141, 192, 207, 209, 210, 214, 215, 221
elections 208, 212, 215, 216
élites 117, 125, 148, 150–3, 155–60, 205, 210, 215, 254, 267
employers 5, 12, 148, 203, 254, 255, 261, 263, 265, 266
England 3, 14, 15, 16, 20, 27, 30, 33, 34, 39, 44, 58, 60, 66, 67, 69–73, 86, 103, 104, 109–13, 115, 126, 136, 137, 138, 143, 148, 151, 152, 156–8, 160, 217, 225, 236, 258
Enlightenment 5, 10, 123, 125–30, 134, 136, 137
estates 8, 9, 46, 84, 86, 88, 155
Europe 7, 9, 14, 15, 16, 19, 29, 38, 68, 77, 78, 82, 90, 94, 101, 102, 105, 106, 117, 127, 140, 150, 151, 152, 157, 158
exchange rate 12, 29, 30, 32–6, 38, 41, 43
exports 6, 10, 11, 17, 44, 56

family 8, 11, 48, 71, 74, 89, 94, 203, 222–3
famine 3, 4, 7, 53, 66–8, 71–3, 77–89, 109, 173, 175, 177, 181, 182, 188
farmers, farming 8, 74, 82, 86, 92, 93, 100, 110, 111, 133, 156, 157, 265–6
Federation of British Industries 256, 260, 261
fiars 52, 57, 62
finance 1, 3, 12
fishing 60, 83, 87, 183, 184
Fitzgerald, G. 35, 43
Fitzpatrick, D. 4, 9
Flinn, M. W. 66, 93, 97
folklore 110
football 12, 112, 213, 215
France 16, 27, 29, 32, 39, 49, 78, 115, 116, 139, 142
Frazer (house of) 31, 34, 40, 41
Free Church 80, 87
fruit 58–62
furniture 48, 58, 106

Gaelic 93, 104, 105, 107, 110, 112, 135, 136, 141, 142, 144, 147, 157
Gaelic League 12, 112
Galway 22, 24, 26, 92
gambling 52
Geary, F. 11
General Assembly 60
Geneva 69, 70
gentry 48, 60
Germany 16, 17, 78, 102, 259
Gillespie, R. 6, 45
Gilpin, W. 151, 152, 154
Glasgow 10, 11, 19, 23–6, 31, 32, 36–8, 41–3, 58, 63, 68, 84, 98, 131, 133, 189–203, 204–15, 217–27, 230, 231, 232, 233, 235, 237, 257, 258, 259, 260, 261, 262, 263, 264, 265
gold standard 261, 265, 267

Gordon, E. 4, 12
government 2, 4, 9, 12, 13, 84, 86, 87
Greenland 54
Greenock 24
guilds 118, 120, 121, 123, 124

Hanoverian 9, 114, 115, 122, 139
Harland and Wolff 243, 245, 258
harvest 7, 52, 68, 75, 87, 174, 183
hearth tax 15, 17, 21, 22, 64, 66
Hebrides 72, 73, 78, 79, 82, 83, 85
Henry, Dr H. (bishop of Down and Connor) 209, 210, 212, 213
Hepburn, A. C. 11, 220
Highland Land Law Reform Association 172, 179, 185
Highlands 4, 7, 64, 66–9, 72, 77–88, 93, 103, 104, 107, 110–13, 142, 143, 145, 146, 152, 156, 157, 159, 172–88, 205, 213
Hill, J. 9, 114
Home Rule 179, 185, 189, 194, 204, 209
household 64, 66, 68–75, 99, 202
housing 11, 202, 217–27, 232
Houston, R. A. 7, 69, 111
Hume, David 128, 131, 136, 145
hurling 106, 107, 108
Hutterites 94

identity 1, 3, 4, 12, 13, 135, 136
imports 52, 54, 84
improvement 74, 75, 104, 157
independence 3, 13
industry 4, 5, 10, 12, 13, 27, 45, 57, 86, 110, 190, 192–203, 206, 228, 230, 234, 239, 255, 256, 257–8, 260, 261, 263, 265, 266, 267
inequalities 11
integration 2
interest rates 51, 53, 61
investment trusts 233, 238
Irish National Foresters 112

Irish National Land League 172, 179, 181, 183, 184, 185

Jacobites 66, 141, 142, 144
Johnson, Samuel 151, 152, 154, 156
Johnson, W. 11
Jones, Griffith 111

kelp 73, 82–6
Kilmarnock 24, 26
Kincardineshire 71, 74, 75
Kindleberger, C. P. 234, 235
kinship 11, 46
kirk session 2, 161–7
knitting 74, 75

labour 9–11, 82, 87, 88, 94, 175, 181, 191, 193, 194, 200, 201, 202, 203, 206, 210–15, 219, 220, 240, 241, 242, 244, 246–8, 250, 251, 255
labourers 73, 78, 193, 196, 197, 198, 199, 200, 220
Lanarkshire 206, 215
land tenure 7, 55, 58, 131, 172–88, 224
Land Wars (Ireland) 172, 177–9, 181–3, 188
Land Wars (Scotland) 172, 177–9, 181, 183, 188
landless 7, 8
landlords 2, 4, 6–9, 48, 52, 54, 73–7, 82–8, 106, 111, 141, 153, 155, 156, 157, 162–4, 166, 214, 224
landscapes 152, 153, 154, 156, 159, 160
language 11, 103, 104, 105, 107, 109, 110, 112, 146
law 2, 4, 10, 29, 105, 132, 142
lawyers 86, 131, 138, 207, 210, 233
leases 8, 46, 48, 50
Lee, J. J. 13
Leinster 68, 107
leisure 12, 107, 148, 155

Leith 47, 50, 52, 54, 55, 56, 58, 60, 65, 163
Lenman, B. 10
Lewis (isle of) 78, 83, 172, 178
life assurance 232–3
life expectancy 69–73
Limerick 24, 99
linen 7, 57, 58, 74, 75, 190, 219, 263, 266
literacy 92, 98, 104, 110–12, 204
Liverpool 208, 209, 215, 216
livestock 56, 58, 82, 86, 87
London 2, 3, 6, 12, 20, 24, 29–44, 89, 115, 117, 121, 122, 126, 131, 155, 220–1, 224, 234, 235, 236, 255
Londonderry 6, 24
Lucas, Charles 120–4
Lynch, M. 17, 19

markets 6, 11, 17, 23, 52, 56, 58–62, 84, 118
marriage 7, 8, 69, 71, 73–5, 78, 89, 90, 93–6, 99–102, 155
masonic lodges 123
masons 46, 198, 199
Maynooth 129, 134
Mayo 22, 92, 181, 182
meal 52, 57, 58, 60, 80, 84–7
Meath 22, 92
merchants 30, 31, 34, 41, 42, 46, 50, 84, 85, 115, 117, 120–2, 124
Midland Bank 236, 237, 265
Midlothian 64, 65
migration 5, 9, 67, 68, 70, 74, 81–2, 84, 85, 88, 89, 92–3, 110, 113, 136, 158, 189, 200, 205–6, 212, 213, 214, 221
mining 93
Mitchison, R. 9, 69, 161
modernisation 10, 12
Mokyr, J. 73
monarchy 114, 117, 119, 123
Morris, R. J. 9

mortality 8, 26, 69–73, 85, 86, 105, 112
Mull (isle of) 71, 80, 83, 84
Munn, C. 7, 12
Munster 68, 92
music 12, 107, 109, 110, 112, 113
Mussleburgh 56
myths 10, 135–40

Napoleonic wars 81–3
National Union of Dock Labourers 206–7, 214
nationalism 3, 9, 13, 107, 120, 205, 208, 209, 210, 211, 212, 213, 214, 215, 216
neighbourhood 11
Nenadic, S. 9, 10, 148
New Statistical Account 80, 83
Newcastle 34, 42
newspapers 59
Nicolson, W. 6
nobility 31, 48, 116, 126
Northern Ireland 2, 12, 13, 99
Northern Star 210, 211, 213
novelists 113, 149, 155

O'Brien, P. 5, 9, 11,, 125
O'Connor, Charles 127, 128, 134, 141–5, 147
Ó'Gráda, C. 5, 83, 87, 89, 90, 92
O'Halloran, C. 9, 135
Old Statistical Account 18, 19, 66, 69
Ossian 10, 141, 142, 144, 145, 147, 152
Oxford 10, 129

Paisley 24, 26
Paris 102
parish 2, 17, 19, 48, 60, 64–7, 69, 71, 72, 74, 76, 78, 80, 87, 130, 161–4, 166
parliament (Irish) 2, 116, 120, 121, 126, 130
parliament (Scottish) 116, 117

partition 13, 266
partnerships 46
paternalism 4
patriotism 105, 112, 120, 151, 212
patronage 2, 105–7, 141
penal laws 123, 132, 144, 147
Pennecuik, Alexander 116, 118, 119, 122, 124
Perth 23, 24, 65
Phoenicians 107, 143–5
Picts 136, 139, 141–3
placemen 50
plague 22, 26, 27
poetry 107, 143, 145, 152
poll tax 17, 21
Poor Law 2, 87, 161
poor 2, 11, 52–4, 62, 76, 77, 81, 84, 112, 158, 203, 220, 226
potato 73, 74, 77–80, 82, 83, 86, 88
pre-christian era 107, 108, 142–4
Presbyterian(s) 10, 133, 140, 141
professions 4, 206, 207, 218, 220, 262
Protestants 2, 9, 11, 105, 112, 120, 123, 124, 127, 131, 132, 140, 189, 193, 194, 200, 206, 209, 211, 214, 215, 220
public houses 194, 207, 210–15

quakers 72, 73, 167

regions 19, 25, 64–5, 255
religion 1, 2, 4–5, 92, 104, 105, 108, 112, 114, 121–3, 128, 136, 137, 144
rent 17, 26, 39, 40, 46, 53, 56, 71, 75, 218, 222–3, 225
riot 11, 194, 203
roads 54, 56
romanticism 152, 153
Roscommon 92, 147
roup (auction) 46, 47, 50, 51, 56, 58, 59
Royal Bank 30–2, 35, 37, 38, 42, 43
Royal Irish Academy 127, 134

Scott, Walter 149, 152, 159
Scottish Financial Enterprise 229
Scottish Unionist Party 13
sectarianism 11, 194, 195, 198, 201, 203
servants 52, 74, 75, 201, 218–19
Seven Years War 7
Shetland 65, 66
shipbuilding 11, 55, 190, 193, 194, 196, 201, 206, 219, 239–51, 258, 266
shore dues 47, 48–50, 54–8
Sinclair, Sir J. 67, 156
Skye 172, 179, 184, 185, 187
Sligo 81, 212
slogans 10
Smith, Adam 38, 131
Smollett, T. 149, 150
Smout, T. C. 6, 9, 10, 15, 17, 152
smuggling 58
society 1–3, 5, 7, 9–12
Spain 137, 143
spinning 74–5
sport 204, 210, 213, 215
squatters 182, 183
standard of living 76, 110, 196–200, 202, 222
Stopes, Marie 89, 97–100

tariffs 258–60, 264, 265
taxation 15, 17, 18, 21, 26, 31, 66, 214, 251, 258
tea 108, 109
technology 5, 12, 241–2
temperance movement 207, 209, 213, 215
tenants 8, 74, 80, 84, 106
tenements 11, 218, 223, 224, 225, 226
textiles 73, 74, 81, 100, 193, 206, 219
theatre 106, 109
timber bush 47, 54, 55, 56, 61
Tiree 70, 80, 84, 85
tithes (teinds) 46
tobacco 7, 30, 31, 35, 37, 38, 43

tourism 84, 148–59, 230
towns 2, 9, 11, 14, 15, 17, 19–22, 26–8, 46, 68, 69, 92, 95–6, 112, 189–203
trade 3, 18, 22, 27, 30, 31, 35, 36, 38, 39, 40, 44, 47, 50, 54, 55, 74, 84, 111, 116, 118, 121, 124, 142, 192, 256, 259
Trainor, R. 4, 12
travel writing 10, 149, 151, 152, 154–7
Trinity College, Dublin 10, 128–34
Tyrone 22, 100, 101, 201
Tyson, R. 4, 7, 48

Ulster 2, 6, 12, 81, 92, 97, 112, 124, 133, 192, 201, 203, 206, 211, 212, 266
unemployment 11, 219–20, 230, 233, 239–51
Union (act of) 12, 31, 34, 116, 117
Unionists 12, 189, 194, 209, 212, 263, 264
United Irish League 204, 211, 213, 214, 215
United States 1, 11, 82, 94, 113

universities 10, 128–32
urbanisation 6, 14–28, 232

wages 11, 60, 62, 75, 196–200, 201, 202–3, 214, 220–2, 224, 239–51
Wales 15, 16, 103–13, 127, 143, 221
Waverley 149, 155
Webster, A. 17, 48, 64, 67, 69, 167
weigh house 50, 51, 56, 57, 61
Western Isles 4, 70, 76, 84, 177, 183, 184, 186
Westminster 2, 13, 126, 217, 254, 255, 266, 267
Whatley, C. 54, 56
whisky/whiskey 82, 84, 103, 113
Whyte, I. 6, 7, 8, 14, 48
wine 46–8, 52, 109
Withers, C. 4, 9
women 55, 69, 89, 90, 94, 98, 100, 192, 203, 206, 219, 224
Woodward, D. 4
wool 50, 56, 58, 84, 86
workhouse (Edinburgh) 60, 62

Young Ireland movement 12, 107
Young, A. 7, 10